This book is dedicated to every
Floridian who has ever killed a plant.

BEST GARDEN COLOR FOR FLORIDA

Pamela Crawford

Color Garden Inc.

Published by Color Garden, 5596 Western Way, Lake Worth, FL 33463

First printing: 2003
Printed in Korea by Asian Printing.com

Library of Congress Catalog Card Number pending

ISBN number 0-9712220-1-0

The book is available though most booksellers and many garden centers. To locate your nearest source or to order wholesale, call Color Garden at 561-964-6500.

All photos by Pamela Crawford, except for:

Bill Allen: Gardens on page 8. Pansies on page 15. Daylilies on pages 94, 95, 278, 286, 314, 338. Gaillardia on page 106, 278, 286, 290, 312.
Gene Joyner, Golden Rain Tree, close-up, pages 244, 282.
Jon's Nursery, Eustis: 'La Marne' Rose on page 174.
Judith King, www.hydrangeashydrangeas.com: Hydrangea photos on pages 156, 157, 270, 271, 317.
Henry P. Leu Botanical Gardens, Orlando: Camellias on pages 124, 125, 263, 270, 271. Magnolias on pages 245, 271, 282, 289, 307, 308.
Nelsons' Florida Roses, Apopka: 'Belinda's Dream' Rose on page 174.
Elise Ryan, Color Garden Farms Nursery, Loxahatchee: Gold Mound Duranta flower on page 89.
Suzanne Williams: Azaleas on pages 172, 173, 268, 269, 270, 307, 338, 339.

Computer consulting: Roger Rosenthal, Affordable Computer Training, Palm Beach Gardens, Florida

Editing and proofreading: Barbara Iderosa, Best Editing Service, Wellington, Florida

Landscape design: Pamela Crawford, Color Garden Inc., Lake Worth, Florida, unless otherwise noted

Landscape installation: Tom Homrich Landscaping, Lake Worth, Florida, unless otherwise noted

Plants: The majority of the plants were grown by Color Garden Farms, Loxahatchee, Florida

Software consulting (Quark Express and Adobe Photoshop), Myke Briskman, Margate, Florida (myke@advanceddesignstudios.com).

CONTENTS

Acknowledgments

Many people were very generous with their time and attention regarding the plants and gardens in this book. I would especially like to thank the following:

A & W Annuals, Lake Worth: annual information

Melodie Abell, Abell's Nursery, Lake Worth: horticultural information

Sheila and Bill Allen, Jackson, Mississippi: in charge of Mississippi trial gardens and southern photography

Lee Asbeck, Beck's Nursery, Delray: Hibiscus information

Brandon Balch, Woodfield Country Club, Boca Raton: general information on garden color

Helen BeVeir, Harry P. Leu Gardens, Orlando: information about central Florida plants; photos of Camellias and Magnolias

Boynton Botanicals Nursery, Boynton Beach: horticultural information

Wayne Bowron, Jon's Nursery, Eustis: information on Roses

Dr. Frank Brown, Valkaria: information on Crotons and Ti Plants

Patricia Bullis, Bullis Bromeliads, Miami: Bromeliad information

Derek Burch, Plantation: clarification of botanical names

Tony Cardinale, BallenIsles Country Club, Palm Beach Gardens: annual information

Joel Crippen, Morningstar Nursery, Delray: information on Plumerias

Alex Dewar, Dewer's Nursery, Apopka: information on Roses

Ellen Dudek, Master Gardener, Duval County Extension, Jacksonville: information about gardening in Jacksonville

Jesse Durko, Jesse Durko's Nursery, Fort Lauderdale: horticultural information

Andy Easton, American Orchid Society, Delray: information on Epidendrum Orchids

Mark Finklestien, Boca West Country Club, Boca Raton: annual information

Mark Gordley, Ritz Carlton, Manalapan: horticultural information

Chris Griffiths, Runway Growers, Fort Lauderdale: new plants for trial gardens

Tom Homrich, Tom Homrich Landscaping, Lake Worth: information on trees and cold protection

Gene Joyner, Palm Beach County Extension Agent, West Palm Beach: horticultural information

Ray Kaufman, Jesse Durko's Nursery, Fort Lauderdale: information on Acalyphas

John King, King Landscaping, Lakeland: information on plants for central Florida and cold protection

Wayne Bowron, Jon's Nursery, Eustis: information on Roses

Michael Marino, Tropical World Nursery, Boynton Beach: horticultural information

David McLean, Ft. Lauderdale: horticultural information

Danny Miller, The Breakers, Palm Beach: annual information

David McLean, Ft. Lauderdale: horticultural information

Scott Nelson, Nelsons' Florida Roses, Apopka: Rose information

Eva Pabon, Osceola County Extension Office, Kissimmee: information on plants for central Florida

Elaine Pawlikowski, Central Florida Rose Society, Sanford, Florida: information about easy roses

Bruce Pearson, Tropical World Nursery, Boynton Beach: horticultural information

Steve Pearson, Falls Country Club, Lake Worth: horticultural information

Bobby Reese, Camellia Society, Jacksonville: extensive information about Camellias

Bill Reeve, Botanical Visions, Fort Lauderdale: horticultural information

Elise Ryan, Color Garden Farms Nursery, Loxahatchee: grower of most of the plant material

Larry Schokman, The Kampong Botanical Garden, Coconut Grove: information on flowering trees

Dave Self, Wyld West Annuals, Loxahatchee: annual information

Elinor Schlosser, Coastal Cuttings, Lake Worth: annual information

Peter and Debra Strelkow, Strelkow and Associates, Fort Lauderdale: information on Bulbine

Elinor Schlosser, Coastal Cuttings, Lake Worth: annual information

Murray Sweetser, Master Gardener, Alachua County Extension Office: information about gardening in north Florida

Donna Torre, The Garden Gate Nursery, Pompano: information on butterfly and hummingbird gardens

Vanderlaan's Nursery, Lake Worth: information about dwarfing Hibiscus

Annual: Plant that lasts for only one season.

Central Florida: The part of Florida located in zone 9. See map on page 12.

Growth Rate: The growth rate depends on the plants' environment. More water and fertilizer, for example, cause plants to grow faster, so the categories are estimates only. *Slow* refers to a plant that increases its size by less than 20 per cent the first year. *Medium* refers to a plant that increases its size by 20 to 50 per cent the first year. *Fast* refers to plants that grow more than 50 per cent during their first year in the ground.

North Florida: The part of Florida located in zone 8. See map on page 12.

On Center: Measurement from the center of one plant to the center of another.

Perennial: Perennials are plants that last more than one season. Some people differentiate between woody perennials (plants with woody stems) and herbaceous perennials (plants with soft stems). This book defines perennials as all herbaceous perennials, bulbs, groundcovers, shrubs, vines, and trees that last for more than one season.

Salt Tolerance: *Low* refers to plants that do not tolerate salt spray on their leaves. *Medium* refers to plants that take some salt on their leaves. *High* refers to plants that take direct oceanfront conditions, provided they are somewhat back from the shoreline. Chapter 11 (Salt and Wind Gardens) in this book's companion, "Easy Gardens for Florida"*, gives much more detail.

South Florida: The part of Florida located in zones 10 and 11. See map on page 12.

Subtropical: Areas that do not routinely have freezing temperatures.

Wind Tolerance: *Low* refers to plants that like fairly protected locations. *Medium* refers to plants that take winds produced in more open locations but not extreme sites, like oceanfront or in a wind tunnel created by buildings. *High* refers to plants that are the most wind-tolerant we have. In storms where winds reach 30 to 40 miles per hour for more than a few hours, even plants with high-wind tolerance suffer leaf burn. However, the plants with high-wind tolerance sustain less damage than the ones with low-wind tolerance. The leaf burn does not heal. New leaves grow and eventually replace the ones that are damaged. None of the plants in this book can sustain severe tropical storm or hurricane-force winds without damage.

Ruellia 'Purple Showers', Golden Shrimp Plants, and Cranberry Pentas are perennials that are layered for color impact. These plants bloom most of the time and last for years.

After

Before

* My current book, "Easy Gardens for South Florida", will be expanded to include the entire state in 2004.

Background and Trial Gardens

Background: Growing up with an English mother gave me a love of gardening. However, I found Florida gardening quite a challenge. After making every mistake imaginable, I enrolled in the graduate school of landscape architecture at Florida International University. I began to do plant research to find plants that were naturally well-adapted to south Florida.

Many gardeners work very hard to change their environment to fit the plant. I search for something different - plants that like it here and are well adapted to the Florida environment. I want plants that are easy, and I want beautiful flowers.

At the end of three years of graduate school, I had a masters' degree in landscape architecture and began my landscaping business. I bought 8 acres in Lake Worth to live and work on, started a small nursery, and built a business renovating gardens for south Florida homeowners. We grew the plants, planned the gardens, installed the plants, and maintained them. I have renovated gardens for 1500 homeowners and many country clubs. The experience has been invaluable and has sensitized me to many of the needs of Florida gardeners.

My trial garden in December

Florida Trial Gardens: The luxury of having eight acres of land meant I could plant whatever I wanted. My graduate school research had been mainly from books, and it was time to get my hands dirty. Since I was constantly shopping the wholesale nurseries for interesting plants, I was regularly exposed to numbers of new ones. Some of them were Florida natives, while others were from up north, California, and other tropical or subtropical areas of the world. I even ordered plants I had never heard of from several seed catalogs. I was like a kid in a candy store, madly planting everything I could get my hands on.

Alas, most of the plants in my trial gardens died. After 10 years of testing, I had tried about 2500 plants; 2300 were dead. Many people would consider my project a complete failure, but I was thrilled. I had found *200 plants* that were fabulous, most of them producing beautiful flowers or leaves.

Why did so many plants die? Florida is a difficult environment for plants. The soils are largely devoid of organic matter. The temperatures are not clearly tropical or subtropical, varying from one decade to the next. The rainfall is extreme, characterized by wet summers and dry winters. Most of the trial garden plant fatalities occurred either as a result of our summer heat and water deluge or our cold in January or February.

When I experienced my first drought, I thought plant choices for a low-water garden would be easy: just copy what they do in a desert. My trial gardens soon sported cacti and succulents in many locations. They did great the first winter. Then came the August rains. They started to yellow and swell with growth, filling with water. The large ones fell over. The small ones simply died.

Many of our new plants come from up north. They usually do well during the first winter but then expire from excessive heat and water during the first summer. If they don't actually die, they simply *ugly away* - looking worse and worse as they wait for the cold that doesn't come.

Many of the glamourous tropicals come from areas where the temperatures never drop below 50 degrees. They love our hot summers but die during our first cold spell, when the temperatures slip into the 40's.

You can see why I am so excited when I find a plant doing well in my trial gardens after two years. Once I identify a survivor, I begin maintenance trials. Many of my initial gardening mistakes were not because I planted the wrong plants but because I didn't know how to care for them. I look for plants that require the same types of care because it is more complicated to water and fertilize each plant differently. But, the trimming has to be done at different times of the year. Most flowering plants need trimming after the bloom period has stopped, and, if you trim them at the wrong time of year, they may not bloom at all until the following year.

My sister, Elise Ryan, moved to Florida from New Jersey in 1998. She bought 20 acres of land and started a nursery called Color Garden Farms in Loxahatchee, which is west of West Palm Beach. She began by specializing in the plants that had done well in my trials and started her own trial gardens as well. Loxahatchee is on the border of zones 9 and 10. Her trial gardens have not only resulted in the discovery of new plants that do well here but also increased our knowledge about cold tolerance of plants in general.

My sister Elise's trial garden in December

Background and Trial Gardens

Mississippi Trial Gardens: My mother and stepfather, Sheila and Bill Allen, are master gardeners in Jackson, Mississippi (zone 7), where I grew up. They have extensive gardens at their home. After seeing my trials in south Florida, they became curious about which of the Florida plants would work in Mississippi. Summer heat is their biggest problem.

And, I was curious about the cold tolerance of many of our south Florida plants. Jackson, Mississippi, is colder than any place in Florida. I knew that if they did well in south Florida <u>and</u> in Mississippi, they would thrive in central and north Florida.

For the next eight years, my sister and I shipped plants from Florida to Mississippi to see how they did. We had expected to find some good subtropical perennials that would be ideal annuals there. However, we were surprised at how many perennials we found - plants that came back year after year. Angel's Trumpets, Cape Honeysuckle, Firespike, and Dwarf Chenille are but a few that have breezed through 15 degree temperatures to bloom dependably the next summer. They not only bloomed longer than most traditional southern perennials, like Azaleas, but also had absolutely no problem with the summer heat!

Mississippi trial garden in fall. Pentas, Plumbago, Firespike, Ruellia 'Purple Showers', Salvia leucantha, and Angel's Trumpets are all in full bloom at the same time. These plants started in our Florida gardens, and were sent north for more testing.

We also discovered many subtropical perennials that performed beautifully as annuals. The summer heat of Mississippi is too much for many traditional annuals. Few make it into August, when Jackson still has four more months of the growing season! Many of our subtropical perennials were blooming when they were planted in April and were still going strong until the first frost in November. For example, Pentas, Blue Daze, and Plumbago bloom from April until the first frost, usually in November. Although they may come back the next year, their performance is far superior to many annuals, which would only live for a few months.

We are excited about this opportunity to share this information, especially with north Florida gardeners, who share a lot of the same problems as Mississippi. We hope they will enjoy trying some of our solutions.

Books: One of the biggest problems I faced in the landscaping business was teaching my customers how to care for their plants after they were installed. Many of my clients were new to Florida and had no idea what to do. They needed written instructions about gardening basics, like watering, fertilizing, mulching, pest control, and trimming. I had learned so much about these chores since my arrival to Florida that and I wanted to share it.

My book, "Easy Gardens for South Florida", is the first in a series of books designed to educate both the gardeners - and the professionals who work with them - about the keys to achieving a beautiful landscape. It describes in detail the first (and easiest) 100 plants that survived my trials and includes chapters on garden planting and maintenance that are critical to the success of the south Florida garden. It tells you how to water, plant, fertilize, control pests, mulch, trim, and control weeds. I hope that these maintenance instructions will keep people from making all the mistakes I made when I began gardening here. I share with you years of research and experience that should save you years of mistakes and frustration.

This book also includes a lot of design ideas from 65 local gardens. Readers are especially fond of the many before-and-after photos.

My first book will be expanded to include the whole state in 2004. The new title will be "Easy Gardens for Florida". I use my own data from our Florida and Missisippi trial gardens as well as information from experts throughout the state.

My second book, "Best Garden Color for Florida", is for the gardener who loves color! It details the second 100 plants that survived our trials - plus some traditional choices for further north in the state. While most are easy, some are more maintenance-intensive than the ones described in the "Easy Gardens" book. Bougainvillea is a good example. It didn't fit in a low-maintenance plant book because of the work involved in trimming it each summer. However, it certainly fits well in a book about color, since it is one of our most spectacular winter bloomers. Annuals are also included. <u>This book does not duplicate any of the plants or care information included in my "Easy Gardens" book. The two work together to give you the necessary information for beautiful garden color.</u>

Criteria for inclusion in this book:

First: Plants that are naturally adapted to the Florida environment.

Second: Plants that offer the most color for the longest period of time with the least amount of care.

Third: Plants that offer the most spectacular color for this area, even if they bloom a short time, like Tabebuias.

Right: My trial garden in January. The Salvias, Petunias and Pansies thrive in south Florida winters.

Goal of My Books

The goal of my books is to make Florida gardening easy and successful by helping you avoid my many mistakes! Here are some of the most important things you need to know:

1. Which plants do well in Florida. I once bought 100 Gerber Daisies, thinking they would bloom constantly and live forever. They lasted only 10 days. In the years since, I've tested 2500 plants to determine which ones adapt best to our difficult environment. 2300 died. The 200 survivors are described in detail in my first two books.

2. Ultimate size of the plants. I planted six major shade trees in the tiny front yard of my second Florida home. I had no idea that a single one would have filled the space, and quickly. A few years later, I paid the price of having most of them removed. **The most common mistake Floridian gardeners make is to install plants that quickly outgrow their space.** *(See "Average Size" in the left, green sidebar of each plant page.)*

We test plants in our trial gardens prior to writing about them to learn first-hand how they perform.

3. Maintainable size of the plants. I planted Ixora 'Nora Grant' in a spot where I needed something 18 inches tall. I kept trimming it and wondering why it never flowered. This plant needs to be maintained at least 36 inches tall to bloom! Each plant has its comfortable size range. *(See "Average Size" in the left, green sidebar of each plant page.)*

4. How long the plants live. Plants in Florida generally don't live as long as they do up north. Before making a substantial investment in landscaping, you should know how long each one will live. *(See "Lifespan" in the left, green sidebar of each plant page.)*

5. Proper plant spacing. Each plant requires a certain amount of space. Your garden may seem sparse on planting day, but the plants will live longer, flower more, and be much easier to maintain if given the proper space. *(See "Spacing" in the left, green sidebar of each plant page.)*

6. Any negatives about the plants. I planted a gorgeous Helinconia right next to my front door, having no idea it would look bad in the winter. Had I known, I would have planted it somewhere in the side or back yard, where it wouldn't be a key focal point in winter. *(Negatives are clearly stated in the "General" section of each plant page.)*

7. When and how long the plants bloom. It is important to know how long a plant blooms. I planted Daylilies once, thinking they bloomed all summer, and was disappointed to find out that the ones I chose only flower four to six weeks. In addition, understand when a plant blooms. For example, Royal Poincianas bloom in summer and are bare in winter. They are not a good choice for a winter resident. *(See "Season" on each plant page.)*

8. Companion plantings. To achieve the beautiful, flower-garden look you see in the magazines, plants that bloom at the same time are layered in the same section of the garden. When I first began designing, I kept getting the order wrong, planting the plants that would eventually be the tallest in front of the shorter ones. *(See the "Companion" section of each plant page for some great combinations for each plant.)*

9. Proper fertilization. In my first Florida gardening years, my plants had frequent nutritional deficiencies. I fertilized with the wrong fertilizer in the wrong amounts at the wrong time of year. I even killed my first lawn with too much! Correct fertilization is easy, if you only know how! *(See the Index under "Fertilization".)*

10. Proper trimming. I used to trim my Hibiscus monthly and wonder why it never bloomed. Most flowering plants in Florida need infrequent, hard cutbacks shortly after they have stopped blooming. The timing is critical. If you trim Brunfelsia after August, for example, it will not bloom that winter. Detailed trimming instructions are given for each plant. *(See "Trimming" section of each plant page for specifics and the index under "Trimming'" for general guidelines.)*

11. Low-water landscaping. Most of the plants in my books require water twice a week or less. I devoted an entire chapter to this topic in "Easy Gardens for Florida"*.

12. Weeds and pest control. Avoid using toxic and expensive chemicals as much as possible. *(See the index under "Weeding" or "Pest Control".)*

13. Proper mulching. I used large pine bark mulch once and found giant palmetto bugs nesting in it. After that nightmarish experience, I set out to learn everything I could about mulches. *(See the index under "Mulch".)*

Visitors to my nursery and gardens are surprised to learn that one person takes care of all eight acres. Miguel Olivares-Popoca (pictured) is a very hard-working man. And, we apply the principles from my research to keep his work to a minimum. **Here is our work schedule:**

- **Fertilize** three times a year.
- **Water** twice a week, if we don't get enough rain.
- **Mulch** once or twice a year.
- **Trim** most of the plants once a year (Bougainvillea requires the most trimming time).
- **Ignore** most garden pests. If we can see a pest on a plant, like aphids or eggs of caterpillars, we remove them and throw them away. If the pests are completely devouring a plant, we remove the plant and never plant another one.
- **Weed** as needed.
- **Enjoy** as much as possible!

* My current book, "Easy Gardens for South Florida", will be expanded to include the entire state in 2004.

Climate and Zone Information

Range of this book: This book covers the state of Florida, which includes zones 8, 9, 10, and 11. "South Florida" refers to zones 10 and 11. "Central Florida" is zone 9, and "North Florida" is zone 8.

The Truth about Zone Hardiness Maps: I used to think that the zone maps were always right. My trial gardens are in zone 10a. I assumed if I plant something that is listed in a book as growing in zone 10b to 11, it would definitely die at my place the next winter. Not so! I have planted hundreds of 10b plants in my 10a garden and never lost one to cold! The Zone Hardiness Maps are more of a 'be careful' than a 'do not plant in your zone or it will quickly die'. And, it's not as easy as the zone map makes it look. Technically, a zone map would look like a Doppler Radar screen, with zones 9 and 10 being mixed up all over Tampa. Many zone 10 plants are traditionally planted all over central Florida, which is zone 9. Bromeliads and Hibiscus are good examples. Both are quite common in Tampa and Orlando, which is zone 9. The Bromeliad Society was even founded in Orlando, where Bromeliads are not supposed to survive the winters! (Since Bromeliads like shade, most are planted under trees, which usually gives the necessary protection from the cold.) The individual plants in this book are classed by USDA zone *as well as local use patterns.*

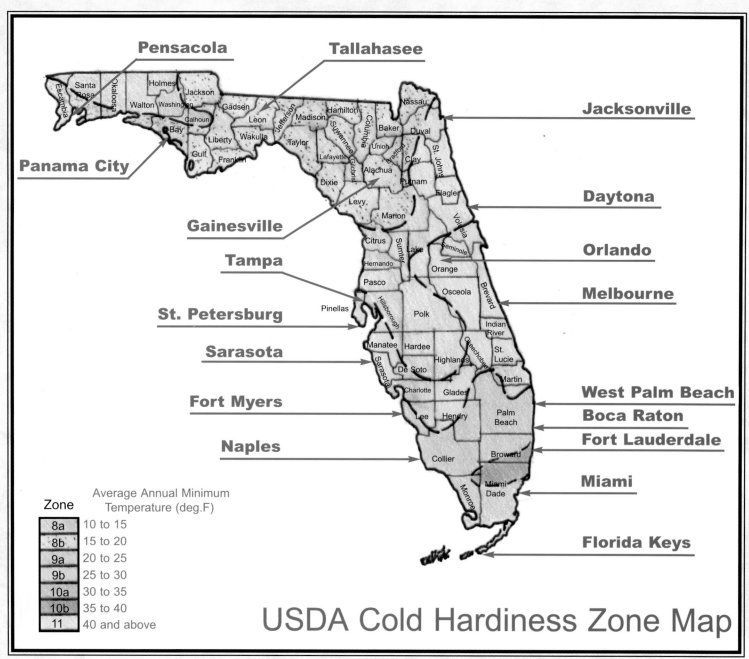

Zone	Average Annual Minimum Temperature (deg.F)
8a	10 to 15
8b	15 to 20
9a	20 to 25
9b	25 to 30
10a	30 to 35
10b	35 to 40
11	40 and above

USDA Cold Hardiness Zone Map

Cold in south Florida: South Florida is defined as zones 10a, 10b, and 11. The pink, green, and small aqua areas (Florida Keys) of the map delineate these areas. Temperatures seldom reach freezing in south Florida, which opens the door to using many of the subtropical plants shown in this book. But, south Florida does have its freezes. It even snowed in Miami in 1977! I was living in Coral Gables at the time and had just planted my front landscape. Within a few weeks, it looked as if it had been burned by a blow torch. Luckily, the plants recovered when temperatures warmed up. But, my next door neighbor's Orchid collection took quite a hit, with many of them dying.

Even if your south Florida garden doesn't freeze in January or February, it normally will not look its best. Our temperatures routinely drop into the 40's, which doesn't damage the plants, but their growth slows way down. They just don't look as good as they do the other 10 months of the year. The only thing to do is have a bit of patience and wait until it warms up. The change can be so subtle that many people do not notice it. In unusually warm years, the winter lack of vigor doesn't happen.

Differences between 10a, 10b, and 11: Zone 11 is the Florida Keys. Temperatures seldom go under 40 degrees. It is the warmest area of Florida, and very few if any plants in this book have historically shown much cold damage in the Keys. The difference between zones 10a and 10b are much hazier and not completely accurate on the map because it cannot show all the microclimates of this large area. There are subtle differences in these areas of a few degrees, which can make a difference in cold damage of plants. I lived in western Boca Raton (west of 441) for seven years in the early 80's and experienced much more cold damage than I did in the late 80's when my home was in the eastern part of the city. The two homes were only a few miles apart! The severe freeze of 1989 damaged Homestead much more than eastern Boca Raton, which was sixty miles to the north!

The 1980's decade was cold for south Florida with a total of 12 freezes in West Palm Beach and 5 in Miami. Many commonly-used subtropical shrubs died back in these freezes, but most recovered when temperatures warmed up. However, many of the cold-sensitive Palms, like Alexander Palms, died in the northern and western parts of south Florida in these freezes. I even lost Areca Palms in the western part of Boca Raton in the 1980's.

Above: 'Red Sister' Ti Plants, Golden Shrimp Plants and Orchids in a south Florida garden. These subtropical plants can be grown outside in south Florida.

The 1990's were much warmer in south Florida, with no freezes reported in West Palm Beach from 1990 to 2000. This warming trend has eased our fears about plants dying from freezes. No one knows why our temperatures are so much warmer.

Read the plant pages carefully to assess your risk of freeze damage. Risks of most of the perennial plants in this book dying from cold in south Florida is minimal based on the climate data from 1975 to 2000. (Of course, we could have another ice age!) A few, like Anthuriums, may die from cold, and this fact is clearly spelled out on the Anthurium pages. You may experience some leaf damage on many tropical perennials, but the majority of them recover when the weather warms up. Be careful of Palms, as they are the most vulnerable to actually dying in a freeze. Also, take

Climate and Zone Information

care with shade trees that are very cold-sensitive, as this could represent quite a financial loss if one was to die. And, some annuals, especially Impatiens, literally melt away in even a light frost.

Cold in central Florida: **Central Florida is defined as zones 9a and 9b.** The blue and yellow sections of the map delineate these areas. **Temperatures routinely reach freezing in central Florida,** meaning much more care is needed with many of the subtropical plants in this book because many are adversely affected by freezes.

The 1980's decade was also cold for central Florida, with a total of 32 freezes in Tampa and 36 in Orlando. **The 1990's were much warmer,** with 4 freezes reported in Tampa and 7 in Orlando from 1990 to 2000. If the temperatures would simply stay the same every year, choosing plants would be a lot easier! But, with these dramatic changes over just one decade, choosing plants for central Florida is becoming pretty tricky. It's almost too warm for plants that like it colder and a bit too cold for those that like it warmer.

Why not simply use colorful plants that aren't hurt by freezes in central Florida? There are some great choices, like Crepe Myrtle, that do quite well through central Florida's freezes. However, the sheer number of colorful plants one can grow in central Florida is greatly increased by planting some that might be adversely affected by cold. Hibiscus is a good example. It is traditionally planted throughout central Florida and frequently dies back in a freeze. But, it comes back as soon as the weather warms up in many central Florida locations. While others might not come back, their low cost is a consolation.

Above: Pansies do well throughout Florida in the winter.

Central Florida is too hot and wet for many northern flowers, like Daffodils and Tulips. Subtropical plants take the heat beautifully but sometimes balk at the cold. They are great choices for most of the year but require care in their placement. Subtropical plants are becoming more popular in northern climates for summer patio plants. Plants like Mussaendas would be spectacular all summer long in containers in Central Florida, even in the worst hot spells.

Jacksonville: **Although located on the northern edge of Florida, Jacksonville is warmer than areas further south,** like Gainesville and Ocala. It's on the border of zone 8 and zone 9, while the rest of what we think of as north Florida is clearly in zone 8. Areas near the beach and along the St. Johns River are warmer than areas further inland. Freeze-tolerant plants, like Azaleas and Camellias co-exist with subtropicals, like Bougainvillea and Hibiscus. Temperatures are similar to New Orleans. Jacksonville gardeners would benefit from an excellent book written for New Orleans, "The New Orleans Garden: Gardening in the Gulf South", by Charlotte Seidenberg (University of

Mississippi Press, 1997).

North Florida: Outside of Jacksonville, north Florida is well above the severe freeze line and not the place for subtropical plants in the permanent landscape. Roses, Hydrangeas, Azaleas, and Camellias are traditional perennials for this area. <u>I am excited to share our eight years of trial gardens in Mississippi with north Florida gardeners.</u> North Florida is very hot in the summer, and many of the plants in this book will thrive in this heat. We have not only discovered some great perennials for north Florida but also some excellent subtropical perennials that can be used as annuals.

However, the basis of this book is the subtropics. I suggest that north Florida gardeners combine this knowlege with many good books that cover gardens in the deep south, Louisiana, and Texas. Southern Living publishes many of them, as does Cool Springs Press, Taylor Publishing, and Timber Press. All of these companies have easily-accessible Web sites.

Microclimates: A few degrees make a big difference in a light freeze. Learn to judge the following:

1. Areas closer to salt water are warmer than inland areas. For example, St. Petersburg is warmer than Tampa. Boca Raton is warmer than Homestead, which is further inland but much further south.

2. Sheltered areas are warmer than open areas. Plants under trees suffer less cold damage than plants in the open.

3. Areas open to winds from the northwest are colder than areas sheltered from these winds. Eva Pabon of the Osceola County Extension office told me that, when she worked at Disney, they planted Lantana around a lake. When the temperatures froze, the Lantana that received the cold wind from the northwest died, while the rest of it lived.

4. Areas close to buildings are warmer than more open areas, particularly if they are on the south side of the building.

Areas close to houses are warmer than open areas.

Areas open to winds are colder than protected spots.

Container gardens can be moved inside if a freeze threatens.

Climate and Zone Information

If you are new to the area and want to test your garden microclimates, buy several high-low thermometers from your local home improvement store. When a freeze is forecast, place them in different areas of your garden. They will record the low temperatures without you staying up all night to watch them.

Look around your neighborhood to see which plants have thrived over the years. You can call your county extension office for local expertise.

Containers are great places for plants that might be damaged by freezes since you can move them inside whenever a freeze threatens. I have very heavy containers that are difficult to move. I bought a small dolly at a home improvement store and was amazed at how much weight I can easily move with it. It comes in quite handy for freeze or hurricane warnings.

Above: Salvia leucantha and Cranberry Pentas thrive throughout Florida.

Cold Protection: South Florida gardens seldom need cold protection. I have tried everything imaginable over the years when a possible freeze was forecast. My efforts usually seemed to cause more harm than good. Remember that more care is needed in central Florida. North Florida gardeners do best to keep cold-sensitive plants in containers and simply move them inside in case of potential damaging cold. However, all gardeners should know about freeze protection, because you never know... Find some ingenious ideas in a book called "Hot Plants for Cool Climates: Gardening with Tropical Plants in Temperate Zones" by Susan A. Roth and Dennis Schrader (Houghton Mifflin Company, New York, 2000). This book deals with tropical gardens in northern locations like Pennsylvania. It is a must-have for any gardener in central or north Florida. If they can show how to grow tropical plants that far north, your Florida garden should be a piece of cake!

Your first line of defense is to plant cold-sensitive materials with as much natural protection as you can. Find your warm microclimates, and use them intelligently. Bromeliads, for example, have survived many a freeze in Orlando when planted under the protection of trees.

Watering: During a freeze warning, it is commonplace for local television stations and newspapers to call local growers to find out about their freeze preparations. Some growers in south and central Florida turn on their water during freezes. I heard this years ago on the evening news and thought I, too, should water. I turned my timer on so that the sprinklers would come on in the middle of the night for 30 minutes in each zone. This proved to be another big gardening blunder! I had far more cold damage than my neighbors, who didn't water at all! Regardless of what anyone tells you, don't even think about turning your sprinklers on during freezing weather. You can do serious damage to the plants. **Be sure to turn off your sprinkler timer if a freeze is forecast. The plants should be well-hydrated before the cold weather arrives.** Cold weather is normally accompanied by drying winds that usually cause more damage than the cold weather itself. Finish watering before nightfall, so that the leaves are dry before the cold hits. If you have wet leaves and stems on a plant when freezing temperatures begin, you will have a lot more cold damage to it.

Some growers do water continuously in a severe freeze, but many lose plants in the process. The theory is that, if a severe freeze hits (e.g., one in the mid-20's or below), the running water will keep the leaves at 32 degrees, and less damage will occur. The water has to stay on the whole time the temperatures are low. If it is off for only a few minutes and the leaves are wet, they will turn to ice. But, often the plants are so wet that they die from root fungus instead of the freeze. It is a very complicated process, and one I have never been successful with. So, just keep your water off in a freeze!

Covering: Growers use freeze cloth, which is sold by the 12 foot wide roll. I have tried this several times. The first time, my nursery workers spent all day neatly covering our plants and holding the cloth down with other potted plants. When the winds hit, all the cloth sailed off into the night. It was a real mess! A few years later, I covered my plants again, this time using bricks to hold down the cloth. It didn't blow away, but I left it on too long. The cold warnings went on for several days. And, after all the trouble of putting it on, I certainly wasn't about to remove it too soon. The plants ended up suffering from light deprivation rather than cold! They looked pretty sad for the next few months. The ones I didn't cover at all fared much better.

Never cover a plant with plastic because it gets cold and burns the leaves. Sheets help somewhat, but they are too small to be of much good. I have heard of some people covering palm buds (the new fronds) with cloth, but if you damage the new fronds, the palm might die. Some commercial establishments, like Disney, use heaters on cold nights.

Is it worth the trouble to grow cold-sensitive plants?

It depends on your priorities. Large trees and exotic Orchids that can't be moved inside pose quite a financial loss if they die. Shrubs and groundcovers are inexpensive in Florida. Most of the plants in this book retail for under five dollars in a one-gallon pot and under twelve dollars in a three-gallon pot. I have never hesitated to buy a plant that was questionable, provided it didn't cost too much. And, I do nothing now if a freeze warning occurs! It is easier to replace the plant than try in vain to protect it!

In central and north Florida, use cold-tolerant plants for the backbone of your garden. Plant the subtropical color for fun, balancing the risks with the potential pleasure you will get from a ten dollar investment that might last for the next 20 years!

Or, use tropicals simply as summer annuals or container plants.

After the freeze:

Some cold damage shows up immediately. Impatiens are a good example. They look as if they melted the day after a freeze. But, most of the damage doesn't show up for a few weeks. You'll notice the leaves dropping off or browning, either all over or just on the tips. If you can stand it, just leave them alone for a while. The damaged branches do no harm to the plant and can actually insulate the healthy part of the plant from another freeze.

Above: Subtropical plants like these Golden Shrimps, Ti Plants, and Bromeliads are more protected from cold near this house than out in the open.

If possible, wait until after March 15 to trim the dead portions off the plant. (I have never been able to wait this long with plants in key locations!) Test the plant before you trim it to see what's dead or alive. With your fingernail, scrape off a tiny piece of the bark. If you see green underneath, that part of the branch is alive. If you see brown underneath, that part is dead. Many of the shrubs that have simply lost their leaves will have no branch damage at all. Just trim the tips off the branches on these.

CHAPTER 1

ANNUALS

Annuals are plants that last just one season.
With the ready availability of so many perennials which can last many years, why plant annuals? Annuals have a higher percentage of color, stay lower, and fill in faster than perennials. They are also less expensive than perennials. Many are less than a dollar!

Trends are changing. For many years, green hedges bordered by Impatiens were the norm in Florida. No more. Layers of color are now the trend, with long-lasting, flowering shrubs and trees forming the main backbone of the landscape. Annuals are the accessory, the color accents of the garden. And many varieties other than thirsty Impatiens are appearing on the scene.

Annuals are fussier than perennials. They need better soil and more consistent temperatures and rainfall. Impatiens, for example, have good years and bad. If temperatures are unusually warm, they do not last as long, growing leggy early. If it rains too much, they get fungus. Easy perennials are more tolerant of varying weather variations.

Annuals are planted several times a year in Florida. Ideally, twice a year is sufficient. In south Florida, plant cool-season flowers from November thru January and warm-season flowers in April or May. In central and north Florida, times vary more and are covered under each individual plant.

Annuals fall into two broad categories, warm season and cool season. This chapter details the easiest of these flowers.

I used an excellent article as a reference for this chapter that you can get for free! Find an article titled "Bedding Plants: Selection, Establishment and Maintenance" by Robert J. Black on the internet at http://edis.ifas.ufl.edu/BODY_MG319. That Web site takes you right to it. (Circular 1134, Florida Cooperative Extension Service, Institute of Food and Agricultural Sciences, University of Florida, March, 1994.)

Left and above: Cosmos (pages 28 and 29)

Botanical Name: *Antirrhinum majus*

Common Name: **Snapdragon**

CHARACTERISTICS

PLANT TYPE: Annual

AVERAGE SIZE: Many varieties available, ranging from 6 inches to 36 inches tall. The most common varieties are in the 12 inch range. The dwarf varieties are more popular than the old-fashioned, tall ones. Try the tall ones for a spectacular, mid-layer display.

GROWTH RATE: Medium

LEAF: Small and narrow, medium green. Size varies by variety.

FLOWER: Spiky clusters in shades of yellow, white, orange, pink, and purple.

AVERAGE LIFE: 5 to 6 months.

ORIGIN: Mediterranean area.

CAUTIONS: None known

SPACING: 8 to 12 inches on center.

Pink bi-colored Snapdragon

Great cool-season annual for Florida. Easy to grow. Tolerant of light frost.

Tall Snapdragons in January in south Florida. Since Snapdragons take longer to establish, Impatiens were planted as a border for faster color. (Design: Tony Cardinale, BallenIsles Country Club, Palm Beach Gardens. Flowers were custom grown by Dave Self, Wyld West Annuals,

General: Snapdragons are traditional annuals being re-discovered in Florida. They offer ease of care and a high percentage of color. Almost as showy as Impatiens, Snapdragons require far less water. They are grown in a wide variety of sizes, from six-inch dwarfs to three-feet tall mid to background plants. I have a lot of experience with the small ones and have been very happy with their performance. They offer a useful carpet of high-impact color and are very useful in areas where low stature is required. I have only recently become acquainted with the tall ones and cannot recommend them based on personal experience. But, they are spectacular, with tall, spire-like flowers that look like the kind of flower that would never grow in Florida. My sources tell me they are quite easy but take longer to become showy than Impatiens. The lovely flowers are ideal for cutting.

Season: Snapdragons are cool-season annuals. Expect five to six months of flowering, if planted from October until December. If the weather is unusually hot, cold, or wet, they do not last as long. If you change annuals three times a year, Snapdragons also do well when planted in March, lasting until about June. Do not plant in the summer.

To locate plants, go to www.easygardencolor.com

Companions: The vertical shape of the Snapdragon's flowers offers great textural contrast with round flowers like Petunias, Geraniums, or Pansies. Try bright pink Snapdragons for the back layer, Midnight Blue Petunias in the middle, and a front border of yellow Pansies. Snapdragons also look good when mixed randomly with Petunias.

Dwarf Snapdragons planted in a mass. They offer excellent low color.

Planting: Every few years, spread two to three inches of potting soil on top of your planting bed shortly before planting. Be sure to use good-quality potting soil, not top soil, because top soil is too heavy for annuals. Plant the Snapdragons high, leaving the top 1/4 inch to 1/2 inch of the root ball out of the ground. *The number one cause of annual death is planting the little plants too deep.* Do not pile mulch up around the base of the plant, or the stem will rot.

Fertilizing: Immediately after planting, fertilize with a well-balanced, slow-release mix that includes minor elements. Repeat in three months. If you have time, spray the Snapdragons with a liquid fertilizer every month instead of the slow-release product. They prefer the liquid but do very well with the easier slow-release.

Trimming: Snapdragons bloom more if dead-headed; in other words, pinch off the old blooms. But, they make very acceptable annual plants without this chore and are seldom dead-headed today. The tallest types benefit most from a dead-heading in January.

Yellow and white Snapdragon

Botanical Name: *Begonia 'Dragon Wing'*
Common Name: **Dragon Wing Begonia**

CHARACTERISTICS

PLANT TYPE: Short-lived herbaceous perennial, often living as long as a year or two. It is more often used as a winter annual.

AVERAGE SIZE: If used as a winter annual, it stays relatively low, about 12 inches tall by 12 inches wide. As a short-lived perennial, it grows to about 24 inches tall by 18 inches wide.

GROWTH RATE: Medium

LEAF: Dark, glossy green. About 3 inches long by 1 1/2 inches wide. Shaped like a wing.

FLOWER: Bright pink or red. Hanging clusters that measure about 4 inches across.

AVERAGE LIFE: 12 months, but most often used as a winter annual for about 6 months because it does much better in winter in south Florida, or early spring in central Florida.

ORIGIN: Begonias are native to the new world tropics. This one is a hybrid.

CAUTIONS: None known

SPACING: 12 inches on center

Pink Dragon Wing Begonia

A beautiful, unique plant for cool-season color. Short-lived perennial most often used as an annual.

Red Dragon Wing Begonias between Golden Shrimp plants and white Wax Begonias. Note the difference between the two types of Begonias. (Design, Brandon Balch, Woodfield Country Club, Boca Raton.)

General: These short-lived perennials are most often used as winter or early spring annuals because they are not as attractive after their first season. When I first planted the Dragon Wings, I thought they were perennials, like the larger Angelwing Begonias. I was disappointed to find that they did not look good after the first winter in most situations in south Florida. Some gardeners have reported Dragon Wings living for years, but most lost them after the first winter. After watching them for a number of years, I realized how valuable they are as winter or early spring annuals in areas that don't freeze. They are beautiful in shade gardens, with a high percentage of color, low water requirements, and a distinctive appearance. They offer about as much color as Impatiens without the high water use. And they are one of our most dependable and durable annuals for our cooler months.

Season: Dragon Wing Begonias flower in summer or winter but do much better in cooler weather. Expect five to six months of flowering, if planted from October until December in south Florida. Because they could freeze, central Florida gardeners may want to wait to plant until late February, or plant in a protected location. North Florida gardeners should wait until the danger of frost is over to plant these outdoors. Or, plant them in containers and move them inside when a freeze threatens.

To locate plants, go to www.easygardencolor.com

Companions: Use bright colors with the red Dragon Wing. Try Stoplight Crotons as the back layer, Justicia 'Fruit Cocktails' in the middle, and a front border of Dragon Wings. Or, plant Giant Shrimp Plants as the back layer, Persian Shields in the middle, and border with red Dragon Wings. The pink Dragon Wing looks good with paler colors, like the pale purples of Brunfelsia.

The red Dragon Wing with some companions that thrive during the cool months.

Planting: Every few years, spread two to three inches of potting soil on top of your planting bed shortly before planting. Be sure to use good-quality potting soil, not top soil, because top soil is too heavy for annuals. Plant the Begonias high, leaving the top 1/4 inch to 1/2 inch of the root ball out of the ground. *The number one cause of annual death is planting the little plants too deep.* Do not pile mulch up around the base of the plant, or the stem will rot.

Fertilizing: Immediately after planting, fertilize with a well-balanced, slow-release mix that includes minor elements. Repeat in three months. If you have time, spray the Begonias with a liquid fertilizer every month instead of the slow-release product. They prefer the liquid but do very well with the easier slow-release.

Trimming: None needed, if used as an annual. As a perennial, trim back drastically in June of each year.

Botanical Name: *Begonia x semperflorens-cultorum*

Common Name: **Wax Begonia**

CHARACTERISTICS

PLANT TYPE: Annual

AVERAGE SIZE: About 12 inches tall by 8 to 12 inches wide.

GROWTH RATE: Medium

LEAF: Dark, glossy green or bronze. About 1 inch long by 1 inch wide. Rounded.

FLOWER: White, pink, or red. Rounded. About 1 inch in diameter. Most are single, but new, beautiful doubles are appearing in the garden centers.

AVERAGE LIFE: 5 to 6 months.

ORIGIN: Brazil

CAUTIONS: Do not over-water.

SPACING: 8 to 12 inches on center.

Single Wax Begonia plant

One of the most dependable cool-season annuals for sun or shade.

Mixed Wax Begonias lining a path. These flowers are a good choice for a manicured, formal look. Insets show Begonia flowers.

General: Wax Begonias are the most common Begonias planted in Florida. They are not only easy to grow but also one of our most dependable cool-season annuals. They take sun or shade and are not demanding of water. These Begonias are available with green or bronze leaves and red, white, or pink flowers. Since Wax Begonias stay compact and neat, they are more often used as a border, as shown above. I use them frequently to border other taller, cool-season annuals, like Salvias or Impatiens. Although most often used in formal plantings, these orderly plants also provide an appropriate edge for wilder, cottage gardens.

Season: Wax Begonias are cool-season annuals. Plant from October until March in south Florida. There are two choices in central Florida: plant in October and expect them to last until the first freeze, or plant from February 15 until March 30 for spring color. In north Florida, plant in spring when danger of freeze has ended. Expect five to six months of flowering, or until June, whichever comes first. Do not plant in the summer.

Companions: For a spectacular color display with a formal look, use masses of bright Impatiens (lipstick, violet, red, orange) bordered by white Begonias (see photo on page 37). Borders using these Begonias also unify wild cottage gardens, as shown opposite. Wax Begonias bordering Dragon Wing Begonias are shown on page 18. Begonias can also be planted in masses of different colors, as shown below.

Mixed Begonias planted in a mass

Planting: Every few years, spread two to three inches of potting soil on top of your planting bed shortly before planting. Be sure to use good-quality potting soil, not top soil, because top soil is too heavy for annuals. Plant the Begonias high, leaving the top 1/4 inch to 1/2 inch of the root ball out of the ground. *The number one cause of annual death is planting the little plants too deep.* Do not pile mulch up around the base of the plant, or the stem will rot.

Fertilizing: Immediately after planting, fertilize with a well-balanced, slow-release mix that includes minor elements. Repeat in three months. If you have time, spray the Begonias with a liquid fertilizer every month instead of the slow-release product. They prefer the liquid but do very well with the easier slow-release.

Trimming: None needed.

Caladium x hortulanum

Botanical Name: Caladium x hortulanum

Common Name: Caladium

CHARACTERISTICS

PLANT TYPE: Technically, an herbaceous perennial. Most commonly used as an annual.

AVERAGE SIZE: 9 inches to 24 inches tall, depending on variety.

GROWTH RATE: Medium

LEAF: Shades of white, green, red, and pink. Size varies by type. Leaves are shaped like either hearts or straps.

FLOWER: Insignificant. Use this plant for its leaf color.

AVERAGE LIFE: Lasts up to 3 years. Normally used for one summer only.

ORIGIN: Tropical South America.

CAUTIONS: Poisonous. All parts of the plant and bulb are irritants.

SPACING: 8 to 12 inches on center.

Note: I got some of my Caladium information from an excellent article you can get for free from the internet. Go to http://edis.ifas.ufl.edu/BODY_EP003 to find the article titled "Caladiums for Florida" by R.J. Black and B. Tija. This document is Circular 469, Department of Environmental Horticulture, Florida Cooperative Extension Service, Institute of Food and Agricultural Sciences, University of Florida. Revised: June 1997.

Use this summer annual for its colorful leaves and tropical look. Very heat-resistant.

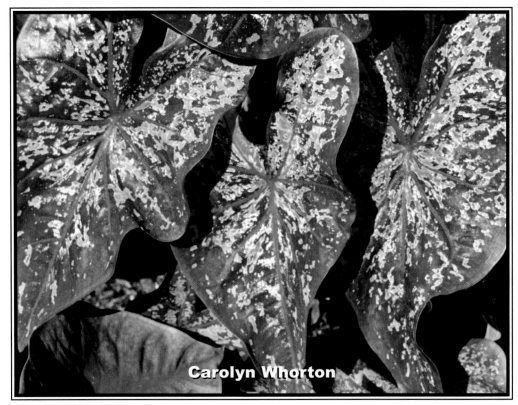
Carolyn Whorton

Caladium leaves are available in many different patterns in shades of green, red, and pink.

General: Caladiums add color in summer, when most other annuals wilt from heat or rot from too much rain. They are native to tropical areas and are well adapted naturally to Florida's summer heat.

Season: Caladiums are perennials, lasting for up to three years if left in the ground in central or south Florida. In an average year, they sprout in the spring, thrive all summer, and die back the following fall. But, if the winter is unusually warm, they can become a problem because they sprout in January if temperatures reach the high 80's. If the bed is filled with winter annuals and the Caladiums unexpectedly appear, they can become a nuisance. In north Florida, the tubers are removed in the winter.

To save tubers: In central and south Florida, it is not necessary to dig up the tubers in the winter because it doesn't get cold enough to damage them. However, north Florida temperatures will kill the tubers, so most gardeners remove them and store them for the next spring. Watch for the leaves to turn yellow and wither. Then, dig up the tubers, taking care to shake off the excess soil, and remove the dead leaves. Allow the tubers to dry in a shady spot for a few days. Store in dry moss or a bag that allows for air flow. Keep inside the house until the following spring.

To locate plants, go to www.easygardencolor.com

Companions: Caladiums are native to tropical areas and fit well with our tropical plants, like Palms and Crotons. They also look good with flowering plants in colors that coordinate with the leaves.

Candidum — Freida Hemple

More Caladium leaves

Planting: Caladiums can be planted as tubers or full-size plants. If planting tubers, they can take poor soil for the first season only. Plant them in February in south Florida, mid-April in central Florida, and the beginning of May in north Florida. Plant the tubers two inches deep with the growing points facing upward. Planting the full-size plants is similar to planting other annuals. Every few years, spread two to three inches of potting soil on top of your planting bed shortly before planting. Be sure to use good-quality potting soil, not top soil, because top soil is too heavy for annuals. Plant the Caladium plants high, leaving the top 1/4 inch to 1/2 inch of the root ball out of the ground. *The number one cause of annual death is planting the little plants too deep.* Do not pile mulch up around the base of the plant, or the stem will rot.

Fertilizing: Immediately after planting, fertilize with a well-balanced, slow-release mix that includes minor elements. Repeat in three months.

Trimming: None needed. Removing the nondescript flowers as they appear increases leaf production but is seldom done in Florida.

GROWING CONDITIONS

LIGHT: Medium shade to full sun. Thick-leafed varieties tolerate more sun than the thinner-leafed types.

WATER: Medium. Plants go dormant without enough water. Water daily the first week or two. Taper off the next 2 weeks. Ideal water is 3 or 4 times a week after the first month. Takes water up to 5 times a week. Requires more water when grown in containers.

SOIL: Wide range, as long as it is well-drained.

SALT TOLERANCE: Medium

WIND TOLERANCE: Medium for strap-leaf type; low for heart-shaped.

ZONE: Grown throughout most of the world as a summer annual. Dies back at 64 degrees. Thrives in all of Florida.

PEST PROBLEMS: Slugs or snails

PROPAGATION: Tubers. The larger the tuber, the fuller the plant.

Botanical Name: *Canna x generalis*

Common Name: **Canna Lily**

CHARACTERISTICS

PLANT TYPE: Most often used as a summer annual. Technically, Cannas grow from rhizomes that keep producing plants for several years. I keep them in my garden as long as they look decent, which varies from 6 months to a few years.

AVERAGE SIZE: Dwarfs to quite large. The dwarfs that only grow to about 18 inches up north reach 3 feet in south Florida. Larger varieties top 5 feet. They are all rather narrow, about 12 to 18 inches wide.

GROWTH RATE: Medium

LEAF: Green, bronze, purple or burgundy; solid, striped, or variegated. Tropical looking. Size varies by type.

FLOWER: Pink, yellow, peach, coral, red, orange. Showy, about 4" across. Grows in clusters. Solids and bicolors.

AVERAGE LIFE: One summer to several years.

ORIGIN: Most of the original Cannas came from South America. The spectacular ones today are mainly hybrids. One variety, *Canna flaccida*, is native to wet areas of Florida.

CAUTIONS: None known

SPACING: 12 to 18 inches on center for the small to medium types. Up to 3 feet on center for the large ones.

Spectacular color impact. High maintenance, especially when planted to be viewed from a close distance.

Canna Lilies in May in my garden

General: I shied away from Cannas in my trial gardens for many years because of their reputation for requiring a lot of care. But, their flowers are so spectacular that I gave into temptation one year and purchased some rhizomes from a bulb catalog. I was pleasantly surprised by their performance. The biggest problem was holes in the leaves from caterpillars. However, the caterpillars only ate the leaves and not the flowers, so I put up with them and did not spray. Do not use this plant if you do not like holes in the leaves or you want to spray because the caterpillars eat LARGE holes throughout the plant! The next problem was brown blotches on the leaves from fungus. We simply cut these leaves off. When the flowers die, the whole stalk dies back with the bloom, so we cut these off, too. All in all, we groomed the plants about once a month, which is more care than any other plant in this book. But, we loved the flowers and found the effort well worth it. The simple plants with green leaves and solid flowers lasted about three years. The fancy hybrids with striped leaves and bicolored flowers only made it a few months.

Season: Canna Lilies are perennials that are most often used as summer annuals throughout Florida. The leaves die back in the cold of central and north Florida and reappear the next spring. Occasionally, they are used in winter in south Florida.

To locate plants, go to www.easygardencolor.com

Companions: Plant Canna Lilies in masses of at least five because the plants are too thin to plant alone. They look best with other plants that peak in summer, like Mussaenda, Plumbago, Thryallis, and Spathoglottis.

Red Canna flower

Planting: Every few years, spread two to three inches of potting soil on top of your planting bed shortly before planting. Be sure to use good-quality potting soil, not top soil, because top soil is too heavy for annuals. Plant the rhizomes about three to four inches deep. If you are planting mature plants, be sure to plant them high, leaving the top 1/4 inch to 1/2 inch out of the ground. Do not pile mulch up around the base of the plant, or the stem will rot.

Fertilizing: Immediately after planting, fertilize with a well-balanced, slow-release mix that includes minor elements. Repeat in three months. If you have time, spray the Cannas with a liquid fertilizer every week instead of the slow-release product. They prefer the liquid but do very well with the easier slow-release. If you leave the plants in the ground for more than one summer season, fertilize either weekly with a liquid or three times a year (March, June, and October) with a well-balanced, slow-release mix that includes minor elements.

Trimming: Cannas need a lot of grooming - removing of brown leaves. When a whole plant looks brown, cut the entire plant to the ground. The rhizome will send up another plant shortly.

Cannas come in shades of yellow, pink, orange, red, peach, or coral.

Botanical Name: *Cosmos spp.*

Common Name: **Cosmos**

CHARACTERISTICS

PLANT TYPE: Annual

AVERAGE SIZE: Varies by type. The smallest dwarfs grow to 12 inches tall by 8 inches wide. The tallest grow to 5 feet tall by 18 inches wide.

GROWTH RATE: Fast

LEAF: Size varies by type, from tiny, fern-like foliage to larger leaves that resemble Marigolds.

FLOWER: Many shades of white, pink, orange, and yellow. Singles and doubles. Sizes from 2 to 4 inches across.

AVERAGE LIFE: Each plant lasts 3 to 5 months. Most varieties reseed like wildflowers for years, flowering constantly in the south Florida garden.

ORIGIN: Mexico

CAUTIONS: Plants fall over easily. (I leave mine where they fall and simply enjoy the flowers.)

SPACING: 8 to 20 inches on center.

A great choice for those who love wildflowers. Low water, easy, and a favorite of butterflies.

Cosmos Cosmic Orange, an All-America Selections winner in 2000

General: Most people consider Cosmos a northern plant and are unaware of their wonderful performance in Florida. Cosmos are the best choice I know for those who want wildflowers here. Wildflowers have a short lifespan but reseed, which is exactly what Cosmos do. They have beautiful flowers on very fine-textured plants. They flop and sometimes fall and are not appropriate for a formal landscape. I have enjoyed many varieties in my gardens, and they are one of my favorite flowers.

Season: Plant Cosmos in fall, winter, or spring. Each plant lasts three to five months. They often reseed politely, not enough to be called invasive. They flower on and off throughout the year in south Florida, and in spring, summer, or fall in the rest of the state.

To locate plants, go to www.easygardencolor.com

Companions: Use Cosmos in wild-looking flower gardens. I plant them at random, in between other flowers. Since they reseed, you never know where they may turn up next, so avoid them in formal gardens. The plants themselves are very fine and, alone, do not have a great form. They show very well when mixed in with other flowers. Sold in single colors or mixes, they do well as cut flowers.

Cosmos sulphureus 'Bright Lights'

Cosmos bipinnatus 'Sonata'

Cosmos bipinnatus 'Sonata'

Cosmos sulphureus 'Cosmic Orange'

'Bright Lights' is a tall variety that reseeds freely. 'Sonata' and 'Cosmic Orange' are medium varieties.

Planting: Cosmos do very well in our native soils, provided they drain well. Plant them high, leaving the top 1/4 inch to 1/2 inch of the root ball out of the ground. *The number one cause of annual death is planting the little plants too deep.* Do not pile mulch up around the base of the plant, or the stem will rot.

Fertilizing: Immediately after planting, fertilize with a well-balanced, slow-release mix that includes minor elements. Repeat in three months. Do not over-fertilize, or you will get lots of leaves and few flowers.

Trimming: The taller varieties flop over and may be trimmed back to one foot tall. The tallest stems can be staked to avoid falling. I let mine fall and simply enjoy the flowers.

Botanical Name: *Gloxinia sylvatica*

Common Name: **Bolivian Sunset**

CHARACTERISTICS

PLANT TYPE: Perennial that usually lives for about one year and blooms in winter. Most practically used as an annual because it seldom looks good after its first season.

AVERAGE SIZE: 12 to 18 inches tall by 12 to 18 inches wide.

GROWTH RATE: Medium

LEAF: Narrow and pointed. Dark, olive green. About 1 inch long by 3/8 inch wide.

FLOWER: Tubular, bright, iridescent orange with golden centers. About 3/4 inch long.

AVERAGE LIFE: Lasts up to 2 years. Normally used for one winter only.

ORIGIN: Bolivia and Peru

CAUTIONS: None known

SPACING: 12 inches on center.

An unusual and beautiful small perennial that is wonderful as a winter annual in south Florida.

Bolivian Sunset plant. Although the flowers are small, they are so bright that they show up very well from a distance.

General: Although Bolivian Sunset is technically a perennial, it makes an excellent winter annual for south Florida gardens (untested in central or north Florida). The plant sometimes regrows and flowers the following winter if it is cut back at the end of its flowering season. More often than not, about half the plants die before reaching the next season; the summer heat and rains seem too much for them. As an annual in winter, its performance is excellent, with flowers that almost glow with color.

Season: Bolivian Sunsets are winter bloomers in south Florida. Expect five to six months of flowering, if planted from October until December. Do not expect flowers in the summer.

To locate plants, go to www.easygardencolor.com

Companions: Use Bolivian Sunsets with other bright colors. Violet, hot pink, and red New Guinea Impatiens are the best annual companions. Shrimp Plants and Crotons are excellent shrub companions. And, Bolivian Sunset is spectacular when planted under purple or red Bougainvillea.

New Guinea Impatiens

Giant Shrimp

New Guinea Impatiens

Bolivian Sunset

Bolivian Sunset flowers and some companions. The contrast of the bright colors creates great winter color impact.

Planting: Every few years, spread two to three inches of potting soil on top of your planting bed shortly before planting. Be sure to use good-quality potting soil, not top soil, because top soil is too heavy for annuals. Plant the Bolivian Sunsets high, leaving the top 1/4 inch to 1/2 inch of the root ball out of the ground. *The number one cause of annual death is planting the little plants too deep.* Do not pile mulch up around the base of the plant, or the stem will rot.

Fertilizing: Immediately after planting, fertilize with a well-balanced, slow-release mix that includes minor elements. Repeat in three months. If you have time, spray the Bolivian Sunsets with a liquid fertilizer every month instead of the slow-release product. They prefer the liquid but do very well with the easier slow-release.

Trimming: None needed, if used as an annual. As a perennial, trim back drastically in the spring after flowering.

LIGHT: Medium shade to full sun. Excellent shade color.

WATER: Medium. Water daily the first week or two. Taper off the next 2 weeks. Ideal water is 3 or 4 times a week in sun and twice a week in shade. Takes water up to 5 times a week. Requires more water when grown in containers.

SOIL: Wide range, as long as it is well-drained.

SALT TOLERANCE: Low

WIND TOLERANCE: Low

ZONE: 10B to 11. Untested in 10A, or any parts of central or north Florida.

PEST PROBLEMS: None known

PROPAGATION: Cuttings or division

Botanical Name: *Impatiens double*

Common Name: **Double Impatiens**

CHARACTERISTICS

PLANT TYPE: Annual

AVERAGE SIZE: 18 to 24 inches tall by 12 to 18 inches wide.

GROWTH RATE: Fast

LEAF: Rounded, with a point on the end. Medium green or variegated. About 1 inch long by 1 inch wide.

FLOWER: Beautiful, rose-like, double bloom. About 1 to 1 1/2 inches wide.

AVERAGE LIFE: 5 to 6 months.

ORIGIN: Africa

CAUTIONS: None known

SPACING: 8 to 12 inches on center.

Note: Impatiens are great for pots or areas that can be watered separately from the rest of the garden. I have stopped using them in my beds with the other plants. They need more water than any other plant I use. This high water use is not good for the south Florida environment. It also increases the maintenance of the rest of the garden: the weeds thrive, and the other annuals or perennials in the bed grow much too fast and lanky, requiring more trimming and fertilization. The high water use can also shorten the lifespan of many other plants.

A little-known Impatiens with a beautiful flower that resembles a rose. Great choice for container gardens.

Double Impatiens are available in many shades of red, pink, orange, violet, and white. Some new hybrids even have bi-colored flowers. Leaves are either green or variegated.

General: I have been using double Impatiens for many years with great success. Their flowers are lovely and very unusual for Florida. Be sure to use them in the shade, and understand that they need a lot of water. Plant these Impatiens in areas where they will be viewed up close. They look like single Impatiens from a distance.

Season: Impatiens are cool-season annuals. Plant from October until March in south Florida. There are two choices in central Florida: plant in October and expect them to last until the first freeze, or plant from February 15 until March 30 for spring color. In north Florida, plant in spring when danger of freeze has ended. Expect five to six months of flowering, or until June, whichever comes first. Do not plant in the summer.

Companions: Double Impatiens look best planted in masses of different colors. They are excellent choices for containers. Plant them where they are viewed up close.

Some of the double Impatiens colors. The flowers are solid or bi-colored. The leaves are green or variegated.

Planting: Every few years, spread two to three inches of potting soil on top of your planting bed shortly before planting. Be sure to use good-quality potting soil, not top soil, because top soil is too heavy for annuals. Plant the Impatiens high, leaving the top 1/4 inch to 1/2 inch of the root ball out of the ground. *The number one cause of annual death is planting the little plants too deep.* Do not pile mulch up around the base of the plant, or the stem will rot.

Fertilizing: Immediately after planting, fertilize with a well-balanced, slow-release mix that includes minor elements. Repeat in three months. Supplement with a liquid fertilizer if you have time. *Quality fertilizer is critical to the performance of Impatiens. They do not grow well without it.*

Trimming: Impatiens normally are not trimmed. However, if they get too tall and leggy in late winter or early spring, trim them back by about half. It takes about a month for them to recover.

GROWING CONDITIONS

LIGHT: Medium shade to full sun. Excellent shade color. Because of their high water requirement, I do not recommend Impatiens for full sun.

WATER: High in sun, medium in shade. Water daily the first week or two. Taper off over the next 2 weeks. After the first month, ideal water is 4 or 5 times a week in sun, 2 or 3 times a week in shade. Takes water everyday without damage. Impatiens' big flaw is their thirstiness. When the plants are large and the temperatures rise in spring, they sometimes need water twice a day in full sun. (See *Note* in opposite sidebar.) Requires more water when grown in containers.

SOIL: Wide range

SALT TOLERANCE: Low

WIND TOLERANCE: Low

ZONE: 10A to 11 in winter. Very sensitive to the slightest frost. Zones 8 or 9 in spring. Grown throughout the world in the warmer months.

PEST PROBLEMS: Fungus, slugs

PROPAGATION: Cuttings or seeds

Botanical Name: *Impatiens wallerana*

Common Name: **Impatiens**

The most popular bedding plant in the world

Some of the many Impatiens colors. The camera never gets exact color. If you want true color interpretation, see the real plants at your garden center.

General: Impatiens are fairly dependable and give a high percentage of color. They require more water than any other plant in this book. This makes them difficult in Florida gardens unless they are on a separate watering system (see *Note*, left). Other annuals, like Petunias, Salvias, Snapdragons, Pansies, and Begonias, provide almost as much color with much less water.

Season: Impatiens are cool-season annuals. Plant from October until March in south Florida. There are two choices in central Florida: plant in October and expect them to last until the first freeze, or plant from February 15 until March 30 for spring color. In north Florida, plant in spring when danger of freeze has ended. Expect five to six months of flowering, or until June, whichever comes first. Do not plant in the summer.

To locate plants, go to www.easygardencolor.com

Companions: Impatiens show best with other bright colors for daytime viewing. One of the most beautiful combinations includes lipstick (bright pink), violet, red, and orange. And, don't forget to combine the bright Impatiens flowers with yellow flowers, such as Shrimp Plants and Marigolds. Lighter Impatiens colors, like the whites and pale pinks, show up better at night. Impatiens are great for pots.

Orange and violet Impatiens contrast well with yellow Marigolds.

Planting: Every few years, spread two to three inches of potting soil on top of your planting bed shortly before planting. Be sure to use good-quality potting soil, not top soil, because top soil is too heavy for annuals. Plant the Impatiens high, leaving the top 1/4 inch to 1/2 inch of the root ball out of the ground. *The number one cause of annual death is planting the little plants too deep.* Do not pile mulch up around the base of the plant, or the stem will rot.

Fertilizing: Immediately after planting, fertilize with a well-balanced, slow-release mix that includes minor elements. Repeat in three months. If you have time, spray the Impatiens with a liquid fertilizer every month instead of the slow-release product. They prefer the liquid but do very well with the easier slow-release. *Quality fertilizer is critical to the performance of Impatiens. They do not grow well without it.*

Trimming: Impatiens are not normally trimmed. But, if they get too tall and leggy in late winter or early spring, trim them back by about half. It takes about a month for them to recover.

GROWING CONDITIONS

LIGHT: Medium shade to full sun. Excellent shade color. Because of their high water requirement, I do not recommend Impatiens for full sun.

WATER: High in sun, medium in shade. Water daily the first week or two. Taper off over the next 2 weeks. After the first month, ideal water is 4 or 5 times a week in sun, 2 or 3 times a week in shade. Takes water everyday without damage. Impatiens' big flaw is their thirstiness. When the plants are large and the temperatures rise in spring, they sometimes need water twice a day in full sun. (See *Note,* opposite sidebar.) Requires more water when grown in containers.

SOIL: Wide range

SALT TOLERANCE: Medium

WIND TOLERANCE: Low

ZONE: 10A to 11 in winter. Very sensitive to the slightest frost. Zones 8 or 9 in spring. Grown throughout the world in the warmer months.

PEST PROBLEMS: Fungus, slugs

PROPAGATION: Cuttings or seeds

Botanical Name: *Impatiens x New Guinea Hybrids*
Common Name: New Guinea Impatiens

CHARACTERISTICS

PLANT TYPE: Annual

AVERAGE SIZE: 12 to 18 inches tall by 12 to 18 inches wide.

GROWTH RATE: Fast

LEAF: Rounded, with a point on the end. Medium green or variegated. About 1 inch long by 1 inch wide.

FLOWER: Iridescent pinks, oranges, reds, purples, peaches, whites, and multicolored. Larger than regular Impatiens; about 1 1/2 inches in diameter.

AVERAGE LIFE: 5 to 6 months.

ORIGIN: New Guinea

CAUTIONS: None known

SPACING: 12 inches on center.

Note: Impatiens are great for pots or areas that can be watered separately from the rest of the garden. I have stopped using them in my beds with the other plants. They need more water than any other plant I use. This high water use is not good for the south Florida environment. It also increases the maintenance of the rest of the garden: the weeds thrive, and the other annuals or perennials in the bed grow much too fast and lanky, requiring more trimming and fertilization. The high water use can also shorten the lifespan of many other plants.

One of the most colorful annuals in the world

Hot Pink

Orange

Purple

New Guinea Impatiens lining a path

General: New Guinea Impatiens are the most colorful annuals currently available in Florida. They do not use as much water as the regular Impatiens but are still very thirsty plants (See *Note,* left). They do better in sun than regular Impatiens but prefer some shade.

Season: Impatiens are cool-season annuals. Plant from October until March in south Florida. There are two choices in central Florida: plant in October and expect them to last until the first freeze, or plant from February 15 until March 30 for spring color. In north Florida, plant in spring when danger of freeze has ended. Expect five to six months of flowering, or until June, whichever comes first. Do not plant in the summer.

To locate plants, go to www.easygardencolor.com

Companions: Impatiens show best with other bright colors for daytime viewing. One of the most beautiful combinations includes lipstick (bright pink), violet, red, and orange. And don't forget combining the bright Impatiens flowers with other yellow flowers, such as Shrimp Plants and Marigolds. Lighter Impatiens colors, like the whites and pale pinks, show up better at night. New Guineas are great for pots.

Violet, orange, and red New Guinea Impatiens bordered by white Wax Begonias.

Planting: Every few years, spread two to three inches of potting soil on top of your planting bed shortly before planting. Be sure to use good-quality potting soil, not top soil, because top soil is too heavy for annuals. Plant the Impatiens high, leaving the top 1/4 inch to 1/2 inch of the root ball out of the ground. *The number one cause of annual death is planting the little plants too deep.* Do not pile mulch up around the base of the plant, or the stem will rot.

Fertilizing: Immediately after planting, fertilize with a well-balanced, slow-release mix that includes minor elements. Repeat in three months. If you have time, spray the Impatiens with a liquid fertilizer every month instead of the slow-release product. They prefer the liquid but do very well with the easier slow-release. *Quality fertilizer is critical to the performance of Impatiens. They do not grow well without it.*

Trimming: Impatiens are not normally trimmed. But, if they get too tall and leggy in late winter or early spring, trim them back by about half. It takes about a month for them to recover.

GROWING CONDITIONS

LIGHT: Medium shade to full sun. Excellent shade color.

WATER: High in sun, medium in shade. Water daily the first week or two. Taper off over the next 2 weeks. After the first month, ideal water is 4 or 5 times a week in sun, 2 or 3 times a week in shade. Takes water everyday without damage. Impatiens' big flaw is their thirstiness. When the plants are large and the temperatures rise in spring, they sometimes need water twice a day in full sun. (See *Note*, opposite sidebar.) Requires more water when grown in containers.

SOIL: Wide range

SALT TOLERANCE: Medium

WIND TOLERANCE: Medium

ZONE: 10A to 11 in winter. Very sensitive to the slightest frost. Zones 8 or 9 in spring. Grown throughout the world in the warmer months.

PEST PROBLEMS: Fungus, slugs

PROPAGATION: Cuttings or seeds

Botanical Name: *Lobularia maritima*
Common Name: Alyssum, Sweet Alyssum

CHARACTERISTICS

PLANT TYPE: Annual

AVERAGE SIZE: 3 to 6 inches tall by 8 inches wide.

GROWTH RATE: Medium

LEAF: The leaf is so tiny it is hardly seen when the plant is in full flower.

FLOWER: White, light or dark purple, rose. Tiny clusters form a mat that looks like solid color when it is in full bloom.

AVERAGE LIFE: 4 to 5 months.

ORIGIN: Mediterranean region.

CAUTIONS: None known

SPACING: 6 to 8 inches on center. Closer than most other annuals.

Alyssum has a cascading growth habit when planted in a planter or container.

A beautiful, low-growing winter annual that's great for borders and pots.

White Alyssum lining a path of Starburst Pentas and Yellow Lantana. This plant is an excellent choice for winter borders in full sun.

General: Alyssum is a beautiful, sweet-smelling annual that is grown throughout the world in the summer, but thrives in Florida's winter and spring. Since it cannot take the heat that we sometimes experience in October and November, plant it later than most other cool-season annuals. It thrives in our cool, dry winters and springs, provided it is given a lot of sun. Alyssum is not as dependable as Petunias or Pansies. I have had some years when the plants have not done well, and there was no explanation as to why. But, they are so lovely and smell so wonderful that I believe they deserve more use in Florida. Take care with watering, because they do not like to dry out but get fungus if over-watered. I have never had a problem with them in containers, where they are well-adapted to cascading over the edges. The white did better than the purple or rose in my trials.

Season: Alyssum is a cool-season annual. Expect four to five months of flowering. If the weather is unusually hot, cold, or wet, they do not last as long. Plant in December or January in south Florida and around February 15 in central Florida. In north Florida, plant after danger of freeze had ended. Do not plant in the summer.

To locate plants, go to www.easygardencolor.com

Companions: Plant Alyssum with other plants that bloom in winter and spring. An easy container idea features hot pink Geraniums in the middle, Victoria Blue Salvias on the sides, and white Alyssum around the edges. The Alyssum will cascade over the edges of the pots. Alyssum also makes a great border for Pansies, Petunias, or Snapdragons.

Alyssum covers the ground in a carpet of rose, white, and different purples. (Design: Tony Cardinale, BallenIsles Country Club, Palm Beach Gardens. Flowers were custom grown by Dave Self, Wyld West Annuals, Loxahatchee.)

Planting: Every few years, spread two to three inches of potting soil on top of your planting bed shortly before planting. Be sure to use good-quality potting soil, not top soil, because top soil is too heavy for annuals. Plant the Alyssum high, leaving the top 1/4 inch to 1/2 inch of the root ball out of the ground. *The number one cause of annual death is planting the little plants too deep.* Do not pile mulch up around the base of the plant, or the stem will rot.

Fertilizing: Immediately after planting, fertilize with a well-balanced, slow-release mix that includes minor elements. Repeat in three months. If you have time, spray the Alyssum with a liquid fertilizer every month instead of the slow-release product. They prefer the liquid but do very well with the easier slow-release.

Trimming: None needed during most years. If the plants go to seed, trim or brush off the tiny pods, and the plants may bloom again.

GROWING CONDITIONS

LIGHT: Full sun. Alyssum does not like even a little bit of shade.

WATER: Medium. Water daily the first week or two. Taper off the next 2 weeks. Ideal water is twice a week after the first month. Takes water up to 3 times a week. Do not overwater, or the plant will get fungus. On the other hand, if you allow the plant to dry out completely, parts of it will turn brown. Requires more water when grown in containers.

SOIL: Wide range, as long as it is well-drained.

SALT TOLERANCE: Medium

WIND TOLERANCE: Medium

ZONE: Spring or summer annual in cooler areas of the world. Late winter and spring annual in Florida. Tolerant of light frost but not freeze. Protect from freezes if used during winter in central or north Florida.

PEST PROBLEMS: None known

PROPAGATION: Germinates quickly from seed, in about a week. Blooms in about 6 weeks.

Botanical Name: *Melampodium paludosum*

Common Name: **Melampodium**

CHARACTERISTICS

PLANT TYPE: Most commonly used as an annual. Occasionally lives more than one season.

AVERAGE SIZE: 12 to 18 inches tall by 12 to 16 inches wide.

GROWTH RATE: Fast

LEAF: Lime green, small and pointed. About 3/4 inch long.

FLOWER: Small and yellow. Shaped like a daisy. About 1/2 inch wide.

AVERAGE LIFE: 5 to 6 months. Occasionally lasts a year.

ORIGIN: Tropical America

CAUTIONS: Reseeds occasionally but not enough to be a nuisance.

SPACING: 12 inches on center.

Great plant for summer color. Small flower resembles a daisy. Deserves much more use.

Melampodium planted in a formal garden with an Ilex border. (Design: Danny Miller, Breakers Hotel, Palm Beach. Flowers custom grown by Dave Self, Wyld West Annuals, Loxahatchee.)

General: This little-known plant is good choice for yellow color in summer. Some years it is not as dependable as others, but its overall performance is good. Its daisy-like flower and mounding growth habit are appropriate for formal or informal gardens. With its low water use and ability to adapt to sun or shade, this flower will be used much more in the future.

Season: Melampodiums are summer annuals. Plant in spring, and expect them to last until late fall. Most years, they thrive all summer long, occasionally lasting a full year. If the weather is unusually wet, their lifespan shortens. The winters are normally too cold for them.

Melampodium planted in an informal garden.

To locate plants, go to www.easygardencolor.com

Companions: For bright summer color, plant Red or Cranberry Pentas for the back layer, Melampodium in the middle, and trailing blue Torenias for the front border. Or, use Melampodium to border a combination of Firespike and Plumbago. Melampodium is also a great border for Red Spot or Stoplight Crotons.

Melampodium flowers with some companions. The red, yellow, and blue combination are ideal for Florida because they show well in our bright sun-

Planting: Every few years, spread two to three inches of potting soil on top of your planting bed shortly before planting. Be sure to use good-quality potting soil, not top soil, because top soil is too heavy for annuals. Plant the Melampodiums high, leaving the top 1/4 inch to 1/2 inch of the root ball out of the ground. *The number one cause of annual death is planting the little plants too deep.* Do not pile mulch up around the base of the plant, or the stem will rot.

Fertilizing: Immediately after planting, fertilize with a well-balanced, slow-release mix that includes minor elements. Repeat in three months.

Trimming: None needed, if used as a one-season annual. If the plant is doing well after one season, trim as needed to restore form.

Botanical Name: *Pelargonium x hortorum*

Common Name: **Geranium**

CHARACTERISTICS

PLANT TYPE: Annual that sometimes grows for more than one season. Normally used as a single-season annual because it seldom looks good after its first winter.

AVERAGE SIZE: 12 to 24 inches tall by 12 to 18 inches wide.

GROWTH RATE: Medium

LEAF: Medium green and rounded. About 2 to 3 inches across. Some varieties have ivy-shaped leaves. These take less heat but are better suited for hanging baskets.

FLOWER: Many shades of red, pink, peach, white, and lavender. Flower is made of clusters. The cluster measures about 3 to 4 inches across.

AVERAGE LIFE: 5 to 6 months.

ORIGIN: South Africa

CAUTIONS: None known

SPACING: 12 to 18 inches on center.

Medium pink Geranium

Beautiful, traditional flowers that love Florida's cool season.

Hot pink Geraniums planted as a low border for mixed Snapdragons and white Cleome. (Design: Brandon Balch, Woodfield Country Club, Boca Raton.)

General: Geraniums do well in our average, dry, cool seasons but do not thrive in wet ones. They also need more maintenance than the other annuals in this book. They require dead-heading: pinching off the dead flowers and brown leaves. Without dead-heading, the old flowers turn brown and persist for quite a while. But, well maintained Geraniums are beautiful, particularly in pots. I usually plant a few in a key location but would not plant hundreds in a bed. Geraniums are historically popular in Spain and Italy, particularly in red clay pots. Since Mediterranean architecture is so prevalent in Florida, Geraniums have a sense of fit with our barrel tile roofs and stucco walls.

Season: Geraniums are cool-season annuals. Plant from October until March in south Florida. There are two choices in central Florida: plant in October and expect them to last until the first freeze, or plant from February 15 until March 30 for spring color. In north Florida, plant after danger of frost has ended. Expect five to six months of flowering, or until June, whichever comes first. Do not plant in the summer.

To locate plants, go to www.easygardencolor.com

Companions: Geraniums are great companions for Salvias, Snapdragons, Marigolds, and Petunias. Use the bright red, orange, or pink Geraniums with other bright flowers that have yellow and blue tones. Dark, bluish-purple Petunias, Pansies, or Salvias and yellow Marigolds, Snapdragons, or Pansies work well. The paler pink and peach Geraniums look better with paler companions.

Bright pink Geraniums and some companions. The intensity of the pink contrasts well with the other bright colors.

Planting: Every few years, spread two to three inches of potting soil on top of your planting bed shortly before planting. Be sure to use good-quality potting soil, not top soil, because top soil is too heavy for annuals. Plant the Geraniums high, leaving the top 1/4 inch to 1/2 inch of the root ball out of the ground. *The number one cause of annual death is planting the little plants too deep.* Do not pile mulch up around the base of the plant, or the stem will rot.

Fertilizing: Immediately after planting, fertilize with a well-balanced, slow-release mix that includes minor elements. Repeat in three months. If you have time, spray the Geraniums with a liquid fertilizer every month instead of the slow-release product. They prefer the liquid but do very well with the easier slow-release.

Trimming: Geraniums need dead-heading to look good (pinching off the dead flowers). They also look better if old leaves are pinched off. Other trimming is not necessary unless you want to attempt to keep them going over the summer.

GROWING CONDITIONS

LIGHT: Light shade to full sun

WATER: Medium. Water daily the first week or two. Taper off the next 2 weeks. Ideal water is twice a week after the first month. Takes water up to 3 times a week. Do not overwater, or the plant will get fungus. If the soil dries out, the leaves yellow. Requires more water when grown in containers.

SOIL: Wide range, as long as it is well-drained.

SALT TOLERANCE: High

WIND TOLERANCE: High

ZONE: Grown all over the world as a summer annual. In zones 9-11, sometimes lives for a year or two with freeze protection.

PEST PROBLEMS: Whiteflies and fungus

PROPAGATION: Seeds or cuttings. Very difficult to start from seed.

Peach Geranium

Botanical Name: *Pentas lanceolata 'New Look'*

Common Name: **Dwarf or New Look Pentas**

CHARACTERISTICS

PLANT TYPE: Annual that occasionally grows for more than one season, especially if the summer is drier than normal.

AVERAGE SIZE: 12 to 18 inches tall by 12 to 18 inches wide. The plants with dark purple flowers are the smallest, the reds mid-range, and the pinks the tallest.

GROWTH RATE: Medium

LEAF: Medium green and pointed. About 2 to 3 inches long by 1/2 inch wide.

FLOWER: Red, pink, white, or purple. Clusters about 2 inches across.

AVERAGE LIFE: 3 to 6 months.

ORIGIN: Africa

CAUTIONS: Dwarf Pentas are very compact, making air circulation difficult in very wet weather. If it rains too much in the summer, they can die from fungus. The purple is the most susceptible.

SPACING: 8 to 12 inches on center.

One of the smallest Pentas. Works best as a summer annual. Great butterfly plant.

Dwarf Pentas are available in shades of pink, red, purple, and white.

General: There are at least sixteen different types of Pentas on the market. The taller ones are short-term perennials, lasting for three to five years. The dwarfs or New Look Pentas do not live as long, lasting for three to six months on the average. But, they offer the advantage of staying low, making them very valuable for annual beds and borders. And, since Pentas are native to Africa, they are very tolerant of south Florida's summer heat. They are not as dependable as other summer annuals, like Coleus and Caladiums. They frequently get fungus, more so than the larger Pentas. Plan on spraying with a fungicide if you choose this Penta. Nor are they as colorful as the perennial Pentas, like the red or Cranberry. Use the dwarfs only if you want a maximum height of eighteen inches.

Season: Because of their heat tolerance, dwarf Pentas are most often used as summer annuals. They grow in the winter in south Florida but are not as colorful as other winter annuals, like Petunias or Salvia. In all of Florida they do best planted in May or June, and should live until November. Sometimes these small Pentas live as long as two years in frost-free areas, but, more often, only six months. If the summer is unusually wet, they may not make it through one summer.

To locate plants, go to www.easygardencolor.com

Companions: Dwarf Pentas look good massed in beds of mixed colors. They also work well with Caladiums and Coleus. Use flower colors that appear in the Caladium or Coleus leaves. Dwarf Pentas also make great borders for summer perennial beds, including plants like Plumbago, Mussaenda, and Thryallis.

The individual, five-petaled flowers have white centers. The perennial Cranberry Pentas have hot pink centers.

Planting: Every few years, spread two to three inches of potting soil on top of your planting bed before planting. Be sure to use good-quality potting soil, not top soil, because top soil is too heavy for annuals. Plant the Pentas high, leaving the top 1/4 inch to 1/2 inch of the root ball out of the ground. *The number one cause of annual death is planting the little plants too deep.* Do not pile mulch up around the base of the plant, or the stem will rot.

Fertilizing: Immediately after planting, fertilize with a well-balanced, slow-release mix that includes minor elements. Repeat in three months.

Trimming: Trimming is not necessary, unless you want to attempt to keep your Pentas going beyond their first summer. If the plants become leggy, trim back to about half. The plants recover well from this cutback about fifty to seventy-five percent of the time. These little Pentas are not as strong as the larger, perennial Pentas, which take cutbacks well.

GROWING CONDITIONS

LIGHT: Light shade to full sun.

WATER: Low. Water daily the first week or two. Taper off over the next two weeks. Ideal water is twice a week after the first month. Takes water up to 3 times a week at the most. The number one cause of early death of Dwarf Pentas is too much water.

SOIL: Wide range, as long as it is well-drained.

SALT TOLERANCE: Medium high

WIND TOLERANCE: Medium high

ZONE: Grown all over the world as a summer annual. In zones 10 to 11, sometimes lives for a year or two. Not as cold tolerant as the larger Pentas.

PEST PROBLEMS: If sections of a plant become brown and die back, the plant has fungus. Cut back on water, if possible, or spray with a fungicide if problem becomes severe.

PROPAGATION: Seeds or cuttings.

Botanical Name: *Petunia spp.*

Common Name: **Petunias**

CHARACTERISTICS

PLANT TYPE: Annual

AVERAGE SIZE: 6 to 18 inches tall by 10 to 24 inches wide.

GROWTH RATE: Medium

LEAF: Medium green and pointed. About 2 inches long by 3/4 inch wide.

FLOWER: Many colors and sizes available. Pinks, purples, reds, whites, salmons. Some bicolored, like red and white stripes. Singles and doubles. Sizes range from 1 inch wide to 5 inches wide. Generally, the smaller and simpler the flower, the higher the percentage of color on the plant. Petunias with simpler flowers are also usually easier to grow.

AVERAGE LIFE: 5 to 6 months.

ORIGIN: South Africa

CAUTIONS: None known

SPACING: 12 inches on center. The 'Wave' series, which does very well in Florida, grows wider, reaching about 18 to 24 inches.

Mini purple Petunias

Great color for sunny spots in our cool season. Gives almost as much color as Impatiens without the high water use.

'Ramblin Peach Glow' Petunias

General: Petunias are easy, very colorful, and deserve much more use in Florida. Thriving in our cool winters and warm springs, they require almost no care. They are also very low-growing, making them quite useful for borders. Petunias are available in many sizes and colors. The flowers range in size from tiny to quite large. The very large-flowered Petunias generally have fewer flowers than the small to medium ones. The newer 'Wave' Petunias are particularly well suited both for containers and to be planted in the ground. The tiny 'Mini Petunias' (shown in both lower corners) are one of the best new container plants I have seen in many years.

Season: For the longest life, plant in fall, from October until December in south or central Florida. They last about five or six months when planted at this time of year. If the weather is unusually hot, cold, or wet, they do not last as long. In north Florida, plant after danger of frost has ended. Do not plant in the summer.

To locate plants, go to www.easygardencolor.com

Companions: Petunias mix beautifully with Snapdragons, Salvias, Pansies, and Geraniums. They also look great planted in mixed colors of all Petunias. One color I find particularly useful is the midnight blue (looks like dark blue velvet), shown below. It mixes well with red or yellow, like red Salvias and yellow Pansies.

Petunias have solid or bi-colored flowers.

LIGHT: Light shade to full sun.

WATER: Medium. Water daily the first week or two. Taper off over the next two weeks. Ideal water is twice a week after the first month. Takes water up to 4 times a week.

SOIL: Wide range, as long as it is well-drained.

SALT TOLERANCE: High. Petunias thrive near the sea.

WIND TOLERANCE: High

ZONE: Grown all over the world as a summer annual. Plant in winter in central and south Florida, spring in north Florida. Withstands a light frost. Protect from hard freezes.

PEST PROBLEMS: I have never seen a pest on these plants. Have heard of aphids and caterpillars occasionally.

PROPAGATION: Seeds or tip cuttings.

Planting: Every few years, spread two to three inches of potting soil on top of your planting bed before planting. Be sure to use good-quality potting soil, not top soil, because top soil is too heavy for annuals. Plant the Petunias high, leaving the top 1/4 inch to 1/2 inch of the root ball out of the ground. *The number one cause of annual death is planting the little plants too deep.* Do not pile mulch up around the base of the plant, or the stem will rot.

Fertilizing: Immediately after planting, fertilize with a well-balanced, slow-release mix that includes minor elements. Repeat in three months. If you have time, spray the Petunias with a liquid fertilizer every month instead of the slow-release product. They prefer the liquid but do very well with the easier slow-release.

Trimming: None needed. There is a common misconception that Petunias require dead-heading (removing of dead flowers). This is not so.

Mini white Petunias

Botanical Name: *Portulaca grandiflora*

Common Name: **Moss Rose**

CHARACTERISTICS

PLANT TYPE: Annual

AVERAGE SIZE: 4 to 8 inches tall by 8 to 14 inches wide.

GROWTH RATE: Medium

LEAF: Tiny and thick like a succulent plant. About 1/4 inch wide by 3/4 inch long. Olive green.

FLOWER: Bright pinks, oranges, yellows, purples, and whites. Looks like jelly bean colors. Singles or doubles. About 1 inch wide.

AVERAGE LIFE: 2 to 3 months.

ORIGIN: Brazil

CAUTIONS: Shorter-lived than most other summer annuals. Flowers only open in sunny weather.

SPACING: 6 to 8 inches on center.

Short-lived but beautiful flower for summer gardens. Flower opens only in sunny weather.

Portulacas planted in blocks of colors as a border

General: Use Moss Rose if you love the flowers. It is shorter-lived than its cousin, Purslane, but prettier, especially when viewed close up. The "Samba" series is particularly well-suited to south Florida. Although the Moss Rose is well-adapted to heat, its flowers close by noon on extremely hot days, especially if the soil is dry. Flowers may not open at all on cloudy days.

Season: Moss Rose is a summer annual. It does not bloom well in cool weather. Plant it in May or June, and expect it to live a few months. If the summer is unusually wet, it may not make it that long.

To locate plants, go to www.easygardencolor.com

Companions: Use Moss Rose with other plants that bloom in summer and prefer full sun. They make an excellent border for Plumbago, Thryallis, or Firespike. Or, try them with leaf color, like Crotons and Ti Plants.

Moss Rose flowers. The colors resemble jelly beans.

Planting: Every few years, spread two to three inches of potting soil on top of your planting bed shortly before planting. Be sure the soil drains well. Plant the Moss Roses high, leaving the top 1/4 inch to 1/2 inch of the root ball out of the ground. *The number one cause of annual death is planting the little plants too deep.* Do not pile mulch up around the base of the plant, or the stem will rot.

Fertilizing: Immediately after planting, fertilize with a well-balanced, slow-release mix that includes minor elements. Repeat in three months.

Trimming: None needed.

LIGHT: Full sun

WATER: Low. Water every other day the first week or two. Taper off over the next two weeks. Ideal water is once or twice a week after the first month. Takes water up to 4 times a week. Overwatering shortens the life span. Needs more water when grown in containers.

SOIL: Wide range, as long as it is well-drained.

SALT TOLERANCE: High

WIND TOLERANCE: High

ZONE: Grown all over the world as a summer annual.

PEST PROBLEMS: Mites

PROPAGATION: Seeds

Botanical Name: *Portulaca oleracea*

Common Name: **Purslane**

CHARACTERISTICS

PLANT TYPE: Annual that occasionally grows for more than one season, especially if the summer is drier than normal.

AVERAGE SIZE: 2 to 3 inches tall by 12 inches wide.

GROWTH RATE: Medium

LEAF: Tiny, green, succulent leaf. Spoon-shaped. About 1/2 inch long.

FLOWER: Pink, white, yellow, orange, or peach. About 3/4 inch across.

AVERAGE LIFE: 5 to 6 months.

ORIGIN: Unknown

CAUTIONS: None known

SPACING: 8 to 12 inches on center.

Summer annual that hugs the ground with color. Flower closes in shade and in the evening.

Purslane in mixed colors planted as a border

General: Purslane is a low-growing, summer annual that takes heat well. It is stronger than its cousin, Moss Rose. Its flowers are quite colorful when they are open, but they close in the evening and on really shady days. Occasionally, it lives beyond the summer as a short term perennial.

Season: Because of its heat tolerance, Purslane is most often used as a summer annual. Plant it in May or June, and expect it to live until November. If the summer is unusually wet, it may not make it through one summer.

To locate plants, go to www.easygardencolor.com

Companions: Purslane looks great in simple plantings of mixed colors, as shown opposite. Yellow Purslane is also a great border for New Look Purple Pentas. Or, try alternating hot pink and yellow Purslane in front of Crotons.

Purslane flowers are so bright, they glow.

Planting: Every few years, spread two to three inches of potting soil on top of your planting bed before planting. Be sure to use good-quality potting soil, not top soil, because top soil is too heavy for annuals. Plant the Purslane high, leaving the top 1/4 inch to 1/2 inch of the root ball out of the ground. *The number one cause of annual death is planting the little plants too deep.* Do not pile mulch up around the base of the plant, or the stem will rot.

Fertilizing: Immediately after planting, fertilize with a well-balanced, slow-release mix that includes minor elements. Repeat in three months. If you have time, spray the Purslane with a liquid fertilizer every month instead of the slow-release product. They prefer the liquid but do very well with the easier slow-release.

Trimming: None needed.

LIGHT: Full sun

WATER: Low. Water every other day the first week or two. Taper off over the next two weeks. Ideal water is once or twice a week after the first month. Takes water up to 4 times a week. Requires more water when grown in containers. Overwatering shortens the life span.

SOIL: Wide range, as long as it is well-drained.

SALT TOLERANCE: High

WIND TOLERANCE: High

ZONE: Grown all over the world as a summer annual. Occasionally lasts longer in zones 9 to 11.

PEST PROBLEMS: Occasional snails

PROPAGATION: Cuttings. Purslane does not grow from seed, like Moss Rose does.

Botanical Name: *Salvia farinacea*

Common Name: **'Victoria Blue' Salvia**

CHARACTERISTICS

PLANT TYPE: Annual that occasionally grows for more than one season. A common misconception is that this plant is a perennial in Florida. Although it is a perennial further north, it very seldom lasts for more than one season in south Florida.

AVERAGE SIZE: 18 inches tall by 12 inches wide.

GROWTH RATE: Medium

LEAF: Medium green and pointed. About 1 1/2 inches long by 1/3 inch wide.

FLOWER: Blue spike, about 5 inches tall.

AVERAGE LIFE: 5 to 6 months.

ORIGIN: New Mexico, Mexico, and Texas.

CAUTIONS: None known

SPACING: 8 to 12 inches on center.

Note: There are many different types of Salvias, both annual and perennial. See the index for many other Salvias that grow well in south Florida.

Beautiful blue flower that is very well-adapted to the Florida's cool season.

Blue Salvia shows up well with contrasting, bright-colored flowers, like these red Salvias and yellow Marigolds.

General: Victoria Blue Salvia deserves much more use in Florida. Although used as a perennial in northern climates, this Salvia seldom lasts more than one season in south or central Florida, although it may last as a perennial in north Florida. However, its low price, coupled with attractive appearance and low water requirements, makes it a great choice as a winter or spring annual. Use this blue flower with other bright colors, as shown above. It does not show up well alone or mixed with only green plants.

Season: Plant these Salvias from October to March in south or central Florida. In north Florida, plant after danger of freeze has ended. Expect them to last about five months, or until early June. If the weather is unusually wet, they do not last as long. Do not plant in the summer.

To locate plants, go to www.easygardencolor.com

Companions: Use Blue Salvia with bright colors. Petunias, Pansies, Marigolds, and Snapdragons are good annual choices. Florida Hydrangeas and Giant Shrimps are good shrub companions.

Blue Salvia with some companions

Planting: Every few years, spread two to three inches of potting soil on top of your planting bed before planting. Be sure to use good-quality potting soil, not top soil, because top soil is too heavy for annuals. Plant the Salvias high, leaving the top 1/4 inch to 1/2 inch of the root ball out of the ground. *The number one cause of annual death is planting the little plants too deep.* Do not pile mulch up around the base of the plant, or the stem will rot.

Fertilizing: Immediately after planting, fertilize with a well-balanced, slow-release mix that includes minor elements. Repeat in three months. If you have time, spray the Salvias with a liquid fertilizer every month instead of the slow-release product. They prefer the liquid but do very well with the easier slow-release.

Trimming: Trimming is not necessary, unless you want to attempt to keep your Salvias going beyond their first season. If the plants become leggy, trim back to about half. The plants recover well from this cutback about one-third of the time.

Botanical Name: *Salvia splendens*
Common Name: **Salvia or Scarlet Sage**

CHARACTERISTICS

PLANT TYPE: Annual

AVERAGE SIZE: 12 to 18 inches tall by 8 to 12 inches wide.

GROWTH RATE: Medium

LEAF: Medium green and pointed. About 1 3/4 inches long.

FLOWER: Showy spike, about 5 inches tall. Available in many shades of red, peach, white, and purple.

AVERAGE LIFE: 5 to 6 months.

ORIGIN: Brazil

CAUTIONS: None known

SPACING: 8 to 12 inches on center.

Note: There are many different types of Salvias, both annual and perennial. See the index for many other Salvias that grow well in south Florida.

A fabulous winter annual now available in many beautiful shades. Great color. Needs much less water than Impatiens.

Red Salvia — Snapdragon — Petunia — Marigold

Red Salvia with some companions. It looks good with other intense colors, like bright yellow, orange, and purple.

General: This Salvia is an annual that is most commonly known in red. Its colors have expanded, however, to include many shades of purple, peach, and white. Although disappointing in mid-summer, the plant is a stellar performer in Florida's dry winter and spring. It requires little care or water. Consider Salvia splendens to replace your thirsty Impatiens. It is also a favorite food of Hummingbirds. Try some in a window box in winter to attract these birds up close. This plant is an excellent choice for containers.

Season: Salvia are cool-season annuals that take some heat as well. Plant from October until March in south Florida. There are two choices in central Florida: plant in October and expect them to last until the first freeze, or plant from February 15 until March 30 for spring color. In north Florida, plant after the danger of freeze has ended. Expect five to six months of flowering, or until July, whichever comes first. Do not plant in summer.

To locate plants, go to www.easygardencolor.com

Companions: Plant the new mixes of different-colored Salvias together, as shown below. The shades contrast well, giving almost as much color as Impatiens. If using other annuals with your Salvias, consider red Salvias with other bright-colored flowers, as shown opposite.

Salvias in mixed colors with a background of Marigolds

Planting: Every few years, spread two to three inches of potting soil on top of your planting bed shortly before planting. Be sure to use good-quality potting soil, not top soil, because top soil is too heavy for annuals. Plant the Salvias high, leaving the top 1/4 inch to 1/2 inch of the root ball out of the ground. *The number one cause of annual death is planting the little plants too deep.* Do not pile mulch up around the base of the plant, or the stem will rot.

Fertilizing: Immediately after planting, fertilize with a well-balanced, slow-release mix that includes minor elements. Repeat in three months. If you have time, spray the Salvias with a liquid fertilizer every month instead of the slow-release product. They prefer the liquid but do very well with the easier slow-release.

Trimming: If the flowers lighten and lose their vigor mid-season, dead-head (remove the flowers). The plant may get a second wind and do well for a few more months.

LIGHT: Light shade to full sun.

WATER: Medium. Water daily the first week or two. Taper off the next 2 weeks. Ideal water is twice a week after the first month. Takes water up to 3 times a week. Requires more water when grown in containers.

SOIL: Wide range, as long as it is well-drained.

SALT TOLERANCE: Medium

WIND TOLERANCE: Low

ZONE: Summer annual in cooler areas of the world. Winter annual in south Florida. Tolerant of light frost but not freeze. Protect from freezes if used during winter in central Florida.

PEST PROBLEMS: I have never seen a pest on this plant but have heard of occasional thrips, mites, caterpillars, and slugs.

PROPAGATION: Seeds or cuttings.

Botanical Name: *Solenostemon scutellarioides*

Common Name: **Coleus**

'Duck's Foot' Coleus is very low-growing.

One of the most dependable choices for summer color. Lives longer than most summer annuals. Use for leaf color.

'Alabama Sunset' Coleus bordered by orange Marigolds. This Coleus grows lighter in the sun. Shade grown 'Alabama Sunset' is darker, as shown on the facing page. The green specimen tree in the middle of the bed is a Pandanus. (Design: Danny Miller, Breakers Hotel, Palm Beach.)

General: Coleus produce some of the most interesting leaf patterns in the world. Many different shapes, sizes, and colors are available - from low groundcovers to tall, shrub-like plants. It is important to know the growth habits of the type you buy. Many people are surprised to find out that the little plants they thought were groundcovers are growing much taller than the taller plants behind them. Coleus are one of the most dependable summer annuals, however, they may require a trimming in mid-summer. Although it takes some time, many people remove the flowers from their Coleus. The flowers are rather non-descript and removing them makes the plants more attractive. I find it therapeutic to pinch them off!

Season: Coleus are summer annuals. Throughout Florida, plant in spring, and expect them to last until the cool weather starts in fall. I have had some varieties live through the winter, particularly if the winter is unusually warm. Usually, they die with the first cool spell.

To locate plants, go to www.easygardencolor.com

Companions: One of the best Coleus combinations features a solid burgundy plant for the back layer, outlined by a low-growing chartreuse border. Be sure that the burgundy variety you purchase for the back layer grows taller than the border. Coleus are also available in mixes that are very attractive when planted together.

Alabama Sunset

Pineapple Speckles

Golden Bedder

Oxblood

Some popular Coleus varieties

Planting: Every few years, spread two to three inches of potting soil on top of your planting bed shortly before planting. Be sure to use good-quality potting soil, not top soil, because top soil is too heavy for annuals. Plant the Coleus high, leaving the top 1/4 inch to 1/2 inch of the root ball out of the ground. *The number one cause of annual death is planting the little plants too deep.* Do not pile mulch up around the base of the plant, or the stem will rot.

Fertilizing: Immediately after planting, fertilize with a well-balanced, slow-release mix that includes minor elements. Repeat in three months.

Trimming: Short, full types of Coleus (like 'Duck's Foot', shown in opposite sidebar) seldom require trimming. The taller varieties benefit greatly from a mid-summer cutback. They recover within a few weeks. Removing flowers as they form greatly increases the fullness and attractiveness of this plant.

GROWING CONDITIONS

LIGHT: Prefers some shade. Frequently used in full sun. Expect to water much more in full sun. Some varieties take more sun than others.

WATER: Medium in shade, high in sun. Water daily the first week or two. Taper off the next 2 weeks. Ideal water is 3 times a week in shade after the first month. Needs up to daily waterings in sun. Requires more water when grown in containers. Lower leaves drop if Coleus dries out.

SOIL: Wide range, as long as it is well-drained.

SALT TOLERANCE: Medium

WIND TOLERANCE: Low

ZONE: Used as a summer annual in most parts of the world, except where the temperatures fall into the 40's.

PEST PROBLEMS: Relatively pest-free in the landscape. Occasional aphids, mites, or mealybugs. Holes in the leaves indicate caterpillars or slugs.

PROPAGATION: Seeds or cuttings.

'Golden Bedder' Coleus bordering Ixora Nora Grant.

Botanical Name: *Tagetes spp.*
Common Name: **Marigolds**

CHARACTERISTICS

PLANT TYPE: Annual

AVERAGE SIZE: 6 to 30 inches tall by 8 to 18 inches wide. Size depends on variety. Smaller types are usually called French Marigolds, while larger ones are commonly called African.

GROWTH RATE: Medium

LEAF: Finely cut, strong-scented. Medium green; sizes vary with variety.

FLOWER: Yellow, orange, burnt orange, white, and burgundy. Solid colors and bicolors. Flowers range from simple, 1 inch blooms to large, 3 inch pom-poms on larger plants. Even larger plants produce 5 inch mum-like blossoms.

AVERAGE LIFE: 4 to 5 months in winter; 3 months in summer.

ORIGIN: Southwestern US and Mexico.

CAUTIONS: None known

SPACING: 8 to 12 inches on center.

A traditional annual that does well for much of the year in south and central Florida.

Yellow Marigolds with violet and red Impatiens

General: Marigolds are traditional annuals of unequaled yellow color. They are not quite as easy as Salvias or Petunias but worth the extra trouble and shorter life if you love the flowers. Marigolds are available in many different sizes and bloom types. It is very important that you know what size you are buying so that you do not expect the plant to grow about 12 inches tall and have it peak at 24 inches, covering the lower layers behind it. Newer varieties have less of an odor than older ones.

Season: Marigolds love our cool season and take quite a bit of heat as well. Plant from October until March in south Florida. There are two choices in central Florida: plant in October and expect them to last until the first freeze, or plant from February 15 until March 30 for spring and early summer color. In north Florida, plant after danger of frost has ended. Expect five to six months of flowering, or until July, whichever comes first. Do not plant in mid-summer.

To locate plants, go to www.easygardencolor.com

Companions: Marigolds look great planted in mixed colors, like orange and yellow, in the same bed. They also make an excellent accent to bright purples or reds. Use them with other plants that peak in winter. They are great companions for bright-colored Petunias and Salvias.

Yellow Pom-Pom Marigold

Orange Pom-Pom Marigold

French Marigolds

Above: Yellow and orange pom-pom Marigolds. Below: Smaller, French Marigolds.

Planting: Every few years, spread two to three inches of potting soil on top of your planting bed shortly before planting. Be sure to use good-quality potting soil, not top soil, because top soil is too heavy for annuals. Plant the Marigolds high, leaving the top 1/4 inch to 1/2 inch of the root ball out of the ground. *The number one cause of annual death is planting the little plants too deep.* Do not pile mulch up around the base of the plant, or the stem will rot.

Fertilizing: Immediately after planting, fertilize with a well-balanced, slow-release mix that includes minor elements. Repeat in three months. If you have time, spray the Marigolds with a liquid fertilizer every month instead of the slow-release product. They prefer the liquid but do very well with the easier slow-release. Marigolds tolerate fair nutrition but grow fuller and bloom more with good fertilization.

Trimming: Flowering increases with dead-heading (pinching off the faded blooms). Not many people do this in south Florida. Smaller varieties recover and benefit from a mid-season trimming. Many of the larger varieties do not.

GROWING CONDITIONS

LIGHT: Full sun

WATER: Medium. Water daily the first week or two. Taper off the next 2 weeks. Ideal water is twice a week after the first month. Takes water up to 3 times a week. Requires more water when grown in containers.

SOIL: Wide range, as long as it is well-drained.

SALT TOLERANCE: Medium

WIND TOLERANCE: Medium

ZONE: Used as a spring and summer annual throughout the world. Sometimes planted in the fall in the southern U.S. Does best in the winter in south Florida. Protect from freezes in central and north Florida or plant in March.

PEST PROBLEMS: Occasional spider mites, particularly in dry weather.

PROPAGATION: Seeds. Quite easy to propagate. Flowers in about 10 weeks from seed.

Botanical Name: *Torenia fournieri*

Common Name: **Torenia, Wishbone Flower**

CHARACTERISTICS

PLANT TYPE: The more common, upright 'Clown' Series is an annual that often reseeds. The trailing 'Summer Wave' form is stronger, sometimes lasting a full year.

AVERAGE SIZE: Upright form grows to about 12 inches tall by 10 inches wide. Trailing form is about 6 inches tall by 14 inches wide.

GROWTH RATE: Fast

LEAF: Medium green. About 3/4 inch long.

FLOWER: Small flower that resembles a tiny Pansy. Blues, purples, whites, and combinations. The 'Clown' series features yellow centers. 'Summer Wave' is solid blue or purple.

AVERAGE LIFE: The upright form lasts 4 to 5 months. The trailing form lasts up to a year.

ORIGIN: Vietnam

CAUTIONS: The 'Clown' series reseeds. I like the seedlings because they fill in the same area most summers. Some people consider them a nuisance.

SPACING: 8 to 12 inches on center.

One of the best summer annuals available for the Florida heat.

The 'Clown' series grows upright. It is available in many shades of pinks, whites, blues, and purples.

General: Torenia lasts longer than most of our summer annuals. It also sometimes reseeds politely, exactly where you had planted it last summer. It does not show up too well from a distance but is quite beautiful up close. The flower resembles a small Pansy. Torenia is available in two forms, trailing ('Summer Wave') and upright ('Clown Series'). Although the Clown Series did well in our trials, the 'Summer Wave' lasted much longer.

Season: Torenia is a summer annual. Expect four to five months of flowering with the upright form, if planted from April to June. The trailing form may last a full year if the winter is unusually warm. If the weather is unusually cold or wet, it may not last as long.

To locate plants, go to www.easygardencolor.com

Companions: The 'Clown' series looks beautiful planted in mixed colors, as shown opposite. 'Summer Wave', the trailing form, is available in blue or purple. One of the best groupings I know for summer annual plantings features Cranberry or red Pentas for the back layer, Melampodiums in the middle, and trailing Torenias as a border.

Trailing Torenia

Red Pentas

Melampodium

Trailing Torenia ('Summer Wave') and some companions. The Trailing Torenia is lower than the 'Clown' series on the opposite page.

Planting: Every few years, spread two to three inches of potting soil on top of your planting bed shortly before planting. Be sure to use good-quality potting soil, not top soil, because top soil is too heavy for annuals. Plant the Torenia high, leaving the top 1/4 inch to 1/2 inch of the root ball out of the ground. *The number one cause of annual death is planting the little plants too deep.* Do not pile mulch up around the base of the plant, or the stem will rot.

Fertilizing: Immediately after planting, fertilize with a well-balanced, slow-release mix that includes minor elements. Repeat in three months.

Trimming: Upright Torenia seldom requires trimming. If your trailing Torenia looks leggy, trim it at any time. Sometimes it will not recover, but it usually grows back well.

GROWING CONDITIONS

LIGHT: Medium shade to full sun.

WATER: Medium. Water daily the first week or two. Taper off the next 2 weeks. Ideal water is twice a week after the first month, if the plants are in shade. In sun, during the hottest days of summer, they may require water 4 times per week. Requires more water when grown in containers.

SOIL: Wide range, as long as it is well-drained.

SALT TOLERANCE: Medium

WIND TOLERANCE: Medium

ZONE: Summer annual in many parts of the world. Not tolerant of even cool, 50-degree temperatures.

PEST PROBLEMS: None known

PROPAGATION: Seeds or cuttings.

| Botanical Name: | *Viola x Wittrockiana* |
| Common Name: | **Pansies** |

CHARACTERISTICS

PLANT TYPE: Annual

AVERAGE SIZE: 4 to 6 inches tall by 6 to 8 inches wide.

GROWTH RATE: Medium

LEAF: Medium green and scalloped. About 2 inches long by 3/4 inch wide.

FLOWER: White, yellow, blue, purple, brown, red. Sizes range from 1 3/4 inches to 4 1/2 inches, depending on variety. Some are solid colors; others are patterned.

AVERAGE LIFE: 4 to 5 months.

ORIGIN: Europe

CAUTIONS: None known

SPACING: 6 to 8 inches on center.

One of the most beautiful annuals. Takes cold well and loves Florida winters.

White, blue, and orange Pansies with red Salvia, purple Pentas, and silver Dusty Millers. (Design by Brandon Balch, Woodfield Country Club, Boca Raton.)

General: Most people are unaware of how well Pansies do throughout Florida in winter, even in north Florida. I have used the smaller-flowered 'Multiflora' variety for years with much success. The 'Multifloras' have smaller but much more plentiful flowers than the larger varieties. They are also more heat tolerant, lasting well into our warm spring months.

Season: Pansies are late-season winter annuals. Expect four to five months of flowering, if planted in January or February in any part of Florida. Do not plant in the summer.

Companions: Pansies' low, full form makes them ideal for borders. They also are lovely planted in masses of mixed colors. The yellow Pansies are especially useful for mixing with red Salvias and purple Petunias.

Pansies come in many different colors and patterns.

Planting: Every few years, spread two to three inches of potting soil on top of your planting bed shortly before planting. Be sure to use good-quality potting soil, not top soil, because top soil is too heavy for annuals. Plant the Pansies high, leaving the top 1/4 inch to 1/2 inch of the root ball out of the ground. *The number one cause of annual death is planting the little plants too deep.* Do not pile mulch up around the base of the plant, or the stem will rot.

Fertilizing: Immediately after planting, fertilize with a well-balanced, slow-release mix that includes minor elements. Repeat in three months. If you have time, spray the Pansies with a liquid fertilizer every month instead of the slow-release product. They prefer the liquid but do very well with the easier slow-release.

Trimming: Very little trimming required. If the plants flop over, trim lightly. Removing spent flowers increases blooming but is not necessary for an impressive landscape planting.

LIGHT: Light shade to full sun. Happier with light shade at noon.

WATER: Medium. Water daily the first week or two. Taper off the next 2 weeks. Ideal water is twice a week after the first month, if the plants are in partial shade. In full sun, water 3 to 4 times per week. Requires more water when grown in containers.

SOIL: Wide range, as long as it is well-drained.

SALT TOLERANCE: Medium

WIND TOLERANCE: Medium

ZONE: Grown throughout the world. In zones 8 to 11, tolerant of all winter cold spells. Many selections take temperatures as low as 15 degrees.

PEST PROBLEMS: Occasional slugs or aphids

PROPAGATION: Seeds or cuttings.

Catharanthus roseus
Periwinkle

White, pink, or purple flowers that do best in sun. Some have naturalized, like wildflowers, and come back each year. These are strong but short-lived plants. Many hybrids have serious fungus problems in our rainy season.

Cleome hasslerana
Spider Flower

Beautiful flower traditionally used in the deep south with few problems. New to Florida. I'm hearing raves from some and a few problems from others. Many sizes available. I will be testing this one much more in the future.

Crossandra infundibuliformis
Peach Crossandra

Attractive peach flowers. Erratic performer, blooming a full summer some years and only a few weeks the next. Occasionally keeps going as a perennial shrub in south Florida, but not too often. Sun or shade. Reseeds.

Eustoma grandiflorum
Lisianthus

Beautiful pink, purple, or white flowers. I have tried this one a few times with no success. If you have had luck with this plant, share your experience with me at my Web site, www.easygardencolor.com.

Helianthus annuus
Sunflower

Hundreds of different colors and sizes are available. Easy to grow from seed in Florida. Avoid the heat of mid to late summer. Each plant is very short-lived, usually lasting for only one, brief, flowering period. Full sun.

Heliotropium spp.
Heliotrope

Many different varieties in lovely shades of purple or white. I have tried a few in south Florida's winters with very mixed results. I will be doing many more trials with this beautiful plant.

Liatrus spp
Blazing Star

Many different types available. Grows in sun as a wildflower in much of Florida, blooming for about a month and then disappearing until the next year. Many hybrids are available that only last a month or so.

Verbena spp.
Verbena

Commonly used as an annual in commercial plantings, like Disney and country clubs. 'Homestead Purple' works well as a perennial in north Florida. I never had much luck with it in my garden because of whiteflies.

Zinnia spp
Zinnia

Commonly planted in commercial gardens. I have had a lot of fungus problems with Zinnias but like them so much that I keep planting them anyway. New, narrow-leafed types show promise of high performance.

This chapter on annuals is just a beginning! There are thousands more to try. I am expanding my annual trial gardens and will report the results of our ongoing trials in future editions of this book.

The tallest layer of this annual garden is made up of Spider Flowers. The lower layers are made up of Salvias, Impatiens, Marigolds, Petunias, and Begonias. The manicured Ilex hedge formalizes this mixed arrangement. (Design: Danny Miller, The Breakers, Palm Beach. Flowers custom grown by Dave Self at Wyld West Annuals, Loxahatchee.)

CHAPTER 2

GROUNDCOVERS AND SMALL PERENNIALS
6 TO 24 INCHES

This chapter details 17 groundcovers and small perennials that are easy to maintain at 24 inches or less and last for more than one year. These plants include herbaceous perennials, bulbs, and small shrubs. This category of plant has the highest demand and the least availability. Fronts of houses need low plants to accentuate the architecture without growing taller than the window sills. Most of our subtropical plants grow much taller than 24 inches, or they have a very short lifespan, like annuals.

Rule of thumb for Florida: The larger the plant, the longer the lifespan. A Live Oak tree might live 100 years. A low-growing groundcover might make it one to five years. Look closely at the average life of each plant in this chapter. It is important to know how long a plant is expected to live before buying it.

More outstanding, colorful groundcovers are detailed in this book's companion, "Easy Gardens for Florida"*, by Pamela Crawford. They are located in Chapter 1, Groundcovers and Small Shrubs.

Left: Orange Ground Orchid (Epidendrum ibaguense, pages 82 and 83).
Above: Justicia 'Fruit Cocktail' (pages 86 and 87)

Botanical Name: *Aechmea fendleri x*

Common Name: # Blue Moon or Blue Tango Bromeliad

CHARACTERISTICS

PLANT TYPE: Perennial epiphyte.

AVERAGE SIZE: 24 inches tall by 30 inches wide.

GROWTH RATE: Slow

LEAF: Lime green. About 18 inches long by 2 inches wide. Sharp spines along the edges.

FLOWER: Spectacular pink and blue spike. About 12 inches long by 3 to 4 inches wide.

AVERAGE LIFE: Single plant lives abut 2 years but sends up babies to replace itself. A clump of good landscape Bromeliads lasts indefinitely.

ORIGIN: Tropical America

CAUTIONS: Painful to handle because of spines. Wear a heavy, long-sleeved shirt and gloves.

SPACING: 24 inches on center.

Spectacular winter or spring bloomer that flowers for up to four months with little care.

Blue Moon

Tricolor Tis

Pink Angelwing Begonia

The 'Blue Moon' flower is over a foot long. It combines beautifully with the Tricolor Ti and Pink Angelwing Begonia, shown above and opposite.

General: This Bromeliad is a must for winter and spring gardens. It is so beautiful that no one can believe its ease of care. The bloom period is long and timed perfectly for when we want to be outside.

Season: This plant blooms four to six months each year, normally from winter to spring. It bloomed quite dependably for four of its five years of trials. The fifth year, it bloomed late, starting in March. When the plant is not in flower, its leaves are attractive. A clump of landscape Bromeliads lasts indefinitely.

To locate plants, go to www.easygardencolor.com

Companions: Use this Bromeliad to accent other winter colors with a tropical look. Tricolor Tis and Pink Begonias are good choices, as shown opposite. Other great companions include Dombeyas, Giant Shrimps, Golden Shrimps, Pink Firespikes, and Justicia 'Fruit Cocktails'. Plant in the ground or in containers.

Blue Moon in a winter garden. It is an excellent container plant that can be moved indoors if freeze threatens.

Planting: Plant any time of the year in native soil. Leave the root ball slightly out of the ground, about 1/4 inch. This plant is so top-heavy in bloom that it sometimes falls out of the pot, breaking the root ball. Plant whatever is left, and prop it up until it re-roots. This is a tough plant and lives with a small root system. (See detailed planting instructions in "Easy Gardens for Florida"*, Chapter 11.)

Fertilizing: Immediately after planting, fertilize the ground around the plant with a well-balanced, slow-release mix that includes minor elements. Repeat in March, June, and October of each year. Do not put fertilizer in the center of this plant; spread it on the ground so that it will reach the roots. (See detailed fertilization instructions in "Easy Gardens for Florida"*, Chapter 11.)

Trimming: The mother plant dies after flowering and producing pups (babies). Trim off the dead plant after it becomes brown. Leave the remaining pups to grow where they are or separate them to cover more ground. Since this only has to be done every few years, this is truly an easy plant.

* My current book, "Easy Gardens for South Florida", will be expanded to include the entire state in 2004.

GROWING CONDITIONS

LIGHT: Light to medium shade. Takes more sun than most Bromeliads.

WATER: Low. Ideal watering is once every week or two after the initial establishment period. Tolerates water up to 3 times per week but rots with too much. Requires more water when grown in containers. (For detailed information on watering, see Chapter 8 in "Easy Gardens for Florida"*.)

SOIL: Wide range, as long as it is well-drained.

SALT TOLERANCE: High

WIND TOLERANCE: High

ZONE: 9b to 11. Protect from freezes. Great for containers in zones 8 or 9a so that it can be easily moved in during the cold.

PEST PROBLEMS: None known

PROPAGATION: Offshoots

Note: The Bromeliad pictured was hybridized as the Blue Moon by Patricia Bullis of Bullis Bromeliads in Miami. It was replaced by Bullis with a newer variety, the Blue Tango.

Botanical Name: *Aechmea chantinii x Aechmea rubrens*

Common Name: **'Little Harve' Bromeliad**

CHARACTERISTICS

PLANT TYPE: Perennial epiphyte.

AVERAGE SIZE: 24 to 30 inches tall by 24 inches wide.

GROWTH RATE: Slow

LEAF: Grey-green. About 18 inches long by 2 inches wide. Sharp spines along the edges.

FLOWER: Showy orange and yellow spike. About 6 inches long by 4 inches wide.

AVERAGE LIFE: Single plant lives about 2 years but sends up babies to replace itself. A clump of good land-scape Bromeliads lasts indefinitely.

ORIGIN: Tropical America

CAUTIONS: Painful to handle because of spines. Wear a heavy, long-sleeved shirt and gloves.

SPACING: 24 inches on center.

Note: I tested many Bromeliads in the south Florida landscape. Most were planted in bloom, and many never re-bloomed. This one was very dependable and consistent.

A traditional Florida landscape Bromeliad that has consistently performed for a generation.

Little Harve Bromeliad in full bloom. It is an excellent container plant that can be moved indoors if freeze threatens.

General: New Bromeliads are frequently appearing on the market. Many of them are bred for the indoors and do not re-bloom in the Florida landscape. The 'Little Harve' is an exception, a tried-and-true plant that is easy to grow and beautiful in bloom.

Season: 'Little Harve' blooms for two to three months of each year. The season varies, normally from winter to spring. When the plant is not in flower, its leaves are attractive. A clump of landscape Bromeliads lasts indefinitely.

To locate plants, go to www.easygardencolor.com

Companions: Since the 'Little Harve' can bloom in any season, use it with plants that offer constant, bright color. It looks good with exotic, tropical flowers, like Anthuriums, Begonias, and Golden Shrimp Plants. Or, plant it among plants with colored leaves, like Crotons and Ti Plants.

'Little Harve' Bromeliad and some companions. The Icetone Croton and the Golden Shrimp Plant offer year-round color.

Planting: Plant any time of the year in native soil. Leave the root ball slightly out of the ground, about 1/4 inch. This plant is so top-heavy in bloom that it sometimes falls out of the pot, breaking the root ball. Plant whatever is left, and prop it up until it re-roots. This is a tough plant and lives with a small root system. (See detailed planting instructions in "Easy Gardens for Florida"*, Chapter 11.)

Fertilizing: Immediately after planting, fertilize with a well-balanced, slow-release mix that includes minor elements. Repeat in March, June, and October of each year. Do not put fertilizer in the center of this plant. Spread it on the ground so that it will reach the roots. (See detailed fertilization instructions in "Easy Gardens for Florida"*, Chapter 11.)

Trimming: The mother plant dies after flowering and producing pups (babies). Trim off the dead plant after it becomes brown. Leave the remaining pups to grow where they are or separate them to cover more ground. Since this only has to be done every few years, this is truly an easy plant.

✱ My current book, "Easy Gardens for South Florida", will be expanded to include the entire state in 2004.

GROWING CONDITIONS

LIGHT: Light to medium shade. Takes more sun than most Bromeliads.

WATER: Low. Ideal watering is once a week after the initial establishment period. Tolerates water up to 4 times per week. Requires more water when grown in containers. (For detailed information on watering, see Chapter 8 in "Easy Gardens for Florida"*.)

SOIL: Wide range, as long as it is well-drained.

SALT TOLERANCE: High

WIND TOLERANCE: High

ZONE: 9b to 11. Protect from freezes. Great for containers in zones 8 or 9a so that it can be easily moved in during the cold.

PEST PROBLEMS: None known

PROPAGATION: Offshoots

Botanical Name: *Agapanthus africanus*
Common Name: **Lily-of-the-Nile, African Lily**

CHARACTERISTICS

PLANT TYPE:
Herbaceous perennial

AVERAGE SIZE: Size varies by type. Dwarfs are about 18 inches tall. Taller types grow up to 30 inches tall.

GROWTH RATE: Slow

LEAF: Medium green and strap-like. Size varies with type.

FLOWER: Different shades of blue or white. Large and showy clusters that grow up to 4 to 6 inches across.

AVERAGE LIFE: Short-lived in south Florida. Some clumps have lived for 15 years in central Florida.

ORIGIN: Southern Africa

CAUTIONS: None known

SPACING: 12 inches on center. Blooms better if roots are crowded.

White Agapanthus

A beautiful spring flower best for central and north Florida gardens. Short-lived in south Florida.

Bright blue Agapanthus flower

General: Agapanthus was disappointing to me in my south Florida trial gardens. It bloomed for a short time the first year and erratically for the next few years before disappearing completely. But, plant it a bit further north and it shines. Central and north Florida are ideal for Agapanthus. I have enjoyed the beauty of the Agapanthus at the entry to Epcot at Walt Disney World for years. Different varieties exist, some doing better in colder areas than Florida. Evergreen varieties do better in warmer climates, and deciduous types that die back in winter prefer more cold. Although Agapanthus does not bloom as long as many Florida perennials, it offers the advantage of very easy care. It is also ideal for short-term use in containers in south Florida.

Season: Blooms for about six weeks in early spring or summer in central and north Florida. I have seen years when they did not bloom at all in south Florida.

To locate plants, go to www.easygardencolor.com

Companions: Agapanthus works well with many landscape styles, from casual cottage gardens to clipped, formal hedges. It looks great in the center of an annual bed surrounded by Torenia and Wax Begonias. Or, use it as a border for spring perennials.

LIGHT: Light shade to full sun.

WATER: Medium. Ideal watering is twice a week after the initial establishment period. Tolerates water up to 4 times per week. Requires more water when grown in containers. (For detailed information, see Chapter 8 in "Easy Gardens for Florida"*.)

SOIL: Wide range, as long as it is well-drained.

SALT TOLERANCE: Low

WIND TOLERANCE: Medium

Wax Begonia

Agapanthus

Wax Begonia

Light blue Agapanthus with some companions. The color looks good with light pink, pale yellow, and white.

Planting: Plant mature plants any time of the year in native soil. Leave the root ball slightly out of the ground, about 1/4 inch. (See detailed planting instructions in "Easy Gardens for Florida"*, Chapter 11.) Rhizomes do best if planted in fall, winter, or early spring. Plant rhizomes slightly below the ground.

Fertilizing: Immediately after planting, fertilize with a well-balanced, slow-release mix that includes minor elements. Repeat in March, June, and October of each year. If the summer is unusually hot and rainy, inspect the leaf color of the plant in August. If it appears washed out, add an additional fertilization at that time. (See detailed fertilization instructions in "Easy Gardens for Florida"*, Chapter 11.)

Trimming: For optimum flower production, cut the old flower stalks off after the plant has flowered. Keep the leaves in place. If the plants show signs of fungus in the summer, cut the leaves back. The rhizomes can be divided but don't do it too often. Older plants with crowded root systems do better than new ones.

ZONE: 8 through 11, although performance is poor in zones 10 and 11. Evergreen types hardy to 25 degrees. Deciduous types take the lower temperatures of zone 8.

PEST PROBLEMS: Caterpillars, grasshoppers

PROPAGATION: Rhizomes

My current book, "Easy Gardens for South Florida", will be expanded to include the entire state in 2004.

Botanical Name: *Alcantarea imperialis* (formerly *Vriesia imperialis*)

Common Name: **Imperial Bromeliad**

CHARACTERISTICS

PLANT TYPE: Perennial epiphyte.

AVERAGE SIZE: 2 feet tall by 2 feet wide. Eventually reaches 3 feet by 3 feet but takes a very long time.

GROWTH RATE: Slow

LEAF: Large and dramatic. About 2 feet long by 6 inches wide at maturity. Grey on top and purple on bottom.

FLOWER: Huge, 6 foot tall spike that is not as attractive as most bromeliads. Use this plant for its foliage.

AVERAGE LIFE: Tested for 10 years and still going strong.

ORIGIN: Brazil

CAUTIONS: None known. No spines on the leaves.

SPACING: 3 feet on center.

Use this Bromeliad for its large-scale size and drama rather than a spectacular flower.

Imperial Bromeliad featured at the Bullis Bromeliad booth (a bromeliad grower from Miami) during the Tropical Plant Industry Exposition in Fort Lauderdale. The Bullis displays won a well-deserved ribbon for seven years in a row. The Imperial Bromeliad is displayed in a raised position so that the beauty of the sides shows at eye level. It is a great container plant.

General: The Imperial Bromeliad is useful for its elegant form and its adaptability to harsh environments. It is one of the few Bromeliads that reaches three feet in height, takes full sun, and has no spines on its leaves. Use it as an accent, like a Sago Palm. I find it very useful in landscape design because it adapts to many different environments and many different styles.

Season: No seasonal variation.

To locate plants, go to www.easygardencolor.com

Companions: Use the Imperial Bromeliad as an accent in the landscape. Since it mixes well with many different styles, use it in manicured, tropical, or even cottage gardens. I use these Bromeliads instead of Sago Palms, which are now very susceptible to cycad scale. Imperial Bromeliads are also excellent choices for containers, especially taller containers that lift the plant high enough for viewers to see the beautiful purple undersides to its leaves.

Imperial Bromeliads planted in the ground. These plants have been in this location receiving full western sun for eight years.

Planting: Plant any time of the year in native soil. Leave the root ball slightly out of the ground, about 1/4 inch. (See detailed planting instructions in "Easy Gardens for Florida"*, Chapter 11.)

Fertilizing: Immediately after planting, fertilize with a well-balanced, slow-release mix that includes minor elements. Repeat in March, June, and October of each year. (See detailed fertilization instructions in "Easy Gardens for Florida"*, Chapter 11.)

Trimming: The mother plant dies after flowering and producing pups (babies). Trim off the dead plant after it becomes brown. Leave the remaining pups to grow where they are or separate them to cover more ground. Since this only has to be done every few years, this is truly an easy plant.

* My current book, "Easy Gardens for South Florida", will be expanded to include the entire state in 2004.

GROWING CONDITIONS

LIGHT: Full sun to medium shade. This is one of the few bromeliads I put in very hot situations.

WATER: Low. Ideal watering is once every week or two after the initial establishment period. Tolerates water up to 3 times per week but rots with too much. Requires more water when grown in containers. (For detailed information on watering, see Chapter 8 in "Easy Gardens for Florida"*.)

SOIL: Wide range, as long as it is well-drained.

SALT TOLERANCE: High

WIND TOLERANCE: High

ZONE: 9b to 11. Protect from freezes. Great for containers in zones 8 or 9a so that it can be easily moved in during the cold.

PEST PROBLEMS: None known

PROPAGATION: Offshoots

Botanical Name: *Anthurium spp.*
Common Name: **Anthurium**

CHARACTERISTICS

PLANT TYPE: Epiphyte

AVERAGE SIZE: 12 to 18 inches tall by 8 to 12 inches wide.

GROWTH RATE: Slow

LEAF: Dark, glossy green. Average leaf is about 3 to 5 inches long by 3 inches wide. Size varies by type.

FLOWER: Large and heart-shaped. Size varies by type. Average is about 2 inches long by 2 to 3 inches wide. Colors include shades of pink, peach, orange, red, and white. *Anthurium andreanum,* or Flamingo Flower, has a larger flower than the Lady Jane, but it is more temperamental in the landscape.

AVERAGE LIFE: 2 to 10 years.

ORIGIN: Tropical America or hybrids.

CAUTIONS: Irritant

SPACING: 8 to 12 inches on center for the smaller, flowering varieties.

Note: Anthuriums are frequently used indoors, but I have never gotten them to live for more than a month in my living room.

Other types: Many Anthuriums are grown for the leaves rather than the flowers. The Bird's nest Anthurium has large, tropical leaves. The 'A. crystallinum' has dark green, velvety leaves with white veins.

A beautiful, tropical plant. Too cold-sensitive to last too long for most of south Florida but easy and gorgeous. Great container plant.

Anthurium 'Lady Jane'

Anthurium andreanum Peach

Anthurium andreanum Red

Anthurium 'Lady Jane', one of the best performers in my trials, is the large plant in the background. The insets are the heart-shaped Anthurium andreanum. They are showier than 'Lady Jane' but not quite as strong.

General: Anthuriums were one of my favorite shade plants until the winter of 1995 when they all died in south Florida from cold. And, it didn't even freeze that year! They do not like temperatures in the 40's, which is routine in south Florida. But, they are so beautiful and offer so much color in shade that I still keep a few in my garden. Anthuriums bloom in less light than any other plant in this book. They are ideal for pots not only because they are horticulturally well-suited for pots but also because you can bring them inside during cold spells. Varieties with simple flowers, like the 'Lady Jane' pictured above, did better in my trials than the fancier ones.

Season: Anthuriums flower all the time.

To locate plants, go to www.easygardencolor.com

Companions: Use Anthuriums with tropical plants, like Palms, Bromeliads, Crotons, and Shrimp Plants. They are particularly well suited for containers. The heart-shaped Anthuriums look good when planted in masses of mixed colors, like orange, red, and peach.

Lady Jane Anthuriums on the far right. Two kind of Bromeliads: 'Perfecta' (the smaller ones) in the center and 'Mend' (the larger ones) to the left.

Planting: Plant any time of the year in native soil. Leave the root ball slightly out of the ground, about 1/4 inch. Anthuriums are very sensitive to being planted too deep. (See detailed planting instructions in "Easy Gardens for Florida"*, Chapter 11.)

Fertilizing: Immediately after planting, fertilize with a well-balanced, slow-release mix that includes minor elements. Repeat in March, June, and October of each year. If the summer is unusually hot and rainy, inspect the leaf color of the plant in August. If it appears washed out, add an additional fertilization at that time. (See detailed fertilization instructions in "Easy Gardens for Florida"*, Chapter 11.)

Trimming: If the plant becomes straggly, cut it back hard to about six inches tall in summer. (This method is not always successful but is better than looking at a straggly plant!) Trim off yellow leaves as they appear. This plant seldom needs any trimming.

GROWING CONDITIONS

LIGHT: Deep to medium shade.

WATER: Low. Ideal watering is once or twice a week after the initial establishment period. Tolerates water up to 3 times per week.

SOIL: Wide range, as long as it is well-drained.

SALT TOLERANCE: Low

WIND TOLERANCE: Unknown

ZONE: 11 for the least amount of cold damage. If you plant Anthuriums in zones 8, 9, or 10, be prepared to keep them in pots so that you can move them inside during temperatures in the 40's. If some of the leaves turn bright yellow while the others remain dark green, the plant is cold damaged.

PEST PROBLEMS: If holes appear in the leaves, it is probably snails. Also susceptible to leaf spot diseases.

PROPAGATION: Division or tissue culture. Some varieties by seed or cuttings.

Botanical Name: *Asclepias curassavica*

Common Name: **Milkweed**

CHARACTERISTICS

PLANT TYPE:
Herbaceous perennial

AVERAGE SIZE: 24 inches tall by 8 to 12 inches wide.

GROWTH RATE: Medium

LEAF: Olive green, long and pointed. About 3 inches long by 3/4 inch wide.

FLOWER: Orange and yellow cluster. About 1 inch across.

AVERAGE LIFE: Each plant lasts only 6 months or so; but, they reseed.

ORIGIN: Tropical America. Naturalized in Florida.

CAUTIONS: None known

SPACING: 12 to 18 inches on center.

Plant this lovely wildflower and watch the Monarch butterflies come.

Milkweed plants are light in texture, appropriate for informal butterfly gardens.

General: Most butterfly plants either provide food for the caterpillars (larval food plants) or the adult butterflies (nectar food plants). Milkweed does both. Many butterflies drink the nectar, and the Monarch butterfly lays her eggs on the leaves. The caterpillars that hatch on the leaves eat them, politely staying off the rest of your plants. This is a fascinating process to watch, especially for children.

Season: Milkweed is a wildflower with no particular season in south and central Florida. The plant lives about six months. Its fluffy seeds spread by the wind and pop up throughout the garden. In north Florida, plant in spring and enjoy as a summer annual.

To locate plants, go to www.easygardencolor.com

Companions: Use Milkweed in butterfly gardens. It is not appropriate in formal gardens because of its habit of disappearing from one spot and reseeding in another. Some excellent butterfly companions include Blue Porterflower, Lantana, Pentas, Jatropha, and Firebush. Plant lots of Milkweed in different parts of your garden so that, hopefully, it will reseed prolifically. The Monarch butterflies will thank you.

Milkweed and some companions. This grouping of flowers attracts many different kinds of butterflies.

Planting: Plant any time of the year in south Florida, and in spring in central and north Florida. Leave the root ball slightly out of the ground, about 1/4 inch. (See detailed planting instructions in "Easy Gardens for Florida"*, Chapter 11.)

Fertilizing: Immediately after planting, fertilize with a well-balanced, slow-release mix that includes minor elements. Repeat in March, June, and October of each year. Milkweed lives fairly well with no fertilization at all. (See detailed fertilization instructions in "Easy Gardens for Florida"*, Chapter 11.)

Trimming: Cut back hard any time the plant appears leggy.

My current book, "Easy Gardens for South Florida", will be expanded to include the entire state in 2004.

GROWING CONDITIONS

LIGHT: Full sun. Milkweed takes all the heat Florida has to offer.

WATER: Low. Lives in the wild with no irrigation after the initial establishment period. Tolerates water up to 4 times per week. Requires more water when grown in containers. (For detailed information about watering, see Chapter 8 in "Easy Gardens for Florida"*.)

SOIL: Wide range, as long as it is well-drained.

SALT TOLERANCE: Unknown

WIND TOLERANCE: Unknown

ZONE: 9 to 11 as a reseeding perennial. Zone 8 as an annual.

PEST PROBLEMS: Although Milkweed occasionally gets aphids and a few other innocuous bugs, never spray it. Spraying could kill Monarch butterfly eggs or caterpillars. The bugs that occasionally appear on Milkweed do no harm.

PROPAGATION: Seeds

Botanical Name: *Begonia rubra*

Common Name: **Orange Angelwing or Rubra Begonia**

CHARACTERISTICS

PLANT TYPE:
Herbaceous perennial

AVERAGE SIZE: 12 to 18 inches tall by 12 to 15 inches wide.

GROWTH RATE: Slow

LEAF: Dark green, glossy, with faint white spots. Shaped like a wing. About 3 inches long by 2 inches wide.

FLOWER: Bright orange clusters. About 3 to 4 inches wide by 2 inches long.

AVERAGE LIFE:
Unknown. I have had them in my gardens for 4 years now, and they show no signs of slowing down.

ORIGIN: Guadeloupe

CAUTIONS: None known

SPACING: 12 to 16 inches on center.

A fabulous (but rare) groundcover that blooms all the time in shade with very little care. Great in the ground or in containers.

The Orange Angelwing surprised me when I first grew it. I had expected it to grow large, like the Pink Angelwing, but it has never grown taller than two feet. It is much smaller than most other Angelwing Begonias.

General: Many different kinds of Begonias thrive in Florida, from small annuals to huge Angelwings. Perennial Begonias should be used much more in Florida - in the landscape in protected areas and in containers where freeze may threaten. Many of them are very well-adapted to our difficult environment. The Angelwing Begonias last for many years and vary in size, from groundcovers to very large shrubs. This Angelwing is a groundcover, growing to only about 18 inches tall. Its intense orange color shows beautifully, both up close and at a distance. It is very slow-growing, adding to its low maintenance character. But its slowness makes it difficult for the nursery industry to produce, making it rare in the marketplace. If you see one for sale, do not hesitate to purchase it because you may not see it again.

Season: This Begonia lasts for many years, blooming all the time. Flowering peaks in the winter and spring.

To locate plants, go to www.easygardencolor.com

Companions: This Begonia looks great with large, yellow flowers or bright-colored leaves that grow in shade. Giant Shrimps or Golden Shrimps are the best yellow-flowered companions. Red Spot or Mammey Crotons are the best choices for companions with colored leaves. And, for pure drama, mix the Orange Angelwing with the short-lived but spectacular Persian Shield.

The Orange Angelwing flower is so bright it almost glows.

Planting: Plant any time of the year in native soil. Leave the root ball slightly out of the ground, about 1/4 inch. (See detailed planting instructions in "Easy Gardens for Florida"*, Chapter 11.)

Fertilizing: Immediately after planting, fertilize with a well-balanced, slow-release mix that includes minor elements. Repeat in March, June, and October of each year. If the summer is unusually hot and rainy, inspect the leaf color of the plant in August. If it appears washed out, add an additional fertilization at that time. (See detailed fertilization instructions in "Easy Gardens for Florida"*, Chapter 11.)

Trimming: Trim this Begonia once a year in summer, when it has the least flowers and recovers fastest from a cutback. Trim back hard to about six inches tall. It takes about a month or two for the plant to recover and bloom again. If the Begonia gets leggy in between annual cutbacks, trim lightly as needed.

✱ My current book, "Easy Gardens for South Florida", will be expanded to include the entire state in 2004.

GROWING CONDITIONS

LIGHT: Medium shade is ideal. Does well with light shade in winter but might burn in summer. Does not flower in dense shade.

WATER: Medium. Ideal watering is twice a week after the establishment period. Tolerates water up to 4 times per week. Requires more water when grown in containers. Do not overwater this plant, or it will get fungus. (For detailed information about watering, see Chapter 8 in "Easy Gardens for Florida"*.)

SOIL: Wide range, as long as it is well-drained.

SALT TOLERANCE: Medium

WIND TOLERANCE: Medium

ZONE: 9b to 11. Protect from freezes. Great for containers in zones 8 or 9a so that it can be easily moved in during the cold.

PEST PROBLEMS: Brown spots on the leaves indicate fungus or bacteria. These routinely occur during the rainy season. Cut back on water, if possible. Do not spray unless they become severe.

PROPAGATION: Cuttings

Botanical Name: *Begonia odorata 'Alba'*
Common Name: **White Begonia, Odorata Begonia**

CHARACTERISTICS

PLANT TYPE:
Herbaceous perennial

AVERAGE SIZE: 18 to 30 inches tall by 18 inches wide.

GROWTH RATE: Medium

LEAF: Medium-green, glossy and rounded. About 3 inches across.

FLOWER: White cluster. About 3 to 4 inches wide.

AVERAGE LIFE: 3 to 8 years. (I have only had this plant for 2 years, so I am guesstimating its life span.)

ORIGIN: Guadeloupe

CAUTIONS: None known

SPACING: 18 inches on center.

A prolific winter bloomer with lovely, white flowers in shade.

White Begonias show well up close or from a distance.

General: The White Begonia is a must for the winter garden. It blooms quite heavily during the cooler months. The plant lasts for years, giving a dramatic show up close or from a distance. Many different kinds of Begonias thrive in Florida, from small annuals to huge Angelwings. This one is small to mid-sized, growing two to three feet in height.

Season: White Begonias last for many years, flowering for six to nine months, predominantly during the cooler months. When the plant is not in flower, its leaves are attractive.

Pink Angelwing Begonias — Brunfelsia

Some companions for the White Begonia. The Pink Angelwing Begonia and the Brunfelsia bloom at the same time as the White Angelwing.

To locate plants, go to www.easygardencolor.com

Companions: This Begonia works well in any style garden. Plant it with other shade plants that bloom in winter. For a delicate combination, plant the Pink Angelwing Begonias as the tallest layer, Brunfelsias in the middle, and border with the White Begonias. For a tropical look in a large area, use the Scarlet Red Cloaks as a back layer, Giant Shrimps or Pink Firespikes in the middle, and White Begonias as a border.

LIGHT: Medium shade is ideal. Does well with light shade in winter but might burn in summer. Does not flower in dense shade.

WATER: Medium. Ideal watering is twice a week after the initial establishment period. Tolerates water up to 4 times per week. Requires more water when grown in containers. Do not overwater this plant, or it will get fungus. (For detailed information about watering, see Chapter 8 in "Easy Gardens for Florida"*.)

SOIL: Wide range, as long as it is well-drained.

SALT TOLERANCE: Medium

WIND TOLERANCE: Medium

ZONE: 9b to 11. Protect from freezes. Great for containers in zones 8 or 9a so that it can be easily moved in during the cold.

PEST PROBLEMS: Brown spots on the leaves indicate fungus or bacteria. These routinely occur during the rainy season. Cut back on water, if possible. Do not spray unless they become severe.

PROPAGATION: Cuttings

The White Begonia flower is a cluster that measures up to four inches across. It shows well up close or from a distance.

Planting: Plant any time of the year in native soil. Leave the root ball slightly out of the ground, about 1/4 inch. (See detailed planting instructions in "Easy Gardens for Florida"*, Chapter 11.)

Fertilizing: Immediately after planting, fertilize with a well-balanced, slow-release mix that includes minor elements. Repeat in March, June, and October of each year. If the summer is unusually hot and rainy, inspect the leaf color of the plant in August. If it appears washed out, add an additional fertilization at that time. (See detailed fertilization instructions in "Easy Gardens for Florida"*, Chapter 11.)

Trimming: Trim this Begonia once a year in summer, when it has the least flowers and recovers fastest from a cutback. Trim back hard to about twelve inches tall. It takes about a month or two for the plant to recover. If the Begonia gets leggy in between annual cutbacks, trim lightly as needed.

* My current book, "Easy Gardens for South Florida", will be expanded to include the entire state in 2004.

Botanical Name: *Bulbine frutescens*

Common Name: **Bulbine**

CHARACTERISTICS

PLANT TYPE: Ground-cover.

AVERAGE SIZE: 12 inches tall by 8 to 12 inches wide. Clumps spread with age and need to be separated every 3 years or so.

GROWTH RATE: Medium

LEAF: Long and thin, needle-like. About 6 to 8 inches tall by 1/4 inch wide. Succulent, like an Aloe.

FLOWER: Clusters of tiny yellow flowers measure about 2 inches long.

AVERAGE LIFE: Unknown but at least 10 years.

ORIGIN: South Africa

CAUTIONS: None known

SPACING: 8 to 12 inches on center, depending on size of plant at planting time. Plant it fairly close together.

A delightful, new groundcover that stays low, requires little care, and blooms during the dry months. Lasts for years.

Bulbine planted in front of Mammey Crotons

General: Peter and Debra Strelkow, landscape architects from Fort Lauderdale, gave me a clump of Bulbine from their garden a few years ago. Peter heard about it from Burle Marx, the famous Brazilian landscape architect. They have ten years' experience working with the plant and recommend it highly. I am equally impressed with its toughness, ability to stay low, and almost constant blooms. Very few groundcovers offer these advantages and live more than a few years. This one appears to have a very long life span, at least 10 years, with very little care. Just be sure it gets a lot of sun and not too much water.

Season: Bulbine blooms mainly during the dry months, including winter. When the plant is not in flower, it is rather non-descript.

To locate plants, go to www.easygardencolor.com

Companions: Bulbine is one of the most versatile plants in this book. It blooms most of the time and stays quite low. It blends well with many different landscape styles, from tropical to informal cottage gardens. Use it in masses as the smallest layer in any planting scheme.

Costus barbatus

Bulbine

Stoplight Croton

Bulbine with some companions

Planting: Plant any time of the year in native soil. Leave the root ball slightly out of the ground, about 1/4 inch. (See detailed planting instructions in "Easy Gardens for Florida"*, Chapter 11.)

Fertilizing: Immediately after planting, fertilize with a well-balanced, slow-release mix that includes minor elements. Repeat in March, June, and October of each year. (See detailed fertilization instructions in "Easy Gardens for Florida"*, Chapter 11.)

Trimming: None needed. Separate the clumps about every three years. Take the whole mass out of the ground and break it up with a sharp shovel. Re-plant the smaller pieces and give the rest to deserving friends or neighbors.

* My current book, "Easy Gardens for South Florida", will be expanded to include the entire state in 2004.

GROWING CONDITIONS

LIGHT: Full sun. This plant does not do well in shade.

WATER: Low. Ideal watering is once or twice a week after the initial establishment period. Tolerates water up to 3 times per week. Do not overwater this plant or plant it in wet areas. (For detailed information about watering, see Chapter 8 in "Easy Gardens for Florida"*.)

SOIL: Wide range, as long as it is well-drained.

SALT TOLERANCE: Medium

WIND TOLERANCE: Medium

ZONE: 10a through 11. It shows no cold damage when temperatures go down to the mid-30's. Some sources say it will do quite well in zone 9, but we did not test it there.

PEST PROBLEMS: None known, provided the plant is not overwatered.

PROPAGATION: Division of clumps.

Botanical Name: *Duranta erecta 'Gold Mound'*

Common Name: **Gold Mound Duranta**

CHARACTERISTICS

PLANT TYPE: Evergreen shrub

AVERAGE SIZE: After its first few years of trials, it appears to be maintainable as low as 12 inches tall by 12 inches wide. The largest specimen we can find is 4 feet tall after 4 years.

GROWTH RATE: Slow for its first year or two in the ground. Faster in subsequent years.

LEAF: Yellow-green, small and pointed. About 3/4 inch long by 1/2 inch wide.

FLOWER: Seldom flowers but has a lovely, small, blue flower when it blooms that is the same as the large Golden Dewdrop.

AVERAGE LIFE: Unknown. Has lived for 4 years so far in our trials and looks great. Other types of Durantas live for over 10 years.

ORIGIN: Unknown

CAUTIONS: Golden berries are poisonous to people. According to Julia F. Morton in her book, "Plants Poisonous to People", children in Australia have died from eating the berries. In Florida, one instance of illness but no deaths have been reported.

SPACING: 12 to 18 inches on center.

A new groundcover that can be maintained as low as one foot tall.

Gold Mound Duranta planted in front of burgundy Coleus and Mussaenda frondosa.

General: Most groundcovers that can be maintained as low as twelve inches have a very short life span or require a lot of care. Not so for the Gold Mound Duranta. It is very slow-growing, adding to its low maintenance character. The gold color is unique, contrasting well with bright-colored tropicals. New to the market, Gold Mound has been in our trial gardens for just four years. There is still a lot to learn about this plant, but it's off to a good start.

Season: No seasonal variation.

To locate plants, go to www.easygardencolor.com

Companions: Gold Mound Duranta is very useful as a border or mass with other colorful plants. It is very versatile, stylewise, working well with manicured or cottage gardens. For high color contrast, use it with bright colors, like Crotons, Ti Plants, or *Costus barbatus*. It also contrasts well with dark colors, like burgundy Coleus or Purple Queen.

Gold Mound Duranta

Mammey Croton   *Costus barbatus*   Purple Queen

Gold Mound Duranta plant and some companions. Note how well it contrasts with dark or bright colors.

Planting: Plant any time of the year in native soil. Leave the root ball slightly out of the ground, about 1/4 inch. (See detailed planting instructions in "Easy Gardens for Florida"*, Chapter 11.)

Fertilizing: Immediately after planting, fertilize with a well-balanced, slow-release mix that includes minor elements. Repeat in March, June, and October of each year. (See detailed fertilization instructions in "Easy Gardens for Florida"*, Chapter 11.)

Trimming: Machine shear at any time. Or, for a less manicured look, hand prune as needed. This plant grows so slowly that frequent trimmings are not necessary.

* My current book, "Easy Gardens for South Florida", will be expanded to include the entire state in 2004.

GROWING CONDITIONS

LIGHT: Light shade to full sun

WATER: Low. Ideal watering is once or twice a week after the initial establishment period. Tolerates water up to 4 times per week. Requires more water when grown in containers. (For detailed information, see Chapter 8 in "Easy Gardens for Florida"*.)

SOIL: Wide range, as long as it is well-drained.

SALT TOLERANCE: Medium

WIND TOLERANCE: Medium

ZONE: 10a to 11. Leaves burn slightly at 38 degrees but recover in warm weather. Untested in zones 8 or 9.

PEST PROBLEMS: None known.

PROPAGATION: Cuttings

Gold Mound Duranta flower

Botanical Name: *Echinacea purpurea*
Common Name: **Purple Coneflower**

CHARACTERISTICS

PLANT TYPE:
Herbaceous perennial

AVERAGE SIZE: 18 to 30 inches tall by 24 to 36 inches wide.

GROWTH RATE: Fast

LEAF: Medium green and pointed.

FLOWER: Daisy-like blooms in pink, white, or lilac with orange centers. Large, up to 4 inches across.

AVERAGE LIFE: In our Mississippi trial gardens, Coneflowers have lived for 10 years. Lifespan shortens as you go further south. Expect a few years in central Florida.

ORIGIN: Southeastern United States.

CAUTIONS: None known

SPACING: 18 to 24 inches on center.

Echinacea 'White Lustre'

Excellent perennial for central and north Florida. Great butterfly plant.

Purple Coneflowers look more pink than purple.

General: Coneflowers need some cold weather to perform really well. They do best in north Florida, not quite as well in the central part of the state, and poorly in the south. They are quite easy to grow, and attract butterflies. The blooms resemble Daisies with an orange center that is raised like a cone. They do well as cut flowers. Coneflowers self-seed a lot, but the plants that grow from them may differ in appearance from their parents.

Season: The performance of Coneflowers varies in different parts of Florida. In central and north Florida, the plants die back with the first freeze and re-appear in spring. They begin blooming in May, continuing for about two months. If the previous winter was unusually warm, they may bloom again in the fall. They do better in north Florida than central Florida. I tried Coneflowers several times in south Florida with no luck. I plan on trying them again but as an annual that only blooms for about two months.

To locate plants, go to www.easygardencolor.com

Companions: These plants resemble wildflowers and are at home in informal gardens. Since they can look a bit scraggly, border Coneflowers with smaller plants that bloom at the same time. Pentas, Yellow Lantana, and Milkweed are good companions that also attract butterflies.

The flower resembles a daisy, with a raised, orange cone in the middle.

Planting: Fall is the best time to start small plants in your garden. Leave the root ball slightly out of the ground, about 1/4 inch. Plant seeds directly in the garden in spring once the danger of frost has past. Water the seeds daily so they don't dry out. (See detailed planting instructions in "Easy Gardens for Florida"*, Chapter 11.)

Fertilizing: Immediately after planting, fertilize with a well-balanced, slow-release mix that includes minor elements. Repeat in March, June, and October of each year. (See detailed fertilization instructions in "Easy Gardens for Florida"*, Chapter 11.)

Trimming: The plant dies back after the first freeze. Your garden will look neater if you trim away the dead top-growth, though the plant will emerge in the spring even if you don't. For fuller growth, pinch the plant back slightly in late spring. If you have time, remove spent flowers and their stalks to encourage more blooms as well as neaten the appearance of the plant. Divide the clumps into sections every two to four years in the fall. Be sure that each section has some well-developed roots.

* My current book, "Easy Gardens for South Florida", will be expanded to include the entire state in 2004.

GROWING CONDITIONS

LIGHT: Light shade to full sun. More blooms in full sun.

WATER: Low. Ideal watering is once or twice a week after the initial establishment period. Tolerates water up to 3 times per week. Requires more water when grown in containers. (For detailed information, see Chapter 8 in "Easy Gardens for Florida"*.)

SOIL: Wide range, as long as it is well-drained. This plant does not do well in poorly-drained soil.

SALT TOLERANCE: Low

WIND TOLERANCE: Medium

ZONE: 3 to 9. Use as a short-lived annual in zone 10 or 11.

PEST PROBLEMS: None known

PROPAGATION: Seeds or divisions.

CHARACTERISTICS

PLANT TYPE: Epiphyte

AVERAGE SIZE: 2 to 3 feet tall. The width of this plant depends on how it is thinned, as it grows in a clump that keeps spreading until it is separated.

GROWTH RATE: Medium

LEAF: Medium green, oblong, with a rounded tip. About 2 to 3 inches long by 3/4 inch wide.

FLOWER: Striking orange and yellow cluster of small Orchids. Each individual flower measures about 1 inch across. Clusters measure about 3 to 4 inches across.

AVERAGE LIFE: At least 10 years.

ORIGIN: Central and South America.

CAUTIONS: None known

SPACING: 2 to 3 feet on center.

I am currently testing a purple Epidendrum that shows great promise.

Beautiful, tried-and-true Orchid that grows in the ground and flowers for about six months a year. Drought-tolerant and easy.

This Orchid grows in the ground with other landscape plants. It is planted with white Firecracker.

General: An easy Orchid! This ground Orchid is an old Florida plant that is undergoing a resurgence of popularity. The flowers are lovely, and the plant usually blooms for at least six months a year. Although the individual flowers are small, they grow in clusters that show well up close or from a distance. The color is almost iridescent - orange and yellow combined. Like most Orchids, the plant itself is not particularly attractive, a bit of a sprawler. Use it in an informal garden, clustered with other flowering plants. It is also very attractive growing up a trellis, either in the ground or in a container. Since they need to be moved inside during freezes, grow them in containers in central or north Florida.

Season: Ground Orchids last for many years. Unlike the Spathoglottis Orchids, this one's leaves stay green and healthy, even in winter in south Florida. It flowers in the warm months, generally from spring to fall. Some years, its bloom period surprises you. The photo above was taken in March (2003), when the plant shouldn't be blooming! The warm weather came a bit early that year. Nature does not always go by the calendar.

Companions: Use this Orchid with other bright-colored plants that offer color in the warmer months. Crotons are a great choice, as are Thryallis, any of the Mussaendas, Golden Shrimp Plants, Cranberry Pentas, and Ruellia Purple Showers.

Orange Orchid with a background of Lobelia

Planting: Plant any time of the year in native soil. Leave the root ball slightly out of the ground, about 1/4 inch. (See detailed planting instructions in "Easy Gardens for Florida"*, Chapter 11.)

Fertilizing: Immediately after planting, fertilize with a well-balanced, slow-release mix that includes minor elements. Repeat in March, June, and October of each year. This plant is well adapted to our native soils and not particularly demanding of fertilizer. (See detailed fertilization instructions in "Easy Gardens for Florida"*, Chapter 11.)

Trimming: As the plant sprawls, it can be trimmed to stay within the desired bounds. However, it seems a shame to trim off and throw away valuable Orchid plants. I divide the clumps every few years, taking the whole plant out of the ground and cutting it into pieces. The individual pieces with roots can be rooted to make new plants. Pull out any weeds that sprout in the middle of the Orchids.

GROWING CONDITIONS

LIGHT: Medium to high

WATER: Low. I have had this plant for years in a bed that gets water twice a week. It thrives under those conditions after the initial establishment period. I have seen it in many old gardens that look like they have no irrigation, but I have never tested it. (For detailed information about watering, see Chapter 8 in "Easy Gardens for Florida"*.)

SOIL: Wide range, as long as it is well-drained. Unlike many other Orchids, this one does not require special soil.

SALT TOLERANCE: Medium

WIND TOLERANCE: Medium

ZONE: 10a to 11. More cold-tolerant than the Spathoglottis Orchids. Makes a great container plant in zones 8 and 9 so that it can be moved inside when freezes threaten.

PEST PROBLEMS: None known.

PROPAGATION: Division or cuttings.

My current book, "Easy Gardens for South Florida", will be expanded to include the entire state in 2004.

Botanical Name: *Hemerocallis spp.*

Common Name: **Daylily**

CHARACTERISTICS

PLANT TYPE: Herbaceous perennial

AVERAGE SIZE: Many different sizes available, from 9 to 40 inches tall.

GROWTH RATE: Medium

LEAF: Long and thin, size varies by type.

FLOWER: Many different colors, sizes, and shapes. Red, yellow, pink, purple, orange. Single colors or bicolors.

AVERAGE LIFE: In our Mississippi trial gardens, Daylilies have lived for 10 years. Lifespan shortens as you go further south. Expect only a few years in south Florida.

ORIGIN: Original Daylilies were from China. Most modern varieties are hybrids.

CAUTIONS: None known

SPACING: 18 to 24 inches on center. Although this may seem sparse at first, the plants will spread to cover the space. Planting too close decreases flower production.

Note: I got some of my Daylily information from an excellent article you can get for free from the internet. Go to http://edis.ifas.ufl.edu/BODY_EP006 to find the article titled "Daylilies for Florida" by Robert J. Black. This document is Circular 620, Department of Environmental Horticulture, Florida Cooperative Extension Service, Institute of Food and Agricultural Sciences, University of Florida. Revised: June 1997.

One of the most popular flowers in the country. Performs better in north and central Florida than the southern part of the state.

Hybrid Daylily

General: Daylilies do better in central and north Florida than further south. I have tried them several times in south Florida with disappointing results. I bought twelve varieties that were supposed to flower in succession so that I had constant blooms. It didn't work. Some didn't bloom at all, and others bloomed for so short a time period that I almost missed them! Now that there are so many Daylily growers in Florida (some of the best in the nation), I am going to try again, looking for varieties that are well-adapted to our tough south Florida conditions. Central and north Florida gardeners rave about Daylilies, which have been a garden staple there for generations. Choose plants carefully because different varieties have very different habits. Some are evergreen and some dormant. The evergreen types do better in Florida. Many Daylilies that do well up north don't thrive in Florida so buy from a nursery that specializes in Daylilies in Florida. Find local sources at the Florida Daylily Society's excellent and informative web site, http://www.daylilies.org/ahs/AHSreg12.html. They know most about which types are best for your area. Although each flower lasts only for a day, each scape (flower stalk) has several buds that bloom in succession.

Season: Bloom periods vary greatly, depending on type. Some bloom off and on all year, others for only a few weeks.

To locate plants, go to www.easygardencolor.com

Companions: In central and north Florida, Daylilies look great planted in clumps of at least 12 of the same color. This mass has more of a showy effect than singles. In south Florida, where plants are not as spectacular, tuck one here and there in a cottage garden to enjoy the beauty of the flowers rather than the impact of a mass of color. Mark Finklestein of Boca West Country Club in Boca Raton uses the 'Gertrude Condon' variety (the gold one, below) in his annual beds, with one planted here and there. For most of the year, the little clumps are almost invisible. They bloom, mixed in with his summer annuals for about six weeks in spring, and the effect is beautiful.

Daylilies are available in many different colors.

Planting: Plant any time of the year in native soil. Spring and fall are ideal. Leave the root ball slightly out of the ground, about 1/4 inch. (See detailed planting instructions in "Easy Gardens for Florida"*, Chapter 11.)

Fertilizing: Immediately after planting, fertilize with a well-balanced, slow-release mix that includes minor elements. Repeat in March, June, and October of each year. If the summer is unusually hot and rainy, inspect the leaf color of the plant in August. If it appears washed out, add an additional fertilization at that time. (See detailed fertilization instructions in "Easy Gardens for Florida"*, Chapter 11.)

Trimming: Dead-heading (removing spent blooms) improves the appearance of Daylilies but is not essential. Divide the clumps every three to five years.

GROWING CONDITIONS

LIGHT: Lighter colors tolerate light shade or sun. Darker colors do better in full sun.

WATER: Medium. Ideal watering is twice a week after the initial establishment period. Tolerates water up to 4 times per week. Requires more water when grown in containers. (For detailed information, see Chapter 8 in "Easy Gardens for Florida"*.)

SOIL: Wide range, as long as it is well-drained. Daylilies are not picky about the type of soil, doing well in sand or clay. But, they require good drainage.

SALT TOLERANCE: High

WIND TOLERANCE: Medium

ZONE: 3 to 10

PEST PROBLEMS: Fairly pest-free in the Florida Landscape. Occasional caterpillars, aphids, thrips, and grasshoppers. When pests strike, they can severely damage the plants.

PROPAGATION: Division, seed, or proliferation (offsets from the flower stalk).

My current book, "Easy Gardens for South Florida",
will be expanded to include the entire state in 2004.

Botanical Name: *Hibiscus rosa-sinensis*

Common Name: **Dwarf Hibiscus**

CHARACTERISTICS

PLANT TYPE: Evergreen shrub.

AVERAGE SIZE: This plant grows to 8 feet tall if never sprayed with a growth retardant. It is frequently used as a large shrub (see pages 154 and 155) or a small tree (see pages 218 and 219).

GROWTH RATE: Medium

LEAF: Dark green. Size and shape vary with type. Average is about 1 1/2 inches wide by 3 inches long.

FLOWER: Many colors. Most often available as a dwarf in yellow, white, pink, double peach, and red. Size varies by color, averaging about 4 inches wide.

AVERAGE LIFE: 3 to 4 years, if kept dwarfed.

ORIGIN: China

CAUTIONS: None known

SPACING: 12 to 16 inches on center.

Note: If some of the leaves become bright yellow all at the same time while most remain green, it is a change in the weather. Leave the plant alone, and it will recover quickly.

Regular Hibiscus that are periodically sprayed with a growth retardant to maintain their low, compact form. Look out for pests.

Dwarf Hibiscus in mixed colors planted around peach Canna Lilies

General: Dwarf Hibiscus are beautiful planted in mixed colors or in a single-colored border or mass. The large flowers on the small plants are a delightful contrast. They are also quite useful, as we have few groundcovers that give as much color and last as long. But, they are tricky to care for, requiring spraying once or twice a year with a growth retardant, which is sometimes difficult to buy and apply. I have seen many people, including myself, pull them out instead of keeping up with the dwarfing process. They seem to work best when maintained by professionals who are very experienced with the process. Hibiscus are also very susceptible to a multitude of pests. Two new ones, Pink Hibiscus Mealybug and Lobate lac scale, have the potential of damaging many of the Hibiscus in south Florida. The US Department of Agriculture is working closely with local nurseries to control them. Call your county extension for the latest controls if you get pests on your Hibiscus.

How to Dwarf: Vanderlaans Nursery in Lake Worth, Florida, is a major grower of dwarf Hibiscus. They recommend a growth retardant called Bonsai. When plants have begun to grow normally, trim them back to 2/3 of the desired size. Once the new growth is one to two inches long, spray with Bonsai at the strongest recommended rate, getting as much spray as possible on the stems of the new growth. A single application should be sufficient. Repeat this process each time the plants grow too big. Average repetition rate is every eight months and varies by time of year and variety of Hibiscus.

Season: On and off all year. Dwarf Hibiscus bloom a bit more than regular Hibiscus.

Companions: Buy Hibiscus that have been trained as dwarfs at the nursery. It is difficult, if not impossible, to turn three-foot plants into one-foot plants. Use in masses or borders, in mixed colors or solids. They are very versatile, working well with formal, tropical, or cottage gardens.

Mixed colors of Dwarf Hibiscus. Insets: Pink, white, and red flowers. The 'White Wing' is a particularly good bloomer when dwarfed.

Planting: Plant any time of the year in native soil. Leave the root ball slightly out of the ground, about 1/4 inch. (See detailed planting instructions in "Easy Gardens for Florida"*, Chapter 11.)

Fertilizing: Immediately after planting, fertilize with a well-balanced, slow-release mix that includes minor elements. Repeat in March, June, and October of each year. If the summer is unusually hot and rainy, inspect the leaf color of the plant in August. If it appears washed out, add an additional fertilization at that time. (See detailed fertilization instructions in "Easy Gardens for Florida"*, Chapter 11.)

Trimming: See 'How to Dwarf', left.

GROWING CONDITIONS

LIGHT: Sun or shade. Several months after planting, the growth regulator wears off, and the plants grow more and flower a lot less. If they are in full sun, they will grow and flower like a regular Hibiscus.

WATER: Medium. Ideal watering is twice a week after the initial establishment period. Tolerates water up to 4 times per week. Do not overwater. Requires more water when grown in containers.

SOIL: Wide range, as long as it is well-drained.

SALT TOLERANCE: High

WIND TOLERANCE: High

ZONE: Technically, 10a to 11. Often successful (and commonly planted) in protected areas of zone 9.

PEST PROBLEMS: Pink Hibiscus Mealybug (pink, cottony material) and Lobate lac scale (small, black, raised dots on stems along with blackened leaves) are 2 new serious pests. Check with your county extension for latest controls. Also, scale, spider mites, snails, aphids, and whitefly. These plants attract a lot of pests in some locations and none in others. They attract more if a lot of them are planted on the same site. Do not use Malathion on Hibiscus - it will defoliate them.

PROPAGATION: Cuttings

Botanical Name: *Justicia 'Fruit Cocktail'*

Common Name: **Shrimp 'Fruit Cocktail'**

CHARACTERISTICS

PLANT TYPE: Evergreen shrub.

AVERAGE SIZE: 18 to 24 inches tall by 15 to 24 inches wide.

GROWTH RATE: Slow

LEAF: Light green and pointed. About 1 1/2 inches long by 3/4 inch wide.

FLOWER: Yellow and red. About 2 inches long by 2 inches wide. Very pretty.

AVERAGE LIFE: Unknown. I have had it in my test gardens for 3 years, and it shows no sign of slowing down.

ORIGIN: Unknown

CAUTIONS: None known

SPACING: 18 inches on center.

A delightful, new groundcover that has excelled through three years of tough south Florida trials. Untested in the central and northern parts of the state.

The colors of the 'Fruit Cocktail' flower resemble fruit cocktail.

General: 'Fruit Cocktail' is a new groundcover that is an excellent choice for areas where the flower can be viewed from a close distance. The flower is lovely and features the colors of fruit cocktail for six to eight months a year in south Florida. (It has not been tested in central or north Florida yet, but will be.) The blooms are small, however, and do not show too well from a distance. When I first tried this groundcover, I expected it to live a very short time, like most other flowering groundcovers in Florida. The plant has outlived my expectations by a long shot, living a full three years so far in the trial gardens. It is small enough to fit in the tiniest garden and blooms well in sun or shade.

Season: 'Fruit Cocktails' live for at least three years. They bloom most of the time, peaking in winter. Since they look better if trimmed hard during their dormant periods, plan on about six to eight months of flowers in the average year.

To locate plants, go to www.easygardencolor.com

Companions: Plant 'Fruit Cocktails' with other plants that provide winter color. It forms a great border for Icetone Crotons, Brunfelsias, *Dombeya 'Seminoles'*, and Pink Angelwing Begonias. Be sure to plant the 'Fruit Cocktails' in locations where they can be viewed from up close.

Brunfelsia

'Fruit Cocktail'

Angelwing Begonia

'Fruit Cocktail' and some companions

Planting: Plant any time of the year in native soil. Leave the root ball slightly out of the ground, about 1/4 inch. (See detailed planting instructions in "Easy Gardens for Florida"*, Chapter 11.)

Fertilizing: This plant is a heavy feeder. If the leaves get yellowish, it needs food. Immediately after planting, fertilize with a well-balanced, slow-release mix that includes minor elements. Repeat in March, June, and October of each year. If the summer is unusually hot and rainy, inspect the leaf color of the plant in August. If it appears washed out, add an additional fertilization at that time. (See detailed fertilization instructions in "Easy Gardens for Florida"*, Chapter 11.)

Trimming: Trim two to three times per year, whenever it gets leggy. Time the trimming right after a bloom spurt. The plant recovers much faster from a cutback in the warmer months. The best times for trimming are spring and summer.

* My current book, "Easy Gardens for South Florida", will be expanded to include the entire state in 2004.

GROWING CONDITIONS

LIGHT: Medium shade to full sun.

WATER: Medium. Ideal watering is twice a week after the initial establishment period. Tolerates water up to 4 times per week. Requires more water when grown in containers. (For detailed information about watering, see Chapter 8 in "Easy Gardens for Florida"*.)

SOIL: Wide range, as long as it is well-drained.

SALT TOLERANCE: Unknown

WIND TOLERANCE: Unknown

ZONE: Unknown. Untested outside of zone 10A. No cold damage from 1998 until 2003 in Palm Beach County.

PEST PROBLEMS: None serious

PROPAGATION: Cuttings

| Botanical Name: | *Lantana camara 'New Gold'* |
| Common Name: | **Yellow Lantana** |

CHARACTERISTICS

PLANT TYPE: Evergreen shrub used as a groundcover.

AVERAGE SIZE: 8 to 12 inches tall by 18 to 24 inches wide.

GROWTH RATE: Fast

LEAF: Medium green, serrated and pointed. About 1 inch long by 1/2 inch wide.

FLOWER: Yellow, about 1 inch across.

AVERAGE LIFE: 1 year. Lives longer in salt and wind situations or with little water.

ORIGIN: Tropical America

CAUTIONS: Poisonous to humans, dogs, and livestock. Can cause serious illness or death. Tends to look weedy.

SPACING: 18 to 24 inches on center. This plant spreads quite a bit and lives longer, if properly spaced.

Note: I tried many different types of Lantanas in my trials. The yellow and purple groundcovers did better than the rest. Many of the others are quite short-lived, only surviving a few months. Others had a very short bloom period and looked bad when not flowering. So, be careful with Lantana. It also behaves very differently in different parts of the state. Many that do well in north Florida are very short-lived in the southern part of the state.

A low-growing, summer groundcover that takes salt, sun, and wind. Great butterfly plant.

Yellow Lantana in June. It seldom blooms in mid-winter unless it is unusually warm.

General: Lantana is a useful groundcover when used in the right environment with the right expectations. It loves sun, salt, and wind but won't take too much water. So, if you plant it in a non-windy, non-salty situation, expect some problems during our rainy summer. It will get leaf spots and not live as long or bloom as much without salt and wind. But, since it offers the advantages of low height and great tolerance for sun, it can be very useful. Understand that the yellow Lantana groundcover blooms mainly in the summer, while the purple peaks in winter. Both are very informal and not appropriate for a manicured garden.

Season: Lantana lives for a year or two, depending on water. It lives longer in a low-water situation. Its blooms peak in summer. Use as a perennial in areas that do not freeze, and as an annual further north.

To locate plants, go to www.easygardencolor.com

Companions: Lantana is most useful in salt or wind or with other plants that peak in summer. For a low-growing flower border, combine it with Pentas and Blue Daze. Or, alternate with three plants, using a New Look Red Penta, a Yellow Lantana, and then a Blue Daze. This combination is also great for pots. Other great companions include Salmon Mussaenda and Plumbago, as shown in the insets below. Lantana sometimes looks wild and is not appropriate in formal gardens.

Yellow Lantana flowers and some companions. The Blue Plumbago and Salmon Musseanda also peak in summer.

Planting: Plant any time of the year in native soil. Leave the root ball slightly out of the ground, about 1/4 inch. (See detailed planting instructions in "Easy Gardens for Florida*", Chapter 11.)

Fertilizing: Immediately after planting, fertilize with a well-balanced, slow-release mix that includes minor elements. Repeat in March, June, and October of each year. If it appears washed out, add an additional fertilization in August. (See detailed fertilization instructions in "Easy Gardens for Florida*", Chapter 11.)

Trimming: Plant Lantana with enough space to grow; trim it hard twice a year, in January and August. If it sends out some wild shoots, groom them back in bounds at any time. Lantana needs much more trimming if it is planted too close together or if you want a manicured look. Accept Lantana as an informal plant if you are looking for low maintenance.

GROWING CONDITIONS

LIGHT: Full sun

WATER: Low. Ideal watering is once or twice a week after the initial establishment period. Tolerates water up to 3 times per week at the most. Requires more water when grown in containers. (For detailed information, see Chapter 8 in "Easy Gardens for Florida".)

SOIL: Wide range, as long as it is well-drained.

SALT TOLERANCE: High

WIND TOLERANCE: High

ZONE: 9b to 11, as a perennial. Used as a summer annual in zones 8 and 9a.

PEST PROBLEMS: If brown spots appear on the leaves, it is a fungus. These spots are routine, especially in the summer. If possible, cut back on water. Spray only if they become quite severe. In most instances, they do not kill the plant. Whitefly is another potential pest.

PROPAGATION: Seeds or cuttings.

Botanical Name: *Lantana montividensis*
Common Name: **Purple Lantana**

CHARACTERISTICS

PLANT TYPE: Evergreen shrub used as a groundcover.

AVERAGE SIZE: 8 to 12 inches tall by 18 to 24 inches wide.

GROWTH RATE: Fast, but not as fast as the Yellow Lantana. If you plant both together, the yellow will dominate.

LEAF: Medium green, serrated and pointed. About 3/4 inch long by 1/2 inch wide.

FLOWER: Purple, about 1 inch across.

AVERAGE LIFE: 1 year. Lives longer in salt and wind situations or with little water.

ORIGIN: South America

CAUTIONS: Poisonous to humans, dogs, and livestock. Can cause serious illness or death. Tends to look weedy.

SPACING: 18 to 24 inches on center. This plant spreads quite a bit and lives longer, if properly spaced.

Note: I tried many different types of Lantanas in my trials. The yellow and purple groundcovers did better than the rest. Many of the others are quite short-lived, only surviving a few months. Others had a very short bloom period and looked bad when not flowering. So, be careful with Lantana. It also behaves very differently in different parts of the state. Many that do well in north Florida are very short-lived in the southern part of the state.

Low-growing groundcover that is a favorite food of butterflies. Use in the cool season. Best as an annual in north Florida.

Purple and Yellow Lantana in a wall pot. Although the yellow blooms more in summer and the purple in cooler weather, they both bloom in spring. The two colors do well in containers or in the ground as a groundcover.

General: Low-growing groundcovers that last more than one season are hard to find in Florida. Purple Lantana fits the bill. It only lasts a year or two but gives a good bit of color in the cool months in the south and central parts of the state. And, the butterflies love it. Understand that it blooms in the cooler months, the opposite season from the Yellow Lantana. They are often planted together with the expectation that they will bloom at the same time, which seldom occurs. The Yellow Lantana is a more aggressive plant, and will overtake the Purple Lantana if planted too close. It is also a wilder-looking plant, although no Lantana fits into a manicured garden. Both the yellow and the purple are excellent for containers.

Season: Purple Lantana lives for a year or two, depending on water. It lives longer in a low-water situation. Its blooms peak in winter in south and central Florida. In summer, its leaves remain full and green; but, do not expect flowers in summer unless we have a dry spell. Use as an annual in areas that freeze.

To locate plants, go to www.easygardencolor.com

Companions: Use Purple Lantana with other plants that provide winter color. It works well as a mass or a border. Great companions include Dombeyas, Giant Shrimps, Crotons, Golden Shrimps, Rondeletias, Bougainvilleas, and Chinese Hats.

Purple Lantana flowers

Planting: Plant any time of the year in native soil. Leave the root ball slightly out of the ground, about 1/4 inch. (See detailed planting instructions in "Easy Gardens for Florida"*, Chapter 11.)

Fertilizing: Immediately after planting, fertilize with a well-balanced, slow-release mix that includes minor elements. Repeat in March, June, and October of each year. (See detailed fertilization instructions in "Easy Gardens for Florida"*, Chapter 11.)

Trimming: Plant Purple Lantana with enough space to grow; trim it hard twice a year, in May and August. If it sends out some wild shoots, groom them back within bounds at any time. Lantana needs much more trimming if it is planted too close together or if you want a manicured look. Accept Lantana as an informal plant if you are looking for low maintenance. The Purple Lantana is easier to maintain than the yellow because it grows more slowly.

My current book, "Easy Gardens for South Florida", will be expanded to include the entire state in 2004.

GROWING CONDITIONS

LIGHT: Full sun

WATER: Low. Ideal watering is once or twice a week after the initial establishment period. Tolerates water up to 3 times per week at the most. Requires more water when grown in containers. (For detailed information about watering, see Chapter 8 in "Easy Gardens for Florida"*.)

SOIL: Wide range, as long as it is well-drained.

SALT TOLERANCE: High

WIND TOLERANCE: High

ZONE: 9 to 11. Dies back in severe freeze but usually reappears when the weather warms up. Use as an annual in zone 8.

PEST PROBLEMS: If brown spots appear on the leaves, it is a fungus. These spots are routine, especially in the summer. If possible, cut back on water. Spray only if they become quite severe. In most instances, they do not kill the plant.

PROPAGATION: Cuttings

Botanical Name: *Spathoglottis spp.*

Common Name: **Ground Orchids, Garden Orchids**

CHARACTERISTICS

PLANT TYPE: Ground-cover.

AVERAGE SIZE: 2 feet tall by 2 feet wide.

GROWTH RATE: Medium

LEAF: Medium green. Looks like they are pleated. Size varies by type.

FLOWER: Lavender, yellow, or dark purple. Size varies by type. Spathoglottis flowers are not as large as the Cattleya Orchids, but they bloom for much longer.

AVERAGE LIFE: 3 to 8 years, if they are kept warm enough in winter.

ORIGIN: Far East and Australia.

CAUTIONS: None known

SPACING: 18 to 24 inches on center.

'Grapette' does best in pots because of its cold sensitivity.

An easy Orchid that grows in the garden among the other flowers and blooms for months at a time. Summer and fall bloomer.

Spathoglottis plicata was the highest performer of all the Spathoglottis in our trials. It is covered in detail on pages 48 and 49 of "Easy Gardens for Florida"*.

General: Orchids are the world's favorite flowers and are traditionally thought of as difficult to grow. Garden Orchids are the exception, blooming in the garden with the same care as other landscape plants. Use these plants in containers only in central and north Florida so that you can easily move them in during cold spells.

Season: Spathoglottis last for many years if they are protected from temperatures in the 40's. They bloom in the warmer months. Bloom time varies from year to year. I have seen *S. plicata* (above) bloom for ten months one year and two months the next. Blooms peak in fall. When the plant is not in flower, its leaves remain but turn yellowish in winter. It seldom flowers in winter.

To locate plants, go to www.easygardencolor.com

Companions: Spathoglottis are a must for summer and fall gardens. A beautiful combination includes Pink Dwarf Poinciana for height, Thryallis as the middle layer, and Spathoglottis massed in front. Other great companions include Firespikes, all Mussaendas, and Golden Shrimp Plants. Do not use Spathoglottis in sections of your garden that are a focal point in winter because they usually do not look good at that time of year. Use the especially cold-sensitive varieties, like the 'Grapette', in containers so that you can move them inside on cold nights.

The Spathoglottis parsonii had the most beautiful flowers of any in our trials; but, its bloom period was shorter than the plicata (shown opposite).

Planting: Plant any time of the year in native soil. Leave the root ball slightly out of the ground, about 1/4 inch. (See detailed planting instructions in "Easy Gardens for Florida"*, Chapter 11.)

Fertilizing: Immediately after planting, fertilize with a well-balanced, slow-release mix that includes minor elements. Repeat in March, June, and October of each year. If the summer is unusually hot and rainy, inspect the leaf color of the plant in August. If it appears washed out, add an additional fertilization at that time. (See detailed fertilization instructions in "Easy Gardens for Florida"*, Chapter 11.)

Trimming: Trim to remove brown leaves. This plant normally has some brown areas on the leaves. These need not be removed unless they become an eyesore. In the winter, quite a few leaves turn yellow. Remove them as needed. This is a very easy plant and only occasionally requires attention.

My current book, "Easy Gardens for South Florida", will be expanded to include the entire state in 2004.

GROWING CONDITIONS

LIGHT: Medium shade to full sun. The ideal light is partial sun, partial shade; but, the plant performs acceptably in a full sun environment.

WATER: Medium. Ideal watering is twice a week after the initial establishment period. Tolerates water up to 3 or 4 times per week. Requires more water when grown in containers.

SOIL: Wide range, as long as it is well-drained.

SALT TOLERANCE: Unknown

WIND TOLERANCE: Unknown

ZONE: 10a to 11. Very cold-sensitive. The Spathoglottis plicata usually gets yellow leaves in the winter, but ours lived through all the winters in Palm Beach County from 1995-2003. The 'Grapette' (pictured in opposite sidebar) is more cold-sensitive. They all died in the winter of 1995. If you keep this one in pots, move it inside during cold spells.

PEST PROBLEMS: None serious.

PROPAGATION: Division

Groundcovers and Small Perennials: *Notes from our ongoing trials*

Allamanda cathartica Hendersonii dwarf
Dwarf Allamanda

Summer-blooming shrub that is mostly bare in the winter in south Florida. Re-appears the next spring. Pretty in bloom. Excellent summer annual in hot areas.

Alternanthera ficoidea
Jacob's Coat

One of my biggest failures. I planted thousands in many different areas, thinking this was a tough perennial for south Florida. They <u>all</u> (100%) died from insect damage within a few months.

Coreopsis spp.
Coreopsis

Although slow to get started in our south Florida gardens, Coreopsis does quite well as an annual. In our Mississippi trial gardens, it is a high-performing perennial, dying back in the winter and reappearing the following spring.

Costus curvibracteatus 'Orange Tulip'
Orange Tulip Costus

Beautiful, summer bloomer that is mostly bare in the winter in south Florida. Highly recommended for summer shade gardens. About 3' wide by 2' tall. Untested further north.

Crossandra infundibuliformis, yellow
Yellow Crossandra

I planted thousands of these in many locations from 1990-1995 and they did very well for at least 5 years. All the new ones I planted after 1995 died within a few months, for no known reason.

Cuphea hyssopifolia
Mexican Heather

Tough groundcover that blooms all year in south Florida, living about 2 years. Use as an annual further north. Very heat-tolerant. Not much impact when used alone. Plant with bright-colored flowers, like Cranberry Pentas.

Dianella ensifolia
Flax

Excellent results from our south Florida trials so far. Untested further north. Variegated groundcover with a tropical look. About 2' x 2'. Does better in shade. Low maintenance. Separate clumps every 5 years or so. Tiny yellow flowers.

Dietes vegetata
African Iris

Disappointing in our south Florida trials because it seldom bloomed. Foliage is relatively attractive, like straight Liriope, adding an interesting texture. Flower is lovely during its brief appearances.

Gaillardia spp.
Blanket Flower

Worked as an annual during the dry months in our south Florida trial gardens, but only lasted a month or so. Somewhat messy-looking, but improved by dead-heading. Bloomed longer and performed better in summer in Mississippi.

Ipomoea batatas 'Tricolor'
Tricolor Sweet Potato

Excellent container plant, one of the best for cascading over the edge of pots. Also works as an annual for a brief period in the ground. Does not last long in the ground in south Florida. Also available in dark purple or lime green.

Iris, Louisiana hybrids
Louisiana Iris

Works beautifully in all of Florida. We planted ours on the edge of a pond. It bloomed each spring. Although the bloom period was quite short (about a week), the beauty of the flower made it worth having.

Ixora 'Petite Pink'
Petite Pink Ixora

Tiny, very slow-growing Ixora that looks fabulous in bloom but doesn't flower too often. I have a few in my summer garden, and that's enough! Very cold-sensitive.

Justica carnea
Brazilian Plume
Spectacular flower on small plant. Difficult to maintain. If you trim it enough to keep it from getting leggy, you inhibit it from blooming. Buy these for short-term container plants and throw them away when they get leggy.

Neomarica caerulea
Twelve Apostles
Fabulous flower that is supposed to bloom every 2 weeks but doesn't. Bloomed very occasionally, and I kept missing the flowers. Very nice, strap-like foliage. Prefers shade.

Orthosiphon stamineus
Cat's Whiskers
Unique, very pretty flower on a small plant that grew to about 2' in our south Florida trials. Untested further north. Short-lived, about 6 months or so, but worth planting a few. Inexpensive and easy to enjoy! White or pale purple.

Otocanthus caeruleus
Brazilian Snapdragon
Pretty, blue flower on a low-growing shrub that blooms in winter. Best used as an annual, because it seldom comes back after its first winter. Grows to about 18" by 18". Untested outside of south Florida.

Peperomia obtusifolia 'Variegata'
Variegated Peperomia
Another one of my biggest blunders. I thought this was a good groundcover and planted thousands of them in hundreds of different locations in south Florida. Within a year, 50% were dead from fungus or snails.

Rudbeckia hirta
Black-eyed Susan
Very short-lived (a month or two) in our south Florida gardens. Much better performance in Mississippi, where it is a perennial that comes back year after year.

Russellia equisetiformis
Firecracker
Beautiful, light-textured groundcover that works well in south Florida. Excellent container plant with good salt-tolerance. Looks straggly after a few years in the ground.

Salvia coccinea
Tropical Sage
An herb that flowers! Just don't plan on it living too long in your south Florida garden. Expect one or two seasons. Untested further north.

Salvia coccinea 'Brenthurst'
Pink and White Salvia
Highly recommended for informal gardens. Beautiful flowers on a strong plant that looks like a wildflower. Each plant lasts about 6 months and reseeds politely. Pops up here and there in the garden.

Salvia splendens 'Purple Fountain'
Salvia 'Purple Fountain'
Low-growing groundcover that lives for a few years in south Florida. I was disappointed with the brevity of its bloom periods. Untested further north.

Turnera subulata
White Alder
Beautiful blooms on a low, short-lived groundcover. The blooms come and go. Also available in yellow. Good plant, if you understand its short lifespan (less than a year) and intermittent bloom periods. Untested outside of south Florida.

Wedelia trilobata
Wedelia
Invasive groundcover that is almost impossible to get rid of. We even tried burning it, and it came right back! If you plant it, it will spread to all of your neighbors' gardens as well. Not recommended for anything!

CHAPTER 3

SHRUBS, 2' TO 8'

The shrubs in this chapter are excellent choices for Florida color.

Together with the shrubs in Chapter 2 of "Easy Gardens for Florida"*, these selections offer some of the best, long-term color available in our area today.

They last for many years, blooming seasonally each year.

This chapter features temperate-zoned favorites, like Roses and Azaleas, along with many great subtropical choices. Each plant page tells you where in Florida each does best.

Subtropical shrubs offer long flowering periods that are very different from northern shrubs. Many northern favorites, like Azaleas, only bloom for a month or so. Most subtropical shrubs average blooming six to eight months a year. If you live in an area with severe freezes, consider some of the subtropicals in containers so that you can move them indoors when a freeze threatens. Or, simply use them as summer annuals.

Layer colorful shrubs for a front landscape that not only delights the eye but also makes your house look better.

And, collect your favorites and display them in your own private botanical garden in your side and back yard.

Left: Scarlet Red Cloak (pages 158 and 159)
Above: Costus barbatus (pages 142 and 143)

* My current book, "Easy Gardens for South Florida", will be expanded to include the entire state in 2004.

Botanical Name: *Acalypha hispida*

Common Name: **Chenille Plant**

CHARACTERISTICS

PLANT TYPE: Shrub

AVERAGE SIZE: Easy to maintain at sizes between 4 feet tall by 4 feet wide and 10 feet tall by 7 feet wide.

GROWTH RATE: Fast

LEAF: Medium green and pointed. About 6 inches long by 5 inches wide.

FLOWER: Red, long and thin. Resembles a pipe cleaner. Size varies, averaging about 6 inches long. Occasionally grows as long as 18 inches. A white variety (*alba*) is also available. I have not tested the white.

AVERAGE LIFE: Over 10 years.

ORIGIN: East Indies

CAUTIONS: None known

SPACING: 3 to 5 feet on center.

An old Florida plant that adds a unique texture to the garden. Ideal for summer and fall.

Chenille in full bloom

General: The Chenille Plant's unique flowers are an excellent source of texture in the garden. They are quite a conversation piece, especially to new south Florida residents. The shrub fits well with a variety of landscape styles, excelling in either tropical or casual flower gardens. Plant it as an accent where it will not be a focal point in winter. And be sure to give it enough space to grow into a medium-to-large shrub.

Season: The Chenille Plant lasts for many years, flowering in spring, summer, and fall. The leaves often burn in winter from routine south Florida temperatures. Do not use it for a winter focal point. *Left: Chenille Plant in full sun in May. The form of the plant is more compact in full sun than in light shade.*

To locate plants, go to www.easygardencolor.com

Companions: Chenille Plants work well in informal flower gardens or tropical gardens. For a tropical look, use them with Palms and large-leafed plants, like Alocasia (Elephant Ear) or White Bird of Paradise. Crotons and Bromeliads are natural companions. For a large, flowering wall in the summer, use the Chenille with Mussaenda frondosa, Thryallis, and Plumbago.

Recently planted Chenille bordered by yellow Marigolds

Planting: Plant any time of the year in native soil. Leave the root ball slightly out of the ground, about 1/4 inch. (See detailed planting instructions in "Easy Gardens for Florida"*, Chapter 11.)

Fertilizing: Immediately after planting, fertilize with a well-balanced, slow-release mix that includes minor elements. Repeat in March, June, and October of each year. If it appears washed out, add an additional fertilization in August. (See detailed fertilization instructions in "Easy Gardens for Florida"*, Chapter 11.)

Trimming: Cut back hard in mid-summer. Prune lightly any time of year. Plant becomes leggy without occasional hard pruning.

* My current book, "Easy Gardens for South Florida", will be expanded to include the entire state in 2004.

Botanical Name: *Acalypha wilkensiana 'Ceylon'*

Common Name: **Fire Dragon Copperleaf**

CHARACTERISTICS

PLANT TYPE: Shrub

AVERAGE SIZE: Easy to maintain at sizes between 4 feet tall by 4 feet wide and 6 feet tall by 5 feet wide. This plant spreads out more than most people realize when they first see the small, new plants. Be sure to give it room to spread.

GROWTH RATE: Fast

LEAF: Copper-colored. About 2 inches long by 3/4 inch wide.

FLOWER: Insignificant

AVERAGE LIFE: Sometimes short-lived, in the 3 year range. Lives longer if well protected from the cold.

ORIGIN: Uncertain. Other *Acalyphas* originate in Malaysia or the Pacific area.

CAUTIONS: None known

SPACING: 3 to 4 feet on center.

Leaf resembles a Japanese Maple. Good specimen plant to highlight green tropicals. Very cold-sensitive.

The copper-colored Fire Dragon is the focal point of this tropical landscape. The Fire Dragon is between a Cardboard Palm to the left and a European Fan Palm to the right. Alexander Palms provide the height, and Juniper forms the front border.

General: The Fire Dragon is an interesting but short-lived accent for a tropical landscape. Its copper color stands out well against dark greens. People frequently plant it without understanding its comfortable size range, which is four to six feet. Be sure to give it enough space, and you will be very happy with this choice.

Season: No seasonal variation. Very cold-sensitive, so use in protected areas only.

To locate plants, go to www.easygardencolor.com

Companions: The Fire Dragon looks best when used as an accent among green tropicals. It adds both color and texture to the landscape. Large-leafed tropicals that contrast well include the Alocasia (Elephant Ear), Traveler's Palm and the White Bird of Paradise. Palms with dark green fronds that look good with the Fire Dragon include Dwarf Royals, Coconut Palms, Alexander Palms, Queen Palms, and Foxtails. Avoid palms that spread a lot, like Fishtail Palms, because they will constantly be running into the Fire Dragon, causing higher maintenance.

The Fire Dragon leaf resembles a Japanese Maple.

Planting: Plant any time of the year in native soil. Leave the root ball slightly out of the ground, about 1/4 inch. (See detailed planting instructions in "Easy Gardens for Florida"*, Chapter 11.)

Fertilizing: Immediately after planting, fertilize with a well-balanced, slow-release mix that includes minor elements. Repeat in March, June, and October of each year. If the summer is unusually hot and rainy, inspect the leaf color of the plant in August. (See detailed fertilization instructions in "Easy Gardens for Florida"*, Chapter 11.)

Trimming: The Fire Dragon will get leggy if not trimmed hard at least once or twice a year. It recovers fastest from a hard cut-back, if done in the summer. Grooming or light trimmings can be done at any time.

* My current book, "Easy Gardens for South Florida", will be expanded to include the entire state in 2004.

GROWING CONDITIONS

LIGHT: High. Colors fade substantially in shade.

WATER: Medium. Ideal watering is twice a week after the initial establishment period. Tolerates water up to 4 times per week. Requires more water when grown in containers. (For detailed information about watering, see Chapter 8 in "Easy Gardens for Florida"*.)

SOIL: Wide range, as long as it is well-drained.

SALT TOLERANCE: Medium

WIND TOLERANCE: Medium

ZONE: 10b to 11. Very cold sensitive. Whereas most of the shrubs in this book recover from temperatures in the high 30's, this one can die. Containers only in central or north Florida. Move it inside if a freeze threatens.

PEST PROBLEMS: None known

PROPAGATION: Seeds or cuttings.

Botanical Name: *Acalypha wilkensiana dwarf*

Common Name: **Mardi-Gras Copperleaf**

CHARACTERISTICS

PLANT TYPE: Shrub

AVERAGE SIZE: Easy to maintain at sizes between 3 feet tall by 2 feet wide and 5 feet tall by 4 feet wide.

GROWTH RATE: Medium

LEAF: Mixed shades of brown, green, and copper. Interesting ruffled appearance, with edges that look like rick-rack.

FLOWER: Insignificant

AVERAGE LIFE: Unknown. Has thrived through 3 years of trials with no signs of slowing down.

ORIGIN: Unknown

CAUTIONS: None known

SPACING: 2 to 3 feet on center.

A new plant that offers constant color and a short, maintainable height. Very cold-sensitive.

The Mardi Gras Copperleaf is much easier to maintain in the three to four foot range than the others in this family.

General: Many members of the Copperleaf family become long and leggy shrubs. Not so for the the Mardi Gras Copperleaf. It is a welcome addition to the south Florida landscape because of its ability to stay at a reasonably short stature. It is quite cold-sensitive, however, and not recommended in important areas (like next to your front door) if it may be exposed to temperatures in the mid-30's. It needs about two months to recover from the average January temperatures of zone 10A, and the Copperleaf is not recommended for zone 9. Copperleafs are common throughout the tropics and subtropics, thriving in forgotten spots that haven't seen much maintenance in years. It is ideal for the low maintenance, south Florida garden.

Season: No seasonal variation. Best used in summer gardens because of its cold sensitivity. When temperatures dip into the high 30's, the leaves burn. It recovers when the weather warms up, but this plant is not recommended in areas where it would be a key focal point in winter. The leaf burn from the cold can remain for 30 to 60 days before the plant really looks good again.

To locate plants, go to www.easygardencolor.com

Companions: The Mardi Gras Copperleaf looks best when used as an accent among green tropicals. It adds both color and texture to the landscape. Large-leafed tropicals that contrast well include the Alocasia (Elephant Ear), Traveler's Palm, and White Bird of Paradise. Palms with dark green fronds that look good with the Mardi Gras Copperleaf include Dwarf Royals, Coconut Palms, Alexander Palms, Queen Palms, and Foxtails. Gold Mound Duranta is an excellent border choice for this Copperleaf.

Mardi Gras Copperleaf and a great companion, Gold Mound Duranta

Planting: Plant any time of the year in native soil. Leave the root ball slightly out of the ground, about 1/4 inch. (See detailed planting instructions in "Easy Gardens for Florida"*, Chapter 11.)

Fertilizing: Immediately after planting, fertilize with a well-balanced, slow-release mix that includes minor elements. Repeat in March, June, and October of each year. (See detailed fertilization instructions in "Easy Gardens for Florida"*, Chapter 11.)

Trimming: This plant requires hand pruning and will not be an acceptable landscape plant without it, growing quite leggy. Cut back hard (to about 12 to 24 inches) at least twice a year during the spring or summer. It takes only a few weeks to recover from this cutback if done during the warm months. Light trimming or grooming can be done at any time of the year.

GROWING CONDITIONS

LIGHT: Full sun

WATER: Medium. Ideal watering is twice a week after the initial establishment period. Tolerates water up to 4 times per week. Requires more water when grown in containers. (For detailed information about watering, see Chapter 8 in "Easy Gardens for Florida"*.)

SOIL: Wide range, as long as it is well-drained.

SALT TOLERANCE: Medium

WIND TOLERANCE: Medium

ZONE: 10b to 11. Leaves burn when the temperatures dip into the high 30's but recovers quickly when warm weather returns. Containers only in central or north Florida. Move it inside if a freeze threatens. (See "Season" on opposite page.)

PEST PROBLEMS: None known

PROPAGATION: Cuttings

---

* My current book, "Easy Gardens for South Florida", will be expanded to include the entire state in 2004.

Botanical Name: *Alpinia purpurata*
Common Name: **Red or Pink Ginger**

CHARACTERISTICS

PLANT TYPE:
Herbaceous perennial

AVERAGE SIZE: Easy to maintain at sizes between 5 feet tall by 4 feet wide and 8 feet tall by 5 feet wide.

GROWTH RATE: Fast

LEAF: Medium green and glossy. About 12 inches long by 5 inches wide.

FLOWER: Spectacular bright red or pink.

AVERAGE LIFE: 5 to 10 years.

ORIGIN: Melanesia

CAUTIONS: None known

SPACING: 4 to 5 feet on center.

Alpinia purpurata 'Eileen McDonald' is the pink Ginger.

One of the most beautiful tropical flowers for summer and fall gardens. Normally dies to the ground in winter, even in south Florida.

Red Ginger in September

General: Gingers are one of our most beautiful summer flowers. However, many people are disappointed to find that the plant turns brown during many winters in most of south Florida (not recommended for central Florida). If the winter is unusually warm, it sometimes breezes through, blooming continuously in zone 10b or 11. But, in an average year, it dies back. From 1991 until 1994, we had a series of warm winters, and the Gingers looked good throughout. I felt confident enough to recommend a large planting of Red Gingers next to the entry of a house in Boca Raton. In January, 1995, they all died back, just as my client's winter house guests were arriving! So, be careful with Gingers! You will be happy with this plant if you plant it in a location that is not a winter focal point, and you understand that the whole plant should be cut back to the ground if it turns brown. Red and Pink Gingers produce fabulous cut flowers.

Season: Ginger plants live for many years. They bloom in summer and fall, dying back in winter during the average year.

To locate plants, go to www.easygardencolor.com

Companions: Use Red Ginger with bright colors that look great in summer shade. Some suggestions include Golden Shrimp Plants, Crotons, and Yellow Mussaendas. Pink Ginger looks good with paler colors, particularly the Tricolor Caricature Plant.

Red and Pink Ginger look good planted together in a summer garden.

Planting: Plant during spring or summer in native soil. Leave the root ball slightly out of the ground, about 1/4 inch. (See detailed planting instructions in "Easy Gardens for Florida"*, Chapter 11.)

Fertilizing: Immediately after planting, fertilize with a well-balanced, slow-release mix that includes minor elements. Repeat in March, June, and October of each year. If the summer is unusually hot and rainy, inspect the leaf color of the plant in August. If it appears washed out, add an additional fertilization at that time. (See detailed fertilization instructions in "Easy Gardens for Florida"*, Chapter 11.)

Trimming: If the plant dies back from cold, trim off all the brown stalks to the ground. This could mean trimming back the entire plant, depending on how much browning occurs from the cold. If the cold is severe, it may take several months before the new shoots sprout. During the rest of the year, groom the plant by trimming off the dead flower stalks. When a flower fades, its entire stalk dies back, sometimes quite slowly, leaf by leaf. It is a lot easier to trim off the entire stalk to the ground than to cut one leaf at a time.

✻ My current book, "Easy Gardens for South Florida", will be expanded to include the entire state in 2004.

GROWING CONDITIONS

LIGHT: Light to medium shade. Burns or yellows in too much sun.

WATER: Medium. Ideal watering is twice a week after the initial establishment period. Tolerates water up to 4 times per week. Requires more water when grown in containers. (For detailed information about watering, see Chapter 8 in "Easy Gardens for Florida"*.)

SOIL: Wide range, as long as it is well-drained.

SALT TOLERANCE: Low

WIND TOLERANCE: Low

ZONE: 10b to 11. Dies back in winter in most of these areas. Containers only in central or north Florida. Move it inside if a freeze threatens.

PEST PROBLEMS: Snails, mealybugs, aphids, scale.

PROPAGATION: Division. Sometimes plantlets appear on the flower tips. These will root.

Botanical Name: *Barleria micans*

Common Name: **Giant Shrimp**

CHARACTERISTICS

PLANT TYPE: Evergreen shrub

AVERAGE SIZE: Easy to maintain at sizes between 3 feet tall by 3 feet wide and 4 feet tall by 4 feet wide. Grows larger in warmer areas, like zones 10b or 11 as compared with zone 10a.

GROWTH RATE: Fast

LEAF: Bright green. About 6 inches long by 3 to 4 inches wide.

FLOWER: Lemon yellow single flowers about 1 inch by 1 inch. Clusters of these flowers appear on stalks.

AVERAGE LIFE: 5 to 10 years.

ORIGIN: Unknown

CAUTIONS: Sprouts from the base but not enough to be considered invasive.

SPACING: 3 to 4 feet on center.

A great winter bloomer for larger areas in sun or shade. Thrived in our south Florida trials. Untested further north.

Giant Shrimp in January in our south Florida trial garden

General: Giant Shrimp is a relatively unknown shrub that is an excellent addition to the south Florida landscape. It is not only larger but also a more seasonal bloomer than the more common Golden Shrimp. Its size is especially deceptive when the plant is young. The flowers appear when it is tiny, about six inches tall. The plants look like they remain small, and many people make the mistake of planting them as a small shrub or groundcover. Make no mistake, this is a wide plant, needing at least four feet to spread. Understand its size requirements and its seasonal bloom period and you will be quite happy with this plant.

Season: Giant Shrimp Plants last for many years. In south Florida, they bloom in winter and spring, generally in two bursts. The first blooms start in November, usually lasting until January. The plant then takes a rest for about a month and blooms again from about March through June. Giant Shrimps look good when they are not blooming but do require a big cutback in summer that leaves them small for a month or two.

To locate plants, go to www.easygardencolor.com

Companions: Use Giant Shrimp with other winter bloomers. It looks particularly good with pinks and purples. Brunfelsias and Dombeyas are great choices. Plant one *Dombeya 'Seminole'* in the center and a few Giant Shrimps and Brunfelsias on either side. This grouping stops traffic when they all bloom at the same time.

Giant Shrimp and some companions

Planting: Plant any time of the year in native soil. Leave the root ball slightly out of the ground, about 1/4 inch. (See detailed planting instructions in "Easy Gardens for Florida"*, Chapter 11.)

Fertilizing: Giant Shrimps are heavy feeders. Immediately after planting, fertilize with a well-balanced, slow-release mix that includes minor elements. Repeat in March, June, and October of each year. If the summer is unusually hot and rainy, inspect the leaf color of the plant in August. If it appears washed out, add an additional fertilization at that time. (See detailed fertilization instructions in "Easy Gardens for Florida"*, Chapter 11.)

Trimming: Removal of the spent flower stalks after the bloom bursts increases blooming. This chore does not take much time to do, only a few minutes per plant. The plant also needs one big cut-back in summer. The best time is July or August. Do not cut back hard from August until May, or you will lose the bloom bursts. Light grooming can be done any time of year.

* My current book, "Easy Gardens for South Florida", will be expanded to include the entire state in 2004.

GROWING CONDITIONS

LIGHT: Medium shade to full sun. Happier with some break from noon sun.

WATER: Medium. Ideal watering is twice a week after the initial establishment period. Tolerates water up to 4 times per week. Requires more water when grown in containers. (For detailed information about watering, see Chapter 8 in "Easy Gardens for Florida"*.)

SOIL: Wide range, as long as it is well-drained.

SALT TOLERANCE: Unknown

WIND TOLERANCE: Low

ZONE: 10a to 11. Some leaf browning when temperatures hit the mid to high 30's. Untested in zones 8 or 9.

PEST PROBLEMS: None known

PROPAGATION: Cuttings

Botanical Name: *Brunfelsia grandiflora*
Common Name: **Yesterday, Today, and Tomorrow**

CHARACTERISTICS

PLANT TYPE: Evergreen shrub.

AVERAGE SIZE: Easy to maintain at sizes between 4 feet tall by 3 feet wide and 6 feet tall by 5 feet wide.

GROWTH RATE: Medium

LEAF: Dark, glossy green and pointed. About 4 inches long by 2 inches wide.

FLOWER: Beautiful clusters of three colors, all different shades of purple. Each flower measures about 1 inch across. The flower starts out dark and gets lighter each day.

AVERAGE LIFE: 5 to 10 years.

ORIGIN: South America

CAUTIONS: Frequently goes through shock after planting, losing many leaves (See "Planting" on opposite page). Also, defoliates much more in windy locations than most plants. Use in a very calm location.

SPACING: 3 to 4 feet on center.

One of our most beautiful winter bloomers. A must for winter gardens in south Florida.

Brunfelsia in full bloom

General: Brunfelsia is an excellent shrub for color in winter, one of the best. It is beautiful and quite a conversation piece, with its three colors of flowers. But it has quirks. It goes through shock frequently after planting, which is lessened by a lot of water. Soaker hoses are ideal. The second year in the ground, it is much more comfortable and less thirsty. And, it will not bloom if trimmed at the wrong time of year (see "Trimming", opposite). It needs a calm spot, defoliating quickly in too much wind. So, plant it in a sheltered location at the beginning of the rainy season, and trim in summer. You will be very happy with this plant under those conditions.

Season: Brunfelsias flower in winter, quite dependably from late November until spring. The plant lasts for many years, looking good while not blooming.

To locate plants, go to www.easygardencolor.com

Companions: Plant Brunfelsia with other plants that bloom in winter. It looks good with pinks and yellows. A great combination for shade includes Pink Angelwing Begonias for the tallest layer, Brunfelsias in the middle, and a border of Golden Shrimp Plants. See Chapter 10, "Cool-Season Color", for more ideas with Brunfelsia.

Brunfelsia flowers are three colors. The first day the flower is purple. The next day, it lightens to lilac. The third day, it is almost white. These three colors on subsequent days have led to the common name, "Yesterday, Today, and Tomorrow".

Planting: Brunfelsias can be planted at any time. Since they need a lot of water after planting, it is easier to get them established in summer, when we have a lot of rain. If planted in fall, soaker hoses are ideal to avoid transplant shock. Brunfelsias frequently lose their bottom leaves after planting, but this occurs much less with a lot of water. Be sure to leave the root ball slightly out of the ground, about 1/4 inch. (See detailed planting instructions in "Easy Gardens for Florida"*, Chapter 11.)

Fertilizing: Brunfelsias are heavy feeders. Immediately after planting, fertilize with a well-balanced, slow-release mix that includes minor elements. Repeat in March, June, and October of each year. If the summer is unusually hot and rainy, inspect the leaf color of the plant in August. If it appears washed out, add an additional fertilization at that time. (See detailed fertilization instructions in "Easy Gardens for Florida"*, Chapter 11.)

Trimming: Trim hard by hand once or twice a year during the summer months when it is not blooming. If trimmed after August, this plant will not bloom the following winter.

* My current book, "Easy Gardens for South Florida", will be expanded to include the entire state in 2004.

LIGHT: Medium shade to full sun. Ideal light is light shade.

WATER: Very high water during the establishment period. Soaker hoses for a few hours a day are ideal for the first month or two. Medium water after plant is well-rooted in the ground. Ideal watering is twice a week after the initial establishment period. Tolerates water up to 4 times per week. Requires more water when grown in containers. (For detailed information about watering, see Chapter 8 in "Easy Gardens for Florida"*.)

SOIL: Wide range, as long as it is well-drained.

SALT TOLERANCE: Low

WIND TOLERANCE: Low. Defoliates in wind.

ZONE: 10a to 11. Other cold-tolerant Brunfelsias grow in zone 9.

PEST PROBLEMS: Snails and scale

PROPAGATION: Seeds or cuttings.

Botanical Name: *Buddleia davidii*

Common Name: **Butterfly Bush**

CHARACTERISTICS

PLANT TYPE: Shrub

AVERAGE SIZE: In north Florida, shrubs that are trimmed in February will be about 6 feet tall the next fall. Untrimmed shrubs reach 13 feet tall by 10 feet wide. In south Florida, the shrubs are so short-lived that they don't get more than a few feet tall. Butterfly Bushes in central Florida are somewhere in the middle.

GROWTH RATE: Fast

LEAF: Green on top and silvery underneath. Pointed.

FLOWER: White, pink, blue, burgundy, or purple. Tiny, fragrant flowers make up spikes about 4 to 8 inches long in south Florida, increasing to 6 to 18 inches long in north Florida. Butterflies like the blues and purples best.

AVERAGE LIFE: In our Mississippi trial gardens, Butterfly Bushes have lived for 10 years. Lifespan shortens as you go further south. Expect a few years in central Florida and a few months at best in the southern part of the state.

ORIGIN: China

CAUTIONS: None known

Easy shrub with a long bloom period. Best in north Florida. One of the favorite foods of butterflies and hummingbirds.

Butterfly Bush in full bloom

General: The aptly-named Butterfly Bush is one of the butterflies' favorite foods. It does better the further north you go in Florida. While lasting for many years in Tallahassee, it only lasts a few months in my trial gardens in the southern end of the state. But, I buy one from time to time as a special treat for my butterflies. Central Florida gardeners may get a few years out of it. In north Florida, the plants die back with the first frost and reappear in spring. The flowers are fragrant, especially at night.

Season: Butterfly Bush is a summer bloomer, starting about May and lasting until the first frost in north Florida. In the southern end of the state, expect just a few months of life from this beautiful plant. Its performance in central Florida is somewhere in the middle. Its low cost should be some consolation.

Companions: Use the Butterfly Bush as the tallest layer of a butterfly garden. Firebush, Pentas, and Lantana are good, smaller companions that also attract butterflies.

The flowers reach up to 18 inches long in north Florida.

Planting: Plant anytime of the year in south or central Florida. Plant in spring in north Florida. The plant adapts well to our native soils provided they drain well. Leave the root ball slightly out of the ground, about 1/4 inch. (See detailed planting instructions in "Easy Gardens for Florida"*, Chapter 11.)

Fertilizing: Immediately after planting, fertilize with a well-balanced, slow-release mix that includes minor elements. Repeat in March, June, and October of each year. (See detailed fertilization instructions in "Easy Gardens for Florida"*, Chapter 11.)

Trimming: Unpruned shrubs bloom earlier but tend to grow lanky the next summer. To encourage fullness and more blooms, trim back to one foot tall in February. If the plant grows so much that it really looks leggy in mid-summer, cut it back by as much as one-third again. Deadheading (removing of spent blossoms) encourages more blooms, but most people just don't have time to do it.

*My current book, "Easy Gardens for South Florida", will be expanded to include the entire state in 2004.

GROWING CONDITIONS

LIGHT: Full sun

WATER: Medium. Ideal watering is twice a week after the initial establishment period. Tolerates water up to 4 times per week. Requires more water in containers. (For detailed information, see Chapter 8 in "Easy Gardens for Florida"*.)

SOIL: Wide range, as long as it is well-drained.

SALT TOLERANCE: Medium.

WIND TOLERANCE: Medium

ZONE: 10a to 11

PEST PROBLEMS: Caterpillars, spider mites

PROPAGATION: Seeds or cuttings.

Botanical Name: *Camellia spp.*

Common Name: **Camellia**

CHARACTERISTICS

PLANT TYPE: Evergreen shrub that eventually reaches the size of a small tree.

AVERAGE SIZE: Easy to maintain at sizes between 6 feet tall and 6 feet wide and 20 feet tall by 10 feet wide. Size varies by type.

GROWTH RATE: Slow

LEAF: Dark green and glossy. Size varies by type. Leaves on the *sasanqua* Camellias are smaller than the leaves on the *japonicas*.

FLOWER: From 2 to 6 inches wide. Blooms on *sasanqua* Camellias are smaller than the *japonicas*. Single or double. Red, pink, and white are the most common colors. The rare *Camellia nitidsimina* has a yellow bloom that looks like a Magnolia.

AVERAGE LIFE: Very long lifespan, with some living hundreds of years.

ORIGIN: The Orient

CAUTIONS: None known

SPACING: At least 6 feet on center. Further apart for larger plants.

Beautiful flowering shrub for central and north Florida. One of the best for winter blooms.

Camellia japonica 'Anita'

General: Camellias are wonderful plants for central and north Florida, offering a vast array of lovely blooms in winter, when most other plants are not blooming. The shrubs are evergreen and very attractive, even when not in flower. Maclay Gardens in Tallahassee and Leu Botanical Gardens in Orlando offer beautiful displays of Camellias. The Leu Camellia Collection (where these photos were taken) is one of the largest outdoor collections of its kind in the United States. Two species are commonly grown in Florida, *japonicas* and *sasanquas*. Neither type has done well in my south Florida garden, which is just a bit south of their range.

Season: Camellias bloom in winter, starting about November and ending around March. They peak in January. Each type blooms for about a month. For a succession of blooms, collect an assortment of early and late bloomers. The *sasanqua* Camellias start blooming first and generally stop when the *japonica* Camellias are ready to begin flowering. A slight freeze damages the blooms but not the buds. A severe freeze (under 25 degrees) can damage the buds to the point where the plant stops blooming that year.

To locate plants, go to www.easygardencolor.com

Companions: With hundreds of different shapes, colors, and sizes of Camellias available, they are ideal for home collections. Buy them from a Florida nursery so that you can be assured that they do well here. Choose your favorites, and plant each shrub with enough space to stand alone and appear distinctive.

Camellia japonica 'Lallarock'

Camellia japonica 'Kick Off' with ladybug

Camellia japonica 'Mary Jane Leu' with bee

Planting: Plant any time of the year in soil with a ph of 6 to 6.5. (If you don't know the ph, get the soil tested at a soil test lab, which you can find in the yellow pages. Or, call your county extension for instructions on how to test your soil and adjust it for Camellias.) Leave the root ball slightly out of the ground, about 1/4 inch. Planting Camellias too deep is the number one cause of death for this plant. (See detailed planting instructions in "Easy Gardens for Florida"*, Chapter 11.)

Fertilizing: Immediately after planting, fertilize with a well-balanced, slow-release mix that includes minor elements. Repeat in March, June, and August of each year. (See detailed fertilization instructions in "Easy Gardens for Florida"*, Chapter 11.)

Trimming: Prune lightly anytime. February or March is ideal for heavy pruning because the plant has spring, summer, and fall to set buds for the following winter.

---

* My current book, "Easy Gardens for South Florida", will be expanded to include the entire state in 2004.

GROWING CONDITIONS

LIGHT: Filtered sun. Under Pines is ideal. Can take some direct sun for a short period. The *sasanqua* Camellias take more sun than *japonicas*. Camellias will not bloom in too much shade.

WATER: Medium. Ideal watering is twice a week after the initial establishment period. Requires more water in containers. (For detailed information, see Chapter 8 in "Easy Gardens for Florida"*.)

SOIL: Prefers a ph of 6 to 6.5. Be sure soil is well-drained. Pine straw mulch helps keep the ph down.

SALT TOLERANCE: Low

WIND TOLERANCE: Low

ZONE: 7 to 9

PEST PROBLEMS: If you see holes in the new growth in spring, it is probably beetles. Ask your garden center for the least toxic spray. Camellias also occasionally get fungus and tea scale.

PROPAGATION: Cuttings

Botanical Name: *Codiaeum variegatum 'Mrs. Icetone'*

Common Name: **Icetone Croton, Apple Blossom Croton**

CHARACTERISTICS

PLANT TYPE: Evergreen shrub.

AVERAGE SIZE: Easy to maintain at sizes between 3 feet tall by 2 feet wide and 6 feet tall by 5 feet wide.

GROWTH RATE: Medium

LEAF: About 4 to 6 inches long by 1 to 2 inches wide. In spring and summer, the colors are pink, peach, green, and yellow. In winter, the plant becomes darker, predominantly grey and dark pink.

FLOWER: Insignificant

AVERAGE LIFE: 15 to 20 years.

ORIGIN: Crotons originated in Malaysia. This one is a hybrid.

CAUTIONS: Milky sap irritates skin and stains clothes. (I have had no problems, but caution is wise.)

SPACING: 2 to 3 feet on center.

Unusual pink and yellow colorations on Crotons that are normally more orange.

Leaves of the Icetone Croton change colors based on time of year and light conditions. The older growth of this plant shows the darker colors of winter. The new growth at the tips shows the lighter growth of warmer temperatures and a lot of light.

General: Icetone Crotons are beautiful and unique plants. While most Crotons are predominately orange, these boast mainly the pink shades of apple blossoms. They blend beautifully with pink and yellow flowers. And, the colors change throughout the year, giving seasonal interest to the garden. This Croton is very easy to grow, requiring little water, fertilization, or trimming. Icetone Crotons will give your garden years of color for very little care.

Season: Crotons last for at least fifteen years. The plants look good all year. The colors change from dark pink and grey in winter to light pink, light green, and yellow in the heat of summer.

To locate plants, go to www.easygardencolor.com

Companions: Use Icetone Crotons with plants that have yellow or pink flowers. In a light-shade situation, plant them in front of Angelwing Begonias and border with Golden Shrimp Plants. The Shrimp Plants may outgrow the Icetones at first, so keep them trimmed lower until the Icetones catch up. These Crotons look better with a border planted in front of them because they have a tendency towards legginess. In sun, the Gold Mound Duranta makes a great border. Salmon Mussaenda is also a good companion for a summer garden.

Icetone Crotons and some companions. In south Florida, plant them in your garden. In central and north Florida, all three work well in containers.

Planting: Plant any time of the year in native soil. Leave the root ball slightly out of the ground, about 1/4 inch. (See detailed planting instructions in "Easy Gardens for Florida"*, Chapter 11.)

Fertilizing: Immediately after planting, fertilize with a well-balanced, slow-release mix that includes minor elements. Repeat in March, June, and October of each year. Croton's nutritional needs are low, but they do benefit and grow faster with these fertilizations.

Trimming: Trim as needed to maintain desired size. Crotons of the same type planted in a mass grow at different rates. Keep them trimmed to the same height. If the plants look leggy, trim some of the leggy branches to the ground. If you do this in June or July, as many as three branches will sprout from each cut, filling in the bare base.

* My current book, "Easy Gardens for South Florida", will be expanded to include the entire state in 2004.

GROWING CONDITIONS

LIGHT: Full sun to light shade. Color fades in too much shade.

WATER: Low. Ideal watering is once or twice a week after the initial establishment period. Tolerates water up to 4 times per week. Survives without irrigation in average environmental conditions. Requires more water when grown in containers.

SOIL: Wide range, as long as it is well-drained.

SALT TOLERANCE: Medium-high

WIND TOLERANCE: Medium-high

ZONE: 10a to 11 in the ground. Excellent container plant anywhere in Florida. Bring it inside when a freeze threatens.

PEST PROBLEMS: Generally pest-free in the landscape. Scale, mealybugs, and spider mites are problems occasionally. If leaf drop occurs, it is probably spider mites. Wash them off with mild soap and water.

PROPAGATION: Cuttings, which root faster from May to August.

Botanical Name: *Codiaeum variegatum 'Piecrust'*

Common Name: **Piecrust Croton**

CHARACTERISTICS

PLANT TYPE: Evergreen shrub.

AVERAGE SIZE: Easy to maintain at sizes between 3 feet tall by 2 feet wide and 6 feet tall by 5 feet wide. (I have not tried maintaining this Croton under 3 feet.)

GROWTH RATE: Medium

LEAF: Long and thin, with edges shaped like piecrust. About 4 to 6 inches long by 3/4 inch wide. In spring and summer, the colors are green, yellow, dark grey, and red. In winter, the plant is darker.

FLOWER: Insignificant

AVERAGE LIFE: 15 to 20 years.

ORIGIN: Crotons originated in Malaysia. This one is a hybrid.

CAUTIONS: Milky sap irritates skin and stains clothes. (I have had no problems, but caution is wise.)

SPACING: 2 to 3 feet on center.

Use the Piecrust Croton for its unusual leaf shape. The edges resemble piecrust.

Piecrust Croton in its dark stage. The Dracaena reflexa 'Song of India' surrounding the Croton contrasts with the dark leaves. Crotons are good choices for pool edges because they hold their leaves well.

General: Piecrust Crotons offer unique color and texture. They are unusual in today's market and worth the purchase, if you come across one. They offer color with little water, fertilizer, or trimming and are quite happy in sun or light shade.

Season: Crotons last for at least fifteen years. The plants look good all year. The colors change from lighter in summer to darker in winter.

To locate plants, go to www.easygardencolor.com

Companions: The Piecrust Croton is very versatile. It looks great with variegated plants, as shown opposite. It also works well with plants featuring red, pink, purple, or yellow flowers. A beautiful grouping for a summer garden features Red Ginger as a tall specimen, Piecrust as the middle layer, and a border of Torenia. For winter, try Pink Firespike as the tall layer, Piecrust in the middle, and border it with 'Fruit Cocktail' Shrimps.

Piecrust and some companions. In south Florida, plant them in your garden. In central and north Florida, all three work well in containers.

Planting: Plant any time of the year in native soil. Leave the root ball slightly out of the ground, about 1/4 inch. (See detailed planting instructions in "Easy Gardens for Florida"*, Chapter 11.)

Fertilizing: Immediately after planting, fertilize with a well-balanced, slow-release mix that includes minor elements. Repeat in March, June, and October of each year. Croton's nutritional needs are low, but they do benefit and grow faster with these fertilizations.

Trimming: Trim as needed to maintain desired size. Crotons of the same type planted in a mass grow at different rates. Keep them trimmed to the same height. If the plants look leggy, trim some of the leggy branches to the ground. If you do this in June or July, as many as three branches will sprout from each cut, filling in the bare base.

* My current book, "Easy Gardens for South Florida", will be expanded to include the entire state in 2004.

GROWING CONDITIONS

LIGHT: Full sun to light shade. Most color in full sun. This Croton does not do well in too much shade.

WATER: Low. Ideal watering is once or twice a week after the initial establishment period. Tolerates water up to 4 times per week. Survives without irrigation in average environmental conditions. Requires more water when grown in containers.

SOIL: Wide range, as long as it is well-drained.

SALT TOLERANCE: Medium-high

WIND TOLERANCE: Medium-high

ZONE: 10a to 11 in the ground. Excellent container plant anywhere in Florida. Bring it inside when a freeze threatens.

PEST PROBLEMS: Generally, pest-free in the landscape. Scale, mealybugs, and spider mites are problems occasionally. If leaf drop occurs, it is probably spider mites. Wash them off with mild soap and water.

PROPAGATION: Cuttings, which root faster from May to August.

Botanical Name: *Codiaeum variegatum 'Stoplight'*

Common Name: **Stoplight Croton**

CHARACTERISTICS

PLANT TYPE: Evergreen shrub.

AVERAGE SIZE: Easy to maintain at sizes between 3 feet tall by 3 feet wide and 6 feet tall by 5 feet wide. This is a wide-growing Croton.

GROWTH RATE: Slow

LEAF: About 8 inches long by 2 to 3 inches wide. Leaves get larger as plant grows. Colors change with the seasons. Bright yellow, green, and red in summer, like a stoplight. Black and dark red in winter.

FLOWER: Insignificant

AVERAGE LIFE: 15 to 20 years.

ORIGIN: Crotons originated in Malaysia. This one is a hybrid.

CAUTIONS: Milky sap irritates skin and stains clothes. (I have had no problems, but caution is wise.)

SPACING: 2 to 3 feet on center.

According to Dr. Frank Brown, author of "Crotons of the World", Stoplight is the most colorful Croton in existence.

Stoplight Croton in summer. The colorations of the plant above are different from the plant on the opposite page. This Croton changes colors throughout the year.

General: Stoplight Crotons got their name from the bright red, yellow, and green colors of their leaves. They are as bright as stoplights. In winter, some of the leaves darken to almost black. In summer, the growth is lighter and brighter.

Season: Crotons last for at least fifteen years. The plants look good all year. The colors change from lighter in summer to darker in winter.

To locate plants, go to www.easygardencolor.com

Companions: Use Stoplights with plants that have bright red or yellow flowers. The most dramatic companion is the *Costus barbatus*, which has both colors. Red Ginger is another winner for a summer garden. Scarlet Red Cloak is a great winter companion, and the Golden Shrimps are a natural for any season.

Costus barbatus

Golden Shrimp Plant

Stoplight Croton

Stoplight Croton and some companions

Planting: Plant any time of the year in native soil. Leave the root ball slightly out of the ground, about 1/4 inch. (See detailed planting instructions in "Easy Gardens for Florida"*, Chapter 11.)

Fertilizing: Immediately after planting, fertilize with a well-balanced, slow-release mix that includes minor elements. Repeat in March, June, and October of each year. Croton's nutritional needs are low, but they do benefit and grow faster with these fertilizations. (See instructions in "Easy Gardens for Florida"*, Chapter 11.)

Trimming: Trim as needed to maintain desired size. Crotons of the same type planted in a mass grow at different rates. Keep them trimmed to the same height. If the plants look leggy, trim some of the leggy branches to the ground. If you do this in June or July, as many as three branches will sprout from each cut, filling in the bare base.

* My current book, "Easy Gardens for South Florida", will be expanded to include the entire state in 2004.

GROWING CONDITIONS

LIGHT: Full sun to medium shade. Most color in full sun.

WATER: Low. Ideal watering is once or twice a week after the initial establishment period. Tolerates water up to 4 times per week. Survives without irrigation in average environmental conditions. Requires more water when grown in containers.

SOIL: Wide range, as long as it is well-drained.

SALT TOLERANCE: Medium-high

WIND TOLERANCE: Medium-high

ZONE: 10a to 11 in the ground. Excellent container plant anywhere in Florida. Bring it inside when a freeze threatens.

PEST PROBLEMS: Generally, pest-free in the landscape. Scale, mealybugs, and spider mites are problems occasionally. If leaf drop occurs, it is probably spider mites. Wash them off with mild soap and water.

PROPAGATION: Cuttings, which root faster from May to August.

Botanical Name: *Cordyline fructicosa 'Black Magic'*

Common Name: **Black Magic Ti**

CHARACTERISTICS

PLANT TYPE: Evergreen shrub.

AVERAGE SIZE: Easy to maintain at sizes between 4 feet tall by 2 feet wide and 6 feet tall by 3 feet wide.

GROWTH RATE: Medium

LEAF: Very dark burgundy. About 3 feet long by 6 inches wide.

FLOWER: Insignificant

AVERAGE LIFE: 5 to 10 years.

ORIGIN: According to Dr. Brown in his book, "The Cordyline": "Native range of Cordylines is unknown but most likely they are indigenous to the Himalayas, Southeastern Asia, Malaysia, and Northern Australia."

CAUTIONS: None known

SPACING: 2 feet on center. The Black Magic is larger than the better-known Red Sister and covers more ground.

The easiest and strongest Ti we know. Dark, dramatic color and large scale. An ideal landscape or container plant.

Black Magic Tis planted with Crotons and Variegated Arboricolas. The dark color stands out well against the white wall.

General: The Black Magic is larger and chunkier than most other Ti Plants. It also is easier to grow, not getting the brown and white leaf patches that are so common on most Tis in winter. This tough Ti is one of the few that stands up well to tough environments, like full sun and wind. Like all Tis, it is an excellent choice for containers, particularly when it is surrounded with lower, cascading plants. Its color, although darker than the more common 'Red Sister' Ti, shows up very well against light-colored walls. All in all, the Black Magic is an excellent landscape plant, giving years of color for very little care.

Season: Unlike most Tis, the Black Magic has no seasonal variation. It looks equally as good in February as in August. However, the color is darker in shade and lighter and brighter in sun.

To locate plants, go to www.easygardencolor.com

Companions: Light-colored plants, like *Dracaena reflexa 'Song of India'* or Variegated Arboricola, contrast well with the Black Magic Ti. This Ti also works well with tropical-looking plants, like Palms, Alocasias (Elephant Ears), and Bromeliads. And many of the bright-colored Crotons make great companions.

Ti Plants are good choices for color in pool areas because they do not drop flowers. Small Black Magic Ti shown with Mammey Crotons.

Planting: Plant any time of the year in native soil. Leave the root ball slightly out of the ground, about 1/4 inch. (See detailed planting instructions in "Easy Gardens for Florida"*, Chapter 11.)

Fertilizing: Immediately after planting, fertilize with a well-balanced, slow-release mix that includes minor elements. Repeat in March, June, and October of each year. (See detailed fertilization instructions in "Easy Gardens for Florida"*, Chapter 11.)

Trimming: Trim once every year or two in April. Stagger the cuts on the different stalks for a layered effect, or trim the tallest one-third of the stalks to the ground. Stick the cuttings in soil nearby, and about half of them should root (See "PROPAGATION", right). Some grooming (removing of damaged leaves) may be needed intermittently throughout the year.

* My current book, "Easy Gardens for South Florida", will be expanded to include the entire state in 2004.

GROWING CONDITIONS

LIGHT: Medium shade to full sun.

WATER: Medium. Ideal watering is twice a week after the initial establishment period. Tolerates water up to 4 times per week. Requires more water when grown in containers.

SOIL: Wide range, as long as it is well-drained.

SALT TOLERANCE: Medium

WIND TOLERANCE: Medium

ZONE: 10a to 11 in the ground. Excellent container plant anywhere in Florida. Bring it inside when a freeze threatens.

PEST PROBLEMS: If holes appear in the leaves, it is probably snails. Few pests occur in the landscape.

PROPAGATION: Cuttings. Much easier to root in summer. Tip cuttings (the whole top part of the plant, including the leaves) root easier than stem cuttings (the woody part of the stem). Tis root with as little as one, 4-inch piece of stem. Put 2 inches in the soil and leave 2 inches out of the soil.

Botanical Name: *Cordyline fructicosa 'Purple Prince'*

Common Name: **Purple Prince Ti**

CHARACTERISTICS

PLANT TYPE: Evergreen shrub.

AVERAGE SIZE: Easy to maintain at sizes between 3 feet tall by 1 foot wide and 4 feet tall by 2 feet wide.

GROWTH RATE: Slow

LEAF: Dark purple with green accents. About 18 inches long by 2 inches wide at maturity.

FLOWER: Insignificant

AVERAGE LIFE: 5 to 10 years.

ORIGIN: According to Dr. Brown's book, "The Cordyline": "Native range of Cordylines is unknown but most likely they are indigenous to the Himalayas, Southeastern Asia, Malaysia, and Northern Australia."

CAUTIONS: None known

SPACING: 18 to 24 inches on center.

A great plant for a winter garden or your personal botanical collection because of its unique color. Not well-suited as a general landscape plant because of a long recovery period after its annual pruning.

Group of Purple Prince Tis in January. This shade of dark purple is difficult to find in the plant kingdom. It adds a unique touch to a winter garden.

General: This is a great plant for collectors. It is smaller than the better-known Ti Red Sister and larger than the Tricolor Ti described on the pages 138 and 139. The purple color is quite striking and draws a lot of attention in our winter garden. It contrasts well with plants with lighter flowers and leaves. But, it suffers from leaf damage every year and needs severe cutbacks to look good the following winter season. Because of its slow growth, it goes for at least six months in a very small state. So, use a few in your winter garden in a location where it will not be sorely missed for the months when it is out of action. This is not a plant to use a lot of in a key summer location.

Season: The Purple Prince Ti peaks in winter. Because of its slow recovery from its annual spring pruning, do not count on it for much summer impact. It grows slower than either the Red Sister or the Black Magic Tis.

To locate plants, go to www.easygardencolor.com

Companions: Use the Purple Prince with other colorful plants that look good in winter. For a great pink and purple combination, plant Pink Angelwing Begonias as a background for clusters of Purple Prince Tis and Tricolor Tis. Yellows and reds, like red Dragonwing Begonias and Golden Shrimp Plants, also show well with the purple leaves.

Purple Prince Tis and some companions. Plant this grouping in your garden in south Florida or in containers in central and north Florida. All three of these plants do quite well in containers.

Planting: Plant any time of the year in native soil. Leave the root ball slightly out of the ground, about 1/4 inch.

Fertilizing: Immediately after planting, fertilize with a well-balanced, slow-release mix that includes minor elements. Repeat in March, June, and October of each year.

Trimming: The Purple Prince Ti suffers from leaf damage every winter. Parts of the leaves develop brown or white tips or splotches. Trim it every April. Remove the damaged leaves, either just a leaf or the entire head. When removing the heads, stagger the cuts on the different stalks for a layered effect, or trim the tallest one-third of the stalks to the ground. Stick the cuttings in soil nearby and about half of them should root (See "PROPAGATION", right). Some grooming (removing of damaged leaves) may be needed intermittently throughout the year.

* My current book, "Easy Gardens for South Florida", will be expanded to include the entire state in 2004.

GROWING CONDITIONS

LIGHT: Light to medium shade.

WATER: Medium. Ideal watering is twice a week after the initial establishment period. Tolerates water up to 4 times per week. Requires more water when grown in containers.

SOIL: Wide range, as long as it is well-drained.

SALT TOLERANCE: Unknown

WIND TOLERANCE: Low

ZONE: 10a to 11 in the ground. Excellent container plant anywhere in Florida. Bring it inside when a freeze threatens.

PEST PROBLEMS: Occasional leafspot, scale, or mealybugs. If holes appear in the leaves, it is probably snails. Few pests occur in the landscape.

PROPAGATION: Cuttings. Much easier to root in summer. Tip cuttings (the whole top part of the plant, including the leaves) root easier than stem cuttings (the woody part of the stem). Tis root with as little as one, 4-inch piece of stem. Put 2 inches in the soil and leave 2 inches out of the soil.

Botanical Name: *Cordyline fructicosa 'Sherbert'*

Common Name: **Sherbert Ti**

CHARACTERISTICS

PLANT TYPE: Evergreen shrub.

AVERAGE SIZE: Easy to maintain at sizes between 3 feet tall by 1 foot wide and 4 feet tall by 2 feet wide.

GROWTH RATE: Medium

LEAF: In winter, looks like a mix between raspberry and lime sherbert. In summer, appears more green.

FLOWER: Insignificant

AVERAGE LIFE: 5 years

ORIGIN: According to Dr. Brown's book, "The Cordyline": "Native range of Cordylines is unknown but most likely they are indigenous to the Himalayas, Southeastern Asia, Malaysia, and Northern Australia."

CAUTIONS: None known

SPACING: 2 feet on center.

An easy Ti with leaves sporting the colors of raspberry and lime sherbert.

Sherbert Ti in winter. I climbed on a wall to take this picture from above. It is the most spectacular Sherbert Ti I have ever seen and not typical of all of them. The one shown to the left is more typical of Sherberts in a home garden.

General: Sherbert Tis are great choices for a winter garden because of their unique and beautiful leaf colors. They are about the same size as the more common Red Sister but do not share the same severe leaf-spot problems.

Season: Sherbert Tis last for many years, but their colors change dramatically with the seasons. In summer, they are mainly green, with a hint of red. In winter, they are in their glory, with very bright-colored leaves, like sherbert.

To locate plants, go to www.easygardencolor.com

Companions: Crotons, particularly Icetones or Petras, are great companions for the Sherbert Tis. Sherberts also look good planted in clumps with other dark Tis, like Red Sisters or Black Magics. Like most Tis, the Sherbert looks best with a groundcover under it, hiding the woody stem. Justicia 'Fruit Cocktails' are excellent for this use.

Sherbert Ti with some companions. Plant this grouping in the ground in south Florida or in containers in central and north Florida.

Planting: Plant any time of the year in native soil. Leave the root ball slightly out of the ground, about 1/4 inch. (See detailed planting instructions in "Easy Gardens for Florida"*, Chapter 11.)

Fertilizing: Immediately after planting, fertilize with a well-balanced, slow-release mix that includes minor elements. Repeat in March, June, and October of each year.

Trimming: Trim once every year or two in April. Stagger the cuts on the different stalks for a layered effect, or trim the tallest one-third of the stalks to the ground. Stick the cuttings in soil nearby, and about half of them should root (see "PROPAGATION", right). Some grooming (removing of damaged leaves) may be needed intermittently throughout the year.

My current book, "Easy Gardens for South Florida", will be expanded to include the entire state in 2004.

* My current book, "Easy Gardens for South Florida",
will be expanded to include the entire state in 2004.

GROWING CONDITIONS

LIGHT: Light to medium shade.

WATER: Medium. Ideal watering is twice a week after the initial establishment period. Tolerates water up to 4 times per week. Requires more water when grown in containers.

SOIL: Wide range, as long as it is well-drained.

SALT TOLERANCE: Medium

WIND TOLERANCE: Medium

ZONE: 10a to 11 in the ground. Excellent container plant anywhere in Florida. Bring it inside when a freeze threatens.

PEST PROBLEMS: Occasional leafspot, scale, or mealybugs. If holes appear in the leaves, it is probably snails. Few pests occur in the landscape.

PROPAGATION: Cuttings. Much easier to root in summer. Tip cuttings (the whole top part of the plant, including the leaves) root easier than stem cuttings (the woody part of the stem). Tis root with as little as one, 4-inch piece of stem. Put 2 inches in the soil and leave 2 inches out of the soil.

Botanical Name: *Cordyline fructicosa 'Tricolor'*

Common Name: **Tricolor Ti**

CHARACTERISTICS

PLANT TYPE: Evergreen shrub.

AVERAGE SIZE: Easy to maintain at sizes between 2 feet tall by 2 feet wide and 3 feet tall by 2 feet wide.

GROWTH RATE: Slow

LEAF: Pink, white, and green. About 12 inches long by 6 inches wide.

FLOWER: Insignificant

AVERAGE LIFE: 5 to 10 years.

ORIGIN: According to Dr. Brown's book, "The Cordyline": "Native range of Cordylines is unknown but most likely they are indigenous to the Himalayas, Southeastern Asia, Malaysia, and Northern Australia."

CAUTIONS: None known

SPACING: 2 feet on center

Tricolor Ti in summer

A low-growing Ti that is excellent for the winter garden.

Tricolor Tis in January planted in front of Pink Angelwing Begonias. The white and pink leaf colors peak in winter. In the summer, the plant is plainer, as shown to the left.

General: The Tricolor Ti offers the advantages of low stature and great winter color. This Ti stays lower than any other I tested and is one of the best for winter color. However, it is susceptible to a leaf fungus that sometimes spots the leaves, especially in winter. After years of working with this plant, I simply cut back the discolored areas in April and enjoy the plant for the rest of the year, especially in winter. But it is important to understand that the plant does not look as colorful in the summer and will not look good the next winter unless it is hand-pruned in the spring.

Season: Tricolor Tis last for many years. However, the color is much more intense in winter.

To locate plants, go to www.easygardencolor.com

Companions: Tricolor Tis look particularly good with pink, blue, or purple. Choose plants that also peak in winter. Some good choices include Pink Angelwing Begonias, Purple Prince Tis, Icetone Crotons, Blue Moon Bromeliads, and Brunfelsias.

Tricolor Tis with some companions

Planting: Plant any time of the year in native soil. Leave the root ball slightly out of the ground, about 1/4 inch.

Fertilizing: Immediately after planting, fertilize with a well-balanced, slow-release mix that includes minor elements. Repeat in March, June, and October of each year. (See detailed fertilization instructions in "Easy Gardens for Florida"*, Chapter 11.)

Trimming: Trim once every year or two in April. Trim off any damaged leaves. If a stalk looks like most of it is damaged, cut the entire stalk to within two or three inches of the ground. Stick the cuttings in soil nearby, and about half of them should root (see "PROPAGATION", right). Some grooming (removing of damaged leaves) may be needed intermittently throughout the year.

* My current book, "Easy Gardens for South Florida", will be expanded to include the entire state in 2004.

GROWING CONDITIONS

LIGHT: Medium to light shade. Bleach out in full sun.

WATER: Medium. Ideal watering is twice a week after the initial establishment period. Tolerates water up to 3 times per week. Requires more water when grown in containers. Do not over-water, or leaf spots will result.

SOIL: Wide range, as long as it is well-drained.

SALT TOLERANCE: Unknown

WIND TOLERANCE: Low

ZONE: 10a to 11 in the ground. Excellent container plant anywhere in Florida. Bring it inside when a freeze threatens.

PEST PROBLEMS: Fungus, shown by spots on the leaves. If holes appear in the leaves, it is probably snails. Few pests occur in the landscape.

PROPAGATION: Cuttings. Much easier to root in summer. Tip cuttings (the whole top part of the plant, including the leaves) root easier than stem cuttings (the woody part of the stem). Tis root with as little as one 4 inch piece of stem. Put 2 inches in the soil and leave 2 inches out of the soil.

Botanical Name: *Cornutia grandifolia*
Common Name: **Jam Lilac**

A large, sprawling shrub that has gorgeous flowers in summer. Not attractive in winter.

CHARACTERISTICS

PLANT TYPE: The plant has multiple trunks, like most shrubs, but grows as tall as a small tree.

AVERAGE SIZE: Grows to 30' in its native Central America. We cut ours back hard once a year and are maintaining it at about 8 feet tall by 12 feet wide. In zone 9, since it dies back in the winter, it doesn't grow quite as large.

GROWTH RATE: Fast

LEAF: Light green and velvety. About 8 inches long by 5 inches wide.

FLOWER: Light purple spike. About 8 inches long by 4 inches wide.

AVERAGE LIFE: Unknown. Ours has lasted 3 years so far.

ORIGIN: Central America

CAUTIONS: Grows very quickly and can overtake a small area unless the owner understands <u>well</u> its space requirements.

SPACING: 12 feet on center. Give this plant a lot of space to spread.

Jam Lilac's flowers resemble the northern Lilac.

General: Jam Lilac is a good choice for summer color in a large spot that is not a winter focal point. The plant itself is not particularly attractive, with a sprawling, loose, growth habit. Grow this one if you love the flowers, which are quite large and showy. It elicits a lot of 'oohs and aahs' from guests to my summer garden. I also hear people say they do not like it after they have had it for a few years because they never expected it to get so big. And, it does not look good in winter. Care is fairly easy if you trim it once a year, but you'll have a huge pile of cuttings to carry out to the trash.

Season: This plant blooms in the summer and fall for about six months.

To locate plants, go to www.easygardencolor.com

Companions: Do not attempt to plant small shrubs and groundcovers too close to this plant because its sprawling growth may crush them. Give it at least twelve feet to spread. It is a good candidate for a summer specimen garden with other large plants, like Crepe Myrtles, *Costus barbatus*, and especially Mussaendas.

Jam Lilac and some companions

Planting: Plant anytime of the year in native soil. Leave the root ball slightly out of the ground, about 1/4 inch. (See detailed planting instructions in "Easy Gardens for Florida"*, Chapter 11.)

Fertilizing: Immediately after planting, fertilize with a well-balanced, slow-release mix that includes minor elements. Repeat in March, June, and October of each year. If the summer is unusually hot and rainy, inspect the leaf color of the plant in August. If it appears washed out, add an additional fertilization at that time. (See detailed fertilization instructions in "Easy Gardens for Florida"*, Chapter 11.)

Trimming: Trim this plant back very hard in winter after it has stopped blooming. Groom it again in spring to remove any leaves that were damaged by the cold. If possible, let it grow the rest of the year. It may spread too much in summer. Trim off the offending branches as needed.

* My current book, "Easy Gardens for South Florida", will be expanded to include the entire state in 2004.

GROWING CONDITIONS

LIGHT: Light shade to full sun.

WATER: Does well with medium water. We water ours twice a week if we do not get any rain. Untested in a lower or higher water situation. (For detailed information on watering, see Chapter 8 in "Easy Gardens for Florida"*.)

SOIL: Wide range, as long as it is well-drained.

SALT TOLERANCE: Unknown

WIND TOLERANCE: Unknown

ZONE: 10a to 11. Untested in zone 9. According to Edwin Menninger in his book "Flowering Trees of the World", this plant withstands temperatures as low as 25 degrees. The foliage dies back in a freeze and regrows the following spring.

PEST PROBLEMS: None known

PROPAGATION: Cuttings

Botanical Name: *Costus barbatus*
Common Name: **Red Spiral Ginger, Spiral Ginger**

CHARACTERISTICS

PLANT TYPE:
Herbaceous perennial

AVERAGE SIZE: Easy to maintain at sizes between 7 feet tall by 6 feet wide and 8 feet tall by 8 feet wide in south Florida, where it is evergreen. In zone 9, it dies back in the first freeze and re-appears in spring, reaching a height of about 6 feet before the next winter.

GROWTH RATE: Fast

LEAF: Medium green and thick. About 6 inches long by 4 inches wide. Leaves are arranged in a spiral on the stems.

FLOWER: Red cone with yellow, oblong cylinders coming out of the sides. Opens slowly, from very small to over 8 inches long. Droops when mature.

AVERAGE LIFE: At least 10 years.

ORIGIN: Costa Rica

CAUTIONS: None known

SPACING: 8 to 12 feet on center. This plant really spreads.

Spectacular plant for summer gardens. One of the few tropical, flowering plants that is evergreen in south Florida. Cold-tolerant in zone 9 as well. Very easy to grow.

Costus barbatus in an informal flower garden

General: Plants with exotic flowers (like Gingers, Heliconias, and most Costus) are normally bare of leaves in winter in south Florida. This makes placement of them difficult. The *Costus barbatus* is the exception, blooming in summer but keeping its leaves all year. The flower is spectacular, a large red cone with yellow accents. The plant is easy to grow if you give it enough space to spread, at least eight feet. It is appropriate for informal gardens.

Season: In south Florida, *Costus barbatus* usually starts blooming in early spring and continues until winter. Unlike most other plants in this family, this Costus stays green and attractive all year in the southern end of the state. In zone 9, it dies back with the first freeze and re-appears the next spring. It usually begins blooming in mid-summer and continues until the first frost.

To locate plants, go to www.easygardencolor.com

Companions: Use *Costus barbatus* with other plants that bloom in summer. All the Mussaendas and Crotons are great companions for south Florida gardens. And Golden Shrimps make a great border for this plant in zones 9 and 10.

A woodpecker takes a drink of water that has been caught in the Costus flower.

Planting: Plant any time of the year in native soil. Leave the root ball slightly out of the ground, about 1/4 inch. (See detailed planting instructions in "Easy Gardens for Florida"*, Chapter 11.) The plant sometimes flops over just after planting, especially if it is pot-bound. Stake it for a short time, and understand that it stabilizes well after the roots become established.

Fertilizing: Immediately after planting, fertilize with a well-balanced, slow-release mix that includes minor elements. Repeat in March, June, and October of each year. (See detailed fertilization instructions in "Easy Gardens for Florida"*, Chapter 11.)

Trimming: Trim the entire stalk to the ground when each flower dies because all the leaves on the stalk will die shortly thereafter. Since the flowers last a long time, this does not have to be done very often. The plant can also be trimmed all over, but only in winter, just after it has stopped blooming.

✳ My current book, "Easy Gardens for South Florida", will be expanded to include the entire state in 2004.

LIGHT: Medium shade to full sun. Prefers light shade.

WATER: Medium. Ideal watering is twice a week after the initial establishment period. Tolerates water up to 4 times per week. Requires more water when grown in containers. (For detailed information about watering, see Chapter 8 in "Easy Gardens for Florida"*.)

SOIL: Wide range, as long as it is well-drained.

SALT TOLERANCE: Unknown

WIND TOLERANCE: Low

ZONE: According to Stokes Tropicals in New Iberia, Louisiana, *Costus barbatus* thrives in zone 9. They have been growing them for years. It has never shown <u>any</u> cold damage <u>at all</u> from 1996 until 2002 in my trial gardens in zone 10a.

PEST PROBLEMS: None known

PROPAGATION: Division or cuttings.

Botanical Name: *Dombeya 'Seminole'*
Common Name: **Florida Hydrangea**

CHARACTERISTICS

PLANT TYPE: Evergreen shrub.

AVERAGE SIZE: Easily maintained at sizes between 6 feet tall by 6 feet wide and 8 feet tall by 8 feet wide.

GROWTH RATE: Fast

LEAF: Medium green. About 6 inches long by 6 inches wide.

FLOWER: Medium pink, round, and shaped like a Hydrangea. About 4 to 5 inches across.

AVERAGE LIFE: Unknown, but at least 5 to 10 years.

ORIGIN: Dombeyas are native to South Africa or Mascarene Islands. The 'Seminole' was hybridized by Paul Soderholm, USDA, in Miami.

CAUTIONS: Attracts bees

SPACING: 6 to 10 feet on center.

Dombeya wallichii is a tree form of Dombeya. It grows large, to 20 feet tall by 30 feet wide. Since the flowers hang, they need to be viewed from the bottom. The tree is quite beautiful but only blooms for about a month each winter. The tree is featured on pages 232 and 233.

One of our most beautiful winter bloomers. Looks like the northern Hydrangea.

Dombeya 'Seminole' in full bloom. The pink flowers are carried on top of the shrub and show well up close or from a distance.

General: *Dombeya 'Seminole'* is a fabulous plant, a must for winter gardens in south and central Florida. It produces six months of traffic-stopping color with very little care. The flowers resemble northern Hydrangeas but are not related. Many different types of Dombeyas exist. Some are large trees, with attractive, drooping flowers that need to be viewed from below. But, the Seminole holds its flowers on top of the leaves, so they are easily viewed from any angle. The plant is amazingly tough, taking adverse conditions with no problems. The only issue with the plant is that it is somewhat difficult to propagate, so not many nurseries stock it. If you see one, buy it because you might not see it again. But, be sure that it is the Seminole type and not the tree type (Dombeya wallichii), which is much easier to propagate but much different in its size and performance.

Season: *Dombeya 'Seminoles'* usually bloom twice a year. The first period starts in late fall and continues through late January. The plant takes a break for about a month and starts blooming again in March, continuing until late May. The plant itself looks good, even when not blooming.

To locate plants, go to www.easygardencolor.com

Companions: Use *Dombeya 'Seminole'* with other plants that bloom in winter. In south Florida, Brunfelsia, Giant Shrimp, Scarlet Red Cloak and the Chinese Hat Plant are excellent large companions. Piecrust Crotons and Justicia 'Fruit Cocktails' work well for smaller layers. And Golden Shrimp Plants and Purple Lantana make great companions in either south or central Florida.

Dombeya with some companions

Planting: Plant any time of the year in native soil. Leave the root ball slightly out of the ground, about 1/4 inch. (See detailed planting instructions in "Easy Gardens for Florida"*, Chapter 11.)

Fertilizing: Dombeyas are not heavy feeders. Immediately after planting, fertilize with a well-balanced, slow-release mix that includes minor elements. Repeat in March, June, and October of each year. (See detailed fertilization instructions in "Easy Gardens for Florida"*, Chapter 11.)

Trimming: Trim back hard in June. The goal is to round out the shape of the plant, not square it off. This annual trimming is normally enough for superior performance the next winter. Do not trim back after August, or you might not have blooms the following winter.

My current book, "Easy Gardens for South Florida", will be expanded to include the entire state in 2004.

GROWING CONDITIONS

LIGHT: Light shade to full sun.

WATER: Medium. Ideal watering is twice a week after the initial establishment period. Tolerates water up to 5 times per week. Requires more water when grown in containers. (For detailed information about watering, see Chapter 8 in "Easy Gardens for Florida"*.)

SOIL: Wide range, as long as it is well-drained.

SALT TOLERANCE: Medium

WIND TOLERANCE: Medium

ZONE: 9b-11. Cold damage occurs between 25 and 29 degrees.

PEST PROBLEMS: None known.

PROPAGATION: Cuttings or air layers. Difficult to propagate.

Note: Blooms increase if dead flowers are removed in between the two winter bloom periods. Also, since Dombeyas need a lot of room to spread, the planting area around them appears quite empty right after planting. Fill in with annuals for an instant look, and do not replace them the following season.

Botanical Name: *Dracaena reflexa 'Song of India'*

Common Name: **Dracaena Reflexa**

CHARACTERISTICS

PLANT TYPE: Evergreen shrub often used as a small tree.

AVERAGE SIZE: Easy to maintain at sizes between 3 feet tall by 3 feet wide and 8 feet tall by 5 feet wide (see note below).

GROWTH RATE: Slow, even slower than the green variety.

LEAF: Long and thin. About 4 inches long by 1/2 inch wide.

FLOWER: Insignificant

AVERAGE LIFE: 10 years plus.

ORIGIN: Madagascar

CAUTIONS: None known

SPACING: Depends on the overall size. For small, short masses, plant 2 feet on center. For large, tall screening, plant 4 feet on center.

An easy plant to use as a small shrub or a large specimen. Low water in sun or shade.

Mature 'Song of India' bordered by Stoplight Crotons. The bright colors of the Croton leaves contrast well with the light, variegated foliage of the Dracaena.

General: Many different types of Dracaenas are successfully grown in Florida. Most are very well adapted to our tough environment. *Dracaena reflexa* is a green variety often used indoors. The 'Song of India' is a variegated cultivar that works beautifully to set off darker leaf masses or flowers. It is extremely slow growing, which is an advantage if you are looking for low maintenance. This slow growth rate also means that large specimens, like the one above, are quite expensive.

Season: No seasonal variation.

To locate plants, go to www.easygardencolor.com

Companions: Use 'Song of India' to set off dark or bright leaves or flowers. Crotons are ideal companions, especially Piecrusts, Mammeys, or Stoplights. Dracaenas are also appropriate for creating a tropical look, mixing well with Palms and plants with large leaves, like Traveler's Palms and Alocasias.

Young 'Song of India'. It is a good choice for pool areas because it doesn't drop many leaves.

Planting: Plant any time of the year in native soil. Leave the root ball slightly out of the ground, about 1/4 inch. (See detailed planting instructions in "Easy Gardens for Florida"*, Chapter 11.)

Fertilizing: Immediately after planting, fertilize with a well-balanced, slow-release mix that includes minor elements. Repeat in March, June, and October of each year. (See detailed fertilization instructions in "Easy Gardens for Florida"*, Chapter 11.)

Trimming: Trim as needed to maintain desired size. If canes are untrimmed, they become bare at the base. If you prefer fullness at the base, trim some of the canes back very low (six to twelve inches). Two to three branches will sprout at each cut if done in early summer. Stick the cuttings in soil nearby, and some will root. Trim off the leaves at the base of the cutting (about four inches up the stalk) before rooting.

* My current book, "Easy Gardens for South Florida", will be expanded to include the entire state in 2004.

GROWING CONDITIONS

LIGHT: Medium shade to full sun. Prefers some shade.

WATER: Low. Ideal watering is once a week after the initial establishment period. Tolerates water up to 4 times per week. Requires more water when grown in containers. (For detailed information about watering, see Chapter 8 in "Easy Gardens for Florida"*.)

SOIL: Wide range, as long as it is well-drained.

SALT TOLERANCE: Medium

WIND TOLERANCE: Medium

ZONE: 10a to 11. Excellent container plant for anywhere in Florida. Bring inside if a freeze threatens.

PEST PROBLEMS: None known

PROPAGATION: Cuttings

Botanical Name: *Gardenia jasminoides*

Common Name: **Gardenia**

CHARACTERISTICS

PLANT TYPE: Evergreen shrub.

AVERAGE SIZE: Easy to maintain at sizes between 4 feet tall by 4 feet wide and 8 feet tall by 5 feet wide. Other Gardenias range in size from groundcovers to small trees.

GROWTH RATE: Slow

LEAF: Dark, glossy green. Size varies by cultivar.

FLOWER: White. Sizes and shapes vary in different cultivars.

AVERAGE LIFE: 20 years

ORIGIN: China

CAUTIONS: None known

SPACING: 5 feet on center. This plant is best used as a single specimen because it is less likely to attract insects.

Note: In north Florida, Gardenia jasminoides are grown on their own root. In south Florida, these plants are grafted on stocks of Gardenia thunbergia.

If you love sweet-smelling flowers, a Gardenia is a must for your garden.

Gardenias have white blooms and dark green, glossy leaves.

General: Gardenias are one of the best choices for scent in the garden. But, they are a bit tricky. They like soil that is slightly acidic, and many of the soils in Florida (particularly south Florida) are alkaline. And, the bugs love them. I have made a lot of mistakes with Gardenias. In one of my gardens, I planted a hedge of 12 plants right outside my bedroom window. Unfortunately, the concentration of so many Gardenias in the same place attracted every bug in the neighborhood. And, the proximity to the concrete foundation of the house made the soil too alkaline for the Gardenias. They did poorly, so I yanked them out - bug-infested, yellow leaves and all. Years later, I planted *one* in my garden, far from any concrete, and mulched it heavily with pine straw to acidify the soil. It did pretty well for a while, until the bugs found it. One day, it was infested with aphids, and I vowed to throw it away, but got busy and forgot. Then the ants came, and it looked like something from a horror movie. Once again, I forgot to take it out. When I noticed it again, it was covered with blooms and looked completely healthy. The ants had eaten the aphids and gone about their merry way! So much for pulling it out. Nature had done its work without my help.

Season: In central and north Florida, Gardenias usually bloom in spring. In south Florida, the bloom time varies. They flower on and off all year but more in the warm months. I have even seen them bloom at Christmas time in the southern part of the state.

Placement: Plant Gardenias near places where you sit or walk, like along paths and outside windows, provided the plant is not right next to concrete. They do best with good air circulation. Avoid planting them under screening because they attract more bugs there.

To locate plants, go to www.easygardencolor.com

Companions If you love sweet-smelling flowers, plant a variety of different scented plants in your garden. Even if they bloom at the same time, the scent *usually* carries only a few feet away from the plant, so give each scented plant some space. Many of the Jasmines are scented, particularly Confederate Jasmine, which blooms all over Florida. In south Florida, the Ylang Ylang Tree is the longest-blooming, scented plant I have found. Other recommended scented plants include Sweet Allysum and Frangipani.

Gardenia with some scented companions

Planting: Plant any time of the year. Leave the root ball slightly out of the ground, about 1/4 inch.

Fertilizing: Immediately after planting, fertilize with a well-balanced, slow-release, acidic mix that includes minor elements. Fertilizers for Azaleas and Camellias usually work well. Minor elements are very important for Gardenias, especially iron. Repeat in March, June, and October of each year. If the summer is unusually hot and rainy, inspect the leaf color of the plant in August. If it appears washed out, add an additional fertilization at that time.

Trimming: I seldom trim my Gardenias, just lightly every few years. Be sure to wait until they have just finished blooming. If the Gardenias are damaged by cold in central or north Florida, remove the damaged portions in spring.

Yellow Leaves and Bud Drop: Many different causes can account for yellow leaves and bud drop in Gardenias. An excellent article that deals with both these issues completely is available for free on the Internet. Go to http://edis.ifas.usf.edu/BODY_MG336. It is called "Gardenias", by Joan Bradshaw. The article is Circular 1098, Florida Cooperative Extension Service, Institute of Food and Agricultural Sciences, University of Florida. First published: June 1993. Reviewed: June 1994.

GROWING CONDITIONS

LIGHT: Light shade to full sun.

WATER: Medium. Ideal watering is twice a week after the initial establishment period. Tolerates water up to 4 times per week.

SOIL: Prefers acidic soils. Many of the soils in Florida (particularly in south Florida) are alkaline, like mine. I mulch my Gardenias with pine straw, which acidifies it naturally. If soil is too alkaline, expect frequent nutritional deficiencies. The article referred to under "Yellow Leaves and Bud Drop" (on this page) tells more about soil for Gardenias.

SALT TOLERANCE: Low

WIND TOLERANCE: Medium

ZONE: 8 to 11. Plants grafted on Gardenia thunbergia rootstock are not hardy at temperatures below 28 degrees.

PEST PROBLEMS: Aphids, thrips, whiteflies, sooty mold.

PROPAGATION: Cuttings or grafting

Tip: 'Miami Supreme' is a tried-and-true variety for the southern and central parts of the state.

Botanical Name: *Graptophyllum pictum 'Tricolor'*

Tricolor Caricature Plant

Common Name:

Decorative and easy to grow. Unique pink, yellow, and green colorations. Beautiful but very cold-sensitive.

CHARACTERISTICS

PLANT TYPE: Evergreen shrub.

AVERAGE SIZE: Easy to maintain at sizes between 4 feet tall by 3 feet wide and 6 feet tall by 5 feet wide.

GROWTH RATE: Medium

LEAF: About 3 to 4 inches long by 2 inches wide. Produces a shiny, multicolored pattern that includes green, yellow, and pink. The pattern resembles a caricature. Other colors are available, including bronze and pink, as well as green and yellow. See "Easy Gardens for Florida"*, pages 82 and 83, for the bronze and pink one.

FLOWER: Purple, about 4 inches long. Beautiful but occasional. The beauty of this plant is the leaf pattern and color.

AVERAGE LIFE: 5 to 10 years.

ORIGIN: New Guinea

CAUTIONS: Cold sensitive for the northern areas of south Florida.

SPACING: 3 to 4 feet on center.

The unique colors of the Tricolor Caricature show quite well up close or from a distance.

General: This plant gets its name from the shape of the pattern in the leaves, which resembles a caricature. No two leaves are alike. It is quite unusual and deserves more use in south Florida. Caricature Plants are also available in bronze and pink as well as green and yellow. Tricolor Caricatures add a unique accent to a summer tropical garden.

Season: Leaf colors are slightly brighter in summer. This plant is very cold-sensitive and often defoliates or burns (leaves turn brown and fall off) in exposed areas of zones 10 in the winter.

To locate plants, go to www.easygardencolor.com

Companions: Use the Tricolor Caricature with plants that have pink or yellow flowers. For a beautiful shade garden, use them with Pink Angelwing Begonias, Golden Shrimp Plants, and Mend Bromeliads. This combination offers year-round color. Giant Shrimps and 'Fruit Cocktails' are also excellent companions.

Tricolor Caricature and some companions

Planting: Plant any time of the year in native soil. Leave the root ball slightly out of the ground, about 1/4 inch. (See detailed planting instructions in "Easy Gardens for Florida"*, Chapter 11.)

Fertilizing: Immediately after planting, fertilize with a well-balanced, slow-release mix that includes minor elements. Repeat in March, June, and October of each year. If the summer is unusually hot and rainy, inspect the leaf color of the plant in August. If it appears washed out, add an additional fertilization at that time. (See detailed fertilization instructions in "Easy Gardens for Florida"*, Chapter 11.)

Trimming: Caricature Plants are easy, provided they are allowed to grow at least four feet tall. They can be maintained at this height by trimming about three times a year or less. To keep them at three feet tall, trim more frequently. They recover quickly from hard cutbacks in summer. In June, we have cut them as low as 12 inches, and they grew back to a respectable height within a month. Avoid cutting only the tips, or you will produce a leggy plant.

* My current book, "Easy Gardens for South Florida",
will be expanded to include the entire state in 2004.

GROWING CONDITIONS

LIGHT: Medium shade to full sun. Avoid dense shade. Needs a lot of water in full sun.

WATER: Medium to high. Ideal watering is twice a week after the initial establishment period in shade, 3 times a week in sun. Tolerates water up to 4 times per week. Requires more water when grown in containers. (For detailed information about watering, see Chapter 8 in "Easy Gardens for Florida"*.)

SOIL: Wide range, as long as it is well-drained.

SALT TOLERANCE: Unknown

WIND TOLERANCE: Unknown

ZONE: 10b to 11. Shows cold damage routinely in the northern part of zone 10 in the winter. The leaves turn brown and fall off. Recovers when the weather warms up a little, except in severe freezes.

PEST PROBLEMS: Holes in the leaves indicate caterpillars or snails. Occasional scale outbreaks.

PROPAGATION: Cuttings

Botanical Name: *Heliconia psittacorum*

Parrot's Beak Heliconia

CHARACTERISTICS

PLANT TYPE: Herbaceous perennial.

AVERAGE SIZE: Many different types available, from 1 to 9 feet tall by 3 to 10 feet wide. Most commonly-available types in south Florida stay under 4 feet tall.

GROWTH RATE: Fast

LEAF: Long and thin, medium green. Size varies by type.

FLOWER: The flower bracts arise from the same point on the stem, which is different from most other Heliconias. It resembles a Bird of Paradise flower. Colors range from orange to red to yellow. Sizes range from about 2 inches across on the dwarfs to 5 inches across on the larger types.

AVERAGE LIFE: 5 to 10 years.

ORIGIN: Tropical America, Asia, and the Western Pacific.

CAUTIONS: None known

SPACING: Depends on variety. Space the small dwarfs 18 to 24 inches on center. Space the larger types 3 to 4 feet on center. Understand that the plants will send out multiple shoots that spread beyond the desired planting area.

Great plant for cut flowers. Exotic color in the heat of summer. Fairly high maintenance. Not appropriate for winter gardens.

Heliconias quickly fill a planting bed but don't look good in the winter.

General: Botanists have identified between 250 and 400 types of Heliconias. The *psittacorum* species is better than most of the larger Heliconias for the south Florida landscape because of its small stature and long bloom period.

Advantages: These smaller Heliconias offer spectacular flowers. If used correctly in a spot that is not a focal point in winter, they can be a wonderful asset to a Florida summer garden. Plant them in the ground in the southern part of the state or in containers in any part of Florida. Heliconias are great for cut flowers because they last from two to three weeks if you cut them early in the morning.

Disadvantages: Most new south Florida gardeners make the mistake of planting them in the wrong place, like right next to the front door, not understanding that the plant is unattractive in the winter. Sometimes the whole plant turns brown in routine, cold weather. And when it regrows in the spring, it sends up shoots over a very large area. Heliconias are fairly high maintenance, needing frequent grooming to remove brown leaves and flowers as well as a yearly cutback of most of the foliage. Unwanted 'volunteers' also need to be frequently removed.

Season: Most Heliconias love heat and thrive in our hot summers. In winter, expect them to turn brown and go dormant. Trim off the brown leaves at this time. The plant will rebloom the following summer.

To locate plants, go to www.easygardencolor.com

Companions: Heliconias show best when highlighted with adjacent plants that have leaf color, exotic flowers, or very different textures. Mixing different Heliconias next to each other in the same bed usually does not work. Crotons, Tis, and Dracaenas are excellent companions, as are Palms. Bright-flowering plants, like Golden Shrimps and the Spathoglottis Ground Orchids, are good choices. Be sure to use plants that peak in the summer because the Heliconias may be cut all the way back for much of the winter.

'St. Vincent Red' Heliconia

'Lady Di' Heliconia

Heliconias are a good choice for containers in summer anywhere in Florida.

Planting: Plant in spring or summer in native soil. Leave the root ball slightly out of the ground, about 1/4 inch.

Fertilizing: Heliconias are heavy feeders. Immediately after planting, fertilize with a well-balanced, slow-release mix that includes minor elements. Repeat in March, June, and October of each year. If the summer is unusually hot and rainy, inspect the leaf color of the plant in August. If it appears washed out, add an additional fertilization at that time.

Trimming: Groom the plant throughout the year, cutting off dead flowers, stems, and leaves. Expect this chore monthly. After the first cold spell, the plant usually turns brown. Cut the plant to the ground at this time. This winter cutback increases the chances of the roots dying in a severe freeze. But, the alternative is looking at dead leaves all winter. New plants sprout from the roots the following spring unless there was a highly unusual temperature dip.

GROWING CONDITIONS

LIGHT: Light shade to full sun. Flowers lose color in too much shade.

WATER: Medium. Ideal watering is twice a week after the establishment period. Tolerates water up to 4 times per week. Requires more water when grown in containers. (For more detailed information about watering, see Chapter 8 in "Easy Gardens for Florida"*.)

SOIL: Wide range, as long as it is well-drained.

SALT TOLERANCE: Medium

WIND TOLERANCE: Low

ZONE: 10a to 11. Shows leaf damage when temperatures hit the low to mid 40's, which happens every winter, even in the Keys. Grows from the ground again when temperatures warm up unless there is an unusually severe freeze. In central and north Florida, Heliconias are frequently grown in pots so they can be moved inside during cold spells.

PEST PROBLEMS: Fungus is the worst problem. Do not overwater. Spider mites appear occasionally, especially under screening or in greenhouses.

PROPAGATION: Division, seeds, or rhizomes.

My current book, "Easy Gardens for South Florida", will be expanded to include the entire state in 2004.

Botanical Name: *Hibiscus rosa-sinensis*

Common Name: **Hibiscus - grown as a shrub**

CHARACTERISTICS

PLANT TYPE: Evergreen shrub.

AVERAGE SIZE: Easy to maintain at sizes between 4 feet tall by 4 feet wide and 6 feet tall by 5 feet wide. The biggest mistake made with Hibiscus is attempting to maintain it at a size that is too small to produce blooms.

GROWTH RATE: Fast

LEAF: Medium to dark green. Size varies by type from 1 inch long by 3/4 inch wide to 4 inches long by 3 inches wide.

FLOWER: Every color imaginable! Size varies by type, from 2 inch diameter to dinner plate size.

AVERAGE LIFE: 5 to 10 years. If your Hibiscus shrub looks old, leggy AND the bottom stems are thick (3/4 inch or more), it may be time to replace it.

ORIGIN: China

CAUTIONS: Not a good candidate over pavement or pools because the flowers stick and are difficult to remove.

SPACING: 3 to 4 feet on center.

Hybrid Hibiscus

An old Florida favorite that is somewhat difficult to grow as a full, thriving shrub. Beautiful flowers that are wonderful inside the house.

General: Hibiscus is covered in this book in three forms: dwarf, shrub, and tree. Technically, they are all the same type of plant. Take the Seminole Pink Hibiscus, for example: it grows as a dwarf if it is sprayed with the dwarfing compound; it grows as a shrub if trimmed as a shrub; and it can be a small tree, if trimmed as a small tree. The shrub form is, overall, the hardest form of Hibiscus to grow because of its tendency toward a leggy, unattractive growth habit.

Tips for Success with Shrub Hibiscus: One of the most frequent questions I am asked is, "Why doesn't my Hibiscus shrub look good?" Several factors are involved: choosing the right variety, trimming correctly, and planting only a few in the same garden. You need to expect some trouble. Most Hibiscus are susceptible to many Florida pests, including the new and serious Pink Hibiscus Mealybug. Hibiscus are also susceptible to changes in the weather, resulting in bud drop or leaf drop after yellowing.

Ideas for Hybrids: Generally, the fancier the flower, the worse the shrub looks. To enjoy the beauty of the flowers, plant a variety of Hibiscus shrubs on a forgotten side of the house. You won't see the shrub, but can take the flowers inside. The flowers only last a day. Pick them in the morning, and put them dry in the refrigerator. Remove them in late afternoon, and decorate with the flowers dry, simply laid on the table. They will stay open late into the night.

Season: Hibiscus plants last for many years, blooming on and off throughout the year.

Companions: Use Hibiscus for the flowers rather than the form of the shrub. They work best mixed in with other flowering shrubs in informal masses. Try different colored Hibiscus in a cottage garden with Golden Shrimp Plants and Plumbagos.

Double Peach Hibiscus

Hibiscus varieties that work well as shrubs are shown above and below right. The doubles sometimes drop more buds than the singles, but the ones pictured feature dense forms that are ideal for shrubs.

Planting: Plant any time of the year in native soil. Leave the root ball slightly out of the ground, about 1/4 inch. (See detailed planting instructions in "Easy Gardens for Florida"*, Chapter 11.)

Fertilizing: Hibiscus are heavy feeders. Immediately after planting, fertilize with a well-balanced, slow-release mix that includes minor elements. Repeat in March, June, and October of each year. If the summer is unusually hot and rainy, inspect the leaf color of the plant in August. If it appears washed out, add an additional fertilization at that time. (See detailed fertilization instructions in "Easy Gardens for Florida"*, Chapter 11.)

Trimming: Hibiscus does not bloom if trimmed too often. Many people shear Hibiscus monthly and wonder why it never flowers. Trim infrequently but make deep cuts instead of just knocking off the tips each month. This manner allows each branch to grow long enough to produce flowers. The best time to trim is right after the shrub has bloomed. Also, remove any crossed branches from within the shrub.

* My current book, "Easy Gardens for South Florida", will be expanded to include the entire state in 2004.

GROWING CONDITIONS

LIGHT: Light shade to full sun

WATER: Medium. Ideal watering is twice a week after the initial establishment period. Tolerates water up to 4 times per week. Do not overwater.

SOIL: Wide range, as long as it is well-drained.

SALT TOLERANCE: High. Ideal near the sea.

WIND TOLERANCE: High

ZONE: Technically, 10a to 11. Often successful (and commonly planted) in protected areas of zone 9.

PEST PROBLEMS: Pink Hibiscus Mealybug is a serious, new pest that has the capability of wiping out all of our Hibiscus. If you see pink, cottony material on your Hibiscus, call your county extension immediately for instructions. Also, scale, spider mites, snails, aphids, and whiteflies. These plants attract a lot of pests in some locations and none in others. They attract more if a lot of them are planted on the same site. Do not use Malathion on Hibiscus - it will defoliate them.

PROPAGATION: Cuttings

Hibiscus varieties that work well as shrubs, from top to bottom: President Red, Seminole Pink, Double Ruffle.

Botanical Name: *Hydrangea spp.*
Common Name: **Hydrangea**

CHARACTERISTICS

PLANT TYPE: Deciduous shrub.

AVERAGE SIZE: Mopheads grow 3 to 6 feet tall by 3 to 5 feet wide. Oakleafs are larger, some reaching 15 feet tall by 6 feet wide in Florida.

GROWTH RATE: Fast

LEAF: Size varies by type

FLOWER: Blue, purple, pink, or white. With the blue or pink Mopheads and Lacecaps, the percentage of each color varies with the acidity of the soil. Some varieties are bred to be more blue, some more pink. Oakleaf Hydrangeas have white flowers that turn pink and then brown as they age.

AVERAGE LIFE: At least 10 years in areas where it's cold enough. Lifespan shortens in warmer areas, like the southern edges of central Florida.

ORIGIN: Mopheads and Lacecaps are native to Japan. Oakleafs are native to the U.S., some to Florida.

CAUTIONS: None known

SPACING: 3 to 6 feet on center. Plant the larger types farther apart than the smaller ones.

'Masja' Mophead

This old favorite is experiencing a resurgence of popularity in central and north Florida.

Hydrangea macrophylla: Mophead Hydrangea 'Penny Mac'

General: Hydrangeas are excellent choices for large flowers in central and north Florida. Since they need cold to flower, they do better the further north you go in the state (see "Zone" in the green sidebar of the next page). All Hydrangeas drop their leaves in the fall, so don't use them in a spot that would be a key focal point in winter. You can choose between three different flower types, depending on your personal taste.

Mophead and Lacecap: The Mophead flower is big and round, while the Lacecap flower is flat. The blue and pink Mopheads and Lacecaps have the unique ability to change flower colors based on the acidity of the soil. Acidic soils produce bluer blooms, and alkaline soils produce pinker blooms. They both come in white also, which does not change colors.

Oakleaf: The Oakleaf flower grows in a more vertical shape. It is white, turning pink and then brown as it ages. The leaves often change colors in fall - to brilliant reds, yellows, and oranges. The Oakleaf is easier to grow than the Mophead, tolerating less water, more sun, and poorer soil.

Hydrangeas in South Florida: Hydrangeas don't do well in south Florida, but Dombeyas, which look similar to Hydrangeas, thrive in zone 10. Read about shrub Dombeyas on pages 144 and 145, and tree Dombeyas on pages 232 and 233.

Season: Hydrangeas bloom from spring to early summer, peaking for about a month; they then continue to have a few blooms for about a month more.

More Information: I used www.hydrangeashydrangeas.com for these photos and much of this information. I recommend it highly.

To locate plants, go to www.easygardencolor.com

Companions: Hydrangeas look beautiful planted in collections of different colors and flower types. They also look good with other perennials that bloom at the same time. Some possibilities include Gardenias, Roses, Agapanthus, Daylilies, and Camellias.

Hydrangea macrophylla normalis:
Lacecap Hydrangea 'Taube'

Hydrangea macrophylla:
Mophead Hydrangea 'Frillibet'

Hydrangea quercifolia:
Oakleaf Hydrangea 'Snowflake'

Planting: Fall and winter are the best times to plant. Leave the root ball slightly out of the ground, about 1/4 inch.

Fertilizing: Immediately after planting, fertilize with a well-balanced, slow-release mix that includes minor elements. Repeat in May and August of each year. It is very difficult to change the color of a Hydrangea by attempting to adjust the pH if it is in the ground, but it is easier with plants in containers. See www.hydrangeashydrangeas.com for more instructions.

Trimming: Prune off any freeze damage in early spring. After the plant has finished blooming, trim off the old flower heads and shape the plant as needed. Do not prune after July, or you will restrict flower production for the next year. For larger flowers, prune to fewer stems. More stems produce larger quantities of smaller flowers.

Buying tip: Look for Hydrangeas that have been bred as landscape plants for your area. Many are bred for Easter potted plants and do not do as well outdoors in Florida because they don't remain dormant all winter. If there is a warm spell in January, they leaf out. If the leaves freeze, the plants won't bloom that year. Many of the landscape varieties stay dormant all winter and bloom quite dependably the next spring or early summer. And, it is best to purchase Hydrangeas in bloom to be sure of the flower type.

GROWING CONDITIONS

LIGHT: Mopheads and Lacecaps need morning sun and afternoon shade in Florida. Oakleafs take more sun but do better with some afternoon shade.

WATER: Mopheads and Lacecaps need water 2 to 4 times per week after the initial establishment period. They do not do well without irrigation. Oakleafs tolerate more drought. All require more water when grown in containers.

SOIL: Mopheads and Lacecaps prefer good soil enriched with organic matter. Oakleafs thrive in sand. All Hydrangeas require excellent drainage.

SALT TOLERANCE: Low

WIND TOLERANCE: Unknown

ZONE: 7 through 9 for Mopheads and Lacecaps. 5 to 9 for Oakleafs. Hydrangeas need cold and do not thrive in the southern areas of 9b. If you live in the southern end of central Florida, call your local county extension office for advice about the suitability of Hydrangeas for your garden.

PEST PROBLEMS: Caterpillars, scales

PROPAGATION: Cuttings

Purple Mophead

Botanical Name: *Megakepasma erythrochlamys*

Common Name: **Brazilian or Scarlet Red Cloak**

CHARACTERISTICS

PLANT TYPE: Evergreen shrub.

AVERAGE SIZE: Easily maintained at sizes between 7 feet tall by 7 feet wide and 9 feet tall by 9 feet wide. I have not seen it larger than 9 feet in south Florida but have heard of it growing to 15 feet in other countries.

GROWTH RATE: Fast

LEAF: Lime green and tropical looking. About 8 inches long by 6 inches wide. Lighter green in sun than shade.

FLOWER: Large red bracts that enclose white flowers. The white flowers are insignificant and the red bracts spectacular. About 8 inches long by 3 inches wide.

AVERAGE LIFE: 10 years plus.

ORIGIN: Venezuela

CAUTIONS: None known

SPACING: 6 to 9 feet on center. This is a very large plant. Give it room to spread.

One of our most spectacular, large-blooming shrubs. Huge, red spikes for months at a time.

This large shrub is a good choice for major, seasonal, color impact. The lime green of the leaves contrasts beautifully with the red flowers.

General: Scarlet Red Cloak is a wonderful shrub if you love flowers, have a large spot, and can put up with some bugs. Caterpillars chew the leaves occasionally, especially shortly after planting. Spraying is not required unless the damage becomes severe. For most people, it is worth seeing some holes in the leaves in order to experience the beauty of the flower, which is one of the showiest I have ever seen. Since it usually blooms in winter, it is a dramatic addition to winter gardens. Unlike many of our tropical plants with showy flowers, like Gingers and Heliconias, the Scarlet Red Cloak is evergreen. The large, lime-green leaves are attractive, even when the plant is not blooming.

Season: Scarlet Red Cloak's spectacular flowers usually appear in fall and winter for about six months. The plant occasionally surprises you with summer blooms that end before January and do not reappear until the following fall. When the plant is not in flower, its leaves are attractive. The Scarlet Red Cloak plant is evergreen, staying attractive all year, except for minor leaf burn if the temperatures drop to the mid to low 30's.

To locate plants, go to www.easygardencolor.com

Companions: Use Scarlet Red Cloak with yellows and purples that bloom in winter, like Giant Shrimps and Brunfelsias. It also looks great with yellow and red Crotons, like the Stoplight or Mammey. An easy grouping for a large area features Scarlet Red Cloak as the tallest layer, Stoplight Crotons in the middle, Golden Shrimps as a border.

Scarlet Red Cloak and some companions

Planting: Plant any time of the year in native soil. Leave the root ball slightly out of the ground, about 1/4 inch.

Fertilizing: Immediately after planting, fertilize with a well-balanced, slow-release mix that includes minor elements. Repeat in March, June, and October of each year. If the summer is unusually hot and rainy, inspect the leaf color of the plant in August. If it appears washed out, add an additional fertilization at that time. (See detailed fertilization instructions in "Easy Gardens for Florida"*, Chapter 11.)

Trimming: Trim once a year, immediately after it stops flowering. The timing is very important because the plant starts blooming about eight to ten months after trimming. It takes very hard cutbacks well. Do not trim it again until after it has stopped flowering again, or you will prevent it from blooming the next year.

* My current book, "Easy Gardens for South Florida", will be expanded to include the entire state in 2004.

LIGHT: Prefers light shade, but grows in full sun as well. Untested in medium or dense shade.

WATER: Medium. Ideal watering is twice a week after the initial establishment period. Tolerates water up to 4 times per week. (For detailed information about watering, see Chapter 8 in "Easy Gardens for Florida"*.)

SOIL: Wide range, as long as it is well-drained.

SALT TOLERANCE: Unknown

WIND TOLERANCE: Low

ZONE: I tested the plant in zones 10a and 10b with no cold damage from 1990 until 2003 other than minor leaf burn when the temperatures hit the mid 30's. References to tolerances in zone 9 are sparse. David Bar-Zvi, in his book, "Tropical Gardening", states that the plant does well in zone 9 but is sensitive to actual freezing.

PEST PROBLEMS: Caterpillars, scale and mealybugs. Most susceptible to pests shortly after planting. I put up with a few chewed leaves on mine.

PROPAGATION: Cuttings

Botanical Name: *Mussaenda frondosa*
Common Name: **Orange and White Mussaenda**

CHARACTERISTICS

PLANT TYPE: Semi-deciduous shrub.

AVERAGE SIZE: I have had this plant in my summer garden for 3 years. Although it keeps getting a bit bigger each year, I am not sure how low it can be maintained. It is a large plant. With one cutback each year, mine is about 8 feet tall by 12 feet wide. This is the largest Mussaenda in my trial garden.

GROWTH RATE: Fast

LEAF: Bright, lime green. About 6 inches long by about 3 inches wide.

FLOWER: Small, orange, star-shaped flowers form clusters surrounded by large white bracts. Showy, about 1 foot wide.

AVERAGE LIFE: Unknown, but at least 5 years.

ORIGIN: Asia or Africa

CAUTIONS: Partially to completely bare in winter.

SPACING: Give this one a lot of space! At least 12 feet on center.

A striking, large specimen for summer gardens in south Florida. A real attention-getter! Unique and unusual flowers that bloom for a full six to eight months. Bare in winter.

The orange Mussaenda frondosa flower and its surrounding white bract are very large, measuring about one foot across.

General: Mussaendas are the stars of south Florida summer gardens, much like Bougainvillea in the winter. The *Mussaenda frondosa* is larger than most of the other Mussaendas and spectacular in bloom. The flower is quite unique, with large, white bracts surrounding orange, star-shaped flowers. Its drawback is that it's almost bare in winter. Place it in a spot where you can enjoy it in summer and not mind if it is bare in winter. Obviously, it does not belong in a key spot in front of your home. It is perfect for your own personal, botanical collection, mixed with other summer specimens in your back yard. Be sure to give it enough space to spread at least twelve feet.

Season: *Mussaenda frondosa* blooms during the warm months, generally starting about May and ending in November. It is partially to completely bare in winter.

To locate plants, go to www.easygardencolor.com

Companions: Some large specimens that work well in the same garden with this Mussaenda include *Costus barbatus*, Crepe Myrtle, and Frangipani. Smaller companions include the Thryallis, Spathoglottis, Epidendrum Orchid, Canna, and many Crotons.

Mussaenda frondosa and some companions

Planting: Plant any time of the year in native soil. Leave the root ball slightly out of the ground, about 1/4 inch.

Fertilizing: Immediately after planting, fertilize with a well-balanced, slow-release mix that includes minor elements. Repeat in March, June, and October of each year. If the summer is unusually hot and rainy, inspect the leaf color of the plant in August. If it appears washed out, add an additional fertilization at that time. (See instructions in "Easy Gardens for Florida"*, Chapter 11.)

Trimming: Trim once a year in winter, after it has stopped blooming and the leaves start to turn brown. Trim back hard - to sticks. Leave it alone the rest of the year. Trimming in spring or summer can prevent blooming for up to one year.

✱ *My current book, "Easy Gardens for South Florida", will be expanded to include the entire state in 2004.*

GROWING CONDITIONS

LIGHT: Light shade to full sun. Untested in medium shade.

WATER: Medium. Ideal watering is twice a week after the initial establishment period. Tolerates water up to 4 times per week. (For detailed information about watering, see Chapter 8 in "Easy Gardens for Florida"*.)

SOIL: Wide range, as long as it is well-drained.

SALT TOLERANCE:
Unknown

WIND TOLERANCE:
Unknown

ZONE: 10a to 11. Untested further north. Highly recommended for container gardens in central and north Florida, if only for the summer. This is a spectacular plant!

PEST PROBLEMS:
None known

PROPAGATION:
Cuttings

Botanical Name: *Mussaenda phillippica 'Aurorae'*

Salmon Mussaenda
Common Name:

CHARACTERISTICS

PLANT TYPE: Deciduous shrub.

AVERAGE SIZE: Easily maintained in the 6 to 8 feet tall by 6 to 8 feet wide range.

GROWTH RATE: Medium

LEAF: Bright green. About 6 inches long by 3 inches wide.

FLOWER: Small, yellow, star-shaped flowers surrounded by large, salmon bracts. The whole thing gets as large as 1 foot across.

AVERAGE LIFE: Unknown. Mine have lasted 5 years so far.

ORIGIN: Tropical Africa and Asia.

CAUTIONS: Completely bare in winter.

SPACING: 4 to 5 feet on center.

Salmon Mussaenda in garden

The most spectacular plant in our summer garden, with huge flowers that bloom for at least six months each year. Very easy to grow. Completely bare all winter.

Salmon Mussaenda in July

General: Salmon Mussaenda is a spectacular plant. It will be one of your favorites, if you use it correctly. In central and north Florida, use it only in containers and move it inside if a freeze threatens. In south Florida, it can be planted outside in the garden, but understand that it is completely bare in the winter! Just sticks with no leaves. People who see it in its summer glory cannot believe that it will actually lose all that beauty in the winter. Friends who have this plant have called me in a state of shock when it begins its dormancy. Many get ready to throw it away, thinking it is dead. Do not throw it away! The leaves and beautiful flowers will return the following spring. Use this plant intelligently. It does not belong next to the front door of your home, greeting your winter guests with sticks. It shines in a summer garden that is enjoyed during the warm months but not as a winter focal point.

Season: Salmon Mussaenda blooms during the warm months, generally starting about May and ending around November. It is completely bare in winter.

To locate plants, go to www.easygardencolor.com

Companions: Use this Mussaenda with other plants that peak in summer. Some large specimens that work well in the same garden include *Mussaenda frondosa*, Crepe Myrtle, and *Costus barbatus*. Smaller companions for a summer garden include Plumbagos, Thryallis and Ruellia 'Purple Showers'.

Salmon Mussaenda (*Mussaenda phillippica "Aurorae"*)

Peach Mussaenda (*Mussaenda erythrophylla 'Queen Sirikit'*)

White Mussaenda (*Mussaenda erythrophylla*)

Similar Mussaendas are available in peach, white, or red. The peach is nice but not quite as strong. I am just beginning to work with the red and white ones.

Planting: Plant any time of the year in native soil. Leave the root ball slightly out of the ground, about 1/4 inch.

Fertilizing: Immediately after planting, fertilize with a well-balanced, slow-release mix that includes minor elements. Repeat in March, June, and October of each year.

Trimming: I trim mine once a year in spring, just as it is beginning to leaf out. I give it enough time for all the good branches to sprout their leaves. In the three years I have had this plant, I have only trimmed off the branches that are dead, leaving the ones with leaves alone.

Salmon Mussaenda is one of the best choices for color impact in containers for anywhere in Florida.

Botanical Name: *Odontonema callistachyum*

Common Name: **Pink Firespike, Firespike Madeline**

CHARACTERISTICS

PLANT TYPE: Shrub

AVERAGE SIZE: Easy to maintain at sizes between 6 feet tall by 6 feet wide and 7 feet tall by 6 feet wide. Larger than the purple or red Firespike.

GROWTH RATE: Fast

LEAF: Medium green and pointed. About 6 inches long by 3 inches wide. Larger than the purple or red Firespike.

FLOWER: Pinkish lavender, showy spike. About 8 inches long by 2 inches wide.

AVERAGE LIFE: 5 to 10 years.

ORIGIN: Unknown

CAUTIONS: None known

SPACING: 6 feet on center. Give this plant a lot of space.

Firespikes are the hummingbird's favorite food in my garden. The Red Firespike is featured in "Easy Gardens for Florida". The purple one is on page 166 and 167 of this book.*

A beautiful, large shrub that offers great color all winter with very little care. Fabulous for hummingbirds and butterflies.

Pink Firespike is very showy when in bloom.

General: The Pink Firespike is one of the best performers in our south Florida winter garden. (See "Zone" on the next page for information about other areas of Florida.) Everyone who sees it comments on its beauty when it is in full bloom. And it blooms for a long time, easily six months nonstop. It's very easy to grow, provided you have a large spot. Give it at least six to eight feet to spread; then, enjoy the winter flowers. This Firespike is larger than the purple or the red. The hummingbirds and butterflies love it.

Season: Pink Firespikes last for many years, flowering for about six months of each winter. When the plant is not in flower, its leaves are attractive. I recommend a hard cutback in summer, which leaves it quite bare for about a month.

A Note on the Name: Three Firespikes are currently available from local nurseries: pink, purple, and red. This pink one has a slightly lavender cast to the flower. But, to avoid confusion, let's call this one pink and the one on pages 166 and 167 purple.

To locate plants, go to www.easygardencolor.com

Companions: Mix the Pink Firespike with other plants that have color in winter. It looks particularly good with yellow flowers or plants that have pink and yellow leaves. See below for suggestions.

Pink Firespike with some companions for south Florida gardens

Planting: Plant any time of the year in native soil. Leave the root ball slightly out of the ground, about 1/4 inch.

Fertilizing: The Pink Firespike is not a heavy feeder. Immediately after planting, fertilize with a well-balanced, slow-release mix that includes minor elements. Repeat in March, June, and October of each year. Do not over-fertilize this plant. Too much will make it grow much too fast. (See detailed fertilization instructions in "Easy Gardens for Florida"*, Chapter 11.)

Trimming: Trim back hard twice a year, once in spring, right after it stops blooming, and again in August. The Pink Firespike can be cut back as low as 18 inches tall without damage. Do not cut too hard from September through March, or you may inhibit its winter blooms. Slight grooming can be done at any time.

✽ My current book, "Easy Gardens for South Florida", will be expanded to include the entire state in 2004.

Botanical Name: *Odontonema cuspidatum*

Common Name: **Purple Firespike, Firespike Caroline**

CHARACTERISTICS

PLANT TYPE: Shrub

AVERAGE SIZE: Easy to maintain at sizes between 4 feet tall by 3 feet wide and 6 feet tall by 5 feet wide.

GROWTH RATE: Fast

LEAF: Dark green and pointed. About 3 to 4 inches long.

FLOWER: Purple spikes, ranging from 4 to 8 inches long. Dramatic and showy.

AVERAGE LIFE: 10 to 20 years.

ORIGIN: Tropical America

CAUTIONS: None known

SPACING: 3 to 5 feet on center.

Firespike comes in red, purple, or pink. The red and purple (above) are quite similar in size and appearance but bloom in opposite seasons. The pink (above, right) is a larger plant that blooms in the winter. All three are great for hummingbirds.

A long-flowering, winter bloomer that is a favorite food of hummingbirds. Great choice for a winter or wildlife garden. Very easy to grow.

Purple Firespike in January

General: Firespike is a fabulous plant. It gives at least six months of color each year with minimal care. The red Firespike is featured in this book's companion, "Easy Gardens for Florida"*. The purple is very similar in appearance and growth habit to the red, with one very important difference: the purple blooms in the cool months, while the red peaks in summer. Both are favorite foods of hummingbirds. Our hummingbirds arrive in October, when the red is in full bloom. As the red flowers slow down in January, the purple is at its peak. The purple continues blooming until the hummingbirds leave in spring. The purple color is unique and quite an asset to winter perennial gardens or wildlife gardens. Understand that both Firespikes are large shrubs and need room to spread. They are also trimmed at different times of the year: the red in winter and the purple in summer.

Season: Purple Firespike blooms all winter in south Florida, starting in November or December and continuing until May or June. The plant looks good, even when the shrub is not in bloom.

To locate plants, go to www.easygardencolor.com

Companions: Plant Purple Firespike with other winter bloomers. It looks good with Giant Shrimps on either side and a border of Red Dragonwing Begonias. Or, surround it with Red Pentas and a border of 'Fruit Cocktails'. Other tall specimens that work well in the same winter garden include Brunfelsia, Chinese Hat, and Bougainvillea.

Purple Firespike with some companions

Planting: Plant any time of the year in native soil. Leave the root ball slightly out of the ground, about 1/4 inch.

Fertilizing: Immediately after planting, fertilize with a well-balanced, slow-release mix that includes minor elements. Repeat in March, June, and October of each year. (See detailed fertilization instructions in "Easy Gardens for Florida"*, Chapter 11.)

Trimming: The key to the success of this plant is a yearly, hard cutback. Cut it almost to the ground when it stops flowering, generally in May. Do not cut it back again until the following year at the same time. You can groom it in between the hard cutbacks. Occasionally, a branch will fall on the ground. Cut that one back to the base at any time.

GROWING CONDITIONS

LIGHT: Medium shade to full sun. Blooms the same in either situation. Not for dense shade.

WATER: Medium. Ideal watering is twice a week after the initial establishment period. Tolerates water up to 4 times per week. Requires more water when grown in containers.

SOIL: Wide range, as long as it is well-drained.

SALT TOLERANCE: Low

WIND TOLERANCE: Low

ZONE: Untested further north than 10a. The Red Firespike has thrived in our Mississippi trial garden, which is in zone 7. It dies back in the first freeze and re-appears the following spring. It blooms in fall in zone 7, and doesn't get as large as our south Florida Firespikes. If you have experience with the pink or purple Firespike in zones 8 or 9, please let us know at www.easygardencolor.com.

PEST PROBLEMS: Snails occasionally

PROPAGATION: Cuttings. Very easy to root.

Botanical Name: *Pentas lanceolata red*

Common Name: **Red Pentas**

CHARACTERISTICS

PLANT TYPE:
Herbaceous perennial

AVERAGE SIZE: Easy to maintain at sizes between 3 feet tall by 2 feet wide and 5 feet tall by 3 feet wide.

GROWTH RATE: Fast

LEAF: Medium green and pointed. About 2 inches long by 3/4 inch wide.

FLOWER: Bright red clusters of small, star-shaped flowers. Clusters measure about 1 1/2 inches to 2 inches wide.

AVERAGE LIFE: 2 to 4 years.

ORIGIN: Tropical Africa

CAUTIONS: None known

SPACING: 2 to 3 feet on center.

Red Pentas bordered with Juniper

One of the oldest and tallest Penta varieties. Very easy and longer-lived than most Pentas. Fabulous for butterflies and hummingbirds.

Red Pentas sheared into a manicured form. They take shearing well but lose their blooms for at least a month afterward.

General: Red Pentas offer one of the most intense reds of our flower kingdom and are one of the top butterfly plants. This variety, along with the Cranberry and Starburst Pentas covered in "Easy Gardens for Florida"*, are the best, short-term, perennial Pentas we tried. The three live for an average of three years in zones 9 through 11 and are much stronger varieties than many of the others we tested. Considering their constant blooms and low cost, they are an excellent value. Since the Red Penta grows from three to five feet tall, it is not the Penta for low borders. The "New Look" Pentas (see pages 42 and 43) offer much lower height but also a much shorter lifespan.

Season: Pentas bloom all year, except for periods after freezes.

Left: Red Pentas informally trimmed. They are easier to maintain and bloom more if trimmed once or twice a year. This informal look is very different from the manicured plants above.

To locate plants, go to www.easygardencolor.com

Companions: Red Pentas look good with other bright-colored flowers, particularly yellows, blues, and purples. The round flower contrasts nicely with spiky flowers, like Salvias and Blue Porterflowers. Milkweed, Lantana, Jatropha, and the Blue or Pink Porterflower make excellent companions for butterfly gardens.

Blue Porterflower

Red Pentas

Yellow Salvia

Red Pentas and some companions. This combination is excellent for butterflies. The Pentas and Yellow Salvia are a great combination for south or central Florida.

Planting: Plant any time of the year in native soil. Leave the root ball slightly out of the ground, about 1/4 inch. (See detailed planting instructions in "Easy Gardens for Florida"*, Chapter 11.)

Fertilizing: Immediately after planting, fertilize with a well-balanced, slow-release mix that includes minor elements. Repeat in March, June, and October of each year. (See detailed fertilization instructions in "Easy Gardens for Florida"*, Chapter 11.)

Trimming: For the manicured look shown opposite top, machine shear (with electric or gas hedge trimmers) four times a year or as needed to maintain the neat form. They will stop blooming for a few weeks or more after each trimming. The plants will live longer if hand-trimmed hard, all the way back to sticks, once a year in summer. For the informal look shown opposite bottom, the annual, hard cutback may suffice, with some light grooming in between.

* My current book, "Easy Gardens for South Florida", will be expanded to include the entire state in 2004.

Botanical Name: *Rhododendron spp. (Azaleas)*

Common Name: **Azaleas**

CHARACTERISTICS

PLANT TYPE: Evergreen or deciduous shrub.

AVERAGE SIZE: Wide range of sizes available, from low and spreading to quite large.

GROWTH RATE: Medium

LEAF: Medium green. Size varies by type.

FLOWER: Pink, red, white, yellow, or purple. Singles or doubles. Size varies by type.

AVERAGE LIFE: 10 years plus in north Florida. The life-span decreases the further south you go. The plants may only last a few years in the southern part of central Florida.

ORIGIN: Most evergreen Azaleas are native to Eastern Asia. Most deciduous Azaleas are native to North America, some to Florida.

CAUTIONS: None known

SPACING: 3 to 4 feet on center for average-sized Azaleas. More space for larger ones.

Note: There are 4 native azaleas found mainly in the northern part of the state. R. austrimun, R. clalendulcaeaum and R. canescens are deciduous. R. chapmanii is evergreen.

One of the most popular flowering shrubs in the southeastern United States.

Azaleas planted under Oaks and Magnolias

General: Over 800 Azalea selections exist today. They are one of the most popular landscape shrubs in the southeastern United States. However, many of the Azaleas found further north than Florida do not thrive here because they require more cold. It is important to buy Azaleas from a nursery that sells plants suitable for your specific Florida location.

Azalea Regions in Florida: Azaleas need cold weather to do well. They do best in the northern part of Florida, moderately well in central Florida, and not too well in the southern part of the state. During a cold decade, like the 1980's, they did much better than during a warm decade, like the 1990's. The native, deciduous Azaleas should only be planted in the colder, northern part of the state. Many non-native, evergreen Azaleas, particularly hybrids, do relatively well further south and into the central part of the state. The 'Southern India' Azaleas are one of the hybrids more suited for central and north Florida. I have tried many different Azaleas in south Florida without much success. They live a year or two, flowering for a brief time in winter. I have found them very useful for containers in south Florida because the small Azaleas in full bloom have such a high percentage of color.

Season: Most bloom for 3 to 4 weeks from late February to early April. Plants at the southernmost tip of their zone, e.g., Orlando, may only bloom for a week or so, depending on how cold it is that year.

To locate plants, go to www.easygardencolor.com

Companions: Azaleas look beautiful planted in groups of different types, creating a small botanical collection. Or, plant them with other plants that bloom in spring, like Roses, Hydrangeas, and late-blooming Camellias.

Planting: Plant containerized plants any time of the year. Transplant plants from one part of the garden to another in winter. Leave the root ball slightly out of the ground, about 1/4 inch. Planting Azaleas too deep is the number one cause of future problems and premature death.

Fertilizing: Immediately after planting, fertilize with a good-quality mix that is specifically for Azaleas. Repeat in March and July.

Trimming: Prune every three to five years after the plant has stopped flowering. Do not prune after early June because you will inhibit blooming the next season. However, you can remove long, unruly 'water sprouts' at any time. Remove any dead wood and crossed branches. Trim the remainder of the plant to define an attractive, full shape.

For More Information: There is a free article on the internet with extensive information about growing Azaleas specifically in Florida. Go to http://edis.ifas.ufl.edu/BODY-MG019 and find "Azaleas for Florida" by Dewayne L. Ingram and James T. Midcap. Fact Sheet OH-37, a series of the Environmental Horticulture Department, Florida Cooperative Extension Service, Institute of Food and Agricultural Sciences, University of Florida. Publication date: July 1990.

* My current book, "Easy Gardens for South Florida", will be expanded to include the entire state in 2004.

GROWING CONDITIONS

LIGHT: LIght shade, like under Oaks or Pines, is ideal. They do not bloom much in too much shade, nor do they flourish in western or southern sun.

WATER: Medium. Ideal watering is once a week after the initial establishment period. Water deeply, to wet the soil down to 14 to 16 inches. Tolerates water up to 4 times per week. Requires more water in containers. (For detailed information, see Chapter 8 in "Easy Gardens for Florida"*.)

SOIL: Wide range, as long as it is well-drained. Good drainage is critical to the success of this plant. Azaleas prefer an acid soil with a pH of 4.5 to 5.5. See article referenced under "For More Information".

SALT TOLERANCE: Low

WIND TOLERANCE: Unknown

ZONE: 6 to 9

PEST PROBLEMS: Caterpillars, mites, root rot, lacewings, leafminors. See article referenced under "For More Information".

PROPAGATION: Root cuttings of 3 to 4 inches long of evergreen Azaleas in June. Propagate deciduous azaleas by seed or air-layering.

Botanical Name: *Rondeletia leucophylla*
Common Name: **Panama Rose**

A pretty, cool-weather bloomer that is a welcome addition to winter gardens.

CHARACTERISTICS

PLANT TYPE: Evergreen shrub. Also grows as a small tree, if trained into a single trunk from the time it is very small. I have not had experience with it as a small tree.

AVERAGE SIZE: Easily maintained in the 4 to 5 feet tall by 4 feet wide range. I have only been testing the plant for 2 years, trimming it once each summer. This is the size it has attained after this time period. I do not know how large it will be 10 years from now.

GROWTH RATE: Medium

LEAF: Small and medium green. About 2 inches long by 3/4 inch wide.

FLOWER: Pink cluster measuring about 1 1/2 inches across.

AVERAGE LIFE: Unknown. I have seen them alive for 4 years so far and thriving. This looks like a 10 to 15 year shrub. I had one fatality after 3 years in my trial garden.

ORIGIN: Central and South America.

CAUTIONS: None known

SPACING: 3 to 4 feet on center.

Panama Rose is the large pink shrub in the middle of this winter garden. Walking Iris is the spiky plant directly in front. 'Victoria Blue' Salvia forms the border, and Brunfelsia is the purple plant behind the Panama Rose.

General: When I first saw the Panama Rose, it looked small and rather nondescript. I quickly thought the Cranberry Penta was a far superior plant with the same look. But, a few years' experience changed my opinion. The Panama Rose is not a small, short-lived perennial like Pentas; rather, it is a large, woody shrub that lasts many years and blooms for the entire winter. It is very easy to grow and a welcome addition to the winter garden. Although it is not a spectacular specimen that stands alone, like Bougainvillea or Brunfelsia, it works beautifully to accentuate these specimens.

Season: Panama Rose blooms in winter, starting in late October and ending in May or June. When the plant is not in flower, its leaves are attractive. This one flowers in winter.

To locate plants, go to www.easygardencolor.com

Companions: Mix Panama Rose with other winter-blooming plants. For a stunning grouping, plant Brunfelsia as the tallest layer, place Panama Rose in the middle and use 'Fruit Cocktail' as the border. Other great companions include Giant Shrimps, Golden Shrimps, Icetone Crotons, and Purple Firespikes.

Panama Rose and some companions

GROWING CONDITIONS

LIGHT: Full sun to light shade. Untested in medium shade.

WATER: Low. Ideal watering is once or twice a week after the initial establishment period. Tolerates water up to 4 times per week. Requires more water when grown in containers. (For detailed information about watering, see Chapter 8 in "Easy Gardens for Florida"*.)

SOIL: Wide range, as long as it is well-drained.

SALT TOLERANCE: Unknown

WIND TOLERANCE: Medium

ZONE: 10a to 11. Untested in zone 9. Many refer to it as half-hardy in central Florida.

PEST PROBLEMS: None known

PROPAGATION: Cuttings

Planting: Plant any time of the year in native soil. Leave the root ball slightly out of the ground, about 1/4 inch. (See detailed planting instructions in "Easy Gardens for Florida"*, Chapter 11.)

Fertilizing: Immediately after planting, fertilize with a well-balanced, slow-release mix that includes minor elements. Repeat in March, June, and October of each year. (See detailed fertilization instructions in "Easy Gardens for Florida"*, Chapter 11.)

Trimming: Trim after the plant has finished blooming, in spring or early summer. We trim ours just this once, cutting it back hard. I have not tried trimming it back later than August for fear that fall cutbacks will inhibit winter blooming.

My current book, "Easy Gardens for South Florida", will be expanded to include the entire state in 2004.

Botanical Name: *Rosa hybrids*
Common Name: **Roses**

CHARACTERISTICS

PLANT TYPE: Shrub

AVERAGE SIZE: Many different sizes available, from dwarfs to large climbers. Average height in Florida is 4 feet tall.

GROWTH RATE: Medium

LEAF: Varies by type

FLOWER: Every color and size imaginable.

AVERAGE LIFE: 5 to 20 years, if cared for properly. Lives longer in the northern part of the state than the far south.

ORIGIN: Hybrid

CAUTIONS: Thorns

SPACING: Miniature Roses require as little as 12 inches of space, while large Roses need up to 8 feet for a single plant. They need good air circulation around each plant.

New Rose book: "Nelsons' Guide to Florida Roses" by Mark Nelson is available at www.micklers.com. Go to products then gardening. Or, call Mickler's at 407-365-8500. This book covers Roses in Florida in a great deal of detail.

For More Information: I used an excellent article for my research that is available for free on the internet. It is called "Rose Culture" by S. E. McFadden. Go to http://edis.ifas.ufl.edu/BODY_MG0 36. This document is Circular 344, Florida Cooperative extension Service, Institute of Food and Agricultural Sciences, University of Florida. First published: June 1990. Reviewed: March 1991.

One of the most popular flowers in the world.

'Belinda's Dream'   'La Marne'

General: Most Roses are high maintenance plants in Florida, having been bred for flower size, color, and fragrance. Maintaining beautiful blooms on perfectly-formed shrubs is ideal for someone who wants a hobby that requires weekly work. Gardeners who are serious about collecting Roses should check with their county extension office to find the local Rose society, which is the best source for local information about this fulfilling pastime. And, don't expect to have compact shrubs loaded with blooms, like in Connecticut or Oregon. The plants grow longer and lankier in Florida and do not have anywhere near the percentage of color as those grown in colder climates. Most Roses do better here if they are grafted onto the roots of another plant. The rootstock that has the best success is *Rosa fortuniana*, which likes the Florida climate. Alex Dewar, of Dewar's Roses in Apopka (the largest Rose grower in the world), says that 80% of the Roses grown in Florida are grafted onto *Dr. Huey* rootstock because they grow faster that way. Plants grown on the *fortuniana* rootstock live longer and bloom more, but are more expensive.

New, Easy Roses: Nelsons' Florida Roses, a nursery in Apopka, has two new Roses that behave like easy, landscape shrubs. They need the same care as the rest of the plants in your garden and almost never need spraying. "Belinda's Dream" (pictured above) is about ten years old and features dense growth, fragrance, and long stems that allow for attractive arrangements in a vase. "Knock Out" is three years old and, while not as good for cutting, blooms like crazy with very little special care. If you are interested in easy Roses, ask your garden center for the longest-blooming types that require the least care.

Old Garden Roses: Roses planted before 1867 are called Old Garden Roses. They do not look thick and lush like they would in colder climates, but they bloom a lot and do not require as much spraying as many of the newer hybrids. And they require the same care as the rest of the plants in your garden. Old Garden Roses generally have smaller flowers but bloom more profusely than modern ones. Jon's Nursery in Eustis is growing only these old or antique Roses.

To locate plants, go to www.easygardencolor.com

Companions: For a formal rose garden, edge the garden with a low-growing hedge, like Ilex, and plant the Roses in a grid pattern. Keep the bed relatively narrow so that you can reach all the plants to cut the flowers. A bed that is two rows deep is ideal. Old Garden Roses are also appropriate for informal cottage gardens, planted among other loose perennials like Plumbago, Thryallis, and Crepe Myrtle.

'Louis Philippe' or Cracker Rose

Since I had killed every Rose I had ever planted in Florida, I issued a challenge to Jane Burgeff of Jane's Herbs and Things in Fort Lauderdale. She said she had easy Roses, and I asked her to prove it! She sold me this 'Louis Philippe' (an Old Garden Rose) that has lived happily in my low-maintenance garden for the last 3 years with no spraying or special attention.

Planting: Bare-root Roses do best planted in November in south and central Florida, and December or January in north Florida. Containerized Roses can be planted any time. Plant in soil enriched with organic matter, like peat moss, manure, and compost, unless the Roses are among the few that are very well-adapted to your native soil. Leave the root ball slightly out of the ground, about 1/4 inch.

Fertilizing: Roses are heavy feeders. Fertilize immediately after planting, with a well-balanced, slow-release mix that includes minor elements. Repeat each time the plant produces a flush of blooms, usually five times a year in north Florida and seven times a year in south Florida. For easy Roses, fertilize three times per year in March, June, and October.

Trimming: For perfect Roses, groom your plants often. Remove faded flowers, crossed branches, and any dead wood after each bloom flush. Remove suckers that appear from the rootstock below the graft spot. I do not take the time to groom my easy Roses, just prune them twice a year in my south Florida garden. In central and north Florida, prune once a year during December or January. Remove no more than half the plant at each pruning.

Season: Roses grow all year in south and central Florida and for about nine months a year in north Florida. Each plant produces blooms in flushes - five to seven per year. Each flush lasts one to three weeks. Expect a few flowers in between cycles.

Botanical Name: *Salvia leucantha*
Common Name: **Mexican Sage**

CHARACTERISTICS

PLANT TYPE:
Herbaceous perennial

AVERAGE SIZE: Easily maintained in the 2 to 3 feet tall by 2 to 3 feet wide range.

GROWTH RATE: Medium

LEAF: Small, pointed and grey-green. About 1 1/2 inches long by 1/2 inch wide.

FLOWER: Long, velvety spike. About 6 inches long by 3/4 inch wide. Some varieties are all purple, while others are purple and white.

AVERAGE LIFE: 5 years

ORIGIN: Mexico

CAUTIONS: None known

SPACING: 2 feet on center.

Below: Salvia leucantha growing in shade. It has a wispy, wildflower look in a medium-shade situation. The plant grows much thicker in sun, as shown in the other photos on these 2 pages.

An excellent perennial Salvia that thrives throughout Florida.

Salvia leucantha and yellow Lantana in October

General: I tested many perennial Salvias in my south Florida trial gardens. Most lasted only one season. This one lasted a full five years and is well worth its low price. It is cold-hardy for all of Florida, but dies back in the winter in the first freeze. This Salvia comes in many different shades of purple, some tipped with white. The solid purple variety is not as showy as the purple and white. Buy this plant while it is blooming so that you can see what type of flowers it has.

Season: Salvia leucantha flowers in fall and early winter for about two to three months..

Right: Salvia leucantha planted at an entry. Entry plantings should look good all the time. Since Salvia leucantha has to be cut back hard and goes through a bad period, the Blue Potato tree takes over as an entry accent when the Salvia is short. Mixed Pentas and Lantana form the groundcovers.

To locate plants, go to www.easygardencolor.com

Companions: Use Salvia leucantha with other light-textured flowers that bloom in fall. Some excellent choices include Pentas, Lantana, and Milkweed, as shown below.

Salvia leucantha and some companions

Planting: Plant any time of the year in native soil. Leave the root ball slightly out of the ground, about 1/4 inch. (See detailed planting instructions in "Easy Gardens for Florida"*, Chapter 11.)

Fertilizing: Immediately after planting, fertilize with a well-balanced, slow-release mix that includes minor elements. Repeat in March, June, and October of each year.

Trimming: Dead-heading (removing dead flowers as they fade) encourages more blooms and a more upright growth habit. I have never done this, however, and simply cut the whole shrub to the ground once a year in winter, after it has stopped blooming. Wait until it looks like the whole top of the shrub is dying. Then, cut all the old growth off, and you will see new branches sprouting from the base.

My current book, "Easy Gardens for South Florida", will be expanded to include the entire state in 2004.

LIGHT: Light shade to full sun. Flowers some in medium shade, but much more in sun.

WATER: Low. Ideal watering is once or twice a week after the initial establishment period. Tolerates water up to 3 times per week. Requires more water when grown in containers. (For detailed information about watering, see Chapter 8 in "Easy Gardens for Florida"*.)

SOIL: Wide range, as long as it is well-drained.

SALT TOLERANCE: Medium, at least. I have not tested this plant in a high salt situation.

WIND TOLERANCE: Medium

ZONE: Grows well in all of Florida. In south Florida, this plant is evergreen. Further north, it dies back to the ground in the first freeze and reappears the next spring. We tested this Salvia in zone 7, where it has been thriving for the last 10 years.

PEST PROBLEMS: None known

PROPAGATION: Seeds or cuttings.

Botanical Name: *Salvia madrensis*

Common Name:
Yellow Salvia, Forsythia Sage

CHARACTERISTICS

PLANT TYPE:
Herbaceous perennial

AVERAGE SIZE: Easy to maintain at sizes between 4 feet tall by 4 feet wide and 6 feet tall by 5 feet wide.

GROWTH RATE: Medium

LEAF: Medium green and shaped like a heart. About 2 inches long on square stems.

FLOWER: Long, yellow spike up to 12 inches long.

AVERAGE LIFE: Thrived for the first 3 years of our trials. I do not know how long beyond that it continues to live.

ORIGIN: Mexico

CAUTIONS: None known

SPACING: 3 to 4 feet on center.

The longest-blooming perennial Salvia from our trials. Showy and full of blooms all winter long, or until the first frost. Grows well throughout Florida.

The lemon-yellow blooms of this Salvia offer an attractive color and interesting texture to informal gardens throughout Florida.

General: Yellow Salvia is a delightful shrub. It is easy to grow and quite beautiful in the winter, when we like to spend time outside. It bloomed longer than any of the other perennial Salvias in our trials. And, while most perennial Salvias we tested did not live for more than one season, this one kept on going for the entire three-year trial. I do not know how long beyond three years it continues to live. This Salvia is easy to grow and blooms happily in sun or medium shade.

Season: Yellow Salvia blooms all winter, starting in early fall and lasting until spring in frost-free areas. Further north, it blooms from early fall until the first freeze.

To locate plants, go to www.easygardencolor.com

Companions: A beautiful, large grouping for south Florida includes *Dombeya 'Seminole'* in the center, Brunfelsia on either side, and a border of Yellow Salvia. Red Pentas and Purple Lantana are good perennial companions in south or central Florida, or annual companions further north.

Yellow Salvia and some companions

Planting: Plant any time of the year in native soil. Leave the root ball slightly out of the ground, about 1/4 inch. (See detailed planting instructions in "Easy Gardens for Florida"*, Chapter 11.)

Fertilizing: Immediately after planting, fertilize with a well-balanced, slow-release mix that includes minor elements. Repeat in March, June, and October of each year. (See detailed fertilization instructions in "Easy Gardens for Florida"*, Chapter 11.)

Trimming: Trim hard once a year in late spring or early summer, shortly after the shrub stops blooming. Do not trim after August, or it might not bloom the following winter.

* My current book, "Easy Gardens for South Florida", will be expanded to include the entire state in 2004.

Botanical Name: *Stachytarpheta speciosa*
Common Name: Pink Porterflower, Coral Porterweed

CHARACTERISTICS

PLANT TYPE: Evergreen shrub.

AVERAGE SIZE: Easy to maintain at sizes between 5 feet tall by 5 feet wide and 6 feet tall by 8 feet wide.

GROWTH RATE: Fast

LEAF: Light, olive green. Size varies a lot, based on size of the plant and light conditions. The leaf is smallest (about 2 inches long) when the plant is small and growing in full sun. It is largest (to 6 inches long) when the plant is mature and growing in shade.

FLOWER: Unusual, green spikes hold coral flowers. The coral portion is about 3/4 inch long. Sometimes, it is solid coral; other times, it is light and dark on the same flower.

AVERAGE LIFE: 5 to 10 years.

ORIGIN: Tropical America

CAUTIONS: None known

SPACING: 3 to 4 feet on center.

One of our best shrubs for butterflies and hummingbirds. Larger than the Blue Porterflower.

Pink Porterflower in full bloom

General: Pink Porterflower is a great shrub for attracting butterflies and hummingbirds - one of the best. But, it is large, rather straggly looking, and certainly not one of our best landscape plants. Use it sparingly, surrounding it with other lush vegetation. Then, its flowers will peak out from among other leaves, and the unattractive form of the shrub will not be so noticeable. It gets a lot larger than most people expect, spreading horizontally to eight feet wide. But, for all its disadvantages, your butterflies and hummingbirds will thank you for planting one.

Season: The Pink or Coral Porterflower blooms on and off for most of the year, peaking in the warm months.

Swallowtail butterfly happily drinking the nectar of the Pink Porterflower. Whenever I am looking for butterflies to photograph, I always go to my Pink Porterflowers first.

To locate plants, go to www.easygardencolor.com

Companions: Plant the Pink Porterflower with other plants that attract butterflies and hummingbirds. Some good choices include Firespikes, Golden Shrimp Plants, Salvias, Firebushes, and Pentas.

LIGHT: Light shade to full sun.

WATER: Low. Ideal watering is once or twice a week after the initial establishment period. Tolerates water up to 3 times per week. (For detailed information about watering, see Chapter 8 in "Easy Gardens for Florida"*.)

SOIL: Wide range, as long as it is well-drained.

SALT TOLERANCE: Unknown

WIND TOLERANCE: Unknown

ZONE: 10a to 11. Untested further north. If you have experience with this plant in central or north Florida (and would like to share it) contact me at the Web site, www.easygardencolor.com.

PEST PROBLEMS: None known

PROPAGATION: Cuttings

Pink Porterflower and some companions

Planting: Plant any time of the year in native soil. Leave the root ball slightly out of the ground, about 1/4 inch. (See detailed planting instructions in "Easy Gardens for Florida"*, Chapter 11.)

Fertilizing: Immediately after planting, fertilize with a well-balanced, slow-release mix that includes minor elements. Repeat in March, June, and October of each year. (See detailed fertilization instructions in "Easy Gardens for Florida"*, Chapter 11.)

Trimming: Trim as needed to control size. Plan on giving this plant room to spread so that you are not constantly hacking at it in a vain attempt to keep it small.

My current book, "Easy Gardens for South Florida", will be expanded to include the entire state in 2004.

Botanical Name: *Tecomaria capensis*

Common Name: Cape Honeysuckle

CHARACTERISTICS

PLANT TYPE: Evergreen shrub or vine.

AVERAGE SIZE: In areas that don't freeze, it is easy to maintain at sizes between 4 feet tall by 4 feet wide and 6 feet tall by 5 feet wide. If it freezes to the ground, it grows to about 3 1/2 feet before the next winter.

GROWTH RATE: Fast

LEAF: Medium green and pointed. About 1 1/2 inches long by 3/4 inch wide.

FLOWER: Bright orange, tubular flower that grows in showy clusters. Also available in yellow or peach, which did not do well in our south Florida trials. We did not test the yellow or peach further north.

AVERAGE LIFE: 10 years plus.

ORIGIN: South Africa

CAUTIONS: Becoming a weed in parts of Florida. Very fast growing.

SPACING: 4 to 5 feet on center in frost free areas. 2 to 3 feet on center further north.

One of the favorite foods of hummingbirds. Thrives throughout Florida.

General: Cape Honeysuckle is a large, sprawling shrub that will also grow as a vine, depending on how it is trained when young. I attempted to train one into a single-trunked tree, and it did not work. The thin trunk couldn't support the weight of the fast-growing crown, and it toppled over and died. But it has done surprisingly well in our south Florida trial gardens as a large, multi-trunked shrub. And, to our surprise, it performed quite well in our Mississippi trial gardens, dying back in the winter and returning the following spring. It has taken temperatures down to 15 degrees for three winters straight! The shrub is becoming a weed in parts of Florida and is not a plant for those who want a manicured landscape. However, it is one of our hummingbird's favorite foods and provides bright color for people as well.

Season: Cape Honeysuckle blooms in cool months in Florida, starting in early fall and blooming until the next spring in frost-free areas. If the temperatures drop below freezing, it dies back to the ground and remains dormant for the rest of the winter. After sprouting in spring, it begins to bloom again the following fall. This plant is especially valuable in north Florida, where fall-blooming perennials are not common.

To locate plants, go to www.easygardencolor.com

Companions: Plant Cape Honeysuckle with other plants that bloom in fall or winter. Firespike, Mexican Sage, and Yellow Salvia are good choices for all of Florida. Bougainvillea, Golden Shrimp Plants, and Brunfelsia work well with Cape Honeysuckle in the southern end of the state.

Planting: In south Florida, plant anytime of the year in native soil. In central and north Florida, plant in spring or summer. Leave the root ball slightly out of the ground, about 1/4 inch. (See detailed planting instructions in "Easy Gardens for Florida"*, Chapter 11.)

Fertilizing: Immediately after planting, fertilize with a well-balanced, slow-release mix that includes minor elements. Repeat in March, June, and October of each year. (See detailed fertilization instructions in "Easy Gardens for Florida"*, Chapter 11.)

Trimming: In frost-free areas, accept this plant as an informal, wild sprawler and you can get away with trimming it once or twice a year. Trim it once right after it has stopped blooming and again about two months later. Do not trim it shortly before it blooms or you will not have flowers that year. In freeze-prone areas, trimming is usually not necessary because the cold weather keeps the size of the plant in check. Occasionally, the plant sends out a long, unruly sprout about six or eight feet in the air. Trim this off at any time.

My current book, "Easy Gardens for South Florida", will be expanded to include the entire state in 2004.

GROWING CONDITIONS

LIGHT: Full sun

WATER: Low. Ideal watering is twice a week after the initial establishment period. Tolerates water up to 3 times per week. Requires more water in containers. (For detailed information, see Chapter 8 in "Easy Gardens for Florida"*.)

SOIL: Wide range, as long as it is well-drained. This plant will not grow in poorly-drained soil. The roots may rot.

SALT TOLERANCE: Medium

WIND TOLERANCE: Medium

ZONE: 7 to 11. Untested further north.

PEST PROBLEMS: I have never seen a pest on this plant but have heard of isolated instances of scales and mites.

PROPAGATION: Cuttings

Shrubs: *Notes from our ongoing trials*

Alpinia zerumbet 'Variegata'
Variegated Ginger

Let this one grow large, to at least 5'-6'. Requires grooming. Trim the whole stalk back to the ground if the leaves start to brown. Flowers in zones 10-11, but not further north. Dies back to the ground in freezes but foliage returns as far north as zone 8b. Prefers some shade.

Barleria cristata
Philippine Violet

Inconsistent in our south Florida trials. Bloomed beautifully some years, but not the next. Short bloom period. Better for north Florida, where it blooms in the fall, dies back for the winter, and returns the next spring.

Cactus spp
Cactus

Good in dry times. I had a lot of problems with Cactus in our rainy season, where many filled up with water and died in our trial gardens. Some are native, but to very dry, sandy ridges. Skin irritant.

Callicarpa americana
Beautyberry

Wonderful native shrub that has purple berries in summer. Good for wildlife gardens. Grows well throughout Florida. Light shade to full sun.

Costus speciosus 'Variegatus'
Variegated Crepe Ginger

Beautiful plant for summer shade gardens. Striking, variegated leaves with a weird flower that always draws attention. Large, to 6' tall. Dies back completely in winter, even in south Florida. Zone 8b-11.

Crinum americanum
Crinum Lily

Dramatic, tropical-looking plant with white flowers. Sun to partial shade. Native to Florida. Grows throughout the state. High maintenance in south Florida because of frequent fungus and lubber grasshopper attacks. Poisonous.

Cuphea micropetela
Cigar Plant

Did fairly well in our south Florida trials. Bloomed briefly in fall with very interesting flowers. Grew to about 3' and only lived a few years. Attractive to hummingbirds. Also grows in zone 9. Tested only in sun in zone 10.

Datura metel
Devil's Trumpet

Beautiful flowers on a low-growing shrub that only lasts a year or so. Tested in light shade. Untested north of zone 10. All parts extremely toxic. Do not eat or smell. Irritating to skin and eyes. Deaths reported from this plant.

Dichorisandra thursiflora
Blue Ginger

Beautiful flowers on a medium shrub of about 5' tall. Bloomed for brief periods in shade. Did not live very long, only a year or so. Untested north of our south Florida trial gardens. Grows in zones 7-11.

Dieffenbachia spp.
Dieffenbachia

Indoor use only. I tried these outdoors in south Florida, and they all died from cold. Skin irritant. Highly toxic if eaten, with some deaths reported.

Eranthemum pulchellum
Blue Sage

Striking blue flowers for about a month each winter for 5 years (so far) in our south Florida trial gardens. Shrub is rather straggly. Bloom period is shorter than many other winter perennials. Untested outside of zone 10. Partial shade.

Hibiscus mutabilis
Confederate Rose

Large shrub, to 8', with one of the most beautiful flowers in our trial gardens. Lived for about 2 years in south Florida sun. Much better in Mississippi, where it has been going strong for 4 years and shows no signs of slowing down.

Justicia aurea
Golden Plume

Large shrub, to 8' tall, with striking, large, yellow flowers. We tested it in partial shade. Blooms about half the year, on and off. The leaves are constantly chewed by insects. I ignore the bugs and simply enjoy the flowers. Untested north of zone 10.

Leea coccinea 'Rubra'
Leea

Beautiful shrub about 6' tall. Noted for its striking, dark leaves. After a few years of trials, it seems to be a very tough plant. Prefers some shade. Untested outside of zone 10.

Medinella magnifica
Medinella

One of the most beautiful flowers I have ever seen. Unfortunately, it only bloomed once for a week or so and died within a year. Tested in shade in south Florida.

Pachystachys spicata
Giant Red Shrimp

Unattractive, leggy shrub with gorgeous red flowers for about a month or so in winter. This one is worth having, if you have a large garden and can tuck it in the back. Tested only in zone 10 in partial shade.

Pseuderanthemum laxiflorum
Shooting Star

Mediocre performer, blooming sporadically for a few months each year. Tested in sun and partial shade in south Florida.

Rhododendron spp.
Vireya

I would love to know the secret of success for this one because it is lovely! I tested 3 different colors in partial shade in south Florida. They all died after their first winter. There are many Vireyas, so I will test more.

Salvia 'Indigo Spires'
Indigo Spires Salvia

Spreading, informal shrub that was short-lived (6 months) in our south Florida trials. Useful for a quick burst of color, particularly in new gardens that need some fillers while the more permanent plants fill in.

Spathiphyllum spp.
Peace Lily

Tropical plant often used indoors all over the world. Blooms in deep shade in south Florida, but is almost always plagued by snails eating the leaves when it is planted outdoors. Very cold-sensitive.

Strelitzia reginae
Orange Bird of Paradise

Traditionally used in south and central Florida for its spectacular flowers. I frequently had complaints that it didn't bloom enough and it was time consuming to remove the dead leaves. Sun or partial shade.

Strobilanthus dyeranus
Persian Shield

The most beautiful, iridescent leaves I have ever seen. Very short-lived (about 6 months) in sun or shade in our south Florida trials. Inexpensive and worth planting for its short but beautiful life. Good choice for containers.

Thunbergia erecta
Kings Mantle

Easy, tough shrub that has the unique advantage of blooming when trimmed as a hedge. Other than that, it did not bloom as long as many other perennials in our south Florida trials. Sun or shade. Zones 10-11.

Tibouchina compacta
Tibouchina Shrub

Beautiful purple flowers on a shrub that did well for the first 6 months, then began declining. Grew leggy and only lived about a year. Untested outside of zone 10. Good potential as a short-lived container plant.

CHAPTER 4

VINES

This chapter details some vines with outstanding color characteristics. They either bloom for most of the year or offer spectacular seasonal color.

Many other beautiful vines grow well in Florida - many of them too well. Vines, such as Sky Vine and Flame Vine, both shown in this chapter, have spectacular color but are destructive to our natural forests. They grow so aggressively that they can actually kill trees! Vines are the worst of our invasive plants on land, more destructive than invasive shrubs and trees. So, be careful when buying a vine with which you are not familiar.

Chapter 3 in this book's companion, "Easy Gardens for Florida"*, details many other great vines for color.

For more information about vines here, you can get a free article from the internet. Go to http://edis.ifas.ufl.edu/BODY_MC097 to find the article called "Vines for Florida" by Robert J. Black. This document is Circular 860, Florida Cooperative extension Service, Institute of Food and Agricultural Sciences, University of Florida. Publication date: April, 1990.

Left and above: Bougainvillea (pages 192 to 195). This color is a hybrid photographed in California.

Botanical Name: *Allamanda cathartica*

Common Name: **Vine Allamanda (Yellow)**

CHARACTERISTICS

PLANT TYPE: Vine

AVERAGE SIZE: Keeps growing until you stop it!

GROWTH RATE: Fast

LEAF: Medium green and shiny. About 2 to 3 inches long by 3/4 inch wide.

FLOWER: Lemon yellow. About 3 to 4 inches wide.

AVERAGE LIFE: 20 years plus.

ORIGIN: Brazil

CAUTIONS: Poisonous. All parts of the plant are toxic, though not enough to have caused any deaths of record. The sap is irritating to skin and eyes. Also, the plant has the capability of taking over trees, although not even in a league with Air Potato or Old World Climbing Fern.

SPACING: 10 feet on center.

Note: There are many different kinds of Allamandas. Shrub Allamanda is covered in "Easy Gardens for Florida"*. Dwarf Allamanda is found on page 106 of this book.

General: I have had two very different experiences with vine Allamanda in two of my gardens. Once I planted it in a narrow planter near a pool surrounded by concrete. It did not do well, suffering from frequent nutritional deficiencies and seldom blooming. My next experience was in my current garden that has eight acres of natural pineland vegetation. The Allamanda is growing throughout the woods, without any care whatsoever! Luckily, it is not aggressive enough to wipe out my forest! I cannot account for the different behavior of Allamanda in the two locations, so be prepared for some surprises with this plant. Allamanda is an aggressive grower that requires support, like a trellis or large arbor. This vine is much too big for small arches and wall trellises. It is better suited to large, chain link or iron fences.

Season: Vine Allamanda blooms on and off during the warm months of spring, summer, and fall. Do not expect a profusion of flowers in the winter.

To find plants, go to www.easygardencolor.com

Companions: Allamanda is most useful planted along large fences. Alternate it with other vines for a multi-colored display. The lemon-yellow flowers look good mixed with red, blue, or purple. Red Passionflower and Petrea are two excellent choices. Plant the vines at least 10 feet apart.

Allamanda with some companions

Planting: Plant any time of the year in native soil. Leave the root ball slightly out of the ground, about 1/4 inch. (See detailed planting instructions in "Easy Gardens for Florida"*, Chapter 11.)

Fertilizing: Immediately after planting, fertilize with a well-balanced, slow-release mix that includes minor elements. Repeat in March, June, and October of each year. If the summer is unusually hot and rainy, inspect the leaf color of the plant in August. If it appears washed out, add an additional fertilization at that time. (See detailed fertilization instructions in "Easy Gardens for Florida"*, Chapter 11.)

Trimming: Trim Allamanda during the fall when it has stopped blooming. Or, if it has grown completely out of control, cut the vine at the base, about one foot up from the ground. The vine will grow back from the roots, and all the growth above the cut will die and fall down. Do this major pruning in spring or early summer.

* My current book, "Easy Gardens for South Florida", will be expanded to include the entire state in 2004.

GROWING CONDITIONS

LIGHT: LIght shade to full sun.

WATER: Low. Ideal watering is one a week (at the most) after the initial establishment period. Tolerates water up to 4 times per week. Requires more water when grown in containers. (For detailed information, see Chapter 8 in "Easy Gardens for Florida"*.)

SOIL: Wide range, as long as it is well-drained.

SALT TOLERANCE: Low

WIND TOLERANCE: Unknown

ZONE: Technically, zones 10a to 11 because it is frost-sensitive. Frequently planted in the warmer parts of central Florida. Great summer container plant for north Florida gardens.

PEST PROBLEMS: I have never seen a pest on this plant but have heard of occasional caterpillars and mites.

PROPAGATION: Cuttings

Botanical Name: *Aristolochia gigantea*

Common Name: **Dutchman's Pipe, Calico Flower, Pipevine**

CHARACTERISTICS

PLANT TYPE: Vine

AVERAGE SIZE: This vine is large. Plant it only if you have a lot of space, like a large fence for it to climb. It can send out runners that are 15 to 20 feet long.

GROWTH RATE: Fast

LEAF: Medium green and heart-shaped. Varies in size from about 2 to 5 inches across, depending on the age of the leaf.

FLOWER: Brown and white pattern that resembles calico. The bud looks like a pipe. The flower measures about 3 to 4 inches across.

AVERAGE LIFE: At least 10 years.

ORIGIN: Brazil

CAUTIONS: Can escape into natural areas. Nowhere nearly as aggressive as Sky Vine or Flame Vine. Mine is growing up an Oak Tree and has not damaged the tree at all in 3 years.

SPACING: At least 8 feet on center.

The weirdest flower in my garden. Plant this one for the Pipevine Swallowtail butterflies.

Pipevine in full bloom

General: Butterflies need nectar and larval food plants. The nectar plants are the flowers, like Pentas and Firespikes, that the butterflies drink the nectar from. (They drink from thousands of different flowers.) Larval food plants provide food for the caterpillars that will soon become butterflies. And, the caterpillars are quite picky about which plants to eat. The Pipevine Swallowtail caterpillars eat mainly Pipevine leaves and flowers. The female butterflies lay their eggs underneath the leaves so that the baby caterpillars will have lots to eat the minute they hatch. These vines are like pet food - expect to see lots of chewed up leaves and flowers. But, the benefit is lots of Pipevine Swallowtails - I have had up to 15 at a time flying around my Pipevine! And, the Pipevine caterpillars are quite considerate - they do not eat other plants in the garden.

Season: The plant lives for many years, blooming predominantly during the warmer months.

Companions: Plant Pipevines with flowering plants that provide nectar for the Pipevine Swallowtails. Some of the best nectar plants include Pentas, Jatrophas, Lantanas, Firespikes, and the Pink and Blue Porterflowers.

Left: The flower in full bloom looks like calico. Right: The bud resembles a strange pipe.

Planting: Plant any time of the year in native soil. Leave the root ball slightly out of the ground, about 1/4 inch. (See detailed planting instructions in "Easy Gardens for Florida"*, Chapter 11.)

Fertilizing: Immediately after planting, fertilize with a well-balanced, slow-release mix that includes minor elements. Repeat in March, June, and October of each year. (See detailed fertilization instructions in "Easy Gardens for Florida"*, Chapter 11.)

Trimming: I have never trimmed mine because the caterpillars keep it in check. Be sure that this vine does not escape and grow up trees, as it may do damage to the tree.

Left: Don't kill this bug! This is the caterpillar that will become the Pipevine Swallowtail butterfly. It eats your Pipevine leaves and flowers but doesn't touch the rest of the garden. The Pipevine has a substance in the leaves that is bitter. The bad taste goes into the caterpillars, making them quite untasty to birds, which greatly increases their chances of survival. Larval food plants greatly increase the numbers of butterflies in a garden.

* My current book, "Easy Gardens for South Florida", will be expanded to include the entire state in 2004.

GROWING CONDITIONS

LIGHT: Light shade is ideal.

WATER: Medium. Ideal watering is once or twice a week after the initial establishment period. Tolerates water up to 4 times per week. (For detailed information about watering, see Chapter 8 in "Easy Gardens for Florida"*.)

SOIL: Wide range, as long as it is well-drained.

SALT TOLERANCE: Low

WIND TOLERANCE: Unknown

ZONE: 9b to 11. Hardy to 28 degrees.

PEST PROBLEMS: The caterpillars that eat the leaves are not pests. They are baby butterflies.

PROPAGATION: Cuttings

Botanical Name: *Bougainvillea glabra 'Barbara Karst'*
Common Name: **Red Bougainvillea**

CHARACTERISTICS

PLANT TYPE: Vine, shrub, or small tree, depending on how the plant is maintained. See pages 206 and 207 for the small tree.

AVERAGE SIZE: In the wild, climbs up trees to a height of 20 feet. Maintain at a minimum of 8 feet tall by 6 to 8 feet wide.

GROWTH RATE: Fast

LEAF: Medium green or variegated. The variegated forms did not do well in our south Florida trials but seem to thrive in California. Leaf measures about 1 1/2 inches wide by 2 inches long.

FLOWER: Small, white flowers surrounded by bracts of bright magenta or red. Other Bougainvilleas come in peach, orange, yellow, white, or bicolor. The red and purple were the strongest so far in our south Florida trials. There are many new, beautiful colors we plan to test in the near future.

AVERAGE LIFE: 20 years plus.

ORIGIN: Brazil

CAUTIONS: Sharp spines. Do not plant near walkways where the thorns could harm someone. Also, the flowers stick to pavement and are difficult to remove.

SPACING: 4 to 8 feet on center.

The best known and most spectacular vine of the tropics.

Bougainvillea growing (with support) around a window

General: Red Bougainvillea is one of our most spectacular winter bloomers. It is a high maintenance plant, however, requiring heavy pruning in the summer because of its fast growth. And, since it has sharp thorns, the experience can be painful. It takes us longer to trim our Bougainvilleas than any other plants in our gardens. But, the winter flowers make the summer work well worth the effort.

Differences Between Red and Purple: The common red is larger than the purple, does not bloom quite as long, and its flowers are a more intense color. This red Bougainvillea also requires more space than the purple (see pages 194 and 195 for the purple).

Season: Red Bougainvillea blooms mainly in the winter and spring, starting around January and ending around June or July. The bloom period varies, however, based on rainfall. It peaks in the dry season.

To find plants, go to www.easygardencolor.com

Companions: Bougainvillea does very well in containers, growing up walls and fences, or growing up supports that lead to a trellis. If planting along a large area, alternate purple and red Bougainvilleas for great color impact. Add some bright yellow flowers, like Golden Shrimp Plants, in front. Many of our best winter perennials make great companions for red Bougainvillea. Some examples of larger specimens include Brunfelsia, Giant Shrimp, Chinese Hat, Dombeya, and Shooting Star. If combining Bougainvillea with annuals, avoid Impatiens if they are on the same watering system. The high water needs of the Impatiens can inhibit the blooming of the Bougainvillea. Petunias, Salvias, or Snapdragons are better choices.

Butterflies love Bougainvillea.

Planting: Plant any time of the year in native soil. Leave the root ball slightly out of the ground, about 1/4 inch. Cut the bottom out of the pot and trim off the rim. *Plant it with the sides of the pot left on* because Bougainvilleas like their roots restricted. Bougainvilleas transplant very well during the warm months.

Fertilizing: Immediately after planting, fertilize with a well-balanced, slow-release mix that includes minor elements. Repeat in March, June, and October of each year. If the summer is unusually hot and rainy, inspect the leaf color of the plant in August. If it appears washed out, add an additional fertilization in August. (See detailed fertilization instructions in "Easy Gardens for Florida"*, Chapter 11.)

Trimming: Frequent machine shearing of red Bougainvillea greatly inhibits blooming. Each branch needs to be long before the blooms will appear. The tip of the branch darkens as the bloom is forming. If you want a manicured look, use the purple Bougainvillea instead of the red because it accepts machine shearing and still flowers. Trim the red hard by hand early during the summer, right after it has stopped blooming. The plant grows so fast during the warm months that you may need to trim it monthly in the summer to keep it from taking over the whole garden. Do not do a major trimming after August, or you may inhibit the next winter season's blooming. Grooming or cutting off a long, unruly branch that suddenly appears can be done at any time of the year.

Supporting the Vine: To mount against a wall, first attach lattice (PVC lattice is available cheaply at home improvement stores) or sink anchors with screws in the wall about three to four feet apart to form a grid. Use stretchy plastic tape (commonly available at garden centers) to attach the branches to the supports.

* My current book, "Easy Gardens for South Florida", will be expanded to include the entire state in 2004.

GROWING CONDITIONS

LIGHT: Full sun. Blooms best with sun all day.

WATER: Low. Ideal watering is once a week after the establishment period. Tolerates water up to 3 times per week. Requires more water when grown in containers, where it thrives. Bougainvilleas require rather dry conditions to flower. (For detailed information, see Chapter 8 in "Easy Gardens for Florida"*.)

SOIL: Wide range, as long as it is well-drained.

SALT TOLERANCE: High

WIND TOLERANCE: Medium. Survives in high wind situations, but the leaves and flowers suffer, thinning out and browning. They recover when given time to grow back after the winds stop. Bougainvilleas are also somewhat weak-rooted and can blow out of the ground, particularly if the plant is top heavy and not well anchored.

ZONE: 9 to 11. Dies back in a severe freeze, especially in zone 9. Usually recovers.

PEST PROBLEMS: If you see holes in the leaves, it is probably caterpillars. Do not spray, unless it is quite severe.

PROPAGATION: Cuttings

Bougainvillea glabra (purple)

Botanical Name:
Common Name: Purple Bougainvillea, Palm Beach Purple*

CHARACTERISTICS

PLANT TYPE: Vine, shrub, or small tree, depending on how the plant is maintained. See pages 208 and 209 for the small tree.

AVERAGE SIZE: In the wild, grows up trees to a height of 20 feet. Maintain at a minimum of 7 feet tall by 4 to 8 feet wide.

GROWTH RATE: Fast

LEAF: Medium green. Leaf is smaller than the common red, measuring about 1 inch wide by 1 inch long.

FLOWER: Small, white flowers surrounded by purple bracts.

AVERAGE LIFE: 20 years plus.

ORIGIN: Brazil

CAUTIONS: Sharp spines. Do not plant near walkways where the thorns could harm someone. Also, the flowers stick to pavement and are difficult to remove.

SPACING: 4 to 8 feet on center.

Notes: Many new Bougainvilleas are coming on the market. I have not tested many of them but plan to in the near future.

*Referred to by many different common names.

More compact and longer-blooming than the common red variety.

Since it is more compact, this purple variety makes a better choice than the common red for small spaces like this window. Shrimp Plants and Impatiens are planted in the window box.

General: Purple Bougainvillea is one of our most spectacular winter bloomers. It is a high maintenance plant, however, requiring heavy pruning in the summer because of its fast growth. And, since it has sharp thorns, the experience can be painful. It takes us longer to trim our Bougainvilleas than any other plants in our gardens. But, the winter flowers make the summer work well worth the effort.

Advantages of the Purple: Use the common purple for a more manicured look than the red. It even flowers shortly after machine-shearing, which the red will not do. The purple is smaller, blooms longer (sometimes all year), and it offers a more compact growth habit. Its flowers are a more subdued color, however. The common purple requires a bit less space than the larger red.

Season: Purple Bougainvillea blooms mainly in the winter and spring, starting in about January and ending around June or July. The bloom period varies, however, based on rainfall. It peaks in the dry season, occasionally blooming all year, if the weather is unusually dry.

To find plants, go to www.easygardencolor.com

Companions: Bougainvillea does very well in containers, growing up walls or fences, or growing up supports that lead to a trellis. If planting along a large area, alternate purple and red Bougainvilleas for great color impact. Add some bright yellow flowers, like Golden Shrimp Plants, in front. Many of our best winter perennials make great companions for purple Bougainvillea. Some examples of larger specimens include Rondeletia, Giant Shrimp, Chinese Hat, and Dombeya. If combining Bougainvillea with annuals, avoid Impatiens if they are on the same watering system. The high water needs of the Impatiens inhibit the blooming of the Bougainvillea. Petunias, Salvias, or Snapdragons are better choices.

Purple Bougainvillea with some companions

Planting: Plant any time of the year in native soil. Leave the root ball slightly out of the ground, about 1/4 inch. Cut the bottom out of the pot and trim off the rim. *Plant it with the sides of the pot left on* because Bougainvilleas like their roots restricted. Bougainvilleas transplant very well during the warm months.

Fertilizing: Immediately after planting, fertilize with a well-balanced, slow-release mix that includes minor elements. Repeat in March, June, and October of each year. If the summer is unusually hot and rainy, inspect the leaf color of the plant in August. If it appears washed out, add an additional fertilization in August.

Trimming: Purple Bougainvillea takes machine shearing much better than the red. It also benefits from a hard cutback by hand early during the summer, right after it has stopped blooming. The plant grows so fast during the warm months that you may need to trim it monthly in the summer to keep it from taking over the whole garden. Do not do a major trimming after August, or you may inhibit the next winter season's blooming. Grooming or cutting off a long, unruly branch that suddenly appears can be done at any time of the year.

GROWING CONDITIONS

LIGHT: Full sun. Blooms best with sun all day.

WATER: Low. Ideal watering is once a week after the establishment period. Tolerates water up to 3 times per week. Requires more water when grown in containers, where it thrives. Bougainvilleas require rather dry conditions to flower.

SOIL: Wide range, as long as it is well-drained.

SALT TOLERANCE: High

WIND TOLERANCE: Medium. Survives in high wind situations, but the leaves and flowers suffer, thinning out and browning. They recover when given time to grow back after the winds stop. Bougainvilleas are also somewhat weak-rooted and can blow out of the ground, particularly if the plant is top heavy and not well anchored.

ZONE: 9 to 11. Dies back in a severe freeze, especially in zone 9. Usually recovers.

PEST PROBLEMS: If you see holes in the leaves, it is probably caterpillars. Do not spray, unless it is quite severe.

PROPAGATION: Cuttings

Botanical Name: *Holmskioldia sanquinea*

Chinese or Mandarin Hat Plant

CHARACTERISTICS

PLANT TYPE: Vine, shrub, or small tree. See pages 222 and 223 for information on small tree.

AVERAGE SIZE: As a shrub, grows to about 6 feet. As a vine, grows much hIgher, to the tops of palms.

GROWTH RATE: Fast

LEAF: Medium green and pointed. About 2 inches long by 1 1/4 inches wide.

FLOWER: Small flowers. About 3/4 inch wide. Arranged in clusters. Look like Chinese hats.

AVERAGE LIFE: Unknown. Have been thriving in my trial gardens for 5 years.

ORIGIN: India

CAUTIONS: None known

SPACING: 4 to 6 feet on center.

We are currently testing this pink and purple Chinese Hat.

One of the best vines from my trials. Blooms all winter with very little care. Easy to grow.

Chinese Hat is one of the few flowering plants that blooms even when machine-sheared with hedge trimmers.

General: Chinese Hat Plant is technically a shrub but grows into a vine if it has a support. Or, it can be trained as a small tree, as shown on pages 222 and 223. It will grow along fences, if attached to them, or climb trees, if planted nearby. Its growth habit is a lot like Bougainvillea, except it does not grow as fast or have thorns. The plant blooms all winter and is a great asset to winter perennial gardens. It even blooms after being machine-sheared, which is very unusual. Be sure to plant it in full sun because its blooms quickly fade in even a small amount of shade. It is available in orange, red, or a beautiful combination of pink and purple. The orange and red have both done very well in my trials. I have just started testing the pink and purple; the plant seems weaker but the flowers are more spectacular.

Season: Chinese Hat Plants last for many years. The red and orange bloom in winter and spring, starting around November and lasting until around May. The plants look good when not blooming.

Companions: Use this plant with other perennials that bloom in winter. Some of the best companions include Brunfelsia, Dombeya 'Seminole', and the Golden or Giant Shrimp Plant. Some great vine companions include Queen's Wreath and Pink Petticoat.

LIGHT: Full sun. The blooms fade in even the smallest amount of shade.

WATER: Medium. Ideal watering is twice a week after the initial establishment period. Tolerates water up to 4 times a week. Requires more water when grown in containers. (For detailed information about watering, see Chapter 8 in "Easy Gardens for Florida"*.)

SOIL: Wide range, as long as it is well-drained.

SALT TOLERANCE: Medium

WIND TOLERANCE: Medium

ZONE: 10a to 11. Untested further north.

PEST PROBLEMS: None known. I have never seen a pest on this plant.

PROPAGATION: Cuttings

Chinese Hat and some companions

Planting: Plant any time of the year in native soil. Leave the root ball slightly out of the ground, about 1/4 inch.

Fertilizing: Immediately after planting, fertilize with a well-balanced, slow-release mix that includes minor elements. Repeat in March, June, and October of each year. If the summer is unusually hot and rainy, inspect the leaf color of the plant in August. If it appears washed out, add an additional fertilization in August. (See detailed fertilization instructions in "Easy Gardens for Florida"*, Chapter 11.)

Trimming: This plant can be machine-sheared as needed for a manicured look. We keep ours more natural, pruning once heavily in the summer and trimming the edges two or three more times each year. If the plant is allowed to vine up trees, it seldom needs trimming. I have seen it growing in trees for years without damaging them but, to be on the safe side, check your trees for damage from time to time. If the vine damages the tree, cut it off a few feet from the ground The long pieces that are high up in the tree will die and fall off. The plant will re-grow from the remaining trunks.

* My current book, "Easy Gardens for South Florida", will be expanded to include the entire state in 2004.

Botanical Name: *Tecomanthe venusta*

Common Name: **Pink Petticoat**

CHARACTERISTICS

PLANT TYPE: Vine

AVERAGE SIZE: This is a very large vine. It grows way up into trees and is not recommended for small spaces. It is nowhere near as large as others, like Flame Vine or Sky Vine.

GROWTH RATE: Medium. I thought this was a small plant for the first year it was in my garden. Then, it began growing much faster.

LEAF: Medium green and pointed. Grows in groups of five. Each leaf measures from about 3 to 4 inches long by 1 inch wide.

FLOWER: Spectacular pink and white hanging clusters. Each flower measures about 3 inches long by 1 1/2 inches wide. Clusters can reach 18 inches in diameter.

AVERAGE LIFE: Unknown. Thriving in my trial garden for 4 years so far. This one looks like it would live a good 20 years at least.

ORIGIN: New Guinea

CAUTIONS: Can spread too much.

SPACING: 3 to 4 feet on center.

One of the most beautiful flowers of the tropics. The flower clusters are huge, measuring up to 18 inches across.

Most plants produce flowers at the tips of the branches. Not so for the Pink Petticoat. It has the unusual characteristic of producing flowers from the old stems, making it ideal for viewing from below, like from under an arbor.

General: Pink Petticoat is a spectacular vine that blooms in winter, when we enjoy being outside to appreciate its flowers. The flower clusters are huge, measuring up to 18 inches across. This is one of the most beautiful flowers in our trial gardens. It has the unique characteristic of blooming along the old stems on the inside of the vine. I would love to see it growing on a trellis or pergola because the flowers should hang from beneath the structure, making it look good from underneath. Most vines bloom on the top, where they get sun, and look bad from underneath. Although its bloom period is short, the Pink Petticoat is a great addition to the south Florida landscape.

Season: For the first three years of its trials, the Pink Petticoat bloomed for about a month or two in winter, beginning in December or January. In its fourth year, it had a second spectacular bloom period in the spring.

Companions: Plant Pink Petticoats with other plants that bloom in winter. Some ideal candidates include Brunfelsias, Bougainvilleas, White 'Odorata' Begonias, and Shrimp Plants.

Pink Petticoat with some companions

Planting: Plant any time of the year in native soil. Leave the root ball slightly out of the ground, about 1/4 inch. (See detailed planting instructions in "Easy Gardens for Florida"*, Chapter 11.)

Fertilizing: Immediately after planting, fertilize with a well-balanced, slow-release mix that includes minor elements. Repeat in March, June, and October of each year. (See detailed fertilization instructions in "Easy Gardens for Florida"*, Chapter 11.)

Trimming and Supporting: My Pink Petticoats are growing up a Pine Tree. They are intermingled with Bougainvilleas, which support them. The vines are not hurting the tree after three years and not growing higher than about fifteen feet, or up to the tops of the Bougainvilleas. I have never trimmed the tops of the Pink Petticoats. They send runners out along the ground that should be removed several times per year.

✱ My current book, "Easy Gardens for South Florida", will be expanded to include the entire state in 2004.

GROWING CONDITIONS

LIGHT: Medium shade to full sun.

WATER: I tested this plant with medium water twice a week after it was established. I do not know its tolerances other than that.

SOIL: Wide range, as long as it is well-drained.

SALT TOLERANCE: Unknown

WIND TOLERANCE: Unknown

ZONE: 10a to 11. Untested in zone 9.

PEST PROBLEMS: None known

PROPAGATION: Cuttings

Bauhinia punctata
Orange or Red Orchid

This large vine or shrub has beautiful flowers during the warm months. Its growth habit is similar to Bougainvillea, except it does not train well into a small tree. Use it on a large arbor with Bougainvillea because they bloom in opposite seasons. Give this plant a lot of space, at least 8 feet. Our trials found unexplained variability in the bloom times of different plants - some bloomed for 6 months straight, while others only bloomed for about 2 months a year. Requires support to climb. Tested in sun in zone 10.

Cydista aequinoctialis
Garlic Vine

While shopping for vines with a client of mine, we spotted some spectacular Garlic Vines at a nursery and ordered 10. When the delivery truck arrived and the doors opened, the whole area smelled awful! Yes, they smell like Garlic. The client sent them back to the nursery. But the profusion of beautiful flowers makes this vine worth it for some people. There is some name confusion about this plant. Menninger, in his "Flowering Vines of the World", identifies it as *Pseudocalymma alliacea.*

Gloriosa rothschildiana
Gloriosa Lily

This lovely flower grows from a tuber each summer and dies back each winter. It is ideal for small spots, like a little arbor, because it never gets large enough to take over. But understand that it will be completely gone in the winter. It grows throughout Florida in sun to partial shade, but is highly toxic. Deaths have been reported from ingesting the tuber or its extracts. Stems, leaves, flowers, and seeds are also highly poisonous. A poison control specialist told me that this is one of Florida's most toxic plants.

Mandevillea spp
Mandeville Vine

This beautiful vine is used throughout the world as a summer container plant for sunny spots. It dies in winter in north Florida. In south and central Florida, it is dormant in winter, and sometimes does not return the following summer. I buy one each spring and plant it in the ground next to the arbor that marks the entry to my summer garden. Some years, it returns the next summer, and, other years, it doesn't. But, its low cost, coupled with the beauty of its flowers, makes the effort worthwhile.

To find plants, go to www.easygardencolor.com

Podranea ricasoliana
Pink Trumpet Vine

I had one of these on a fence for about 5 years in partial shade. The flowers were lovely but appeared infrequently for only short periods. Pink Trumpet Vine is a good choice for a collector who has a lot of space to display a variety of vines. Gardeners with only a small space would do better with a vine that blooms longer. Untested north of zone 10.

Pyrostegia venusta
Flame Vine

I planted one of these on a wooden fence in March. Within 8 months, it had grown to a width of 15' and was pulling down the fence! This plant is beautiful but highly invasive. One plant can send out tendrils 70'! I have seen it growing over Pine Trees, like Kudzu. Flame Vine is fairly cold-tolerant, taking temperatures down to 28 degrees. Since it dies back to the ground at 32 degrees, this vine may be useful in parts of central Florida, where freezes would keep it from taking over the world.

Thunbergia alata
Black-eyed Susan Vine

A short-lived, pretty vine that is used throughout the world as an annual. Although it grows as a perennial in its native South Africa, it never made it for more than 6 or 8 months in our south Florida trial gardens. The vine blooms heavily from June until October. It adds an interesting touch to a country garden anywhere in Florida. We tested it in full sun.

Thunbergia grandiflora
Sky Vine

I planted one of these at the bottom of a Pine Tree. It grew up the tree to a height of about 25' within a year! Had I left it there, it would undoubtedly have smothered the tree. Luckily, I cut it at the base and removed the roots before it proceeded to take over the rest of my forest. I have seen this plant growing like Kudzu over what's left of a native forest, covering acres and killing much of what is growing underneath.

CHAPTER 5

SMALL TREES, 8 TO 15 FEET

The small trees in this chapter put the flowers at eye level. They add a new dimension to small gardens, which are traditionally planted with smaller shrubs that are lower than our eyes.

Together with the small trees in Chapter 4 of "Easy Gardens for Florida", these selections offer some of the best small-flowering trees available in our area.

They last for many years, blooming seasonally each year.

There are more flowering trees in the subtropics than in temperate areas. The majority of the trees in this chapter are cold-tolerant only in the southern and central parts of Florida. North Floridians should keep Camelias in mind (124 and 125) because many easily attain the height of small trees.

Small trees are very useful in today's growing number of small gardens. Large trees are frequently misplaced in small areas because the owners do not understand their mature size. The trees in this chapter adapt very well to small areas and maintain their small stature throughout their entire life span.

Plant them in a front landscape to make your house look better.

And, collect your favorites to display in your private side or back yard botanical collection.

Left and above: Dwarf Poinciana (pages 214 and 215)

Botanical Name: *Bauhinia acuminata*

Dwarf White Orchid Tree

CHARACTERISTICS

PLANT TYPE: Small tree

AVERAGE SIZE: About 8 feet tall by 5 to 6 feet wide. I trim it once a year lightly to maintain it at that size.

GROWTH RATE: Medium

LEAF: Shaped like a hoof (dual-lobed). Medium to light green. About 3 inches across.

FLOWER: Beautiful, white flower about 3 inches across. Resembles an Orchid.

AVERAGE LIFE: Over 10 years.

ORIGIN: India and Malaysia.

CAUTIONS: None known

SPACING: 8 feet on center.

A delightful, easy, small tree whose flowers resemble Orchids. Bare in winter. Much smaller than most other Orchid trees.

Dwarf White Orchid in July. The tree is much smaller than other commonly-used Orchid trees.

General: The Dwarf White Orchid Tree is very useful in the south Florida landscape because of its small stature, ease of care, and beauty. It fits well in small spots without quickly outgrowing its space. This tree is also beautiful, evoking a lot of positive compliments by viewers. It is quite easy to maintain, unlike some other Bauhinias that sprout hundreds of tenacious seedlings. But, be careful about where you put it because it is bare and ugly in the winter. The Dwarf White Orchid belongs in a garden where it can be enjoyed in the summer and not noticed in the winter. It is a great choice for a summer garden that is not a winter focal point, like in a side or back yard.

Season: This tree blooms all summer and into the fall. It is partially to completely bare in the winter, with unattractive seed pods persisting well into spring.

To locate plants, go to www.easygardencolor.com

Companions: Use the White Orchid with other plants that bloom in summer. Other flowering trees that work well include Frangipani, Orange Geiger, Crepe Myrtle, and Jatropha. All the different Mussaendas, the most spectacular of our summer-blooming shrubs, are great companions. Plumbagos, Dwarf Allamandas, and Pentas are good for planting underneath the Orchid Tree. And, don't forget the real Orchids! Epidendrums and Spathoglottis are naturals.

Spathoglottis Orchid

Dwarf White Orchid

Epidendrum Orchid

Although not a member of the Orchid family, the white flower looks like an Orchid. The purple Spathoglottis and orange Epidendrum are not only easy to maintain but also fit well underneath the White Orchid Tree.

Planting: Plant any time of the year in native soil. Leave the root ball slightly out of the ground, about 1/4 inch. (See detailed planting instructions in "Easy Gardens for Florida"*, Chapter 11.)

Fertilizing: Immediately after planting, fertilize with a well-balanced, slow-release mix that includes minor elements. Repeat in March, June, and October of each year. If the summer is unusually hot and rainy, inspect the leaf color of the plant in August. If it appears washed out, add an additional fertilization in August. (See detailed fertilization instructions in "Easy Gardens for Florida"*, Chapter 11.)

Trimming: Little required. This is an easy tree. Every few years, cut out any dead branches and shape the top as desired. Trim any unwanted branches from the trunk. The seed pods are unattractive, and remain on the tree too long. If they bother you, remove them.

* My current book, "Easy Gardens for South Florida", will be expanded to include the entire state in 2004.

GROWING CONDITIONS

LIGHT: Light shade to full sun.

WATER: Untested in a low water situation. The plant family has a history of thriving in drought. Our trial gardens are watered twice a week after the plants are established. It thrived under these conditions.

SOIL: Wide range, as long as it is well-drained.

SALT TOLERANCE: Medium

WIND TOLERANCE: Medium

ZONE: 10a to 11. Untested in zone 9.

PEST PROBLEMS: None known

PROPAGATION: Seeds

Botanical Name: *Bougainvillea glabra 'Barbara Karst'*

Common Name: **Red Bougainvillea Tree**

CHARACTERISTICS

PLANT TYPE: Vine, shrub, or small tree, depending on how the plant is maintained. See pages 192 and 193 for the vine.

AVERAGE SIZE: As a vine, grows up trees to a height of 20 feet. As a tree, maintain at a minimum of 7 feet tall by 7 to 12 feet wide. Trees will grow to about 10 to 12 feet tall.

GROWTH RATE: Fast

LEAF: Medium green or variegated. The variegated forms did not do well in our south Florida trials but seem to thrive in California. Leaf measures about 1 1/2 inches wide by 2 inches long.

FLOWER: Small, white flowers surrounded by bracts of bright magenta or red. Other Bougainvilleas come in peach, orange, yellow, white, or bicolors. The red and purple were the strongest so far in our south Florida trials. There are many new, beautiful colors we plan to test in the near future.

AVERAGE LIFE: 20 years plus.

ORIGIN: Brazil

CAUTIONS: Sharp spines. Do not plant near walkways where the thorns could harm someone. Also, the flowers stick to pavement and are difficult to remove.

SPACING: 8 to 15 feet on center.

A vine that can be trained into one of our better, small-flowering trees.

Red Bougainvillea Tree. This tree is a bit top-heavy and will eventually fall if not securely staked and trimmed <u>hard</u> once a year.

General: The red Bougainvillea grows as a tree or a vine. The color is more magenta than red, but it is usually referred to as red. The growth habit of the plant is somewhat different from the purple described on the next two pages; it is larger and does not bloom quite as long. And the red Bougainvillea requires a lot more space than the purple, at least six to eight feet across. Since the branches grow much more aggressively than the trunk, it can easily fall over. Plan to keep it permanently staked. And understand that this is a high-maintenance plant.

Season: Red Bougainvillea blooms mainly in the winter and spring, starting in about January and ending around June. The bloom period varies, however, based on rainfall. It peaks in the dry season.

Tips for turning your vine into a tree: Prune your vine to uncover what will become the trunks of the tree. To start the process, trim all of the small branches from the larger-diameter trunks that are growing from the ground. Then assess the multiple trunks that are left. Choose a few that look the strongest and trim away the rest. The first time you do this, you may start with a huge vine and end up with three bare sticks growing out of the ground. These sticks will become the trunks of the tree. Be sure they are at least six feet tall. The smaller branches will quickly re-grow at the top. As the years progress, trim any unwanted branches from these main trunks. The trunks must be permanently staked. Use a large piece of wood - up to six inches in diameter and eight feet long - for the stake. Bury the stake three to four feet in the ground and tie the Bougainvillea trunks to it, taking care not to strangle the trunks. As the tree grows, it can blow over even with the strongest stake. If this occurs, trim off the small branches, stand the bare trunk up and re-stake it. The small branches grow back.

To locate plants, go to www.easygardencolor.com

Companions: If the trunk of the tree is interesting, do not cover it up with large plants. Stick to low groundcovers in bright colors. Annuals, like Snapdragons, Pansies, and Petunias, are ideal. If planting along a large area, alternate purple and red Bougainvilleas for great color impact. Many of our best winter perennials make great companions for red Bougainvillea. Some examples of larger specimens to plant in the same garden (but not underneath!) include Brunfelsia, Giant Shrimp, Chinese Hat, Dombeya, and Shooting Star.

Red Bougainvillea and some companions. Use it with bright-colored purple or yellow flowers that bloom in winter and spring. Pansies and Petunias bloom at the same time and remain low enough to allow the Bougainvillea trunk to be seen.

Planting: Plant any time of the year in native soil. Leave the root ball slightly out of the ground, about 1/4 inch. Cut the bottom out of the pot and trim off the rim. *Plant it with the sides of the pot left on* because Bougainvilleas like their roots restricted. Bougainvillea transplants very well during the warm months. Be sure to stake the trunk securely and permanently when planting.

Fertilizing: Immediately after planting, fertilize with a well-balanced, slow-release mix that includes minor elements. Repeat in March, June, and October of each year.

Trimming: Frequent machine shearing of red Bougainvillea greatly inhibits blooming. Each branch needs to be long before the blooms will appear. The tip of the branch darkens as the bloom is forming. If you want a manicured look, use the purple Bougainvillea instead of the red because it accepts machine shearing and still flowers. Trim the red hard by hand early during the summer, right after it has stopped blooming. The plant grows so fast during the warm months that you may need to trim it monthly in the summer to keep it from taking over the whole garden. Do not do a major trimming after August, or you may inhibit the next winter season's blooming. Grooming or cutting off a long, unruly branch that suddenly appears can be done at any time of the year. Keep unwanted growth off the trunk to keep the plant looking like a tree.

✳ My current book, "Easy Gardens for South Florida", will be expanded to include the entire state in 2004.

Botanical Name: *Bougainvillea glabra (purple)*
Common Name: **Purple Bougainvillea, Palm Beach Purple***

CHARACTERISTICS

PLANT TYPE: Vine, shrub, or small tree, depending on how the plant is maintained. See pages 194 and 195 for the vine. See page 206 for turning a vine into a tree.

AVERAGE SIZE: In the wild, grows up trees to a height of 20 feet. Maintain at a minimum of 7 feet tall by 6 to 10 feet wide.

GROWTH RATE: Fast

LEAF: Medium green. Leaf is smaller than the common red, measuring about 1 inch wide by 1 inch long.

FLOWER: Small, white flowers surrounded by purple bracts. Other Bougainvilleas come in peach, orange, yellow, white, or bicolor. The red and purple were the strongest so far in our south Florida trials. There are many new, beautiful colors we plan to test in the near future.

AVERAGE LIFE: 20 years plus.

ORIGIN: Brazil

CAUTIONS: Sharp spines. Do not plant near walkways where the thorns could harm someone. Also, the flowers stick to pavement and are difficult to remove.

SPACING: 8 to 12 feet on center.

*Referred to by many different common names.

A vine that can be trained into one of our better, small-flowering trees.

Purple Bougainvillea Tree in January. They must be securely staked.

General: Traditionally used as a vine, Purple Bougainvillea is one of our most spectacular winter bloomers. In the last few years, it has begun to be planted as a tree. The old trunks that support the trees take years to develop. Certain landscaping companies are looking for old Bougainvillea vines in people's yards. If they see one, they leave a note in the mailbox, asking if it is for sale. If the homeowner wants to sell it, they remove it and take it to one of several wholesalers who renovate the large vines into trees. It can take at least a year to complete the renovation, and the large trees are expensive. They require a lot of maintenance after planting - at a minimum, they need frequent pruning - and the tree must be permanently staked to keep it from falling over. But, it performs beautifully - flowering for much of the year, especially in winter. The red Bougainvillea on pages 206 and 207 differs from the purple Bougainvillea on these two pages; the purple is smaller and blooms longer, sometimes all year. The purple also offers a more compact growth habit and flowers shortly after machine shearing. Its flowers are a more subdued color, however.

Season: Purple Bougainvillea blooms mainly in the winter and spring, starting in about January and ending around June or July. The bloom period varies, however, based on rainfall. It peaks in the dry season and occasionally blooms all year in dry years.

To locate plants, go to www.easygardencolor.com

Companions: One of the best characteristics of the Bougainvillea Tree is the interesting trunk. Many are knurled and twisted, filled with character. Do not cover up an interesting trunk with plants. Since most Bougainvillea Trees have short trunks, restrict underplantings to low-growing groundcovers. Dwarf Snapdragons and Petunias are great choices. For flowering-tree impact, plant Golden Sennas and Chinese Hat Trees with this Bougainvillea. And, for great (but short - the Yellow Tab only blooms for about a week!) color impact in spring, pair this plant with Yellow Tabs.

LIGHT: Full sun. Blooms best with sun all day.

WATER: Low. Ideal watering is once a week after the establishment period. Tolerates water up to 3 times per week. Requires more water when grown in containers, where it thrives. Bougainvilleas require rather dry conditions to flower.

SOIL: Wide range, as long as it is well-drained.

SALT TOLERANCE: High

WIND TOLERANCE: Medium. Survives in high wind situations, but the leaves and flowers suffer, thinning out and browning. They recover when given time to grow back after the winds stop. Bougainvilleas are also somewhat weak-rooted and can blow out of the ground, particularly if the plant is top heavy and not well anchored. Bougainvillea trees require excellent staking.

ZONE: 9 to 11. Dies back in a severe freeze, especially in zone 9. Usually recovers.

PEST PROBLEMS: If you see holes in the leaves, it is probably caterpillars. Do not spray unless it is quite severe.

PROPAGATION: Cuttings

Purple Bougainvillea and some companions

Planting: Plant any time of the year in native soil. Leave the root ball slightly out of the ground, about 1/4 inch. Cut the bottom out of the pot and trim off the rim. _Plant it with the sides of the pot left on_ because Bougainvilleas like their roots restricted. Bougainvilleas transplant very well during the warm months. Be sure to stake the tree securely and permanently after planting.

Fertilizing: Immediately after planting, fertilize with a well-balanced, slow-release mix that includes minor elements. Repeat in March, June, and October of each year. If the summer is unusually hot and rainy, inspect the leaf color of the plant in August. If it appears washed out, add an additional fertilization in August. (See detailed fertilization instructions in "Easy Gardens for Florida"*, Chapter 11.)

Trimming: Purple Bougainvillea takes machine shearing much better than the red. It also benefits from a hard cutback by hand early during the summer, right after it has stopped blooming. The plant grows so fast during the warm months that you may need to trim it monthly in the summer to keep it from taking over the whole garden. Do not do a major pruning after August, or you may inhibit the next winter season's blooming. But, the purple blooms much faster after a pruning than the red, so do not hesitate to neaten it up when it is in full bloom. Keep unwanted growth off the trunk to keep the plant looking like a tree.

✻ My current book, "Easy Gardens for South Florida", will be expanded to include the entire state in 2004.

Botanical Name: *Brugmansia spp.*

Common Name: **Angel's Trumpet**

CHARACTERISTICS

PLANT TYPE: Shrub or small tree.

AVERAGE SIZE: Easy to maintain at sizes between 7 feet tall by 6 feet wide and 10 feet tall by 12 feet wide in frost-free areas. Grows about half that size further north.

GROWTH RATE: Fast

LEAF: Medium green and pointed. Up to 12 inches long by 5 inches wide.

FLOWER: Long and thin. Shaped like a trumpet. Up to 8 inches long.

AVERAGE LIFE: The peach (some call it pink) type shown here lives at least 10 years. The other colors (whites and yellows) have only lived a few years in my trials. There are many others that I have not tested.

ORIGIN: Ecuador

CAUTIONS: All parts of the plant are very poisonous, even to smell. Some think of it as a hallucinogenic drug. It makes you a lot more sick than high. Do not eat this plant. It could kill you. Be careful when trimming the plant. If you touch any of the sap to your eyes, you could also develop serious eye problems.

SPACING: 6 to 8 feet on center in frost-free areas. 4 to 5 feet on center further north.

Beautiful flowers with a cost: They are extremely poisonous.

Angel's Trumpet planted with a mass of tropical vegetation. Snowbush is to the left and Canna Lilies in front.

General: The Angel's Trumpet is a plant of extremes. The flowers are spectacular and wonderfully scented. But, all parts of the plant are extremely poisonous. Since they have hallucinogenic properties, some young people attempt to take them as a recreational drug. The effect is awful. They quickly become very sick, and some have died from ingesting this plant. It is wonderfully scented at night, but some who sniff too closely become quite ill. But, it is one of the most spectacular flowering plants in all of Florida. In our Mississippi trials, it has come back from the roots every spring for five years now, surviving temperatures as low as 15 degrees.

Season: In frost-free areas, it is evergreen and blooms on and off all year, including winter. Some say they bloom with the full moon, but I have never confirmed that. Further north, it dies back with the first freeze and reappears in spring, blooming heavily on and off in summer and fall.

To locate plants, go to www.easygardencolor.com

Companions: Angel's Trumpets mix very well with tropical vegetation, like Palms and Elephant Ears. They also look great in flower gardens. In frost-free areas, they develop a leggy growth habit and look best mixed with other large plants so you can hide their unattractive form. They are more attractive when frozen to the ground each year because they do not grow so awkwardly.

LIGHT: Medium shade to full sun. Does not flower in deep shade.

WATER: Medium. Ideal watering is twice a week after the initial establishment period. Tolerates water up to 4 times per week. Requires more water when grown in containers. (For detailed information about watering, see Chapter 8 in "Easy Gardens for Florida"*.)

SOIL: Wide range, as long as it is well-drained.

SALT TOLERANCE: Low

WIND TOLERANCE: Low

ZONE: 7 to 11. Dies back in a frost and reappears in spring. We have had this one reappear for 5 years now in zone 7.

PEST PROBLEMS: The leaves never look good on this plant unless you spray a lot for leaf spot fungus and caterpillars. My advice is to leave it alone and enjoy the flowers.

PROPAGATION: Very easy to grow from cuttings.

Angel's Trumpet and some companions for south Florida gardens

Planting: Plant any time of the year in zones 9 through 11. Plant in spring or summer in zone 8. Leave the root ball slightly out of the ground, about 1/4 inch.

Fertilizing: Immediately after planting, fertilize with a well-balanced, slow-release mix that includes minor elements. Repeat in March, June, and October of each year in zones 9 though 11. Leave off the fall fertilization in the colder areas of zone 8. The leaves of this plant do not look good for a lot of the year. (See detailed fertilization instructions in "Easy Gardens for Florida"*, Chapter 11.)

Trimming: The Angel's Trumpet is a fast-growing, ungainly plant that is next to impossible to keep neatly manicured. Plant it in the middle of a lot of vegetation, and leave it alone for most of the year. Cut it back at least once a summer very hard in frost-free areas.

Important tip for success: I tried many different colors of this plant (yellows and whites) with disappointing results. Then, I discovered the one pictured on these two pages, and it thrived. The bud is yellow, and the flower opens to a peachy pink.

Note: This plant used to be called Datura. Datura now refers to plants that look similar to Angel's Trumpets, except the flower points up and not down.

* My current book, "Easy Gardens for South Florida", will be expanded to include the entire state in 2004.

Botanical Name:	*Brunfelsia grandiflora*
Common Name:	**Yesterday, Today, and Tomorrow Tree**

CHARACTERISTICS

PLANT TYPE: Shrub that can be trained into a small tree when young. For information on the shrub, see pages 110 and 111.

AVERAGE SIZE: Easy to maintain at sizes between 6 feet tall by 5 feet wide and 8 feet tall by 7 feet wide.

GROWTH RATE: Medium

LEAF: Dark, glossy green and pointed. About 4 inches long by 2 inches wide.

FLOWER: Beautiful clusters of three colors, all different shades of purple. Each flower measures about 1 inch across. The flower starts out dark and gets lighter each day.

AVERAGE LIFE: 10 years plus.

ORIGIN: South America

CAUTIONS: Frequently goes through shock after planting, losing many leaves (see "Planting" on opposite page). Also, defoliates much more than most plants in wind. Use in very calm locations.

SPACING: 6 to 8 feet on center.

One of our most beautiful, cool-weather bloomers. A must for winter gardens in protected locations of south Florida.

Brunfelsia Tree in winter. This specimen has a single trunk, which is covered by other plant layers in this garden. One of the advantages of planting it in tree form instead of shrub form is the instant height, which is great for layering.

General: Brunfelsia is an excellent plant for color in winter. Like many of our large shrubs, it can be trained into a tree when young. It is beautiful and quite a conversation piece, with its three colors of flowers. But, it has quirks. It goes through shock frequently after planting, which is lessened by a lot of water; soaker hoses are ideal. The second year in the ground, it is much more comfortable and less thirsty. But, it will not bloom if trimmed at the wrong time of year (see "Trimming", opposite). It needs a calm spot because it will defoliate quickly in too much wind. So, plant it in a sheltered location at the beginning of the rainy season, and trim in summer. You will be very happy with this plant under those conditions.

Season: Brunfelsias flower in winter quite dependably from late November until spring. Most plants are not this dependable with their bloom cycles. I have watched Brunfelsias have buds or blooms beginning at Thanksgiving for the last 10 years. And, it blooms for a full six months without any breaks, which is unusual for our winter perennials. When the plant is not in bloom, the dark green leaves are quite attractive.

To locate plants, go to www.easygardencolor.com

Companions: Plant Brunfelsia with other plants that bloom in winter. A great combination for shade includes Brunfelsia with Pink Angelwing Begonias and Golden Shrimp Plants as shown below. Small trees that work well with Brunfelsia include Golden Senna, Red Bougainvillea, Angel's Trumpet, Turk's Cap, and Chinese Hat.

Golden Shrimp

Angelwing Begonia

Brunfelsia

Brunfelsia with some companions

Planting: Brunfelsias can be planted at any time. Since they need a lot of water after planting, it is easier to get them established in summer when we have a lot of rain. If planted in fall, soaker hoses are ideal to avoid transplant shock. Brunfelsias frequently lose their bottom leaves after planting, but fewer are lost with a lot of water. Be sure to leave the root ball slightly out of the ground, about 1/4 inch.

Fertilizing: Brunfelsias are heavy feeders. Immediately after planting, fertilize with a well-balanced, slow-release mix that includes minor elements. Repeat in March, June, and October of each year. If the summer is unusually hot and rainy, inspect the leaf color of the plant in August. If it appears washed out, add an additional fertilization in August.

Trimming: Trim hard by hand once or twice a year in summer, when it is not blooming. If trimmed after August, this plant will not bloom that year. To maintain its form, trim off any branches that appear on the trunk.

∗ My current book, "Easy Gardens for South Florida", will be expanded to include the entire state in 2004.

LIGHT: Medium shade to full sun. Ideal light is light shade.

WATER: Medium. Ideal watering is twice a week after the initial establishment period. Tolerates water up to 4 times per week. Requires more water when grown in containers. (For detailed information about watering, see Chapter 8 in "Easy Gardens for Florida"∗.)

SOIL: Wide range, as long as it is well-drained.

SALT TOLERANCE: Low

WIND TOLERANCE: Low. Defoliates in wind.

ZONE: 10a to 11

PEST PROBLEMS: Snails, scale

PROPAGATION: Seeds or cuttings.

Recently planted Brunfelsia Tree under-planted with 'Lady Jane' Anthuriums

Botanical Name: *Caesalpinia pulcherrima*

Dwarf Poinciana, Pride of Barbados

CHARACTERISTICS

PLANT TYPE: Large shrub or small tree.

AVERAGE SIZE: About 10 feet tall by 10 feet wide. I have not tried to maintain it smaller.

GROWTH RATE: Medium

LEAF: Fern-like foliage similar to a Royal Poinciana or Cassia Tree.

FLOWER: Comes in 4 different colors, as shown on the next page: orange and yellow, red and yellow, pink and yellow, or solid yellow. Flower measures about 4 inches across.

AVERAGE LIFE: Unknown, but thought to be short-lived, in the 4 to 8 year range.

ORIGIN: West Indies

CAUTIONS: Poisonous and thorny.

SPACING: 6 feet on center.

A great choice for those who love the Royal Poinciana but do not have space for it. Summer bloomer that looks poorly in the winter.

Dwarf Poinciana in full bloom

General: Dwarf Poinciana is a good choice for someone who loves flowers and does not mind a large, untidy tree that looks bad in winter. I have been working with this plant for years - attempting to turn it into a manicured, single-trunked, symmetrical specimen - with absolutely no luck. It took me about 10 years to find one symmetrical enough to photograph (see above). Most are much less tree-like and more like a big, sprawling shrub. But, the flowers are spectacular. I look forward to the blooms each year. Use it in an informal garden, surrounded and intermingled with other foliage. The goal is for it to not show up too much in winter but be visible in its summer and fall prime.

Season: Dwarf Poincianas bloom off and on in summer and fall, usually peaking in fall. The total amount of time they stay in bloom varies a lot from year to year, from about two to five months. They lose many leaves and look poorly in the winter.

To locate plants, go to www.easygardencolor.com

Companions: Plant the Dwarf Poinciana with other plants that peak in fall. Three Dwarf Poincianas together (orange, pink, and yellow) make a wonderful color display. Cassia Trees (Senna surattensis), Lonchocarpus, and Floss Silk Trees are additional trees that bloom at the same time. Be sure to plant other lush plants adjacent to your Dwarf Poincianas. Some good choices include Thryallis, Plumbago, and all the Mussaendas.

Four colors of Dwarf Poinciana - pink, orange, red, and yellow. The pink is called 'Compton' and the yellow 'Flava'.

Planting: Plant any time of the year in south Florida, and in spring or summer in central Florida. Leave the root ball slightly out of the ground, about 1/4 inch. Stake the plant, if needed, to keep it from falling over. (See detailed planting instructions in "Easy Gardens for Florida"*, Chapter 11.)

Fertilizing: Immediately after planting, fertilize with a well-balanced, slow-release mix that includes minor elements. Repeat in March, June, and October of each year. (See detailed fertilization instructions in "Easy Gardens for Florida"*, Chapter 11.) In winter, when this plant is partially bare, the leaves are naturally yellowish.

Trimming: Trim back every year or two after it has stopped blooming. It recovers well from hard cutbacks. Do not attempt to trim this plant into a manicured tree. It will not work.

* My current book, "Easy Gardens for South Florida", will be expanded to include the entire state in 2004.

GROWING CONDITIONS

LIGHT: Full sun

WATER: Low. Ideal watering is once a week after the initial establishment period. Tolerates water up to 3 times per week. (For detailed information about watering, see Chapter 8 in "Easy Gardens for Florida"*.)

SOIL: Wide range, as long as it is well-drained.

SALT TOLERANCE: Medium

WIND TOLERANCE: Unknown

ZONE: 9 to 11. Dies back to the ground in a severe freeze but comes back in the spring. Survived 25 degrees in the 1989 freeze.

PEST PROBLEMS: None known

PROPAGATION: Seeds. Wait until the seed pods are brown. Remove the seeds from the pods, like shelling peas. Soak the seeds overnight. Plant them in good potting soil, about 1/2 inch down. These seeds are easy to germinate.

Botanical Name: *Duranta repens*

Common Name: **Golden Dewdrop**

CHARACTERISTICS

PLANT TYPE: Shrub that can be trained into a small tree when young.

AVERAGE SIZE: Prefers to be about 8 feet tall by 6 feet wide.

GROWTH RATE: Fast

LEAF: Medium green and pointed. About 1 1/2 inches long by 3/4 inch wide.

FLOWER: Clusters of small, lavender flowers followed by golden berries. When both appear on the tree at the same time, it looks like a bi-colored tree. There is also a variety with white flowers and a new one that is a darker purple.

AVERAGE LIFE: 5 to 10 years.

ORIGIN: Tropical America

CAUTIONS: Golden berries are poisonous to people. According to Julia F. Morton in her book, "Plants Poisonous to People", children in Australia have died from eating the berries. In Florida, one instance of illness but no deaths have been reported.

SPACING: 6 to 8 feet on center.

Beautiful in bloom, but a bit temperamental. Flowers attract butterflies, and berries attract birds.

Perfectly maintained Golden Dewdrop tree in full bloom

General: Golden Dewdrop is a shrub that can be trained into a tree when it is small. I like it better as a small tree because it becomes quite leggy and scraggly as a shrub. Its thick trunk supports the weight of the top well, but it requires frequent trimming to look as good as the one above. This is not a low-maintenance plant! And, it will not adapt to a tree form in areas that freeze. The name 'Golden Dewdrop' comes from the golden berries that follow the flowers. When both appear on the tree at the same time, it looks like the tree is purple and yellow.

Season: Golden Dewdrop flowers on and off all year, predominantly in the warmer months. It blooms for a total of about three months each year. It dies back in freezes and re-appears in spring as far north as zone 9b.

Companions: For a small butterfly garden, combine Golden Dewdrop with Firebush, Cranberry Pentas, and Yellow Lantana. If you have enough space for a small, flowering tree garden that also attracts butterflies, use the Golden Dewdrop with a Cassia Tree, Jatropha Tree, and Dwarf Poinciana Tree.

Golden Dewdrop flowers with some companions. The purple flowers contrast well with pink and yellow.

Planting: Plant any time of the year in south Florida, and in spring or summer in central Florida. Leave the root ball slightly out of the ground, about 1/4 inch. Stake securely. (See detailed planting instructions in "Easy Gardens for Florida"*, Chapter 11.)

Fertilizing: Immediately after planting, fertilize with a well-balanced, slow-release mix that includes minor elements. Repeat in March, June, and October of each year. If the summer is unusually hot and rainy, inspect the leaf color of the plant in August. If it appears washed out, add an additional fertilization in August. (See detailed fertilization instructions in "Easy Gardens for Florida"*, Chapter 11.)

Trimming: This plant requires a lot of trimming to look good; it benefits from a good, structural pruning in the summer. Other than that, the tips can be machine-sheared on an average of every two months, more in summer than winter. Be sure to remove any branches that appear on the trunk or that sprout from the ground.

My current book, "Easy Gardens for South Florida", will be expanded to include the entire state in 2004.

GROWING CONDITIONS

LIGHT: Full sun

WATER: Low. Ideal watering is once or twice a week after the initial establishment period. Tolerates water up to 3 times per week. (For detailed information about watering, see Chapter 8 in "Easy Gardens for Florida"*.)

SOIL: Wide range, as long as it is well-drained.

SALT TOLERANCE: Medium

WIND TOLERANCE: Unknown

ZONE: 9b to 11

PEST PROBLEMS: None serious

PROPAGATION: Seeds or cuttings.

Botanical Name: *Duranta repens variegata*
Common Name: **Variegated Golden Dewdrop**

CHARACTERISTICS

PLANT TYPE: Shrub that can be trained into a small tree when young.

AVERAGE SIZE: We maintain ours easily at 7 feet tall by 5 to 6 feet wide by trimming 3 times per year.

GROWTH RATE: Medium. Slower than the regular Golden Dewdrop.

LEAF: Medium green and white. Pointed. About 1 1/2 inches long by 3/4 inch wide.

FLOWER: Clusters of small lavender flowers followed by golden berries. When both appear on the tree at the same time, it looks like a bi-colored tree. This variegated form does not flower as much as the regular Golden Dewdrop on the previous page.

AVERAGE LIFE: 5 to 10 years.

ORIGIN: Tropical America

CAUTIONS: Poisonous. Golden berries are poisonous to people. (See Golden Dewdrop on page 216 for more details.)

SPACING: 6 to 8 feet on center.

An excellent, small tree for its variegated leaves and ease of care. Easier to grow and maintain than the regular Golden Dewdrop.

The lavender flowers and golden berries on the Variegated Golden Dewdrop are visible only when viewed up close. From a distance, the variegated leaves show up well.

General: The Variegated Golden Dewdrop is quite different from the regular Golden Dewdrop featured on the previous page. It grows slower, making it much easier to maintain. It does not flower as much, but keeps a smaller, more attractive form. Use this tree for its variegated leaves and golden berries rather than the occasional flowers. When the lavender flowers appear, they show up well against the attractive green and white leaves. This tree deserves much more use in south and central Florida. Many gardens need a tree that stays small and is easy to grow, and there are not many on the market. The Variegated Golden Dewdrop shares the additional benefit of looking good all year (in frost-free areas), making it very useful for Florida gardens.

Season: Golden Dewdrop flowers on and off all year, predominantly in the warmer months. The leaves look great all year in frost-free areas. It dies back to the ground in freezes and returns in spring as far north as zone 9b.

To locate plants, go to www.easygardencolor.com

Companions: The Variegated Golden Dewdrop looks good with dark-leaved plants, like Crotons and Starbursts. It also blends well with other light-textured, flowering plants, like Thryallis, Pentas, and Plumbago. For a small-tree grouping, combine it with Jatropha and Cassia Trees.

Variegated Golden Dewdrop with some companions

Planting: Plant any time of the year in south Florida and in spring or summer in central Florida. Leave the root ball slightly out of the ground, about 1/4 inch. Stake securely. (See detailed planting instructions in "Easy Gardens for Florida"*, Chapter 11.)

Fertilizing: Immediately after planting, fertilize with a well-balanced, slow-release mix that includes minor elements. Repeat in March, June, and October of each year. If the summer is unusually hot and rainy, inspect the leaf color of the plant in August. If it appears washed out, add an additional fertilization in August.

Trimming: We have great results from hand-pruning this tree three times a year. Be sure to remove any branches that appear on the trunk or that sprout from the ground. Trim the crown lightly, and even out the branches at the bottom of the canopy. We have not tried machine shearing this plant. The leaves occasionally develop brown patches. We leave them alone because they have been insignificant.

* My current book, "Easy Gardens for South Florida", will be expanded to include the entire state in 2004.

GROWING CONDITIONS

LIGHT: Full sun

WATER: Low. Ideal watering is once or twice a week after the initial establishment period. Tolerates water up to 3 times per week. (For detailed information about watering, see Chapter 8 in "Easy Gardens for Florida"*.)

SOIL: Wide range, as long as it is well-drained.

SALT TOLERANCE: Medium

WIND TOLERANCE: Unknown

ZONE: 9b to 11

PEST PROBLEMS: None serious

PROPAGATION: Seeds or cuttings.

Note: Variegated Golden Dewdrop berries are poisonous to people.

One of the better varieties of Hibiscus for trees. It develops a thicker trunk, larger size, and more compact form than most other Hibiscus.

CHARACTERISTICS

PLANT TYPE: Shrub that is easily trained into a small tree when young.

AVERAGE SIZE: Easy to maintain at sizes between 8 feet tall by 6 feet wide and 10 feet tall by 8 feet wide. The biggest mistake made with Hibiscus is attempting to maintain it at a size that is too small to produce blooms.

GROWTH RATE: Fast

LEAF: Dark green. About 2 inches wide by 2 inches long.

FLOWER: Bright pink, double flower measures about 2 to 3 inches across.

AVERAGE LIFE: 10 to 15 years.

ORIGIN: China

CAUTIONS: Not a good candidate over pavement or pools because the flowers stick and are difficult to remove.

SPACING: 8 to 15 feet on center.

Carnation Red Hibiscus Tree in full bloom

General: Hibiscus is covered in this book in three forms: dwarf, shrub, and tree. Technically, they are all the same type of plant. Carnation Red grows as a shrub, if trimmed as a shrub, and a small tree, if trimmed as a small tree. It excels in either form. As a tree, it grows larger than most other Hibiscus, developing a thick trunk that supports the top well. The plant recovers quickly from pruning and maintains a more manicured shape than most other Hibiscus. It is also resistant to many common Hibiscus pests (though probably susceptible to Pink Hibiscus Mealybug) and not subject to the frequent nutritional deficiencies of most Hibiscus. It does not have as high a percentage of color as the Seminole Pink or Anderson Crepe Hibiscus in full bloom.

Season: Hibiscus blooms on and off all year. When it is not in bloom, the plant maintains attractive dark green leaves.

To locate plants, go to www.easygardencolor.com

Companions: The Carnation Red Hibiscus works well when repeated in a formal arrangement along roadways. It offers the advantage of not growing tall enough to hit power lines. In a backyard, mix it with other flowering trees or shrubs. Good companion small trees include the Cassia, Golden Senna, and Silver Buttonwood trees.

The flower resembles a Carnation.

Planting: Plant any time of the year in south Florida and in fall or spring in central Florida. Leave the root ball slightly out of the ground, about 1/4 inch. Stake the tree well, and plan on leaving the stakes in for the life of the tree.

Fertilizing: Hibiscus are heavy feeders. Immediately after planting, fertilize with a well-balanced, slow-release mix that includes minor elements. Repeat in March, June, and October of each year. If the summer is unusually hot and rainy, inspect the leaf color of the plant in August. If it appears washed out, add an additional fertilization in August. (See detailed fertilization instructions in "Easy Gardens for Florida"*, Chapter 11.)

Trimming: The most common mistake made with Hibiscus is trimming it too small or too often. Many shear Hibiscus monthly and wonder why it never flowers. Trim infrequently, but make deep cuts instead of just knocking off the tips each month. This manner allows each branch to grow long enough to produce flowers. Also, remove any crossed branches from within the shrub as well as any branches that sprout along the trunk.

* My current book, "Easy Gardens for South Florida", will be expanded to include the entire state in 2004.

GROWING CONDITIONS

LIGHT: Light shade to full sun.

WATER: Medium. Ideal watering is twice a week after the initial establishment period. Tolerates water up to 4 times per week. Do not overwater.

SOIL: Wide range, as long as it is well-drained.

SALT TOLERANCE: High

WIND TOLERANCE: High

ZONE: Technically, 10a to 11. Often successful (and commonly planted) in protected areas of zone 9.

PEST PROBLEMS: Pink Hibiscus Mealybug is a serious new pest that has the capability of wiping out all of our Hibiscus. If you see pink, cottony material on your plant, call your county extension for help. Other potential pests include scale, spider mites, snails, aphids, and whitefly. These plants attract a lot of pests in some locations and none in others. They attract more if a lot of them are planted on the same site. Do not use Malathion on Hibiscus - it will defoliate them.

PROPAGATION: Cuttings

Botanical Name: *Holmskioldia sanquinea*
Common Name: **Chinese or Mandarin Hat Plant**

CHARACTERISTICS

PLANT TYPE: Vine, shrub, or small tree. See pages 196 and 197 for vine.

AVERAGE SIZE: As a small tree, grows 7 to 9 feet tall by 6 to 8 feet wide.

GROWTH RATE: Fast

LEAF: Medium green and pointed; about 2 inches long by 1 1/4 inches wide.

FLOWER: Small flower, about 3/4 inch wide. Arranged in clusters. Looks like a Chinese hat. Orange, red, or a lovely blue and pink combination. The orange is the main one I tested. The red appears to be strong, while the pink and blue has the prettiest flowers but is a weaker plant.

AVERAGE LIFE: Unknown. Have been thriving in my trial gardens for 5 years.

ORIGIN: India

CAUTIONS: None known

SPACING: 6 to 8 feet on center.

One of our better small trees for winter blooms. Long bloom period, dependable, and easy.

Chinese Hat Tree in January. Purple Prince Tis are planted in front.

Left: This is the same tree, 3 years earlier, as shown in the larger picture to the right.

General: The Chinese Hat Plant is technically a shrub or vine but grows into a tree if trained as one when it is young. Its growth habit is a lot like Bougainvillea, except it does not grow as fast or have thorns. The plant blooms all winter and is a great asset to winter perennial gardens. It even blooms after being machine-sheared, which is very unusual. Be sure to plant it in full sun because its blooms quickly fade in even a small amount of shade. It is available in orange, red, or a beautiful combination of pink and purple. The orange and red have both done very well in my trials. I have just started testing the pink and purple, and it appears weaker so far.

Season: Chinese Hat Plants last for many years. They bloom in winter and spring, starting around November and lasting until around May. The plants look good when not blooming.

To locate plants, go to www.easygardencolor.com

Companions: Use this plant with other perennials that bloom in winter. Some of the best companions include Brunfelsias, Dombeyas, and all the yellow Shrimp Plants. Bright-colored Crotons also work well with this plant.

Chinese Hat and some companions. The orange flowers of this plant look like Chinese hats.

Planting: Plant any time of the year in native soil. Leave the root ball slightly out of the ground, about 1/4 inch. (See detailed planting instructions in "Easy Gardens for Florida"*, Chapter 11.)

Fertilizing: Immediately after planting, fertilize with a well-balanced, slow-release mix that includes minor elements. Repeat in March, June, and October of each year. If the summer is unusually hot and rainy, inspect the leaf color of the plant in August. If it appears washed out, add an additional fertilization in August. (See detailed fertilization instructions in "Easy Gardens for Florida"*, Chapter 11.)

Trimming: This plant can be machine-sheared, as needed, for a manicured look. It is one of the few flowering plants that blooms shortly after machine-shearing. We keep ours more natural, pruning once heavily in the summer and trimming the edges two or three more times each year. Remove any unwanted branches from the trunk, as needed.

GROWING CONDITIONS

LIGHT: Full sun. The blooms fade in even the smallest amount of shade.

WATER: Medium. Ideal watering is twice a week after the initial establishment period. Tolerates water up to 4 times per week. Requires more water when grown in containers. (For detailed information about watering, see Chapter 8 in "Easy Gardens for Florida"*.)

SOIL: Wide range, as long as it is well-drained.

SALT TOLERANCE: Medium

WIND TOLERANCE: Medium

ZONE: 10a to 11

PEST PROBLEMS: None known. I have never seen a pest on this plant.

PROPAGATION: Cuttings

* My current book, "Easy Gardens for South Florida", will be expanded to include the entire state in 2004.

Botanical Name: *Malvaviscus arboreus*

Common Name: **Turk's Cap**

CHARACTERISTICS

PLANT TYPE: Shrub that can be trained into a small tree in frost-free areas. Works better in shrub form further north.

AVERAGE SIZE: In frost-free areas grows 7 to 9 feet tall by 6 to 8 feet wide. Further north, it dies back to the ground in the first freeze. It grows to about 4 to 5 feet tall during the next growing season.

GROWTH RATE: Fast

LEAF: Medium green and pointed. Size varies based on age of leaf. Up to about 5 inches long by 4 inches wide.

FLOWER: Pink or red, about 3 inches long. Looks like an upside down, half-opened Hibiscus flower.

AVERAGE LIFE: Unknown. Has lived for 5 years so far in our trial gardens and shows no signs of slowing down.

ORIGIN: Mexico and Texas.

CAUTIONS: None known

SPACING: 8 feet on center in frost-free areas. 4 feet on center further north.

A good, small tree or large shrub for informal gardens. Hummingbirds love the flowers.

General: Turk's Cap looks best maintained as a single-trunked small tree in frost-free areas because the year-round growth turns it into an unattractive, leggy shrub. Further north, it dies back with the first freeze and reappears the next spring. This forced dormancy controls its growth so that it behaves quite well as a shrub in these cooler areas. The flowers look like upside down, half-opened Hibiscus and are not particularly notable. But, the percentage of color is high, particularly on the red ones.

Season: In frost-free areas, Turk's Cap blooms in winter and spring for about six to eight months. Further north, it blooms in spring and fall.

To locate plants, go to www.easygardencolor.com

Companions: In frost-free areas, mix with other winter bloomers like Brunfelsia, Giant Shrimp and Dombeya. Although the plant is not spectacular alone, the length of the bloom period coupled with the percentage of color makes it worthwhile for winter gardens in south Florida. Further north, it works well in a cottage garden with Old Garden Roses, Butterfly Bushes, and perennial Salvias.

The bright color of the red Turk's Cap contrasts well with the blue, winter sky.

Planting: Plant any time of the year in frost-free areas and in spring or summer further north. Leave the root ball slightly out of the ground, about 1/4 inch. Stake securely. (See detailed planting instructions in "Easy Gardens for Florida"*, Chapter 11.)

Fertilizing: Immediately after planting, fertilize with a well-balanced, slow-release mix that includes minor elements. Repeat in March, June, and October of each year in zones 9 through 11. Leave out the fall fertilization in zone 8. (See detailed fertilization instructions in "Easy Gardens for Florida"*, Chapter 11.)

Trimming: Trim any unwanted growth off the trunk at any time. Cut back quite severely once in summer. Trim the ends of the branches off as needed during the rest of the year. This is a fast-growing plant and needs trimming 4 or 5 times per year. If the crown of the tree grows larger than the trunk can hold, trim back the crown and stake the trunk. This tree re-flowers fairly quickly after a cutback, so it can be trimmed in the winter without losing flowers for too long.

* My current book, "Easy Gardens for South Florida", will be expanded to include the entire state in 2004.

GROWING CONDITIONS

LIGHT: Light shade to full sun.

WATER: Low. Ideal watering is once a week after the initial establishment period. Tolerates water up to 4 times per week. (For detailed information about watering, see Chapter 8 in "Easy Gardens for Florida"*.)

SOIL: Wide range, as long as it is well-drained.

SALT TOLERANCE: Low

WIND TOLERANCE: Medium

ZONE: 8 to 11

PEST PROBLEMS: None known

PROPAGATION: Cuttings. Roots well from long, straight cuttings and is ideal for quick, standard crops from growers.

Botanical Name: *Nerium Oleander*
Common Name: **Oleander**

CHARACTERISTICS

PLANT TYPE: Evergreen shrub frequently used as a small tree.

AVERAGE SIZE: Easy to maintain at sizes between 6 feet tall by 6 feet wide and 12 feet tall by 12 feet wide.

GROWTH RATE: Medium

LEAF: Green and pointed. About 3 inches long by 3/4 inch wide.

FLOWER: Showy clusters of flowers. Most are red, white, or pink. Dwarf shrubs come in peach.

AVERAGE LIFE: 5 to 10 years.

ORIGIN: Eurasia

CAUTIONS: Poisonous. All parts of this plant (wood, flowers, leaves) are extremely toxic. Even its smoke is toxic. Grazing animals, birds, and people have been killed by this plant. **Avoid any contact - even with the sap - of this plant.**

SPACING: 6 to 10 feet on center.

For more information, there is an excellent article available for free on the interned. Go to http://edis.ifas.usf.edu/BODY_MG348 and look for "Oleanders for Florida" by Daniel F. Culbert. This document is fact sheet ENH-116, a series of the Environmental Horticulture Department, Florida Cooperative Extension Service, Institute of Food and Agricultural Sciences, University of Florida. Publication date: October 1995.

One of the most common shrubs or small trees planted in Florida, particularly near the sea.

Oleander is mainly used as a small tree or large shrub. Dwarf varieties are also available.

General: Oleander has been a difficult plant in my trial gardens. All of the ones we planted got Oleander caterpillars, which are a nasty pest (see "Pests" in opposite green sidebar). They grew leggy quickly, requiring frequent pruning. And, their toxicity scared me. This plant is really poisonous (see "Cautions" on this page). With so many other beautiful and easy alternatives, this plant had little value, so we removed all of them. But, they are worthwhile in other situations, particularly near the sea. They are very tolerant of salt and wind, which is unusual for plants that produce this much color. They also offer a long bloom period as well as cold hardiness for most of Florida. Plants in cold spots freeze back to the ground when temperatures stay below freezing for long periods. They grow back when temperatures warm up, except in severe freezes in the far northern and northwestern areas of the state.

Season: Oleanders bloom mainly in spring, summer, and fall. They do not bloom continuously during all three seasons, but do bloom a good bit of the time. Occasionally, they bloom in winter, especially in south Florida.

To locate plants, go to www.easygardencolor.com

Companions: For color near the sea in south Florida, combine Oleander with Frangipani and Orange Geiger. Annuals that work well all over Florida in high salt situations include Moss Rose, Petunias, Lantana, Victoria Blue Salvia, and Geraniums.

Planting: Plant container plants any time of the year. Field-grown or transplanted material can be moved any time in south Florida and in winter in central Florida. Leave the root ball slightly out of the ground, about 1/4 inch.

Fertilizing: Oleanders' nutritional needs are few, but they benefit from fertilization immediately after planting, with a well-balanced, slow-release mix that includes minor elements. Repeat in March, June, and October of each year, if the plant appears to need it.

Trimming: The best time to prune Oleander is in winter, when it is not blooming. One annual pruning may be enough in colder areas of the state, if the plant dies back in a freeze. In south Florida, it needs more pruning - at least three times a year to keep it reasonably attractive. Time the prunings to coincide with the end of a bloom spurt. _Do not ever burn the clippings because the smoke is very toxic._ Oleanders are sometimes maintained with a single trunk. If this is desired, remove any suckers that sprout from the base as well as any branches that appear low on the trunk. Additional, excellent pruning tips are in the article referenced in the opposite sidebar under "For More Information".

GROWING CONDITIONS

LIGHT: Full sun

WATER: Low. This plant lives without supplemental water in all but the worst droughts after its initial establishment period. Tolerates water up to 3 times per week. Requires more water in containers.

SOIL: Wide range, as long as it is well-drained.

SALT TOLERANCE: High

WIND TOLERANCE: High

ZONE: 8 to 11. In northern and northwestern Florida, protect from severe freezes.

PEST PROBLEMS: Frequently attacked by the Oleander caterpillar. The caterpillar stings. Children sometimes use Oleander sticks with caterpillars as weapons. This caterpillar does substantial damage to the plant. I have never planted an Oleander that did not get these pests. For more pest information, including photos, see the article referenced in the opposite sidebar.

PROPAGATION: Cuttings

Calliandra haematocephala
Powderpuff

Powderpuff Trees look more like large shrubs than trees. There is also a Dwarf Powderpuff shrub that is quite a bit smaller. My first experience was with the dwarf shrub, which blooms about 8 months each year. I was expecting the same bloom period from the larger Powderpuff and was disappointed to find that it only bloomed for about 2 months the first year of its trials. During the next 10 years, the bloom time varied from year to year. Some years, it bloomed for 6 or 8 months and other years only for 2 months. Plants located in colder areas bloomed more, and all of them bloomed more during cold years. Since the plants grow in south and central Florida, it makes sense that they would flower more in the central part of the state, where the weather is cooler. The tree grows into a large mass of about 15 feet tall and is ideal for screening. Sun or light shade.

Cassia quinquanulatum
West Indian Shower

This is a tree of extremes. I have planted quite a few in my trial gardens, which are about 5 miles inland from the ocean. We tried them in both sun and shade locations. None of them looked particularly good, a big scraggly, but the sulfer butterflies loved them. They laid their eggs on the leaves each winter, and the caterpillars proceeded to eat most of the leaves and all of the flowers. Since the tree didn't look particularly good to begin with, I was happy with its role as pet food. Then, I began to notice spectacular West Indian Shower trees in Palm Beach, which is very near the ocean. So I suggested to the owner of this waterfront garden (right) that she try one. Since it blooms for about 4 months in the winter, it fit into our plans for a winter garden. It is absolutely beautiful! I don't know if it was the salt air that made this one so spectacular, but West Indian Shower is definitely worth trying if you live near the sea. At least you'll get some sulfer butterflies! Edwin Menninger, in his book, "Flowering Trees of the World", refers to the same tree as *Chamaefistula antilllana* and states that it takes temperatures down to 25 degrees.

Sesbania grandiflora
Hummingbird Tree

I planted about 30 Hummingbird Trees in different locations in Palm Beach County. They flowered in winter with a lovely bloom, but all died for no apparent reason within 2 years.

Tecoma stans
Yellow Elder

I have never had much luck with Yellow Elders. They grew tall and scraggly very quickly, not looking anywhere near as nice as the one to the right. Since we look for trees for our trial gardens that only need pruning once or twice a year, this one would get completely out of hand before its next turn came up. However, the plant grows with almost no care, and the flowers are lovely in fall. If you really like to prune, this may be the tree for you! Yellow Elders are partially to completely bare in the winter and grow in light shade or full sun to a height of about 15 feet. According to Edwin Menninger, in his "Flowering Trees of the World", the tree takes temperatures down to 24 degrees. It would probably die down to the ground at that temperature and regrow the following spring.

CHAPTER **6**

MEDIUM TREES, 15' TO 35'

The trees in this chapter, together with the flowering trees in Chapter 5 in 'Easy Gardens for Florida', make up an excellent selection of medium flowering-trees. Flowering trees require little care and keep blooming for many years. They are ideal for someone who loves flowers but has little time or inclination for maintenance.

The fifteen to thirty-five foot size range represented in this chapter is ideal for many residences. Choose your favorites and create your own personal botanical collection.

Left and above: Frangipani (pages 242 and 243)

Botanical Name: *Dombeya wallichii*
Common Name: **Tropical Snowball, Hydrangea Tree**

CHARACTERISTICS

PLANT TYPE: Tree with multiple trunks that looks like a huge shrub. Smaller, shrub *Dombeya 'Seminole'* is featured on pages 144 and 145.

AVERAGE SIZE: 30 feet tall by 30 feet wide.

GROWTH RATE: Fast

LEAF: Leaf size increases as the plant grows larger. Up to about 8 inches long by 8 inches wide.

FLOWER: Beautiful, large, hanging, round flowers that resemble upside down Hydrangeas. Up to 5 or 6 inches across.

AVERAGE LIFE: Unknown. At least 10 years.

ORIGIN: Madagascar

CAUTIONS: None known

SPACING: 30 feet on center.

The flowers brown as they die and persist on the tree for some time.

Winter bloomer with a short bloom period but spectacular flowers.

Dombeya wallichii in January. The flowers are best viewed from underneath the branches. The tree does not show up well from a distance.

General: Over 200 types of Dombeyas exist, both shrubs and trees. When I first planted this one, I thought it was a shrub, like the shrub Dombeya featured on pages 144 and 145. To my surprise, it took off like the beanstalk in "Jack and the Beanstalk", reaching over twenty feet tall and twenty feet wide in just 4 years! And, it is still growing. It is not an attractive tree, growing more like a shrub, with lots of small branches growing out of the lower parts of the trunk. But, the flowers are spectacular, blooming dependably every winter for about two months. The flowers hang down, unlike the shrub Dombeya that displays its flowers on top of the leaves. They brown after a short time and persist on the tree for quite a while. However, the beauty of the blooms is worth it for someone with a lot of space and a love of large, showy flowers.

Season: This Dombeya blooms for about two months in the winter, normally starting in late December. The leaves look good in summer as well.

To locate plants, go to www.easygardencolor.com

Companions: Plant the Dombeya wallichii with other plants that bloom in winter. It looks great with Brunfelsias and White 'Odorata' Begonias. Be sure to leave the area directly under the tree bare of plantings because it needs trimming on the trunk.

Dombeya wallichii and some companions

Planting: Plant any time of the year in native soil. Leave the root ball slightly out of the ground, about 1/4 inch.(See detailed planting instructions in "Easy Gardens for Florida"*, Chapter 11.)

Fertilizing: Immediately after planting, fertilize with a well-balanced, slow-release mix that includes minor elements. Repeat in March, June, and October of each year. If the summer is unusually hot and rainy, inspect the leaf color of the plant in August. If it appears washed out, add an additional fertilization at that time.

Trimming: Let this tree grow into its natural shape of long and lanky, and you will not need to trim it much. The main area of need is the bottom part of the trunk, which frequently sprouts small branches that are out of proportion to the tree. Remove these several times a year. Keep the trunk trimmed up to a height where you can walk under it when it is blooming to enjoy the view of the flowers.

* My current book, "Easy Gardens for South Florida", will be expanded to include the entire state in 2004.

LIGHT: Light shade to full sun.

WATER: Medium. Ideal watering is twice a week after the initial establishment period. Tolerates water up to 4 times per week. Untested in a low water situation. (For detailed information about watering, see Chapter 8 in "Easy Gardens for Florida"*.)

SOIL: Wide range, as long as it is well-drained.

SALT TOLERANCE: Low

WIND TOLERANCE: Unknown

ZONE: We tested this plant in zone 10a with no cold damage at all from 1997 until 2003. The temperatures dipped into the high to mid-30's but never to freezing. This may be a zone 9b plant.

PEST PROBLEMS: None known

PROPAGATION: Easily propagated by cuttings. Much easier to root than the *Dombeya 'Seminole'.*

Botanical Name:	*Erythrina variegata orientalis 'Sunshine'*

Common Name: **Sunshine Tree**

CHARACTERISTICS

PLANT TYPE: Tree

AVERAGE SIZE: 20 to 30 feet tall by 20 feet wide.

GROWTH RATE: Medium

LEAF: Heart-shaped. About 6 inches by 6 inches. Yellow and green.

FLOWER: Beautiful, but occasional flowers. Red, 2 to 3 inches long. Grow this tree for its leaves.

AVERAGE LIFE: At least 20 years.

ORIGIN: India and Malaysia.

CAUTIONS: Poisonous

SPACING: 20 feet on center.

A beautiful tree with bright yellow and green leaves. Looks like its name, 'Sunshine Tree', against the blue skies of Florida. Almost bare in winter.

The leaves of the Sunshine Tree look like the sun against the blue Florida sky.

General: Over 100 species of Erythrina have been identified. Most do better in dry California than in wet Florida. Not so for the Sunshine Tree, which thrives in the state with the same name. While most Erythrinas are grown for their beautiful red flowers, the Sunshine Tree is grown for its striking leaves. They are very unusual and elicit lots of oohs and aahs from visitors to my summer garden. Its flowers are beautiful red clusters, but they only appear occasionally. The leaves make a nice impact in a summer garden, but the plant is bare in winter, so be sure to plant it in a spot where that would not be a problem.

Season: Erythrinas peak in summer and fall. They are partially to completely bare in winter for about two to three months, generally December through February. They begin to leaf out again in March.

To locate plants, go to www.easygardencolor.com

Companions: Use Sunshine Trees with other plants that peak in summer and feature bright colors that contrast with the variegated leaves. Some flowering trees that look good with this tree include Crepe Myrtle, Orange Geiger, Frangipani, and Royal Poinciana. Some large shrubs that work well with this tree include Chenille Plant, Firespike, *Costus barbatus*, and all the Mussaendas.

Sunshine Tree with some companions

Planting: Plant any time of the year in native soil. Leave the root ball slightly out of the ground, about 1/4 inch. (See detailed planting instructions in "Easy Gardens for Florida"*, Chapter 11.)

Fertilizing: Immediately after planting, fertilize with a well-balanced, slow-release mix that includes minor elements. Repeat in March, June, and October of each year. (See detailed fertilization instructions in "Easy Gardens for Florida"*, Chapter 11.)

Trimming: This tree does not need much trimming, as it forms a nice, symmetrical canopy. Remove any branches that appear too low on the trunk. Prune every three or four years to remove dead growth and crossed branches.

* My current book, "Easy Gardens for South Florida", will be expanded to include the entire state in 2004.

GROWING CONDITIONS

LIGHT: Full sun

WATER: Low. Ideal watering is once a week after the initial establishment period. Tolerates water up to 3 times per week. Untested in wetter or drier conditions. (For detailed information about watering, see Chapter 8 in "Easy Gardens for Florida"*.)

SOIL: Wide range, as long as it is well-drained.

SALT TOLERANCE: Medium

WIND TOLERANCE: Unknown

ZONE: 10a to 11

PEST PROBLEMS: None serious

PROPAGATION: Seeds or cuttings.

Botanical Name: *Lagerstroemia indica*
Common Name: **Crepe Myrtle**

CHARACTERISTICS

PLANT TYPE: Shrub or tree.

AVERAGE SIZE: Many different types available, ranging from 2 foot groundcovers to 30 foot trees. Know what you are buying, or you could be in for quite a surprise later. The average tree at Florida nurseries grows to about 20 feet tall.

GROWTH RATE: Medium

LEAF: Medium green in spring, summer, and fall; leaves turn red as the tree is defoliating in early winter. Measures up to 4 inches long by 1 1/2 inches wide.

FLOWER: Showy clusters of white, purple, pink, or red flowers that look wrinkled, like crepe paper. Clusters measure up to 10 inches long by 5 inches wide. *Note: It is often difficult for nurseries to know the color if the plant is not in bloom. If the color is very important to you, buy them in bloom. I have bought trees twice that were not blooming, and they turned out to be different colors than what the nurserymen had thought.*

AVERAGE LIFE: 30 years plus.

ORIGIN: China

CAUTIONS: Flowers drop on pavement if planted near it.

SPACING: 10 to 20 feet on center.

A beautiful, summer-flowering tree that is common from California to Florida.

Left: Hot pink Crepe Myrtle in full bloom. Right: Some other colors.

General: Crepe Myrtles are one of the most common flowering trees in much of the United States. They are hardy to zone 7 and thrive throughout Florida, blooming profusely for about a month or two in summer or fall. Although the bloom period is short compared with many other tropical flowering trees, the color impact of the Crepe Myrtle makes the tree worthwhile. However, they are completely bare in winter and not a good choice for an area that is a cool-weather focal point (except for the interesting peeling, character that the bark develops as the tree ages). And understand that these Crepe Myrtles are smaller than the Queen's Crepe featured on pages 238 and 239. They average about twenty feet tall, although there is a white variety that grows to thirty feet in south Florida.

Season: Crepe Myrtles bloom for about a month every summer. If the seed pods are removed after the initial bloom, they bloom again. Repeat the process for a third bloom. They are completely bare in the winter, even in south Florida.

To locate plants, go to www.easygardencolor.com

Companions: Crepe Myrtles make excellent street trees, either repeating the same color or alternating the colors. Mix them in with evergreen trees, like Palms or Oaks, so that the bare winter branches are not a focal point. Crepe Myrtles are also an excellent specimen for summer gardens. They look great with other summer bloomers, like Copperpods and Royal Poincianas.

GROWING CONDITIONS

LIGHT: Full sun. This tree does not like any shade at all.

WATER: Low. Ideal watering is once a week after the initial establishment period. Tolerates water up to 3 times per week. I have not tested it in wetter conditions. (For detailed information about watering, see Chapter 8 in "Easy Gardens for Florida"*.)

SOIL: Wide range, as long as it is well-drained.

SALT TOLERANCE: Low

WIND TOLERANCE: Medium

ZONE: 7 to 10b

PEST PROBLEMS: None common in the Florida landscape. A few reports of aphids and root rot. Older varieties are prone to powdery mildew. Most newer varieties are resistant.

PROPAGATION: Seeds or cuttings.

Find excellent Crepe Myrtle information in "Southern Living Big Book of Flower Gardening" on pages 164 to 167. The pruning section is the best I have ever seen. See the bibliography for more details.

Purple Crepe Myrtle in full bloom

Planting: Plant any time of the year in frost-free areas and in spring to mid-summer further north. Leave the root ball slightly out of the ground, about 1/4 inch. (See detailed planting instructions in "Easy Gardens for Florida"*, Chapter 11.)

Fertilizing: Immediately after planting, fertilize with a well-balanced, slow-release mix that includes minor elements. Repeat in March, June, and October of each year. If the summer is unusually hot and rainy, inspect the leaf color of the plant in August. If it appears washed out, add an additional fertilization in August. (See detailed fertilization instructions in "Easy Gardens for Florida"*, Chapter 11.)

Trimming: Crepe Myrtles have a nice, natural form and seldom require massive cutbacks. Remove crossed branches and dead wood every few years. It is difficult to maintain a Crepe Myrtle with a single trunk, so let some shoots grow from the base to form a multiple-trunked specimen. Remove any small branches appearing too low on these trunks. After the initial flowering, the tree will bloom again if the emerging seed pods (that look like berries) are removed.

My current book, "Easy Gardens for South Florida", will be expanded to include the entire state in 2004.

Botanical Name: *Lagerstroemia speciosa*

Common Name: **Queen's Crepe Myrtle**

CHARACTERISTICS

PLANT TYPE: Tree. Sometimes sends up multiple trunks in an attempt to look like a huge shrub.

AVERAGE SIZE: 35 feet tall by 30 feet wide. Larger than the *Lagerstroemia indica.*

GROWTH RATE: Medium

LEAF: Dark green, 6 to 12 inches long.

FLOWER: Long spikes that appear above the leaves. Measures from about 10 to 18 inches long by about 8 inches wide. Color varies by individual trees, from pinkish purple to deep purple. The flower opens at night, and the blooms fade over the next few days.

AVERAGE LIFE: Over 20 years.

ORIGIN: East Indies and India.

CAUTIONS: Poisonous

SPACING: 30 feet on center.

One of south Florida's most beautiful summer-flowering trees. Bare in winter.

Queen's Crepe in full bloom

General: Unlike the more temperate Crepe Myrtle featured on the previous two pages, the Queen's Crepe is a subtropical tree that does not take the northern winters. It is also larger than the other Crepe Myrtle. Blooming in summer, it is almost completely bare in winter. The Queen's Crepe is one of our most beautiful flowering trees and deserves much more use in south Florida.

Season: The Queen's Crepe flowers in summer for a relatively short time, four to eight weeks. The flowers may appear as early as May and last until August. It begins to bloom when it is very small.

To locate plants, go to www.easygardencolor.com

Companions: In a large space, plant the Queen's Crepe with other good-sized, flowering trees that bloom in summer. One of the most spectacular color displays I know combines the Queen's Crepe with the Royal Poinciana and the Copperpod. For smaller areas, mix the Queen's Crepe with yellow Frangipani and red Jatropha. The Queen's Crepe also looks good with the Dwarf Poincianas, but they frequently bloom at different times.

LIGHT: Full sun. This tree does not like any shade at all.

WATER: Low. Ideal watering is once a week after the initial establishment period. Tolerates water up to 3 times per week. I have not tested it in wetter conditions. (For detailed information on watering, see Chapter 8 in "Easy Gardens for Florida"*.)

SOIL: Wide range, as long as it is well-drained.

SALT TOLERANCE: Low

WIND TOLERANCE: Unknown

ZONE: 10a to 11. Untested in zone 9. According to Edwin Menninger in his "Flowering Trees of the World", this tree survives 25 degrees.

PEST PROBLEMS: Sooty mold, aphids, scale

PROPAGATION: Seeds

Queen's Crepe and some companions

Planting: Plant any time of the year in native soil. Leave the root ball slightly out of the ground, about 1/4 inch. (See detailed planting instructions in "Easy Gardens for Florida"*, Chapter 11.)

Fertilizing: Immediately after planting, fertilize with a well-balanced, slow-release mix that includes minor elements. Repeat in March, June, and October of each year. (See detailed fertilization instructions in "Easy Gardens for Florida"*, Chapter 11.)

Trimming: Remove any branches that appear low on the trunk. Prune every three or four years to remove dead growth and crossed branches.

My current book, "Easy Gardens for South Florida", will be expanded to include the entire state in 2004.

Botanical Name: *Peltophorum dubium and pterocarpum*
Common Name: **Copperpod or Peltophorum**

CHARACTERISTICS

PLANT TYPE: Tree

AVERAGE SIZE: *P. dubium* grows to 20 feet tall by 20 feet wide. *P. pterocarpum* grows to 35 feet tall by 30 feet wide.

GROWTH RATE: Medium

LEAF: Fern-like, similar to the Royal Poinciana. The individual leaflets are described in the chart below.

FLOWER: Long clusters that form spikes up to 12 inches long.

AVERAGE LIFE: Unknown

ORIGIN: *P. dubium*, South America. *P. pterocarpum*, Philippines.

CAUTIONS: None known

SPACING: 25 feet on center.

The flower buds of the P. pterocarpum (above) are more coppery than the P. dubium. The seed pods are copper-colored and appear at the same time as the yellow flowers, causing the tree to look yellow and copper at the same time.

Beautiful trees for summer color. Partially bare in winter in central Florida. Evergreen in south Florida.

Peltophorum dubium in June. The pterocarpum looks very similar from a distance.

General: Copperpods are lovely trees for summer color. Two are excellent choices: the *Peltophorum dubium* and the *Peltophorum pterocarpum* (also called *inerme*). Although the trees are almost identical in flower, they are different in their temperature range, leaf size and arrangement, bud color, and overall size. The chart below describes their differences. Both are lovely and deserve more use. Some refer to these trees as Yellow Poincianas, which is very confusing because there are other Yellow Poincianas. Let's call them Peltophorums or Copperpods.

Season: The Copperpod blooms in summer. According to Mark Stebbins, in his "Flowering Trees of Florida", the number of blooms varies year to year. Some years, it is covered in flowers and, other years, it just blooms lightly.

	Peltophorum dubium	*Peltophorum pterocarpum (inerme)*
Range	South and central Florida	South Florida only
Leaves	1/2" long, arranged in 20-30 pairs	3/4" long, arranged in 10-20 pairs
Buds	Light copper	Dark copper
Size	20' tall by 20' wide	35' tall by 30' wide

To locate plants, go to www.easygardencolor.com

Companions: Crepe Myrtles are excellent tree companions for the Copperpod. Plant the Copperpod in the center and a red and purple Crepe Myrtle on either side. For shrub companions that bloom at the same time, use Plumbagos and Cranberry Pentas. All of these combinations work well in south or central Florida.

Peltophorum dubium and some companions

Planting: Plant any time of the year in native soil. Leave the root ball slightly out of the ground, about 1/4 inch. Stake the tree securely.

Fertilizing: Immediately after planting, fertilize with a well-balanced, slow-release mix that includes minor elements. Repeat in March, June, and October of each year. If the summer is unusually hot and rainy, inspect the leaf color of the plant in August. If it appears washed out, add an additional fertilization in August. (See detailed fertilization instructions in "Easy Gardens for Florida"*, Chapter 11.)

Trimming: This tree does not need much trimming; it forms a nice, natural canopy. Remove any branches that appear too low on the trunk. Prune every three or four years to remove dead growth and crossed branches.

GROWING CONDITIONS

LIGHT: High

WATER: Low. Ideal watering is once a week after the initial establishment period. No information on its performance in wet conditions. (For detailed information on watering, see Chapter 8 in "Easy Gardens for Florida"*.)

SOIL: Wide range, as long as it is well-drained.

SALT TOLERANCE: Medium

WIND TOLERANCE: Medium

ZONE: *P. dubium*, zone 9 to 11. *P. pterocarpum*, zone 10A to 11.

PEST PROBLEMS: None known

PROPAGATION: Seeds

My current book, "Easy Gardens for South Florida", will be expanded to include the entire state in 2004.

Botanical Name: *Plumeria spp.*
Common Name: **Frangipani**

CHARACTERISTICS

PLANT TYPE: Tree

AVERAGE SIZE: 12 to 25 feet tall by 10 to 16 feet wide. Size depends on type. Know what you are buying if planting the tree in a small spot.

GROWTH RATE: Slow

LEAF: Medium green and pointed. About 3 to 4 inches wide by 12 to 15 inches long.

FLOWER: Fragrant. Red, yellow, white, pink, or beautiful, multicolored blooms called 'Rainbow'. Most varieties are 3 inches across.

AVERAGE LIFE: 20 years plus.

ORIGIN: Throughout the tropical world.

CAUTIONS: Skin irritant

SPACING: 10 to 20 feet on center.

Notes on names: P. acutifolia, white with yellow centers. P. rubra, red-flowered varieties. P. Singapore, white flowers.

Notes on newer Frangipanis: Some new dwarf varieties are evergreen. I have not tested any of them yet but plan to in the future.

One of the most celebrated of all tropical flowers. Most are completely bare in winter.

General: Frangipani is a tree of extremes. The flowers are treasured throughout the world for their beauty and nighttime fragrance. They are even used in Hawaii to make leis. But most are completely bare in the winter. Like sculpture, people respond quite differently to a bare Frangipani. Some love its antler-like, sculptural quality. Others find it particularly ugly. A friend of mine thought it was dead in its first winter and threw it away! Over 45 different species have been identified, and there is much confusion about which is which. It's best to just call them Frangipani. The plant blooms when quite young, if planted from a tip cutting.

Season: Bloom season varies in Florida. Some trees start in spring and bloom all summer. Others start later in the summer and bloom for a shorter time period. Most do not bloom and are completely bare in winter in Florida. The 'Singapore', with a white flower, is evergreen and sometimes blooms in Florida's winter. In Hawaii, many bloom all year.

To locate plants, go to www.easygardencolor.com

Companions: Frangipanis can either be planted with other plants that bloom in summer or in a tropical mass that hides their winter bareness. In a summer, flowering-tree garden, combine them with Crepe Myrtles, Royal Poincianas, and Orange Geigers. Summer shrubs that make great companions include Mussaendas, Chenille Plants, and *Costus barbados*. In tropical masses, combine Frangipanis with Palms and large-leafed tropicals, like Alocasias.

Frangipani flowers

Planting: Plant any time of the year in native soil. Leave the root ball slightly out of the ground, about 1/4 inch. (See detailed planting instructions in "Easy Gardens for Florida"*, Chapter 11.)

Fertilizing: Immediately after planting, fertilize with a well-balanced, slow-release mix that includes minor elements. Repeat in March, June, and October of each year. Since Frangipanis are not demanding of food, they might not notice if you miss a fertilization. (See detailed fertilization instructions in "Easy Gardens for Florida"*, Chapter 11.)

Trimming: Frangipanis require little pruning. Remove dead wood occasionally.

My current book, "Easy Gardens for South Florida", will be expanded to include the entire state in 2004.

LIGHT: High

WATER: Low. Ideal watering is once a week after the initial establishment period. Tolerates water (at least) up to twice per week. Untested in higher or lower water situations. (For detailed information on watering, see Chapter 8 in "Easy Gardens for Florida"*.)

SOIL: Wide range, as long as it is well-drained.

SALT TOLERANCE: High

WIND TOLERANCE: Leaves and flowers may blow off in a wind storm, but they recover fairly quickly if the weather is warm.

ZONE: 10a to 11 for most varieties. Some newer ones are hardy to zone 8.

PEST PROBLEMS: Routinely gets rust on leaves in Florida. Looks like orange spots. Do not spray unless it is very severe because it will go away naturally when the tree defoliates the next winter.

PROPAGATION: Easy to root from cuttings if the cutting is dry and weather is warm. Let it dry for 2 weeks before planting.

Cassia afrofistula
Cassia Tree

Very little is known about this rare tree that I found blooming beautifully at Marie Selby Botanical Garden in Sarasota. It blooms for a few months each summer. We will be adding it to our trial gardens. Since so many Cassias do well here, this may be a great addition to our available flowering trees.

Cordia boissieri
White Geiger Tree

This is a tree of extremes. I had always heard it was easy and have never gotten a single one to do well in my trial gardens. However, I have found gorgeous specimens in other locations. The tree above was photographed at the Ritz Carlton Hotel, which is on the ocean in Manalapan (Palm Beach County). It has been thriving there for years! The White Geiger grows to about 20 feet tall and takes cold well, since it is native to Texas. It's growth habit is varied - some grow like trees and others like shrubs.

Cordia lutea
Yellow Geiger

This tree has been doing very well in our trial gardens for the last 3 years. I make the initial mistake of underestimating its size and spread, and had to transplant it. Its growth habit is shrub-like when it is young. The largest ones I have seen are about 15 to 20 feet tall. The flowers are beautiful, and the tree is quite showy. The leaves show cold damage at about 38 degrees, but it keeps its leaves during the winter. I do not know at what temperature the tree dies.

Koelreuteria elegans
Golden Rain Tree

This unique tree blooms with yellow flowers in fall. The seed pods that follow are peach-colored, and look like flowers. When the flowers and seed pods are on the tree at the same time, it looks like it has two colors of flowers! The tree grows throughout Florida and is bare all winter, even in south Florida. It has one big problem: it reseeds too much, enough to become a nuisance. Hopefully, it will not become a weed tree. Golden Rain Trees grow best in sun and reach a height of about 25 feet.

Lonchocarpus violacius
Florida Lilac or Lancepod

Florida Lilac is a beautiful tree that blooms profusely in the fall. The bloom period is short, about a month, but the percentage of color is high enough to make this a worthwhile choice. It grows very well in south Florida but is too cold-sensitive to survive further north. The tree is partially deciduous in winter. It grows in sun to about 20 feet tall. The roots, wood, and seeds of this tree are <u>extremely</u> poisonous to humans and animals. Do not leave seedpods within reach of pets or children.

Magnolia grandiflora 'Little Gem'
Little Gem Magnolia

This dwarf tree (to 24') is ideal for many small gardens because of its narrow form. It grows well all over Florida, including the south. The Little Gem blooms on and off all year in south Florida, and during the warm months in central and north Florida. Plant it in an area with good sun and air-circulation to diminish the chance of scale insects. The flowers are smaller than the Southern Magnolia but have the same general appearance. Both the foliage and the form of the tree are quite attractive.

Tabebuia impetiginosa
Tab Ipe

We are accustomed to the Yellow Tabs lighting up our spring every year in south Florida. The pink ones had never particularly impressed me because the blooms were sparse and washed-out. When I saw the tree above in Boynton Beach (Palm Beach County), I almost wrecked my car! This is the Tab Ipe, which has traditionally performed well in zone 9b. I will watch this one carefully for the next 5 years to see if it continues this high performance in zone 10. Grows to 25 feet in sun.

Tibouchina granulosa
Tibouchina or Purple Glory Tree

This is one of the prettiest flowering trees in Florida. I planted hundreds of them in the early 1990's throughout Palm Beach County. In 1995, all the new ones we planted died. The old ones kept going. I have tried several in my trial gardens since 1995 with the same results - they died. They seem to do better in central Florida. They may like the colder area or the more acidic soil. Tibouchinas like sun and grow to about 25 feet, if you can keep them alive that long.

CHAPTER 7

LARGE TREES, OVER 35'

The trees in this chapter, together with the flowering trees in Chapter 5 in "Easy Gardens for Florida"*, make up an excellent selection of large-flowering trees.

Large flowering trees require little care and keep blooming for many years. They are an excellent choice for cities and municipalities who want color impact without expensive maintenance.

Pay special attention to the companions suggested in this chapter. Flowering tree gardens that feature groups of different trees that bloom at the same time have incredible color impact. When planting a Royal Poinciana, for example, group it with a Golden Shower and a Queen's Crepe. (see page 249 for photos of this grouping). The three usually bloom at the same time, with a riot of orange, purple, and yellow flowers. These large groupings are especially appropriate for public spaces.

Left and above: Jacaranda

Botanical Name: *Cassia fistula*

Common Name: **Golden Shower**

CHARACTERISTICS

PLANT TYPE: Tree

AVERAGE SIZE: 35 feet tall by 25 feet wide.

GROWTH RATE: Medium

LEAF: Larger than most other Cassias. About 6 inches long. Light to medium green, depending on nutrition.

FLOWER: Hanging yellow flower clusters measure 12 to 18 inches long.

AVERAGE LIFE: 30 years plus.

ORIGIN: Tropical Asia

CAUTIONS: Poisonous

SPACING: 30 feet on center.

Beautiful summer bloomer with a somewhat awkward form. Bare in winter.

Golden Shower in June

General: Golden Shower is a tree of extremes - its flowers are wonderful, but its form is irregular and lanky. And, it is bare in the winter. However, it makes a spectacular street tree when paired with other summer bloomers or evergreens. This Cassia blends well with a variety of landscape styles.

Season: Golden Shower Trees bloom in summer and are briefly bare in winter. They do not look good during these cool months because of bare branches and hanging seed pods.

To locate plants, go to www.easygardencolor.com

Companions: Golden Shower is spectacular when planted with other flowering trees that bloom at the same time. The two best companions are Royal Poinciana and Queen's Crepe. But, you pay a price for all that impact because they all look bad at the same time in winter. Another approach is to use it among evergreens, like Oaks, so that the bareness is not so noticeable in winter.

Golden Shower and some companions

Planting: Plant any time of the year in native soil. Leave the root ball slightly out of the ground, about 1/4 inch. (See detailed planting instructions in "Easy Gardens for Florida"*, Chapter 11.)

Fertilizing: Immediately after planting, fertilize with a well-balanced, slow-release mix that includes minor elements. Repeat in March, June, and October of each year. If the summer is unusually hot and rainy, inspect the leaf color of the plant in August. If it appears washed out, add an additional fertilization in August. (See detailed fertilization instructions in "Easy Gardens for Florida"*, Chapter 11.)

Trimming: Remove any dead growth and crossed branches every few years. Also, remove any unwanted growth on the trunk.

* My current book, "Easy Gardens for South Florida", will be expanded to include the entire state in 2004.

Botanical Name: *Ceiba speciosa (formally Chorisia speciosa)*

Common Name: **Floss Silk Tree**

CHARACTERISTICS

PLANT TYPE: Tree

AVERAGE SIZE: 50 feet tall by 50 feet wide.

GROWTH RATE: Fast

LEAF: Medium green. About 3 to 4 inches long.

FLOWER: The flowers of no two trees are exactly alike. Generally, pink and white; about 4 to 8 inches across.

AVERAGE LIFE: Over 50 years.

ORIGIN: Brazil and Argentina.

CAUTIONS: Spiny

SPACING: 30 to 50 feet on center.

Some trunks are studded with thorns that may drop off with age. Other Floss Silk Trees never have thorns.

One of our most spectacular flowering trees. Deserves much more use, particularly in public places. Thrives in south and central Florida.

Floss Silk in full bloom

General: The Floss Silk Tree is one of the most beautiful flowering trees in the world. Although it is too large for most residences, it should be planted much more in public places. The Floss Silk Tree is quite cold-tolerant, withstanding temperatures down to 20 degrees. It gets its name because of the floating floss expelled from seed pods. These can be a nuisance.

Season: Floss Silk Trees bloom in fall, generally from October until December. They are bare of leaves in winter.

To locate plants, go to www.easygardencolor.com

Companions: For a spectacular floral display, plant your Floss Silk Tree with other flowering trees that bloom at the same time. *Senna surattensis*, Lonchocarpus, and Dwarf Poinciana are three excellent choices. The price you pay for the color impact is that all but the Senna will look bad at the same time. Another approach is to plant the Floss Silk surrounded by evergreens, so that it is not so visible when bare.

LIGHT: High

WATER: Low. Ideal watering is once a week after the initial establishment period. Tolerates water up to 3 times per week. Untested in wetter conditions. (For detailed information about watering, see Chapter 8 in "Easy Gardens for Florida"*.)

SOIL: Wide range, as long as it is well-drained.

SALT TOLERANCE: Medium

WIND TOLERANCE: Unknown

ZONE: 9 to 11

PEST PROBLEMS: None known

PROPAGATION: Seeds or grafting.

Floss Silk flower

Planting: Plant any time of the year in zones 10 through 11 and in spring or summer in zone 9. Leave the root ball slightly out of the ground, about 1/4 inch.

Fertilizing: Immediately after planting, fertilize with a well-balanced, slow-release mix that includes minor elements. Repeat in March, June, and October of each year. If the summer is unusually hot and rainy, inspect the leaf color of the plant in August. If it appears washed out, add an additional fertilization in August. (See detailed fertilization instructions in "Easy Gardens for Florida"*, Chapter 11.)

Trimming: If desired, remove thorns from the trunk. Remove any crossed branches or dead wood every few years. Trim as needed to promote a symmetrical crown.

* My current book, "Easy Gardens for South Florida", will be expanded to include the entire state in 2004.

Note: Ceiba insignis has white to light yellow flowers and is native to Peru. It is rare in Florida.

Botanical Name: *Jacaranda mimosifolia*

Common Name: **Jacaranda**

CHARACTERISTICS

PLANT TYPE: Tree

AVERAGE SIZE: 40 feet tall by 40 feet wide.

GROWTH RATE: Fast

LEAF: Tiny leaflets, about 1/4 inch long, make up long, feathery leaves. Leaves are medium green and measure up to 20 inches long.

FLOWER: Lavender. Each flower is about 2 inches long. Clusters of flowers measure up to 1 foot long. A white variety, *Jacaranda mimosifolia 'alba'*, is sometimes available.

AVERAGE LIFE: 50 years.

ORIGIN: Argentina and Brazil.

CAUTIONS: None known

SPACING: 30 to 40 feet on center.

Beautiful lavender flowers in spring or early summer. Blooms more in central Florida. Bare in winter.

Jacaranda in bloom

General: A Jacarandas is a beautiful sight to behold in spring. Although it blooms more in central Florida than the southern end of the state, it is definitely worth considering in the both areas. Most Jacaranda trees do not bloom when young, taking up to 16 years to bloom from the time the seed is planted. Newer types are much faster. They are all bare in winter.

Season: Jacarandas bloom in spring, usually in May, but occasionally a bit later. They generally flower better in central Florida than south Florida, although, occasionally, the ones in south Florida are spectacular. The specimen above was photographed in Palm Beach County, which is in south Florida.

To locate plants, go to www.easygardencolor.com

Companions: It is difficult to find other flowering trees that dependably bloom the same time as the Jacaranda. Most other flowering trees bloom in winter or later in the summer. Two small ones that are good bets are Bougainvillea and the Cassia Tree (*Senna surattensis*). Another advantage of this combination is that the Cassia and Bougainvillea are evergreen, which diminishes the bad effect of the bare Jacaranda in winter.

Jacaranda with some companions

Planting: Plant any time of the year in native soil. Leave the root ball slightly out of the ground, about 1/4 inch. Stake securely. (See detailed planting instructions in "Easy Gardens for Florida"*, Chapter 11.)

Fertilizing: Immediately after planting, fertilize with a well-balanced, slow-release mix that includes minor elements. Repeat in March, June, and October of each year. (See detailed fertilization instructions in "Easy Gardens for Florida"*, Chapter 11.)

Trimming: Stake seedlings and prune to improve form, trimming to a single trunk. As the tree matures, it does not require much pruning. Every few years, remove any crossed branches or dead wood. Trim as needed to promote a somewhat symmetrical crown.

* My current book, "Easy Gardens for South Florida",
will be expanded to include the entire state in 2004.

GROWING CONDITIONS

LIGHT: High

WATER: Low. Ideal watering is once a week after the initial establishment period. (For detailed information about watering, see Chapter 8 in "Easy Gardens for Florida"*.)

SOIL: Wide range, as long as it is well-drained.

SALT TOLERANCE: Low

WIND TOLERANCE: Unknown

ZONE: 9 to 11. Flowers more in zone 9. According to David Bar-Zvi in "Tropical Gardening", several 50-year-old trees at Bok Tower (central Florida) withstood 26 degrees easily but died at 17 degrees. Young trees are not as frost-hardy as mature ones.

PEST PROBLEMS: None serious. Occasional root rot.

PROPAGATION: Seeds, cuttings, grafting.

Botanical Name: *Magnolia grandiflora*
Common Name: **Southern Magnolia**

A traditional tree throughout the southeastern United States. One of the most widely planted ornamental trees in the world.

CHARACTERISTICS

PLANT TYPE: Evergreen tree.

AVERAGE SIZE: 75 feet tall by 40 feet wide.

GROWTH RATE: Medium

LEAF: Olive green and shiny on top. Bronze and dull on the bottom. 5 to 8 inches long by 3 to 4 inches wide.

FLOWER: White. About 8 inches across.

AVERAGE LIFE: 50 years plus.

ORIGIN: Southeastern United States.

CAUTIONS: None known

SPACING: 50 feet on center

'D.D. Blancher' from Leu Botanical gardens in Orlando.

General: There are 80 species of tree and shrub Magnolias. The Southern Magnolia is known for its beautiful leaves and flowers as well as its stately pyramidal form. And, there are many different cultivars of Southern Magnolias. The large, traditional Southern Magnolia does better in the northern and central parts of the state than in the far south. The 'Little Gem' (a cultivar discussed on page 245) does beautifully throughout the state, including the southern portions. The 'D.D. Blancher' is the large cultivar doing best at Leu Botanical Gardens in Orlando. Its leaves (pictured left) were photographed there.

Season: Southern Magnolias begin blooming in late spring and continue on and off throughout the summer.

To locate plants, go to www.easygardencolor.com

Companions: If possible, don't plant anything under your Magnolia. Not many plants like growing under Magnolias. The low branches should be left to grow almost to the ground to hide the frequent Magnolia droppings. If you have a tree that has already had its lower branches removed and need a groundcover underneath, Liriope and Bromeliads will tolerate life there. But, it will be quite a maintenance chore to remove the fallen leaves from the top of your Bromeliads.

Planting: Plant containerized trees any time of the year in native soil. Field-grown trees do best transplanted in winter or spring. Leave the root ball slightly out of the ground, about 1/4 inch. (See detailed planting instructions in "Easy Gardens for Florida"*, Chapter 11.)

Fertilizing: Immediately after planting, fertilize with a well-balanced, slow-release mix that includes minor elements. Repeat in March, June, and October of each year. (See detailed fertilization instructions in "Easy Gardens for Florida"*, Chapter 11.)

Trimming: None needed. Southern Magnolias naturally grow all the way to the ground. Magnolias are fairly messy, and the low branches hide the droppings. It is a mistake to trim them off.

My current book, "Easy Gardens for South Florida", will be expanded to include the entire state in 2004.

GROWING CONDITIONS

LIGHT: Flowers best in full sun but adapts to partial shade.

WATER: Medium. Ideal watering is once or twice a week after the initial establishment period unless the tree is planted in wet, clay soil. (Be sure to water your Magnolia properly during the establishment period because it is very sensitive to drying out at this time.)

SOIL: Prefers acidic soil

SALT TOLERANCE: High

WIND TOLERANCE: Medium

ZONE: 7 to 10b. Grow better in north and central Florida than in the southern end of the state.

PEST PROBLEMS: Scales

PROPAGATION: Seeds, grafting, or air layering.

For More Information: I used an article called "Magnolias" by Gary Knox for some of my information. It is available for free on the internet. Go to http://edis.ifas.ufl.edu/BODY_MG270. This document is Circular 1089, a series of the Environmental Horticulture Department, Florida Cooperative Extension Service, Institute of Food and Agricultural Sciences, University of Florida. Publication date: June 1993. Revised: April 1994.

Botanical Name: *Spathodea campanulata*
Common Name: **African Tulip Tree**

CHARACTERISTICS

PLANT TYPE: Tree

AVERAGE SIZE: In Florida, grows 30 to 40 feet tall by 30 feet wide.

GROWTH RATE: Fast; up to 6 feet per year.

LEAF: Up to 8 inches long by 5 inches wide.

FLOWER: Looks like Tulips. About 4 to 5 inches long by 3 inches wide. Arranged in clusters. Reddish-orange, with yellow fringe. An all-yellow form is still quite rare.

AVERAGE LIFE: At least 40 years.

ORIGIN: Central Africa

CAUTIONS: Wood is weak and brittle, so it blows down easily in windstorms. Do not plant near buildings. Also, the seeds germinate a bit too easily, making it a possible weed tree. But the trees produce seeds very erratically. I have never had a seedling on my property.

SPACING: 30 feet on center.

Gorgeous flowers on a tree with a long bloom period. Evergreen, but with an awkward form.

African Tulip in full bloom

General: The African Tulip Tree features spectacular flowers during late winter and spring. In south Florida, the tree has a rather awkward form and keeps its leaves all year. In central Florida, the form of the tree is better because it is naturally pruned by frosts. It is partially bare in central Florida winters and dies back to the ground at thirty degrees. The tree grows back from the roots, provided the freeze is not too severe. The buds hold water and will spew it out, if squeezed. Children all over the world use them as toy water pistols. The tree is quite messy and best planted far from pavement. It also blows over easily in windstorms, so plant it far from buildings.

Season: In south Florida, it blooms from late winter into spring. The bloom period is long, up to five months. In central Florida, the bloom period is more varied, sometimes occurring twice a year.

Left: Yellow African Tulip Trees are still quite rare.

Companions: Plant African Tulips with other trees that bloom in late winter to early spring. A beautiful combination includes Purple Bougainvillea, African Tulip, and Yellow Tabebuia.

Bougainvillea

Yellow Tabebuia

African Tulip and some companions

Planting: Plant any time of the year in zones 10 through 11 and in spring or summer in zone 9b. Leave the root ball slightly out of the ground, about 1/4 inch. Stake the tree securely.

Fertilizing: Immediately after planting, fertilize with a well-balanced, slow-release mix that includes minor elements. Repeat in March, June, and October of each year. If the summer is unusually hot and rainy, inspect the leaf color of the plant in August. If it appears washed out, add an additional fertilization in August. (See instructions in "Easy Gardens for Florida"*, Chapter 11.)

Trimming: African Tulip Trees develop an awkward form, if untrimmed when young. Trim to a single trunk and a fairly symmetrical crown. Every few years, remove dead wood and crossed branches.

My current book, "Easy Gardens for South Florida", will be expanded to include the entire state in 2004.

LIGHT: Full sun. No blooms in even the lightest shade.

WATER: Medium. Ideal watering is twice a week after the initial establishment period. Tolerates water up to 4 times per week. (For detailed information about watering, see Chapter 8 in "Easy Gardens for Florida"*.)

SOIL: Wide range, as long as it is well-drained.

SALT TOLERANCE: Medium

WIND TOLERANCE: Low. Blows over easily.

ZONE: 9b to 11. According to Edwin Menninger in his book, "Flowering Trees of the World", the tree freezes to the ground at 30 degrees but grows back from the roots, often flowering the same year.

PEST PROBLEMS: None known

PROPAGATION: The orange and red forms grow from seed or cuttings. The yellow form grows by root cuttings.

CHAPTER **8**

SHADE COLOR

After

Before

Angelwing Begonia

Brunfelsia

Golden Shrimp Plant

This chapter features ideas for shade color as well as charts that organize the plants by size. These plant charts make designing easier by putting all the plants that work in a specific environment in one spot, so that you can see all the possibilities at once. For example, if you are looking for a plant about four to six feet tall for between your windows, simply look at that size range on the plant charts.

The plant charts show plants that thrive in medium shade, light shade, and mixed light. Not much color grows in dense shade. See Chapter 9 in "Easy Gardens for Florida" for dense shade suggestions, as well as thorough explanations of medium shade, light shade, and mixed light. Classifying the amount of shade you have is complex, so do not neglect to read this important chapter. In brief:

Medium shade: Areas that are predominately shady, but do not receive strong sun from the south or west. Many medium-shade plants burn with direct sun.

Light shade: Areas that are predominantly shady, but may receive some strong sun from the south or west.

Mixed light: Areas that receive light extremes, like full sun in summer and shade in winter. Plants that live in mixed light will grow either in sun all day, or shade all day.

Left and above: The 'Before' garden featured mainly green. The 'After' garden features four layers of color: Pink Angelwing Begonias as the tallest layer, Brunfelsia next, Golden Shrimp Plants next, and a border of Lipstick Impatiens

Best Shade Color for Florida Zones 9 through 11

Many colorful plants thrive in light to medium shade in Florida, as shown on the plant charts later in this chapter. So many, in fact, that the shear number of them can make choices difficult. The nine plants below represent some of the best for a high percentage of color that lasts a significant time of the year.

Begonias - Shrubs, groundcovers, or annuals. The Pink Angelwing (above) is the number one performer in shade, blooming every day of the year. The Orange Angelwing and Odorata Begonias are also very high performers, as are the Dragon Wings.

Bromeliads - Groundcovers or accents. Spectacular flowers last up to four months. Some have leaf color that lasts all year. 'Blue Tango' is pictured above. Zone 9b-11, or protected areas further north.

Brunfelsia - Shrubs or small trees that show up very well in shade because of the different colors on the flowers. Bloom for about six months a year in winter. Zones 10 through 11.

Costus barbatus - Large shrub that offers not only unique color but also tropical texture for very little care. One of the few plants with an exotic flower that doesn't die back in winter. Zones 9 though 11.

Crotons - Shrubs and groundcovers that offer constant color with very little care in sun or shade gardens. Collect many different varieties and break them up with plants that have flowers the colors of the Croton's leaves. The Croton above is the Icetone. Zones 10 through 11.

Firespike - Shrubs that come in red, purple, or pink and bloom for six to eight months each year. Offer a high percentage of color for very little care. The favorite food of hummingbirds. Different colors bloom in different seasons. Zones 7 through 11.

Impatiens - Annuals that offer the highest percentage of color in the shade garden. Use much less water in medium shade as compared with full sun. Use regular Impatiens (above) or New Guinea or Double Impatiens for color impact in shade.

Shrimp Plants - Shrubs or groundcovers. The Golden Shrimp (above) is the only Shrimp Plant that blooms all year, and the number two overall performer. Zones 9 through 11. Other types of Shrimps only grow in zones 10 through 11.

Ti Plants - Accent plants that offer color all year for very little care. Collect many different kinds for your shade garden. Available in many different colors and sizes. Tricolor Tis are pictured above. Zones 10 through 11.

Color layers for shade featuring Brunfelsia as the tallest layer, Golden Shrimp Plants in the middle, and a border of Lipstick Impatiens. The Brunfelsia blooms in the winter, while the Shrimp Plants bloom all year. Impatiens are annuals that bloom in the winter. Torenia is a good summer replacement for shade.

Medium Shade Color: Annuals and perennials arranged by size; numbers indicate hardiness zones in Florida.

Under 1'

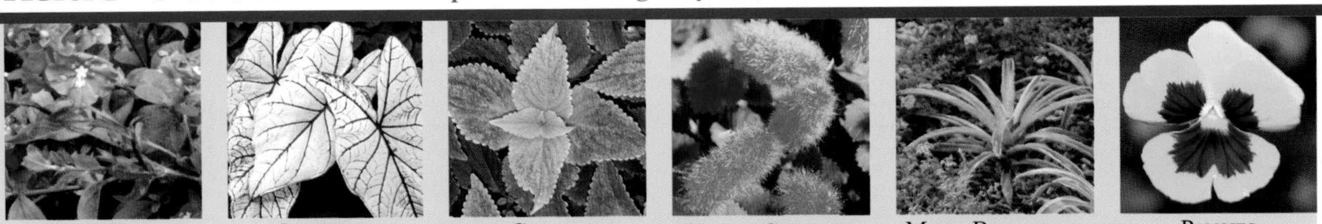

Blue Daze 8-11 | Caladium 8-11 | Coleus 8-11 | Dwarf Chenille 8-11 | Mend Bromeliad 9b-11 | Pansies 8-11

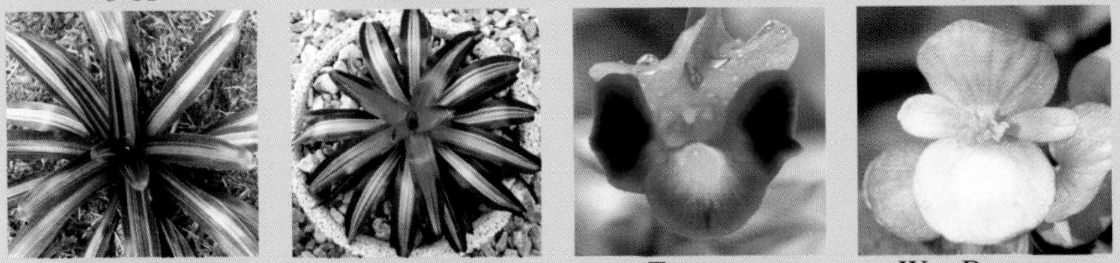

Perfection Bromeliad 9b-11 | Perfecta Bromeliad 9b-11 | Torenia 8-11 | Wax Begonias 8-11

1' - 3'

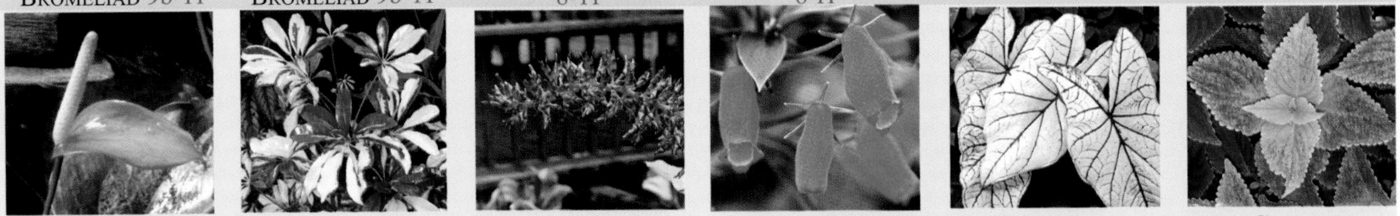

Lady Jane Anthurium 10-11 | Variegated Arboricola 10-11 | Blue Moon Bromeliad 9b-11 | Bolivian Sunset 8-11 | Caladium 8-11 | Coleus 8-11

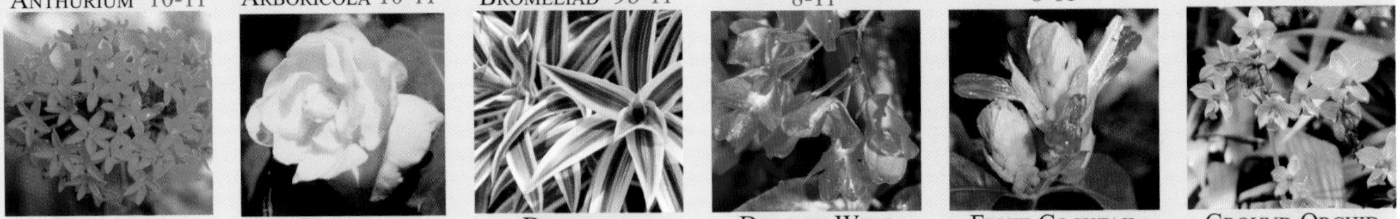

Cranberry Pentas 9-11 | Double Impatiens 8-11 | Dracaena reflexa 10-11 | Dragon Wing Begonia 8-11 | Fruit Cocktail 10-11 | Ground Orchid 10b-11

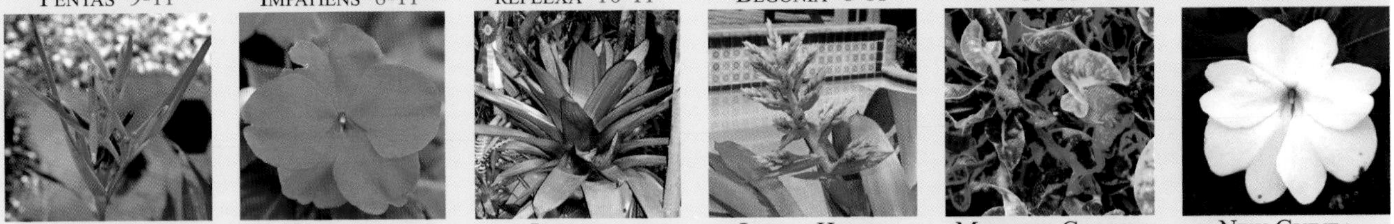

Heliconia Orange 10-11 | Impatiens 8-11 | Imperial Bromeliad 9b-11 | Little Harve Bromeliad 9b-11 | Mammey Croton 10-11 | New Guinea Impatiens 8-11

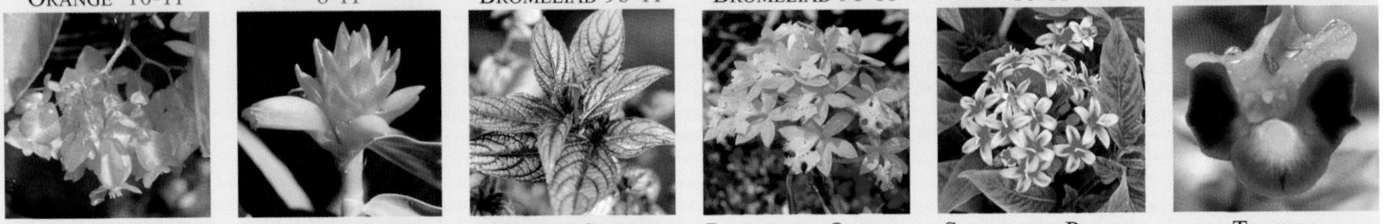

Orange Angelwing Begonia 9b-11 | Orange Tulip Costus 10-11 | Persian Shield 10-11 | Reed-stem Orchid 10-11 | Starburst Pentas 9-11 | Torenia 8-11

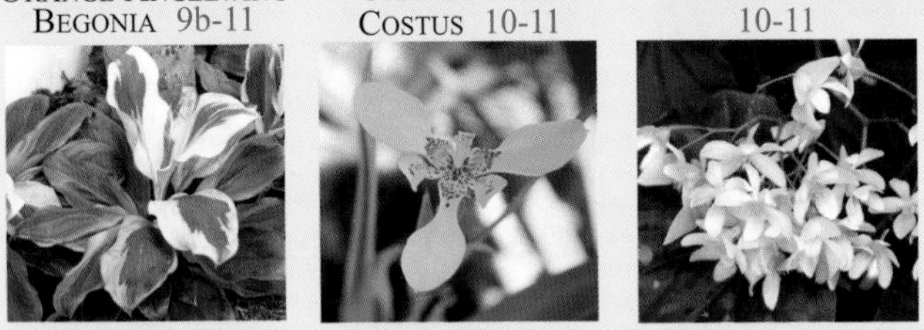

Tricolor Ti 10-11 | Walking Iris 10-11 | White Begonia 9b-11

2.5' - 4'

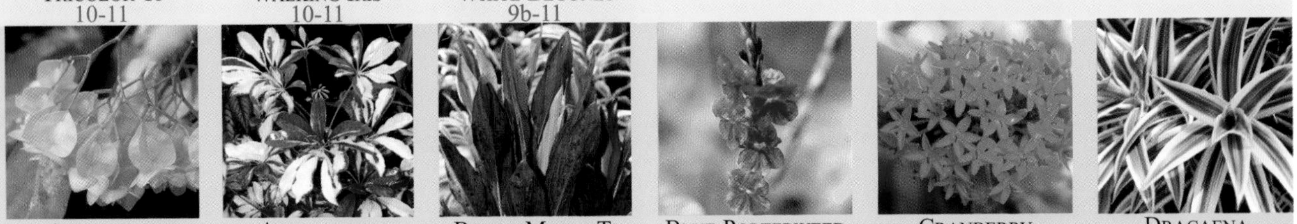

Angelwing Begonia 9b-11 | Arboricola 'Trinette' 10-11 | Black Magic Ti 10-11 | Blue Porterweed 10-11 | Cranberry Pentas 9-11 | Dracaena reflexa 10-11

2.5' - 4'

DWARF
POWDERPUFF 10-11

GIANT SHRIMP
10-11

HELICONIA
LADY DI 10-11

HELICONIA ORANGE
10-11

ICETONE CROTON
10-11

KING'S MANTLE
10-11

MAMMEY CROTON
10-11

PETRA CROTON
10-11

PIECRUST CROTON
10-11

PURPLE PRINCE TI
10-11

RED SPOT CROTON
10-11

SANCHEZIA
10-11

SHERBERT TI
10-11

SHRIMP PLANT
9-11

STOPLIGHT CROTON
10-11

TI RED SISTER
10-11

4' - 6'

ANGELWING
BEGONIA 9b-11

ARBORICOLA
'TRINETTE' 10-11

BRONZE
CARICATURE 10-11

BRUNFELSIA
10-11

DRACAENA
REFLEXA 10-11

DWARF POWDERPUFF
10-11

FIRESPIKE
8-11

GIANT RED SHRIMP
10-11

GIANT SHRIMP
10-11

GINGER
10-11

ICETONE CROTON
10-11

KING'S MANTLE
10-11

PANAMA ROSE
9b-11

PETRA CROTON
10-11

RED SPOT CROTON
10-11

SANCHEZIA
10b-11

SHRIMP PLANT
9-11

STOPLIGHT CROTON
10-11

TI RED SISTER
10-11

TRICOLOR
CARICATURE 10-11

VARIEGATED
GINGER 8-11

6' - 8'

ANGEL'S TRUMPET
8-11

ARBORICOLA
'TRINETTE' 10-11

CAMELLIA
8-9

COSTUS BARBATUS
9-11

DRACAENA
REFLEXA 10-11

GINGER
10-11

6' - 8'

GOLDEN PLUME
10-11

HELICONIA LOBSTER
CLAW 10-11

PANAMA ROSE
9b-11

PINK FIRESPIKE
8-11

SANCHEZIA
10b-11

SCARLET RED
CLOAK 9b-11

TRICOLOR
CARICATURE 10-11

TURK'S CAP
8-11

VARIEGATED
COSTUS 8-11

8' - 15'

ANGEL'S TRUMPET
8-11

STARBURST
10-11

TURK'S CAP
8-11

VINES

BLEEDING
HEART VINE 9-11

PINK PETTICOAT
10-11

PIPEVINE
9b-11

QUEEN'S WREATH
10-11

Orchids are an excellent choice for south Florida shade gardens.

This tropical garden peaks in the shade of our warmer months and features yellows and reds. Three of the plants stay colorful all year - the Ti Red Sisters, Mammey Crotons, and Golden Malayan Coconut Palms. The beautiful red flowers are Red Ginger, which bloom in summer and fall.

This tropical shade garden features exotic color accenting the Areca Palms. Anthuriums, Bromeliads, Bolivian Sunset, Ti Plants, and Ginger add color and a tropical feel.

Use variegated plants to show off dark leaves. The dark Ti Plants would not show up in this shade garden without the light variegation of the Flax in front. The plant with multicolored leaves is the Philodendron 'Kalaidascope'. Gingers and Heliconias complete this tropical garden.

UNDER 1'

BLUE DAZE 8-11	CALADIUM 8-11	COLEUS 8-11	DWARF CHENILLE 8-11	DWARF HIBISCUS 9b-11	MEND BROMELIAD 9b-11
PANSIES 8-11	PERFECTION BROMELIAD 9b-11	PETUNIAS 8-11	PURPLE QUEEN 9-11	SNAPDRAGON 8-11	TORENIA 8-11
WAX BEGONIAS 8-11					

1' - 3'

AGAPANTHUS 8-9	ANNUAL SALVIA 8-11	ARBORICOLA 'TRINETTE' 10-11	AZALEA 8-9	BLUE MOON BROMELIAD 9b-11	BOLIVIAN SUNSET 8-11
CALADIUM 8-11	COLEUS 8-11	CONEFLOWER 8-9	CRANBERRY PENTAS 9-11	DAYLILY 8-9	DOUBLE IMPATIENS 8-11
DRACAENA REFLEXA 10-11	DRAGON WING BEGONIA 8-11	DWARF HIBISCUS 9b-11	FRUIT COCKTAIL 10-11	GERANIUM 8-11	GROUND ORCHID 10-11
HELICONIA 10-11	IMPATIENS 8-11	IMPERIAL BROMELIAD 9b-11	IXORA 'PETITE' 10-11	LITTLE HARVE BROMELIAD 9b-11	MAMMEY CROTON 10-11
MELAMPODIUM 8-11	MEXICAN SAGE 8-11	NEW GUINEA IMPATIENS 8-11	NEW LOOK PENTAS 8-11	ORANGE ANGELWING BEGONIA 9b-11	ORANGE TULIP COSTUS 10-11

See page 259 for an explanation of 'light' shade.

1' - 3'

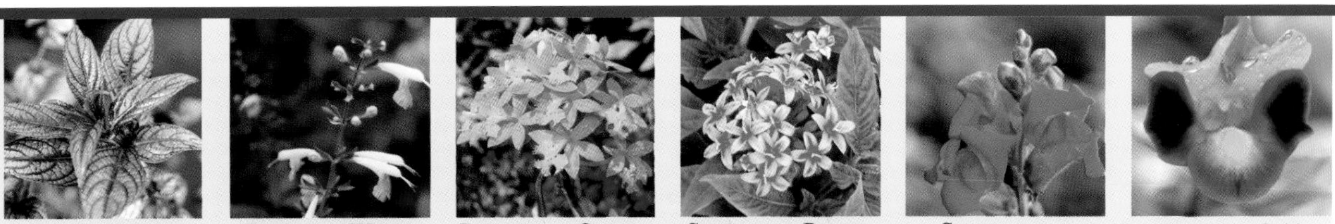

Persian Shield 10-11

Pink and White Salvia 8-11

Reed-stem Orchid 10-11

Starburst Pentas 9-11

Snapdragon 8-11

Torenia 8-11

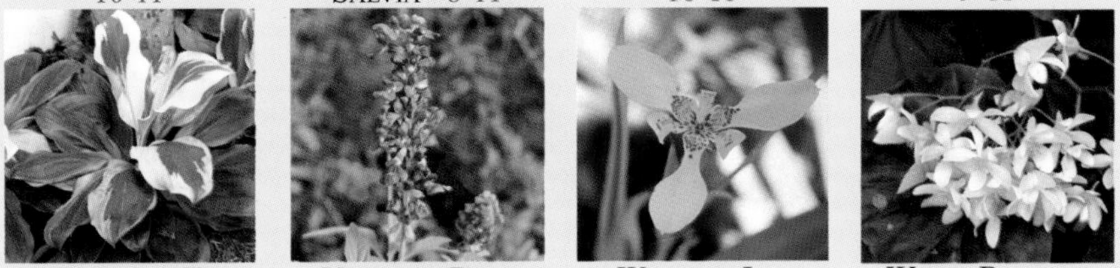

Tricolor Ti 10-11

Victoria Blue Salvia 8-11

Walking Iris 10-11

White Begonia 9b-11

2.5' - 4'

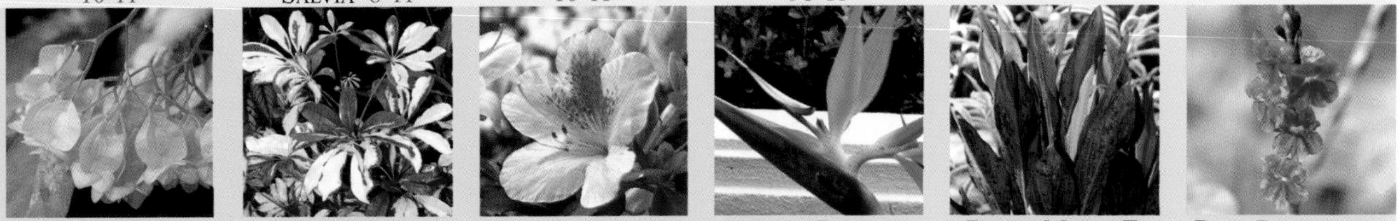

Angelwing Begonia 9b-11

Arboricola 'Trinette' 10-11

Azalea 8-9

Bird of Paradise 9-11

Black Magic Ti 10-11

Blue Porterweed 10-11

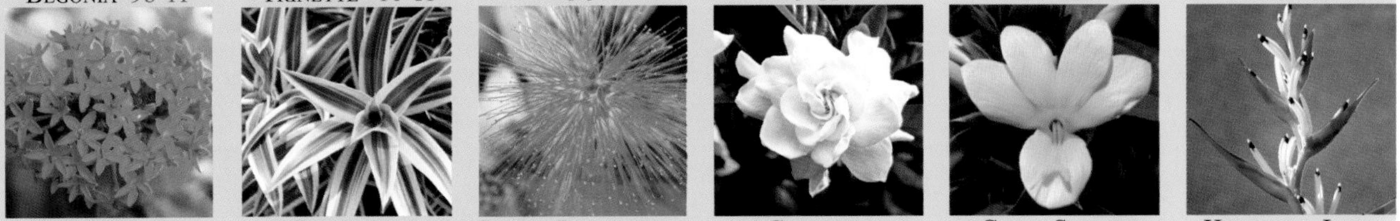

Cranberry Pentas 9b-11

Dracaena Reflexa 10-11

Dwarf Powderpuff 10-11

Gardenia 8-11

Giant Shrimp 10-11

Heliconia Lady Di 10-11

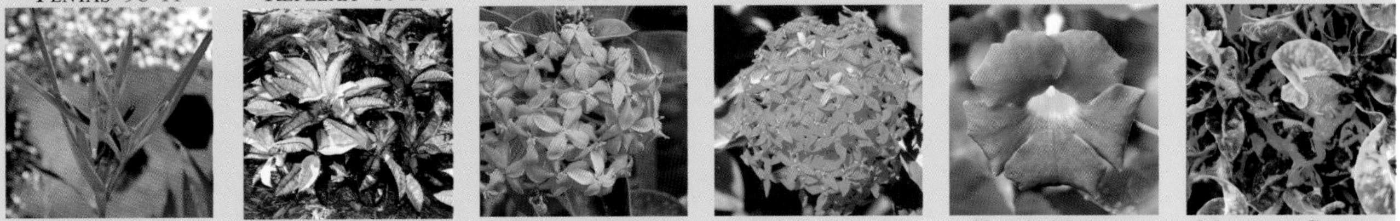

Heliconia Orange 10-11

Icetone Croton 10-11

Ixora 'Nora Grant' 10-11

Ixora 'Super King' 10-11

King's Mantle 10-11

Mammey Croton 10-11

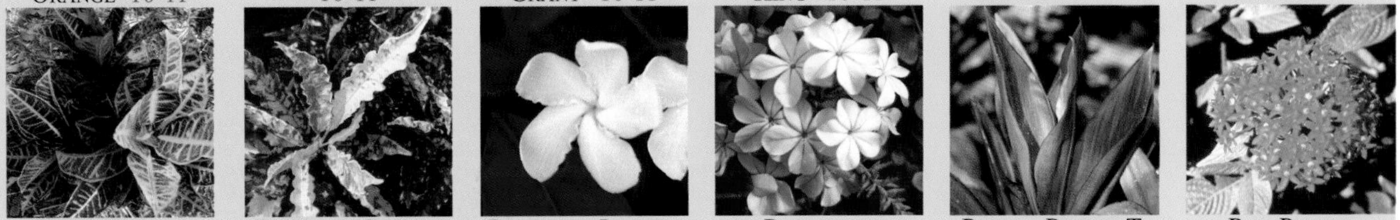

Petra Croton 10-11

Piecrust Croton 10-11

Pinwheel Jasmine 10-11

Plumbago 9-11

Purple Prince Ti 10-11

Red Pentas 9b-11

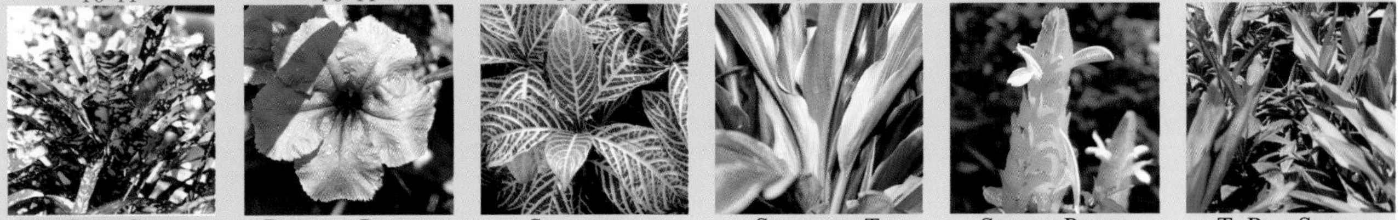

Red Spot Croton 10-11

Ruellia Purple Showers 8-11

Sanchezia 10-11

Sherbert Ti 10-11

Shrimp Plant 9-11

Ti Red Sister 10-11

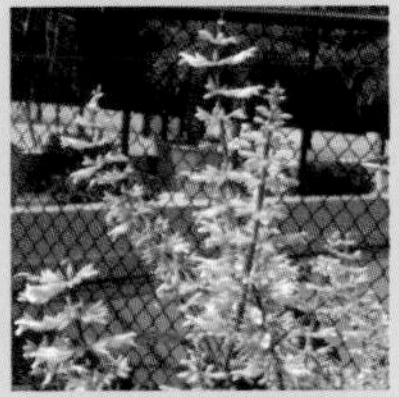

Yellow Salvia 8-11

4' - 6'

| ANGELWING BEGONIA 9b-11 | ARBORICOLA 'TRINETTE' 10-11 | AZALEA 8-9 | BEAUTYBERRY 8-11 | BLUE BUTTERFLY 10-11 | BIRD OF PARADISE 9-11 |

| CARICATURE PLANT 10-11 | BRUNFELSIA 10-11 | CAPE HONEYSUCKLE 8-11 | CHENILLE PLANT 10-11 | CRINUM LILY 8-11 | DRACAENA REFLEXA 10-11 |

| DWARF MUSSAENDA 10-11 | DWARF POWDERPUFF 10-11 | FIREBUSH 9-11 | FIRESPIKE 8-11 | GARDENIA 8-11 | GIANT RED SHRIMP 10-11 |

| GIANT SHRIMP 10-11 | GINGER 10-11 | HIBISCUS 9b-11 | ICETONE CROTON 10-11 | IXORA 'NORA GRANT' 10-11 | IXORA 'SUPER KING' 10-11 |

| JATROPHA 10-11 | KING'S MANTLE 10-11 | MOPHEAD HYDRANGEA 8-9 | PANAMA ROSE 9b-11 | PETRA CROTON 10-11 | PINK PORTERWEED 10-11 |

| PINWHEEL JASMINE 10-11 | PLUMBAGO 9-11 | RED PENTAS 9-11 | RED SPOT CROTON 10-11 | RUELLIA PURPLE SHOWERS 8-11 | SANCHEZIA 10-11 |

| SHRIMP PLANT 9-11 | STOPLIGHT CROTON 10-11 | THRYALLIS 9-11 | TI RED SISTER 10-11 | TRICOLOR CARICATURE 10-11 | VARIEGATED GINGER 8-11 |

6' - 8'

| ANGEL'S TRUMPET 8-11 | ARBORICOLA 'TRINETTE' 10-11 | AZALEA 7-9 | BRONZE CARICATURE 10-11 | BRUNFELSIA 10-11 | CAMELLIA 7-9 |

6' - 8'

CAPE HONEYSUCKLE
8-11

CHENILLE PLANT
10-11

CHINESE HAT
10-11

COSTUS BARBATUS
9-11

DOUBLE RUFFLE
HIBISCUS 9b-11

DRACAENA
REFLEXA 10-11

FIREBUSH
9-11

FLORIDA
HYDRANGEA 9b-11

GARDENIA
8-11

GINGER
10-11

GOLDEN PLUME
10-11

HELICONIA LOBSTER
CLAW 10-11

IXORA 'NORA
GRANT' 10-11

IXORA 'SUPER
KING' 10-11

JATROPHA
10-11

OAKLEAF
HYDRANGEA 8-9

ORANGE & WHITE
MUSSAENDA 10-11

PINK FIRESPIKE
10-11

PINK PORTERWEED
10-11

SANCHEZIA
10-11

SCARLET RED
CLOAK 10-11

TRICOLOR
CARICATURE 10-11

TURK'S CAP
8-11

VARIEGATED
COSTUS 8-11

8' - 15'

AND. CREPE
HIBISCUS 9b-11

ANGEL'S TRUMPET
8-11

CAMELLIA
8-9

CHINESE HAT
10-11

DOUBLE RUFFLE
HIBISCUS 9b-11

GOLDEN SENNA
10-11

HIBISCUS, 'SEMINOLE
PINK' 9b-11

JATROPHA
10-11

OAKLEAF
HYDRANGEA 6-9

STARBURST
10-11

TURK'S CAP
8-11

15' - 35'

MAGNOLIA LITTLE
GEM 8-11

POWDERPUFF
9-11

TROPICAL
SNOWBALL 10-11

VINES

BLEEDING HEART
VINE 9-11

CHINESE HAT
10-11

CONFEDERATE
JASMINE 8-11

PINK PETTICOAT
10-11

PIPEVINE
9b-11

QUEEN'S WREATH
10-11

SHADE COLOR   271

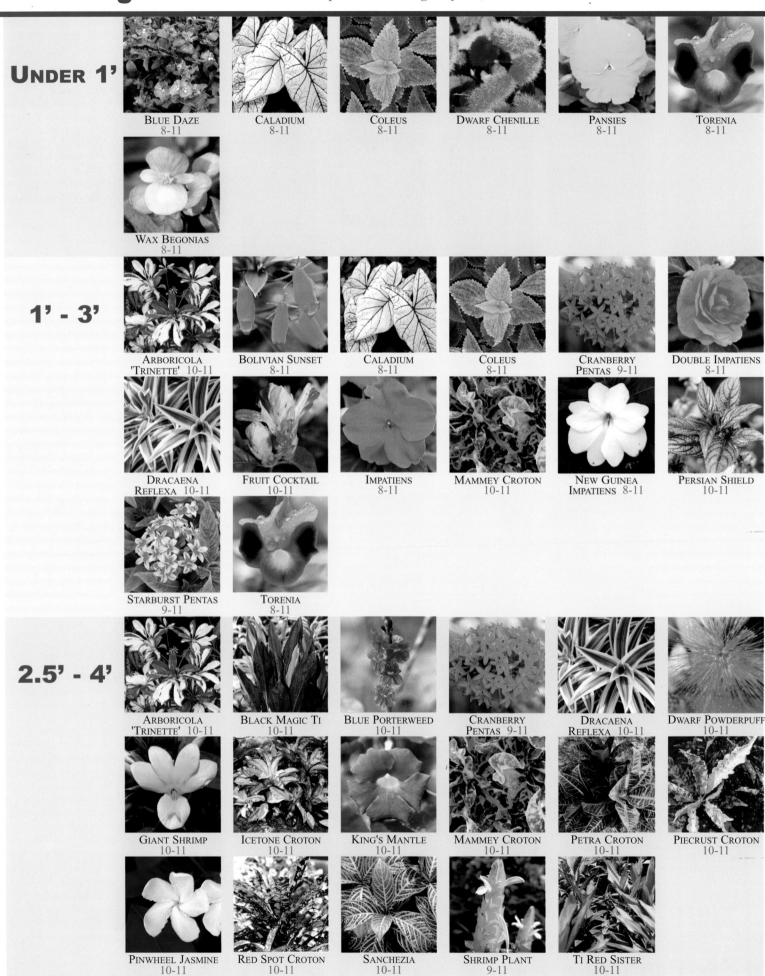

UNDER 1'

BLUE DAZE
8-11

CALADIUM
8-11

COLEUS
8-11

DWARF CHENILLE
8-11

PANSIES
8-11

TORENIA
8-11

WAX BEGONIAS
8-11

1' - 3'

ARBORICOLA
'TRINETTE' 10-11

BOLIVIAN SUNSET
8-11

CALADIUM
8-11

COLEUS
8-11

CRANBERRY
PENTAS 9-11

DOUBLE IMPATIENS
8-11

DRACAENA
REFLEXA 10-11

FRUIT COCKTAIL
10-11

IMPATIENS
8-11

MAMMEY CROTON
10-11

NEW GUINEA
IMPATIENS 8-11

PERSIAN SHIELD
10-11

STARBURST PENTAS
9-11

TORENIA
8-11

2.5' - 4'

ARBORICOLA
'TRINETTE' 10-11

BLACK MAGIC TI
10-11

BLUE PORTERWEED
10-11

CRANBERRY
PENTAS 9-11

DRACAENA
REFLEXA 10-11

DWARF POWDERPUFF
10-11

GIANT SHRIMP
10-11

ICETONE CROTON
10-11

KING'S MANTLE
10-11

MAMMEY CROTON
10-11

PETRA CROTON
10-11

PIECRUST CROTON
10-11

PINWHEEL JASMINE
10-11

RED SPOT CROTON
10-11

SANCHEZIA
10-11

SHRIMP PLANT
9-11

TI RED SISTER
10-11

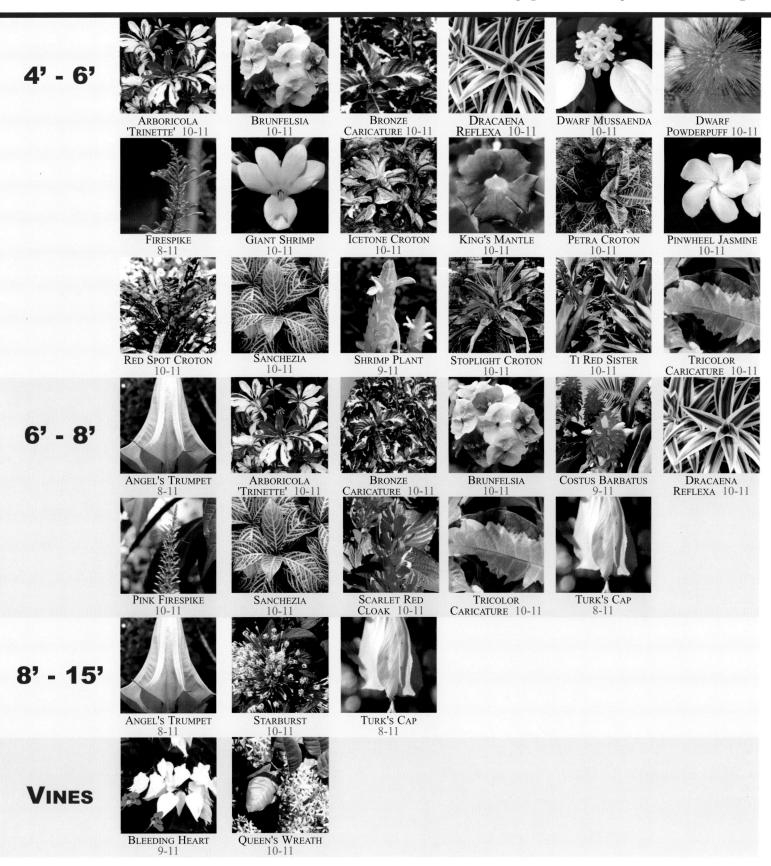

4' - 6'

ARBORICOLA 'TRINETTE' 10-11

BRUNFELSIA 10-11

BRONZE CARICATURE 10-11

DRACAENA REFLEXA 10-11

DWARF MUSSAENDA 10-11

DWARF POWDERPUFF 10-11

FIRESPIKE 8-11

GIANT SHRIMP 10-11

ICETONE CROTON 10-11

KING'S MANTLE 10-11

PETRA CROTON 10-11

PINWHEEL JASMINE 10-11

RED SPOT CROTON 10-11

SANCHEZIA 10-11

SHRIMP PLANT 9-11

STOPLIGHT CROTON 10-11

TI RED SISTER 10-11

TRICOLOR CARICATURE 10-11

6' - 8'

ANGEL'S TRUMPET 8-11

ARBORICOLA 'TRINETTE' 10-11

BRONZE CARICATURE 10-11

BRUNFELSIA 10-11

COSTUS BARBATUS 9-11

DRACAENA REFLEXA 10-11

PINK FIRESPIKE 10-11

SANCHEZIA 10-11

SCARLET RED CLOAK 10-11

TRICOLOR CARICATURE 10-11

TURK'S CAP 8-11

8' - 15'

ANGEL'S TRUMPET 8-11

STARBURST 10-11

TURK'S CAP 8-11

VINES

BLEEDING HEART 9-11

QUEEN'S WREATH 10-11

CHAPTER 9

SUN COLOR

This chapter features ideas for sun color as well as charts that organize the plants by size. These plant charts make designing easier by putting all the plants that work in a specific environment in one spot, so that you can see all the possibilities at once. For example, if you are looking for a plant about four to six feet tall for between your windows, simply look at that size range on the plant charts.

Above: Yellow and Purple Lantana in a wall pot.

Left: A cottage garden that features plants that thrive in the hot Florida sun. White Sweet Alyssum forms the border around Midnight Blue Petunias and Starburst Pentas. This plant selection uses much less water than the more common Impatiens.

Best Sun Color for Florida Zones 9 through 11

Many colorful plants thrive in bright Florida sun, as shown on the plant charts later in this chapter. So many, in fact, that the shear number of them can make choices difficult. The nine plants below represent some of the best for a high percentage of color that lasts a significant time of the year.

Bougainvillea - Shrubs, trees, or vines. One of our most spectacular plants for color in the dry season if you can put up with the high maintenance requirements. Zones 9 through 11. Protect from severe freezes in zone 9.

Crotons - Shrubs and groundcovers that offer constant color with very little care in sun or shade gardens. The Croton above is the Red Spot. Hundreds of different colors, shapes, and sizes of Crotons are now available. Zones 10 through 11.

Firespike - Shrubs that come in red, purple, or pink and bloom for six to eight months each year. Offer a high percentage of color for very little care. The favorite food of hummingbirds. Different colors bloom in different seasons. Zones 7 through 11.

Pentas - 16 different kinds now on the market, from 6 inch annuals to 4 foot shrubs. Large plants have more color and live longer. Red (above) and Cranberry give the best color in sun. Bloom all the time. Perennials in zones 9 though 11.

Petunias - Cool-season annuals that perform extremely well throughout Florida. Many colors, both solids and bicolors available. Very high color impact.

Plumbago - Shrubs that bloom for most of the year (warmer months) in blue or white. Best suited for informal gardens. Very easy to grow. One of our best shrubs for color in zones 9 through 11.

Salvia - Annuals now available in many colors. Very high performers throughout Florida. Offer almost as much color as Impatiens without the need for a lot of water.

Thryallis - Shrubs that offer about 8 months of blooms with very little care. Give them space to grow at least 4 feet tall by 4 feet wide. Most people try to maintain them too short to bloom up to their potential. Zones 9 through 11.

Ti Plants - Many Ti Plants require shade but some of the darker varieties thrive in full sun. The 'Black Magic' (above) performed best in our trials in full sun. Offers year-round color for very little care. Zones 10 through 11.

Color layers for sun: Above, featuring Plumbago and Red Pentas as the back layer, bordered by yellow Marigolds. Below, mixed annual Salvias with yellow Marigolds. The strong color contrast - using blues or purples with yellows and reds - works well in the intense Florida sun. Pale colors do not show well in this much light. Save your pale pinks for shade gardens.

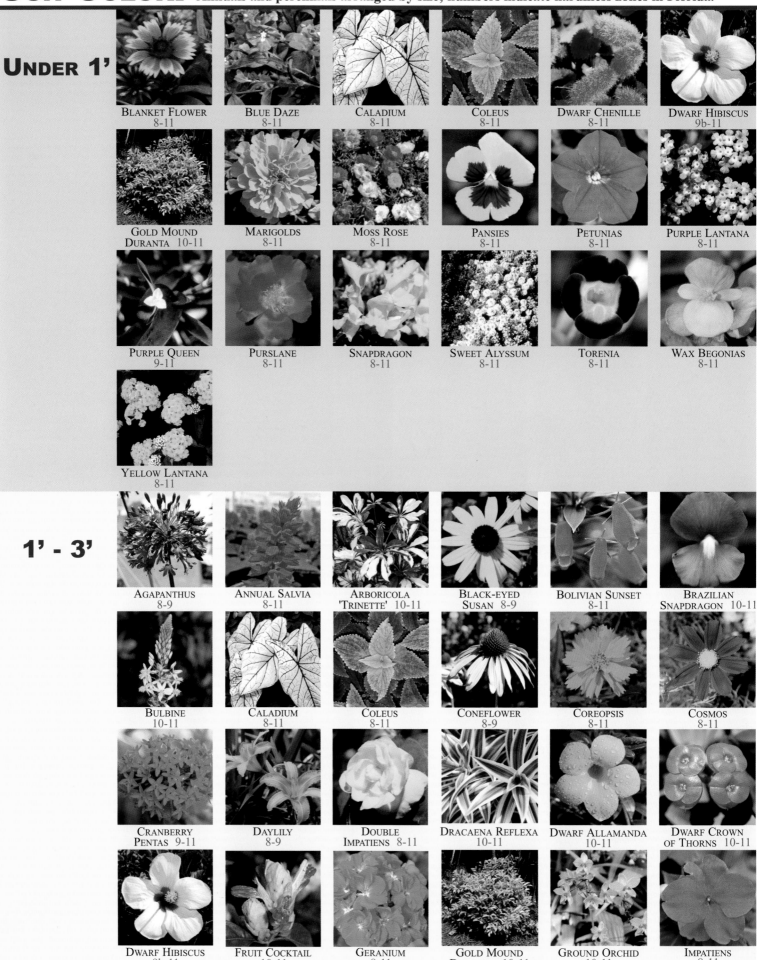

UNDER 1'

BLANKET FLOWER 8-11	BLUE DAZE 8-11	CALADIUM 8-11	COLEUS 8-11	DWARF CHENILLE 8-11	DWARF HIBISCUS 9b-11
GOLD MOUND DURANTA 10-11	MARIGOLDS 8-11	MOSS ROSE 8-11	PANSIES 8-11	PETUNIAS 8-11	PURPLE LANTANA 8-11
PURPLE QUEEN 9-11	PURSLANE 8-11	SNAPDRAGON 8-11	SWEET ALYSSUM 8-11	TORENIA 8-11	WAX BEGONIAS 8-11
YELLOW LANTANA 8-11					

1' - 3'

AGAPANTHUS 8-9	ANNUAL SALVIA 8-11	ARBORICOLA 'TRINETTE' 10-11	BLACK-EYED SUSAN 8-9	BOLIVIAN SUNSET 8-11	BRAZILIAN SNAPDRAGON 10-11
BULBINE 10-11	CALADIUM 8-11	COLEUS 8-11	CONEFLOWER 8-9	COREOPSIS 8-11	COSMOS 8-11
CRANBERRY PENTAS 9-11	DAYLILY 8-9	DOUBLE IMPATIENS 8-11	DRACAENA REFLEXA 10-11	DWARF ALLAMANDA 10-11	DWARF CROWN OF THORNS 10-11
DWARF HIBISCUS 9b-11	FRUIT COCKTAIL 10-11	GERANIUM 8-11	GOLD MOUND DURANTA 10-11	GROUND ORCHID 10-11	IMPATIENS 8-11

1' - 3'

IMPERIAL
BROMELIAD 9b-11

IXORA 'PETITE'
10-11

MAMMEY CROTON
10-11

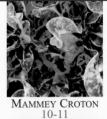
MARIGOLDS
8-11

MELAMPODIUM
8-11

MEXICAN SAGE
8-11

MILKWEED
9-11

NEW GUINEA
IMPATIENS 8-11

NEW LOOK PENTAS
8-11

PERSIAN SHIELD
10-11

PINK AND WHITE
SALVIA 8-11

REED-STEM
ORCHID 10-11

SNAPDRAGON
8-11

STARBURST PENTAS
9-11

ROSE
8-10

TORENIA
8-11

VICTORIA BLUE
SALVIA 8-11

WALKING IRIS
10-11

YELLOW LANTANA
8-11

2.5' - 4'

ARBORICOLA
'TRINETTE' 10-11

BLACK MAGIC TI
10-11

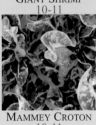
BLUE PORTERWEED
10-11

CANNA LILY
8-11

COSMOS
8-11

CIGAR FLOWER
9-10

CRANBERRY
PENTAS 9-11

DRACAENA
REFLEXA 10-11

DWARF POWDERPUFF
10-11

GIANT SHRIMP
10-11

ICETONE CROTON
10-11

IXORA 'NORA
GRANT' 10-11

IXORA 'PETITE'
10-11

IXORA 'SUPER
KING' 10-11

KING'S MANTLE
10-11

MAMMEY CROTON
10-11

MARDI-GRAS
COPPERLEAF 10-11

PETRA CROTON
10-11

PHILIPPINE VIOLET
8

PIECRUST CROTON
10-11

PINWHEEL JASMINE
10-11

PLUMBAGO
10-11

RED PENTAS
9-11

RED SPOT CROTON
10-11

SUN COLOR: Annuals and perennials arranged by size; numbers indicate hardiness zones in Florida.

2.5' - 4'

RUELLIA PURPLE
SHOWERS 8-11

SANCHEZIA
10-11

SHRIMP PLANT
9-11

ROSE
8-11

SHRUB ALLAMANDA
10-11

SILVER
BUTTONWOOD 10-11

SNOWBUSH
10-11

TI RED SISTER
10-11

YELLOW SALVIA
8-11

4' - 6'

ARBORICOLA
'TRINETTE' 10-11

BEAUTYBERRY
8-11

BIRD OF PARADISE
9-11

BLUE BUTTERFLY
10-11

BRONZE CARICATURE
10-11

BRUNFELSIA
10-11

CAPE HONEYSUCKLE
10-11

CHENILLE PLANT
10-11

CRINUM LILY
8-11

CURLY RUFFLE
10-11

DRACAENA
REFLEXA 10-11

DWARF
MUSSAENDA 10-11

DWARF POWDERPUFF
10-11

FIRE DRAGON
COPPERLEAF 10-11

FIREBUSH
8-11

FIRESPIKE
8-11

GARDENIA
8-11

GIANT RED SHRIMP
10-11

GIANT SHRIMP
10-11

HIBISCUS
9b-11

ICETONE CROTON
10-11

IXORA 'NORA
GRANT' 10-11

IXORA 'SUPER
KING' 10-11

JATROPHA
10-11

KING'S MANTLE
10-11

MARDI-GRAS
COPPERLEAF 10-11

PANAMA ROSE
10-11

PETRA CROTON
10-11

PINK PORTERWEED
10-11

PINWHEEL JASMINE
10-11

PLUMBAGO
9-11

RED PENTAS
9-11

RED SPOT CROTON
10-11

ROSE
8-10

RUELLIA PURPLE
SHOWERS 8-11

SANCHEZIA
10-11

SHRIMP PLANT
9-11

SHRUB ALLAMANDA
10-11

SILVER BUTTONWOOD
10-11

SNOWBUSH
10-11

STOPLIGHT CROTON
10-11

THRYALLIS
9-11

TI RED SISTER
10-11

TRICOLOR
CARICATURE 10-11

ANGEL'S TRUMPET
8-11

ARBORICOLA
'TRINETTE' 10-11

BOUGAINVILLEA
9-11

BRONZE
CARICATURE 10-11

BRUNFELSIA
10-11

BUTTERFLY BUSH
8-9

CAPE HONEYSUCKLE
8-11

CHENILLE PLANT
10-11

CHINESE HAT
10-11

COSTUS BARBATUS
9-11

CURLY RUFFLE
10-11

DOUBLE RUFFLE
HIBISCUS 9b-11

DRACAENA
REFLEXA 10-11

DWARF WHITE
ORCHID 10-11

FIREBUSH
9-11

FLORIDA
HYDRANGEA 9b-11

GARDENIA
8-11

GOLDEN DEWDROP
9b-11

IXORA 'NORA
GRANT' 10-11

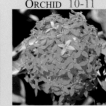
IXORA 'SUPER
KING' 10-11

JATROPHA
10-11

OLEANDER
8-11

ORANGE AND WHITE
MUSSAENDA 10-11

PANAMA ROSE
10-11

PEACH MUSSAENDA
10-11

PINK FIRESPIKE
10-11

PINK PORTERWEED
10-11

RED ORCHID
9b-11

SALMON
MUSSAENDA 10-11

SANCHEZIA
10-11

SCARLET RED
CLOAK 10-11

SNOWBUSH
10-11

TRICOLOR
CARICATURE 10-11

TURK'S CAP
8-11

VAR.GOLDEN
DEWDROP 9b-11

8' - 15'

AND. CREPE
HIBISCUS 9b-11

ANGEL'S TRUMPET
8-11

BOUGAINVILLEA
9-11

BUTTERFLY BUSH
8-9

CASSIA TREE
10-11

CHINESE HAT
10-11

CORNUDIA
10-11

CREPE MYRTLE
8-11

DOUBLE RUFFLE
HIBISCUS 9b-11

DWARF POINCIANA
9b-11

FRANGIPANI
10-11

GOLDEN DEWDROP
9b-11

GOLDEN SENNA
10-11

HIBISCUS 'SEMINOLE
PINK' 10-11

JATROPHA
10-11

OLEANDER
8b-11

SILVER BUTTONWOOD
10-11

STARBURST
10-11

TURK'S CAP
8-11

WEST INDIAN
SHOWER 9b-11

15' - 35'

COPPERPOD
9-11

CREPE MYRTLE
8-11

FRANGIPANI
10-11

GOLDEN RAIN
8-11

MAGNOLIA 'LITTLE
GEM" 8-11

ORANGE GEIGER
10-11

POWDERPUFF
9b-11

QUEEN'S CREPE
10-11

SUNSHINE TREE
10-11

TAB IPE
9-10

TROPICAL
SNOWBALL 10-11

YELLOW TABEBUIA
10-11

35'+

AFRICAN TULIP
TREE 9b-11

QUEEN'S CREPE
10-11

FLOSS SILK TREE
9-11

GOLDEN SHOWER
10-11

HONG KONG
ORCHID 10-11

JACARANDA
9-11

ROYAL POINCIANA
10-11

SOUTHERN
MAGNOLIA 8-10

PELTOPHORUM
10-11

VINES

ALLAMANDA
10-11

**BLEEDING HEART
VINE** 9-11

BOUGAINVILLEA
9-11

CAPE HONEYSUCKLE
8-11

CHINESE HAT
10-11

**CONFEDERATE
JASMINE** 8-11

PINK PETTICOAT
10-11

PIPEVINE
9b-11

RED ORCHID
9b-11

After

Before

A corner of this front yard is transformed into a beautiful garden with a winding path-path and some layers of color. All the plants did well except the purple trees (Tibouchina grandiflora).

CHAPTER 10

COLOR FOR SALT AND WIND

After

Before

This chapter features ideas for garden color in areas susceptible to salt and wind. It also has charts that organize the plants by size. These plant charts make designing easier by putting all the plants that work in a specific environment in one spot, so that you can see all the possibilities at once. For example, if you are looking for a plant about four to six feet tall for between your windows, simply look at that size range on the plant charts.

Most sites that are near salt water are also windy, so the two environments are featured together. These plants are tough, and work well in many challenging environments. They are useful near the sea as well as on windy sites inland.

Assessing the amount of salt and wind is important. Look on page 5 of this book's Glossary to see definitions of medium and high salt and wind tolerance. In addition, see Chapter 11 in this books companion ("Easy Gardens for Florida") for more details.

Above and left: A planter on a salt water canal is planted with Pentas, Lantana, and Blue Daze surrounding Sago Palms and a White Bird of Paradise.

Color for Medium Salt and Wind

Under 1'

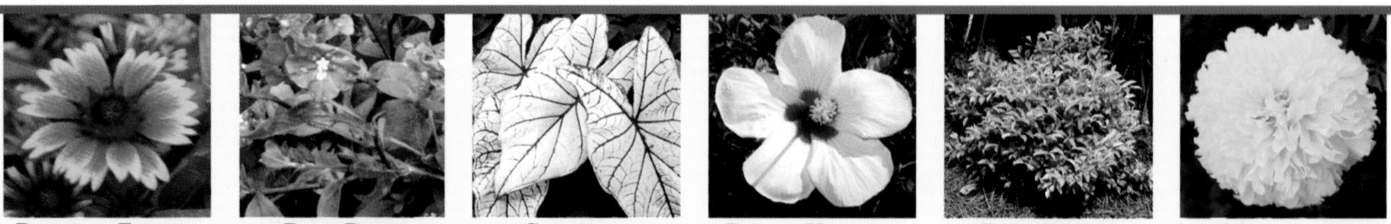

Blanket Flower 8-11	Blue Daze 8-11	Caladium 8-11	Dwarf Hibiscus 9b-11	Gold Mound Duranta 10-11	Marigolds 8-11

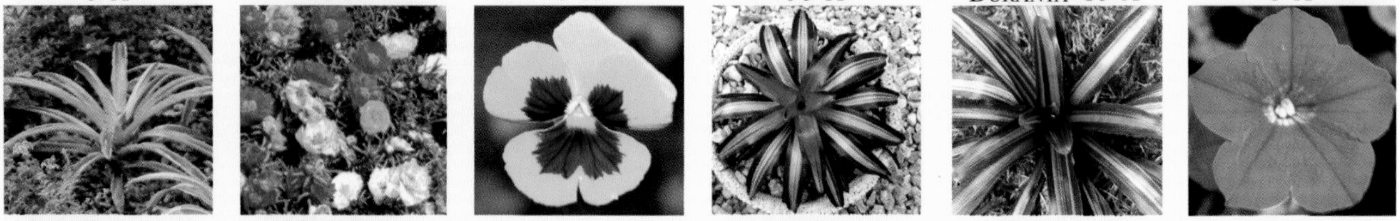

Mend Bromeliad 9b-11	Moss Rose 8-11	Pansies 8-11	Perfecta Bromeliad 9b-11	Perfection Bromeliad 9b-11	Petunias 8-11

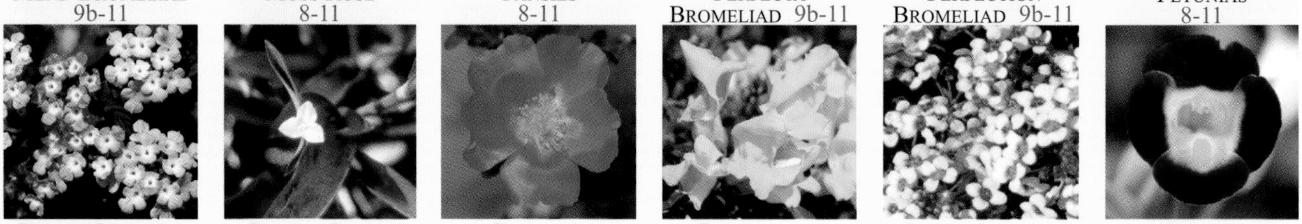

Purple Lantana 8-11	Purple Queen 9-11	Purslane 8-11	Snapdragon 8-11	Sweet Alyssum 8-11	Torenia 8-11

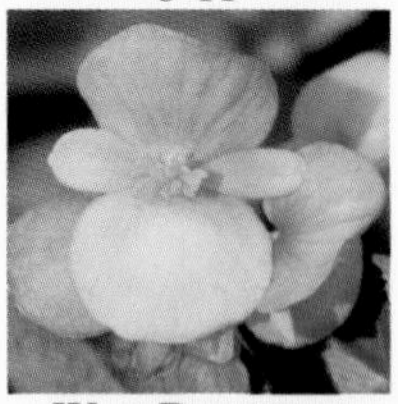

Wax Begonias 8-11

1' - 3'

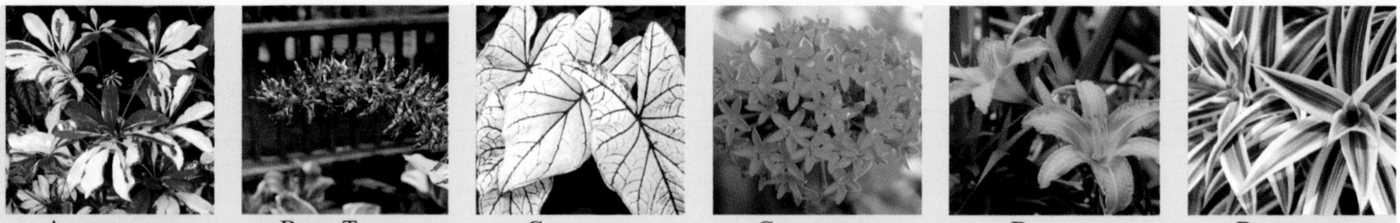

Arboricola 'Trinette' 10-11	Blue Tango Bromeliad 9b-11	Caladium 8-11	Cranberry Pentas 9-11	Daylily 8-9	Dracaena Reflexa 10-11

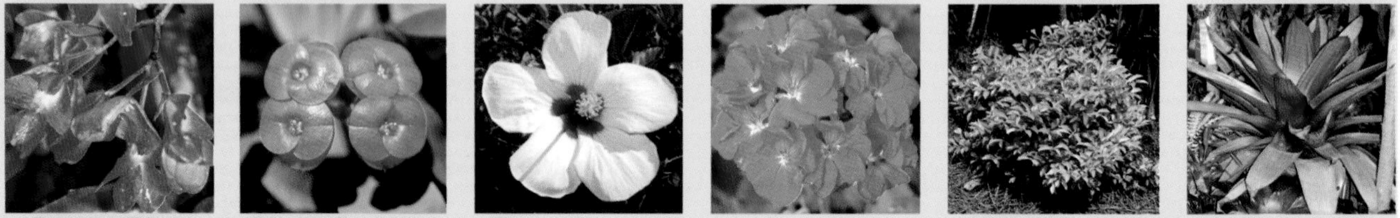

Dragon Wing Begonia 8-11	Dwarf Crown of Thorns 10-11	Dwarf Hibiscus 9b-11	Geranium 8-11	Gold Mound Duranta 10-11	Imperial Bromeliad 9b-11

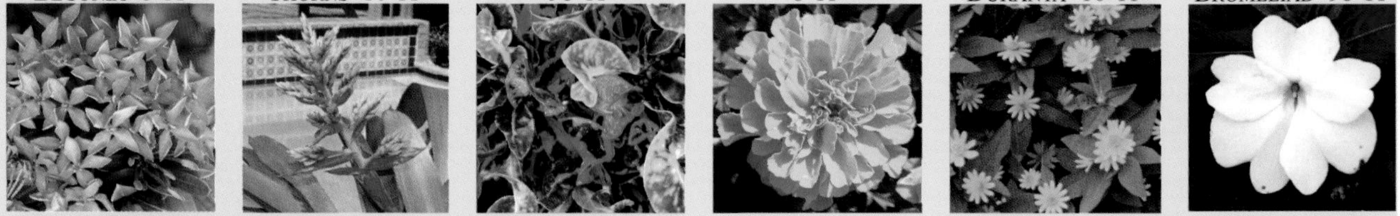

Ixora 'Petite' 10-11	Little Harve Bromeliad 9b-11	Mammey Croton 10-11	Marigolds 8-11	Melampodium 8-11	New Guinea Impatiens 8-11

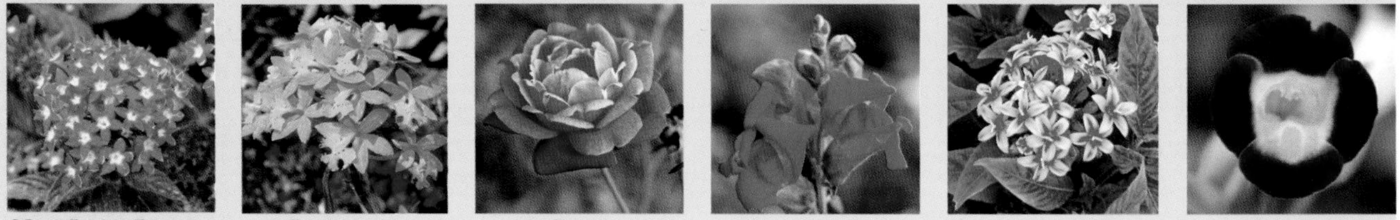

New Look Pentas 8-11	Reed-stem Orchid 10-11	Rose 8-11	Snapdragon 8-11	Starburst Pentas 9-11	Torenia 8-11

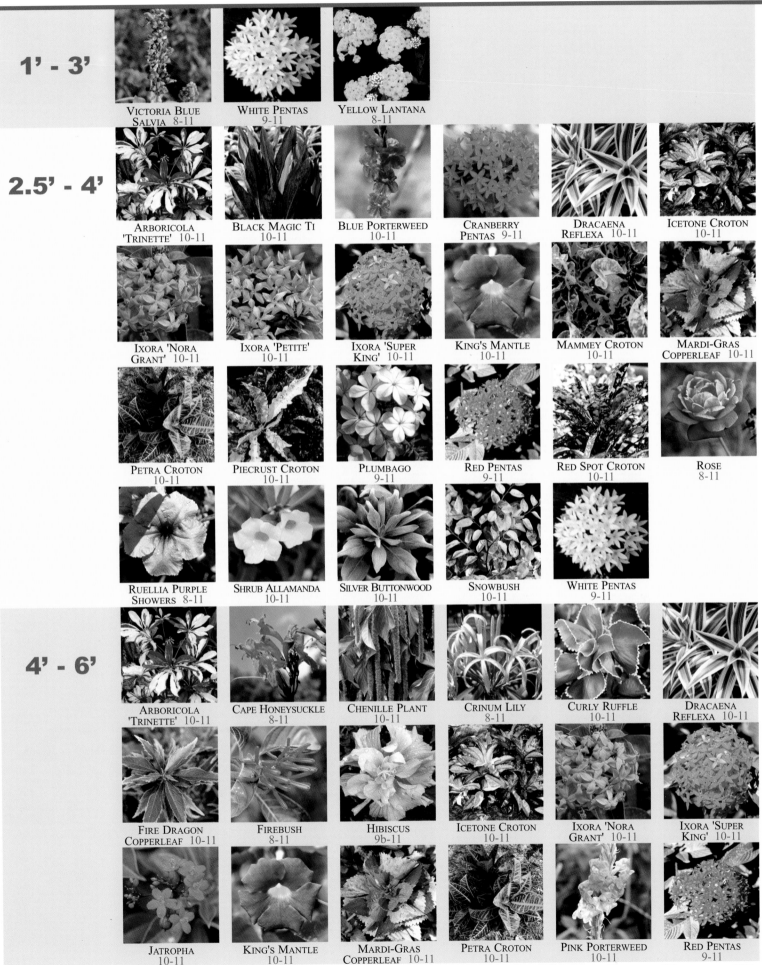

1' - 3'

VICTORIA BLUE
SALVIA 8-11

WHITE PENTAS
9-11

YELLOW LANTANA
8-11

2.5' - 4'

ARBORICOLA
'TRINETTE' 10-11

BLACK MAGIC TI
10-11

BLUE PORTERWEED
10-11

CRANBERRY
PENTAS 9-11

DRACAENA
REFLEXA 10-11

ICETONE CROTON
10-11

IXORA 'NORA
GRANT' 10-11

IXORA 'PETITE'
10-11

IXORA 'SUPER
KING' 10-11

KING'S MANTLE
10-11

MAMMEY CROTON
10-11

MARDI-GRAS
COPPERLEAF 10-11

PETRA CROTON
10-11

PIECRUST CROTON
10-11

PLUMBAGO
9-11

RED PENTAS
9-11

RED SPOT CROTON
10-11

ROSE
8-11

RUELLIA PURPLE
SHOWERS 8-11

SHRUB ALLAMANDA
10-11

SILVER BUTTONWOOD
10-11

SNOWBUSH
10-11

WHITE PENTAS
9-11

4' - 6'

ARBORICOLA
'TRINETTE' 10-11

CAPE HONEYSUCKLE
8-11

CHENILLE PLANT
10-11

CRINUM LILY
8-11

CURLY RUFFLE
10-11

DRACAENA
REFLEXA 10-11

FIRE DRAGON
COPPERLEAF 10-11

FIREBUSH
8-11

HIBISCUS
9b-11

ICETONE CROTON
10-11

IXORA 'NORA
GRANT' 10-11

IXORA 'SUPER
KING' 10-11

JATROPHA
10-11

KING'S MANTLE
10-11

MARDI-GRAS
COPPERLEAF 10-11

PETRA CROTON
10-11

PINK PORTERWEED
10-11

RED PENTAS
9-11

COLOR FOR MEDIUM SALT AND WIND

4' - 6'

RED SPOT CROTON
10-11

OLEANDER
8-11

ROSE
8-11

RUELLIA PURPLE
SHOWERS 8-11

SHRUB ALLAMANDA
10-11

SILVER BUTTONWOOD
10-11

SNOWBUSH
10-11

STOPLIGHT CROTON
10-11

6' - 8'

ARBORICOLA
'TRINETTE' 10-11

BOUGAINVILLEA
9-11

BUTTERFLY BUSH
8-9

CAPE HONEYSUCKLE
8-11

CHENILLE PLANT
10-11

CHINESE HAT
10-11

CURLY RUFFLE
10-11

HIBISCUS
9b-11

DRACAENA
REFLEXA 10-11

FIREBUSH
8-11

FLORIDA
HYDRANGEA 9b-11

GOLDEN DEWDROP
9b-11

IXORA 'NORA
GRANT' 10-11

IXORA 'SUPER
KING' 10-11

JATROPHA
10-11

OLEANDER
8-11

PINK PORTERWEED
10-11

SNOWBUSH
10-11

VAR. GOLDEN
DEWDROP 9b-11

8' - 15'

AND. CREPE
HIBISCUS 9b-11

BOUGAINVILLEA
9-11

CHINESE HAT
10-11

HIBISCUS
9b-11

DWARF POINCIANA
9b-11

FRANGIPANI
10-11

GOLDEN DEWDROP
9b-11

HIBISCUS, 'SEM.
PINK' 9b-11

JATROPHA
10-11

OLEANDER
8-11

SILVER BUTTONWOOD
10-11

WEST INDIAN
SHOWER 9b-11

15' - 35'

| COPPERPOD 9-11 | FRANGIPANI 10-11 | MAGNOLIA LITTLE GEM 8-11 | ORANGE GEIGER 10-11 | SUNSHINE TREE 10-11 | TROPICAL SNOWBALL 10-11 |

35'+

| FLOSS SILK TREE 9-11 | GOLDEN SHOWER 10-11 | PELTOPHORUM 10-11 | SOUTHERN MAGNOLIA 8-11 |

VINES

| CAPE HONEYSUCKLE 8-11 | CHINESE HAT 10-11 | CONFEDERATE JASMINE 8-11 | PINK PETTICOAT 10-11 | BOUGAINVILLEA 9-11 | RED ORCHID 9b-11 |

Yellow Lantana, Blue Daze, and Cranberry Pentas thrive around this windy lake.

COLOR FOR HIGH SALT AND WIND

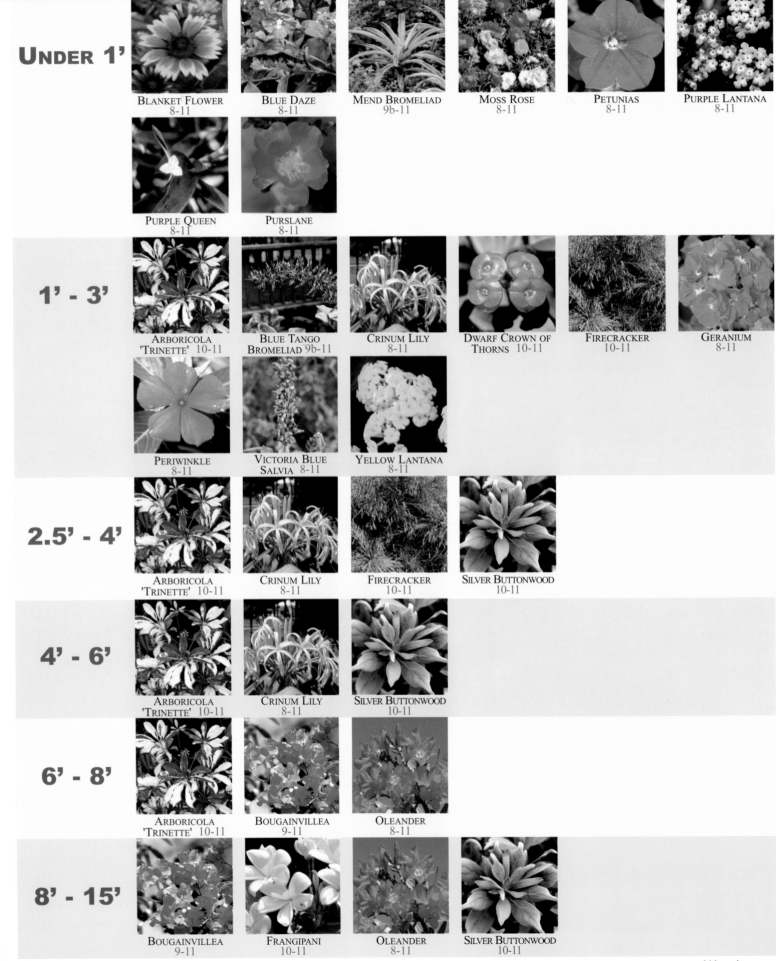

UNDER 1'

BLANKET FLOWER
8-11

BLUE DAZE
8-11

MEND BROMELIAD
9b-11

MOSS ROSE
8-11

PETUNIAS
8-11

PURPLE LANTANA
8-11

PURPLE QUEEN
8-11

PURSLANE
8-11

1' - 3'

ARBORICOLA
'TRINETTE' 10-11

BLUE TANGO
BROMELIAD 9b-11

CRINUM LILY
8-11

DWARF CROWN OF
THORNS 10-11

FIRECRACKER
10-11

GERANIUM
8-11

PERIWINKLE
8-11

VICTORIA BLUE
SALVIA 8-11

YELLOW LANTANA
8-11

2.5' - 4'

ARBORICOLA
'TRINETTE' 10-11

CRINUM LILY
8-11

FIRECRACKER
10-11

SILVER BUTTONWOOD
10-11

4' - 6'

ARBORICOLA
'TRINETTE' 10-11

CRINUM LILY
8-11

SILVER BUTTONWOOD
10-11

6' - 8'

ARBORICOLA
'TRINETTE' 10-11

BOUGAINVILLEA
9-11

OLEANDER
8-11

8' - 15'

BOUGAINVILLEA
9-11

FRANGIPANI
10-11

OLEANDER
8-11

SILVER BUTTONWOOD
10-11

(A) = ANNUAL

15' - 35'

FRANGIPANI
10-11

ORANGE GEIGER
10-11

VINES

BOUGAINVILLEA
9-11

Red Pentas and Crown of Thorns combine with Purple Queen and Yellow Lantana in this planter by the sea.

CHAPTER 11

COOL-SEASON COLOR (OCTOBER - APRIL)

Bougainvillea

Brunfelsia

Dombeya

Golden Shrimp

Salvia

After

Before

Impatiens

Turk's Cap

The cool season is the most pleasant time of the year in Florida because of the wonderful cool-but-seldom-cold temperatures. This is the time we want to be outside enjoying our gardens.

Most annuals do better in cool season than summer because of the cooler temperatures. We are the envy of many gardeners from other places because of our ability to grow such a wide variety of annuals in our ideal cool-season.

But, most of our traditional perennials (groundcovers, shrubs, vines, and trees) peak in summer. Ixora, Plumbago, and Thryallis are examples. They are loaded with blooms at a time when we prefer our air-conditioned houses.

So, I searched the world over for perennials that would peak in cool-season, when we want to spend time outdoors. Twelve years of searches and plant trials paid off. This chapter shows gardens full of perennials that bloom all cool-season. These plants are more applicable to south and central Florida than the colder parts of the state during the coldest months of winter.

Above and left: This garden is almost all cool-season perennials. The "Before" photo (above) shows the old garden, which was hedges and grass. The new "After" garden features all flowering material that peaks in the cool season because this country club is a winter club. The only annuals in the garden are the Impatiens that border this path. See more about this garden on the next page. (Design by the author. Installation by Tom Homrich Landscaping of Lake Worth. Plants from Color Garden Farms Nursery of Loxahatchee.)

Cool-Season Perennial Garden

Landscape style is changing. The *'Before'* photo below shows older type of landscaping which features hedges, grass, and annuals for color.

New landscape designs feature more color and less grass. The effect is lusher and much more colorful.

Perennials are becoming the backbone of new landscapes. Annuals used to be the major source of garden color in Florida. They are now used to accent perennial gardens, or to create color accents in assorted beds.

The Giant Shrimp, Dombeya, and Golden Shrimp are perennials that last for many years. They all bloom in cool-season and are trimmed once or twice a year in summer.

Impatiens and 'Victoria Blue' Salvias are annuals used to accent the perennial garden. The Salvia fills in the areas in between the recently-planted Dombeyas. The Dombeyas will grow to fill those spaces by the next cool-season, and the Salvias will not be replaced. The Impatiens form borders that should be replaced with annuals each cool season.

Giant Shrimp

Before

After

Dombeya

Golden Shrimp

Impatiens

Salvia

Best Cool-Season Perennials for Zones 9 through 11

Many colorful plants thrive in Florida's mild, cool-season, both annuals and perennials. (I am using the dictionary definition of 'perennial', a plant that has color and lasts more than one season.) The plant charts later in this chapter give a complete listing. These are some of the best.

African Tulip Tree - Large tree that blooms from about February until June. Spectacular orange tulips in the sky. Do not plant too close to buildings. Tree looks good all year, even when not blooming. Zone 9b through 11.

Begonias - Perennial angelwing types, including the 'Odorata' (above), the Pink Angelwing, and the Orange Rubra bloom beautifully and very dependably all cool-season long. Zones 9b through 11.

Bougainvillea - Shrubs, trees, or vines. One of our most spectacular plants for color in the dry season if you can put up with the high maintenance requirements. Zones 9 through 11.

Brunfelsia - Shrubs or small trees that show up very well in sun or shade. One of our longest and most dependable cool-season perennials. Blooms for about 6 months, from November until April. Zones 10 through 11.

Chinese Hat - Vine, shrub, or small tree. Blooms heavily with a high percentage of color for most of the cool-season months. Zones 10 through 11.

Dombeya Seminole - Or, Florida Hydrangea. Large shrub that usually blooms from November until January and again from March until May. Spectacular color for very little care. Zone 9b through 11.

Firespike - Especially the pink variety shown above. Large shrub that blooms from November until June. Favorite food of Hummingbirds. Blooms in the opposite season of the more common red Firespike. Zones 7 to 11, depending on type of Firespike.

Hong Kong Orchid - Large tree that blooms from about December until February with beautiful flowers that look like orchids. Does not produce pesky seedlings like some the orchid trees. Looks a bit scruffy at times but keeps its leaves all year. Zone 9b through 11.

Shrimp Plants - The Giant Shrimp (above) usually blooms from November until January and again from March until May. The Golden Shrimp blooms all year, and the 'Fruit Cocktail' for most of the cool-season and spring. Zone depends on type of Shrimp.

Cool-season perennials in a tropical garden, featuring a wild color combination. Tis and Crotons provide leaf color and need to be included in any list of best cool-season perennials. The orange flowers are Bolivian Sunset. The yellow blooms just beginning to appear are yellow Crossandra.

Best Cool-Season Annuals

Many colorful plants thrive in Florida's mild cool-seasons, both annuals and perennials. (I am using the dictionary definition of 'perennial', a plant that has color and lasts more than one season.) The plant charts later in this chapter give a complete listing. These are some of the best annuals.

Dragon Wing Begonias - A beautiful, unique plant for winter color. Short-term perennial most often used as an annual. One of our most dependable cool-season annuals.

Geraniums - Beautiful, traditional flowers that love Florida's cool season. Look best if dead-headed. Great container plants.

Impatiens - The most popular bedding plant in the world. Try the New Guinea Impatiens or Double Impatiens for some variety. Heavy water users.

Marigolds - A traditional annual that does well throughout Florida. Cheerful, orange or yellow blooms. Planted during all but the hottest months.

Pansies - One of the few plants that blooms in the coldest parts of Florida in January. Available in many colors and patterns. Underused in the southern end of the state.

Petunias - Great color for sunny spots during our cooler months. Gives almost as much color as Impatiens without the high water use. Beautiful variety of colors.

Salvia - Very dependable bloomer that comes in many colors and types. Requires little care or water. One of the favorite foods of hummingbirds.

Snapdragon - Great cool-season annual for Florida. Comes in dwarf or tall sizes. Many different colors. Tolerant of light frost.

Wax Begonias - One of the most dependable cool-season annuals for sun or shade. Low water use. Mass different colors together or border other annuals with a single color.

Cool-season annuals in a multi-colored display, featuring blue and white Pansies bordering California Daisies, Pentas, and mixed Salvias. Dusty Miller is the plant with the silver leaves. Design by Brandon Balch, Woodfield Country Club, Boca Raton.

Tall Snapdragons bordered by Impatiens. Design by Tony Cardianale, BallenIsles Country Club, Palm Beach Gardens.

The tallest layer of this annual garden is made up of Spider Flowers. The lower layers are made up of Salvias, Impatiens, Marigolds, Petunias, and Begonias. The manicured Ilex hedge formalizes this mixed arrangement. Design by Danny Miller, The Breakers, Palm Beach. Flowers custom grown by Dave Self at Wyld West Annuals, Loxahatchee.

Impatiens

Snapdragon

Petunia

Petunia

Snapdragon

Petunia

Impatiens, Petunias, and Snapdragons are alternated in this annual planting under Ficus Trees. Design by Mark Finkelstein, Boca West Country Club, Boca Raton.

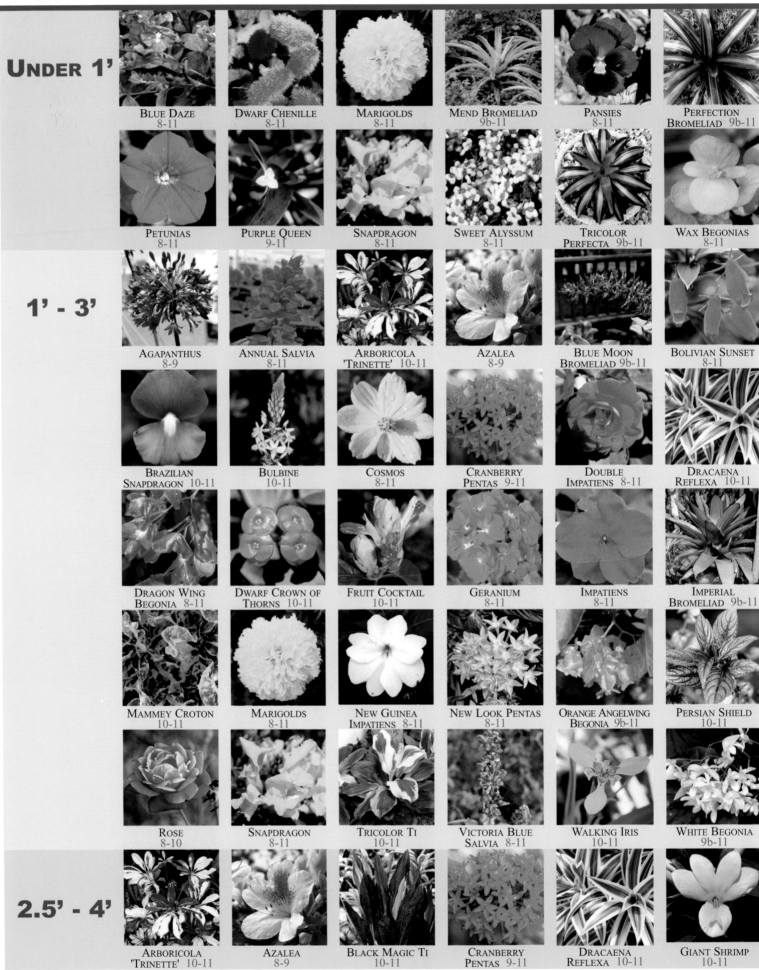

UNDER 1'

BLUE DAZE
8-11

DWARF CHENILLE
8-11

MARIGOLDS
8-11

MEND BROMELIAD
9b-11

PANSIES
8-11

PERFECTION
BROMELIAD 9b-11

PETUNIAS
8-11

PURPLE QUEEN
9-11

SNAPDRAGON
8-11

SWEET ALYSSUM
8-11

TRICOLOR
PERFECTA 9b-11

WAX BEGONIAS
8-11

1' - 3'

AGAPANTHUS
8-9

ANNUAL SALVIA
8-11

ARBORICOLA
'TRINETTE' 10-11

AZALEA
8-9

BLUE MOON
BROMELIAD 9b-11

BOLIVIAN SUNSET
8-11

BRAZILIAN
SNAPDRAGON 10-11

BULBINE
10-11

COSMOS
8-11

CRANBERRY
PENTAS 9-11

DOUBLE
IMPATIENS 8-11

DRACAENA
REFLEXA 10-11

DRAGON WING
BEGONIA 8-11

DWARF CROWN OF
THORNS 10-11

FRUIT COCKTAIL
10-11

GERANIUM
8-11

IMPATIENS
8-11

IMPERIAL
BROMELIAD 9b-11

MAMMEY CROTON
10-11

MARIGOLDS
8-11

NEW GUINEA
IMPATIENS 8-11

NEW LOOK PENTAS
8-11

ORANGE ANGELWING
BEGONIA 9b-11

PERSIAN SHIELD
10-11

ROSE
8-10

SNAPDRAGON
8-11

TRICOLOR TI
10-11

VICTORIA BLUE
SALVIA 8-11

WALKING IRIS
10-11

WHITE BEGONIA
9b-11

2.5' - 4'

ARBORICOLA
'TRINETTE' 10-11

AZALEA
8-9

BLACK MAGIC TI
10-11

CRANBERRY
PENTAS 9-11

DRACAENA
REFLEXA 10-11

GIANT SHRIMP
10-11

2.5' - 4'

ICETONE CROTON
10-11

MAMMEY CROTON
10-11

PETRA CROTON
10-11

PIECRUST CROTON
10-11

PINK ANGELWING
BEGONIA 9b-11

PURPLE PRINCE TI
10-11

RED PENTAS
10-11

RED SPOT CROTON
10-11

ROSE
8-11

SHERBERT TI
10-11

SILVER BUTTONWOOD
10-11

SHRIMP PLANT
9-11

TI RED SISTER
10-11

YELLOW SALVIA
8-11

4' - 6'

ARBORICOLA
'TRINETTE' 10-11

AZALEA
8-9

BRUNFELSIA
10-11

CAPE HONEYSUCKLE
8-11

DRACAENA
REFLEXA 10-11

GIANT RED SHRIMP
10-11

GIANT SHRIMP
10-11

ICETONE CROTON
10-11

JATROPHA
10-11

PANAMA ROSE
10-11

PETRA CROTON
10-11

PINK ANGELWING
BEGONIA 9b-11

RED PENTAS
10-11

RED SPOT CROTON
10-11

ROSE
8-11

SHRIMP PLANT
9-11

SILVER BUTTONWOOD
10-11

STOPLIGHT CROTON
10-11

TI RED SISTER
10-11

6' - 8'

ANGEL'S TRUMPET
8-11

ARBORICOLA
'TRINETTE' 10-11

AZALEA
8-9

BOUGAINVILLEA
9-11

BRUNFELSIA
10-11

CAMELLIA
7-9

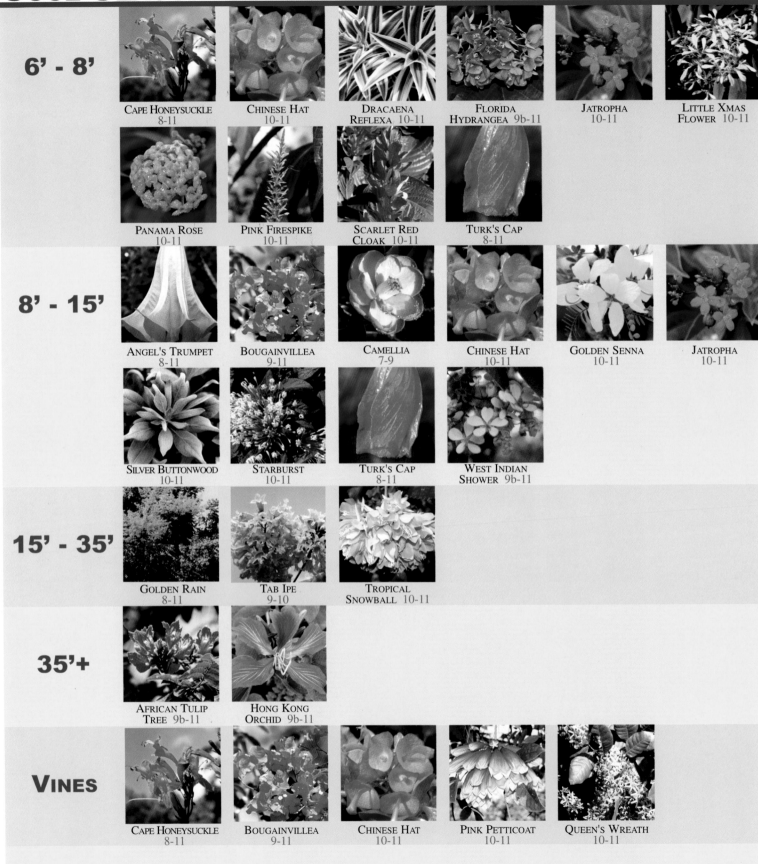

6' - 8'

CAPE HONEYSUCKLE
8-11

CHINESE HAT
10-11

DRACAENA
REFLEXA 10-11

FLORIDA
HYDRANGEA 9b-11

JATROPHA
10-11

LITTLE XMAS
FLOWER 10-11

PANAMA ROSE
10-11

PINK FIRESPIKE
10-11

SCARLET RED
CLOAK 10-11

TURK'S CAP
8-11

8' - 15'

ANGEL'S TRUMPET
8-11

BOUGAINVILLEA
9-11

CAMELLIA
7-9

CHINESE HAT
10-11

GOLDEN SENNA
10-11

JATROPHA
10-11

SILVER BUTTONWOOD
10-11

STARBURST
10-11

TURK'S CAP
8-11

WEST INDIAN
SHOWER 9b-11

15' - 35'

GOLDEN RAIN
8-11

TAB IPE
9-10

TROPICAL
SNOWBALL 10-11

35'+

AFRICAN TULIP
TREE 9b-11

HONG KONG
ORCHID 9b-11

VINES

CAPE HONEYSUCKLE
8-11

BOUGAINVILLEA
9-11

CHINESE HAT
10-11

PINK PETTICOAT
10-11

QUEEN'S WREATH
10-11

Left: Annual planting in the bright Florida sun. The design is different from most annual plantings because the plants are alternated instead of lined up in masses of the same flower. The bed features Victoria Blue Salvia, Impatiens, Petunias, and an occasional Gerber Daisy.

Right: Impatiens, Marigolds, and Salvias are alternated in this garden under the Palms. Design of both of these gardens by Mark Finklestein, Boca West County Club, Boca Raton.

CHAPTER 12

HOT-SEASON COLOR (APRIL-OCTOBER)

After

Before

This chapter features ideas for hot-season color as well as charts that organize the plants by size. These plant charts make designing easier by putting all the plants that work in a specific environment in one spot, so that you can see all the possibilities at once. For example, if you are looking for a plant about four to six feet tall for between your windows, simply look at that size range on the plant charts.

Although annuals are more difficult during the hot season, perennials are easier. More perennials bloom in summer than winter. Some, like Plumbago and Ruellia Purple Showers, bloom almost all year if the weather is particularly warm. Since they peak during warmer months, they are included in this chapter.

Above and left: This white fence is a great backdrop for this profusion of hot-season perennials including Hibiscus, Shrub Allamanda, and Pentas.

HOT-SEASON COLOR:

Three views of a summer garden along a winding path. This garden features some of our best summer perennials - Mussaendas, Salvias, Pentas, and an Angel's Trumpet.

The garden accessories punctuate the plantings, adding focal points at key turns in the path.

Hot-Season Color: Plants that Peak from April to October

Under 1'

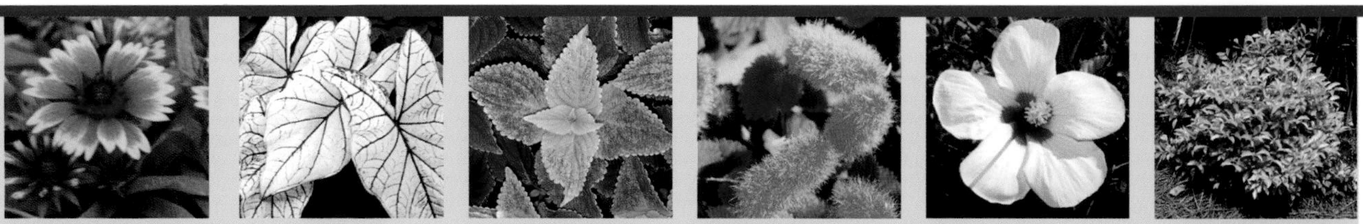

Blanket Flower 8-11 | Caladium 8-11 | Coleus 8-11 | Dwarf Chenille 8-11 | Dwarf Hibiscus 9-11 | Gold Mound Duranta 10-11

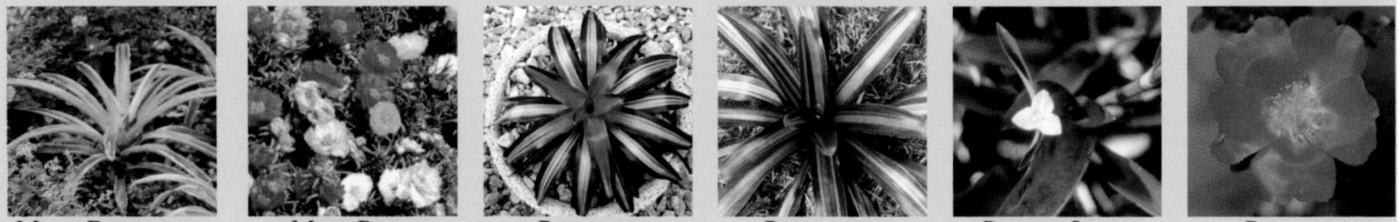

Mend Bromeliad 9b-11 | Moss Rose 8-11 | Perfecta Bromeliad 9b-11 | Perfection Bromeliad 9b-11 | Purple Queen 9-11 | Purslane 8-11

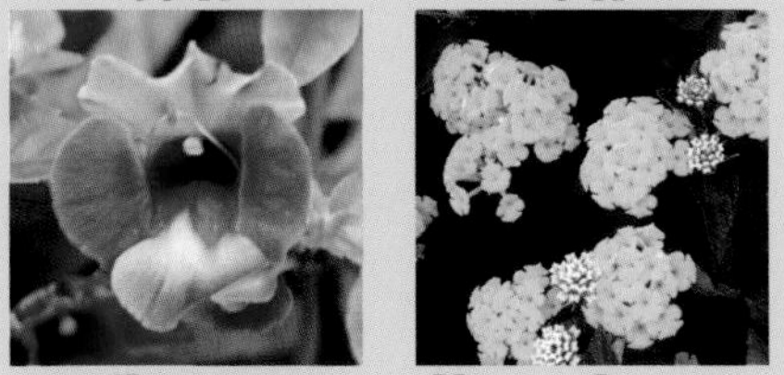

Torenia 8-11 | Yellow Lantana 8-11

1' - 3'

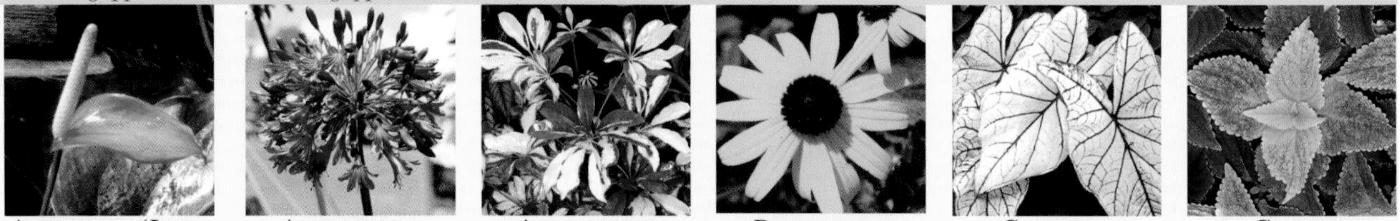

Anthurium 'Lady Jane' 10-11 | Agapanthus 8-9 | Arboricola 'Trinette' 10-11 | Black-eyed Susan 8-9 | Caladium 8-11 | Coleus 8-11

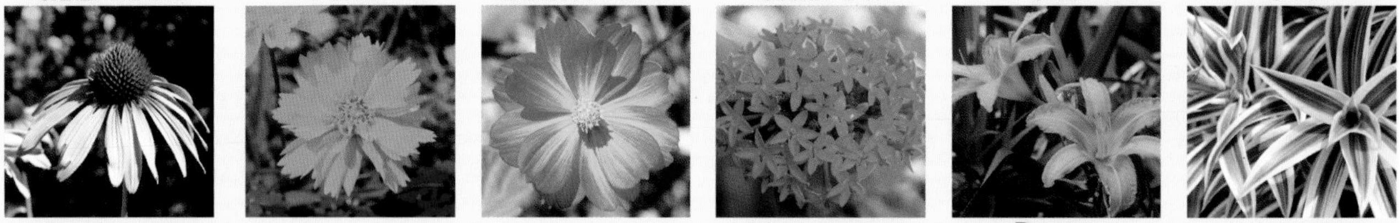

Coneflower 8-9 | Coreopsis 8-11 | Cosmos 8-11 | Cranberry Pentas 9-11 | Daylily 8-9 | Draceana Reflexa 10-11

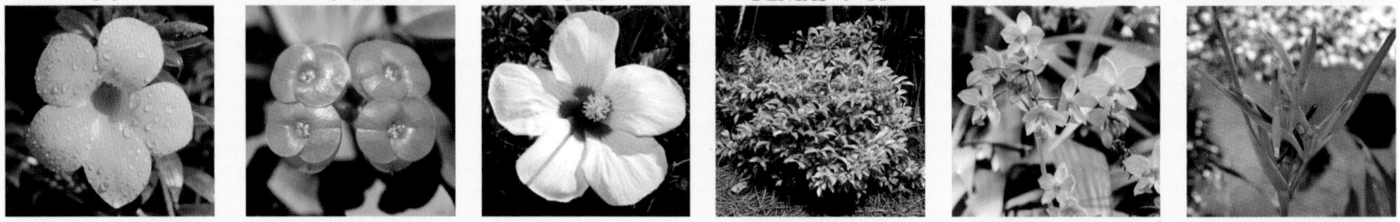

Dwarf Allamanda 10-11 | Dwarf Crown of Thorns 10-11 | Dwarf Hibiscus 9-11 | Gold Mound Duranta 10-11 | Ground Orchid 10-11 | Heliconia 10-11

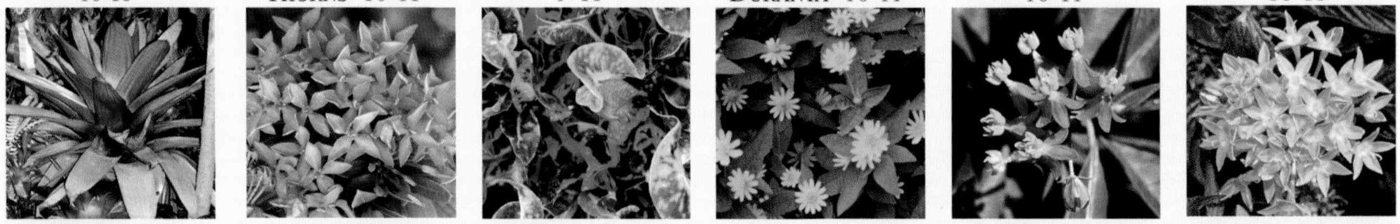

Imperial Bromeliad 9b-11 | Ixora 'Petite' 10-11 | Mammey Croton 10-11 | Melampodium 8-11 | Milkweed 9-11 | New Look Pentas (A)

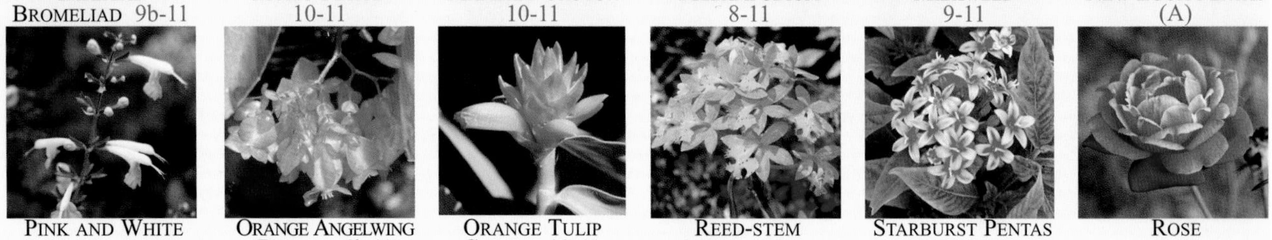

Pink and White Salvia 8-11 | Orange Angelwing Begonia 9b-11 | Orange Tulip Costus 10-11 | Reed-stem Orchid 10-11 | Starburst Pentas 9-11 | Rose 8-10

1' - 3'

TORENIA
8-11

WALKING IRIS
10-11

YELLOW LANTANA
8-11

2.5' - 4'

ARBORICOLA
'TRINETTE' 10-11

BIRD OF PARADISE
9-11

BLACK MAGIC TI
10-11

BLUE PORTERWEED
10-11

CANNA LILY
8-11

CRANBERRY
PENTAS 9-11

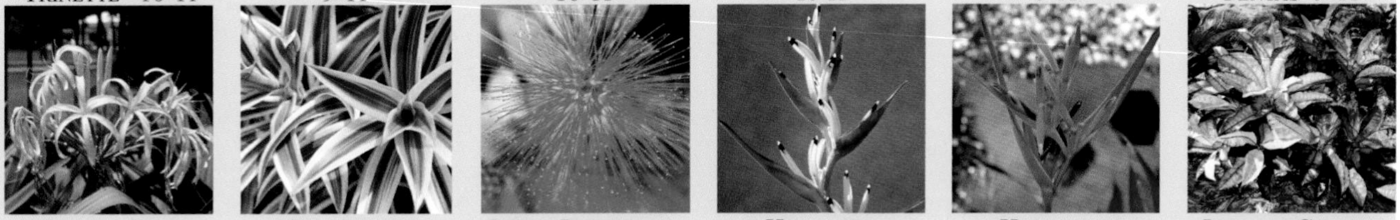

CRINUM LILY
8-11

DRACEANA
REFLEXA 10-11

DWARF POWDERPUFF
10-11

HELICONIA
LADY DI 10-11

HELICONIA
ORANGE 10-11

ICETONE CROTON
10-11

IXORA 'NORA
GRANT' 10-11

IXORA 'PETITE'
10-11

IXORA 'SUPER
KING' 10-11

KING'S MANTLE
10-11

MAMMEY CROTON
10-11

MARDI-GRAS
COPPERLEAF 10-11

PETRA CROTON
10-11

PIECRUST CROTON
10-11

PINK ANGELWING
BEGONIA 9b-11

PINWHEEL JASMINE
10-11

PLUMBAGO
9-11

RED PENTAS
9-11

RED SPOT CROTON
10-11

ROSE
8-10

RUELLIA PURPLE
SHOWERS 8-11

SANCHEZIA
10-11

SHRIMP PLANT
9-11

SHRUB ALLAMANDA
10-11

SILVER BUTTONWOOD
10-11

SNOWBUSH
10-11

TI RED SISTER
10-11

VARIEGATED
GINGER 8-11

4' - 6'

ARBORICOLA
'TRINETTE' 10-11

BEAUTYBERRY
8-11

BIRD OF PARADISE
9-11

BLUE PORTERWEED
10-11

BUTTERFLY BUSH
8-9

BRONZE
CARICATURE 10-11

4' - 6'

CHENILLE PLANT 10-11	CRINUM LILY 8-11	CURLY RUFFLE 10-11	DRACEANA REFLEXA 10-11	DWARF MUSSAENDA 10-11	DWARF POWDERPUFF 10-11
FIRE DRAGON COPPERLEAF 10-11	FIREBUSH 10-11	FIRESPIKE 8-11	GINGER 10-11	GARDENIA 8-11	HIBISCUS 9-11
ICETONE CROTON 10-11	IXORA 'NORA GRANT' 10-11	IXORA 'SUPER KING' 10-11	JATROPHA 10-11	KING'S MANTLE 10-11	MARDI-GRAS COPPERLEAF 10-11
MOPHEAD HYDRANGEA 8-9	PETRA CROTON 10-11	PINK ANGELWING BEGONIA 9b-11	PINK PORTERWEED 10-11	PINWHEEL JASMINE 10-11	PLUMBAGO 9-11
RED PENTAS 9-11	RED SPOT CROTON 10-11	ROSE 8-10	RUELLIA PURPLE SHOWERS 8-11	SANCHEZIA 10-11	SHRIMP PLANT 9-11
SHRUB ALLAMANDA 10-11	SILVER BUTTONWOOD 10-11	SNOWBUSH 10-11	STOPLIGHT CROTON 10-11	THRYALLIS 9-11	TI RED SISTER 10-11
TRICOLOR CARICATURE 10-11	VARIEGATED GINGER 8-11				

6'-8'

ANGEL'S TRUMPET 8-11	ARBORICOLA 'TRINETTE' 10-11	BRONZE CARICATURE 10-11	BUTTERFLY BUSH 8-9	CHENILLE PLANT 10-11	COSTUS BARBATUS 9-11

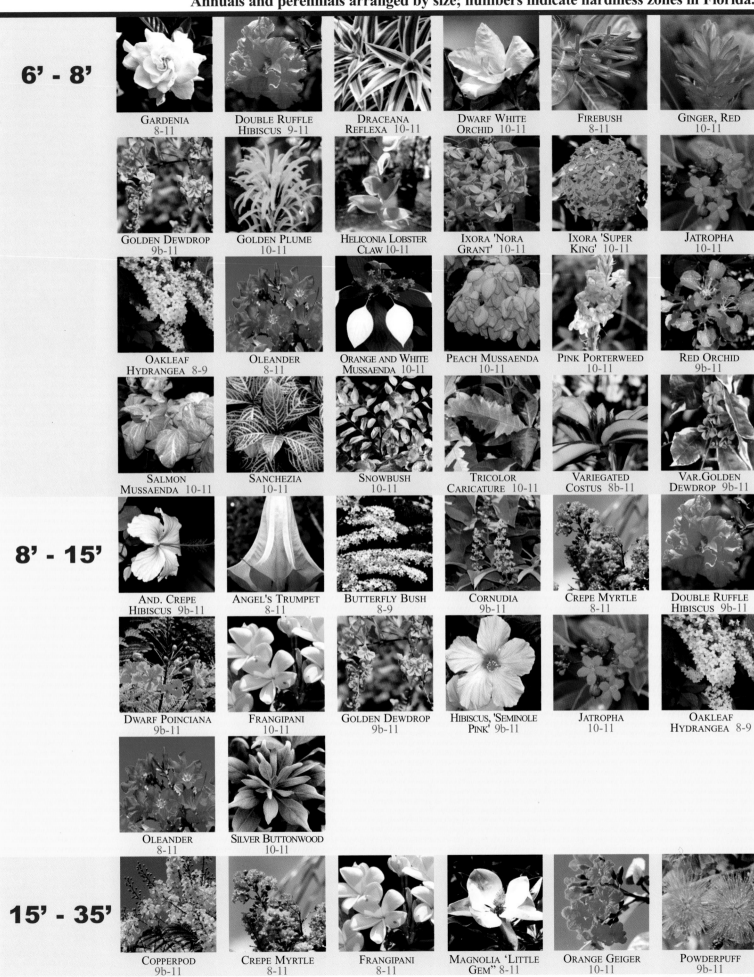

6' - 8'

GARDENIA
8-11

DOUBLE RUFFLE
HIBISCUS 9-11

DRACEANA
REFLEXA 10-11

DWARF WHITE
ORCHID 10-11

FIREBUSH
8-11

GINGER, RED
10-11

GOLDEN DEWDROP
9b-11

GOLDEN PLUME
10-11

HELICONIA LOBSTER
CLAW 10-11

IXORA 'NORA
GRANT' 10-11

IXORA 'SUPER
KING' 10-11

JATROPHA
10-11

OAKLEAF
HYDRANGEA 8-9

OLEANDER
8-11

ORANGE AND WHITE
MUSSAENDA 10-11

PEACH MUSSAENDA
10-11

PINK PORTERWEED
10-11

RED ORCHID
9b-11

SALMON
MUSSAENDA 10-11

SANCHEZIA
10-11

SNOWBUSH
10-11

TRICOLOR
CARICATURE 10-11

VARIEGATED
COSTUS 8b-11

VAR. GOLDEN
DEWDROP 9b-11

8' - 15'

AND. CREPE
HIBISCUS 9b-11

ANGEL'S TRUMPET
8-11

BUTTERFLY BUSH
8-9

CORNUDIA
9b-11

CREPE MYRTLE
8-11

DOUBLE RUFFLE
HIBISCUS 9b-11

DWARF POINCIANA
9b-11

FRANGIPANI
10-11

GOLDEN DEWDROP
9b-11

HIBISCUS, 'SEMINOLE
PINK' 9b-11

JATROPHA
10-11

OAKLEAF
HYDRANGEA 8-9

OLEANDER
8-11

SILVER BUTTONWOOD
10-11

15' - 35'

COPPERPOD
9b-11

CREPE MYRTLE
8-11

FRANGIPANI
8-11

MAGNOLIA 'LITTLE
GEM" 8-11

ORANGE GEIGER
10-11

POWDERPUFF
9b-11

15' - 35'

SUNSHINE TREE
10-11

35'+

QUEEN'S CREPE
10-11

GOLDEN SHOWER
10-11

ROYAL POINCIANA
10-11

PELTOPHORUM
10-11

SOUTHERN
MAGNOLIA 8-10

VINES

  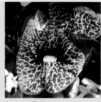   

BLEEDING
HEART VINE 9-11

GLORIOSA LILY
8-11

PIPEVINE
9b-11

PURPLE PASSION
VINE 9-11

RED ORCHID
9b-11

VINE ALLAMANDA
10-11

Above: Blue Plumbago and Red Pentas are bordered by yellow Marigolds and Purslane in this summer planting. Design by Mark Gordly, Ritz-Carlton Hotel, Manalapan.

Right: An entry is improved with a planting of a formal topiary with Thryallis, Lantana, and Pentas.

Before

After

CHAPTER **13**

YEAR-ROUND COLOR

After

Before

Gardeners love year-round color. Of course, who wouldn't want plants that bloom all year? Unfortunately, most plants have a shorter blooming season, like summer or winter. Blooming all the time is similar to being pregnant all the time - a not-too-frequent occurrence.

The plant charts in this chapter are considerably shorter than the charts in the other chapters because of the scarcity of plants that actually bloom all year. Consider leaf color, which is always there. This chapter shows lots of ideas of garden design with Crotons, Ti Plants, and Bromeliads, the three major plants for perennial leaf color.

For year-round color impact, mass the plants in groupings of different colors for maximum contrast. The gardens in this chapter will give you lots of ideas!

Above and left: Simple color layers of yellow, hot pink, and purple offer year-round color for this entry. Golden Shrimp Plants form the tallest layer with Cranberry Pentas in the middle and a border of Purple Queen.

Year-Round Color: Angelwing Begonias

The most spectacular shade plant I ever found is the Pink Angelwing Begonia, featured in this book's companion volume. This perennial Begonia blooms every day of the year with large, beautiful, hanging clusters of pink flowers.

Left: Pink Angelwings behind Golden Shrimp Plants and Bromeliads. Installation by Tom Homrich Landscaping, Lake Worth.

Right: Blooming Bromeliads in bright blue pots accent this grouping of Golden Shrimp Plants and Pink Angelwings. Installation by Color Garden Group, Loxahatchee.

Below: The Pink Angelwing is larger than most Begonias. This clump is four feet tall.

Year-Round Color: Crotons, Tis, Shrimps

Combinations of Tis, Shrimps, and Crotons give dramatic, easy, year-round color in the warmer areas of the state. The Golden Shrimp is one of the few plants that blooms 365 days a year. See this book's companion for more specific information on the Ti Red Sisters, Golden Shrimp Plants, and Mammey Crotons shown on these two pages.

Left: Ti Red Sisters and Golden Shrimp Plants in front of Variegated Ginger.

Right: Ti Red Sisters, Golden Shrimp Plants, and Mammey Crotons.

Below: Golden Shrimp Plants and Mammey Crotons bordered by California Daisies and Blue Daze.

Year-Round Color: Pentas

Sixteen different kinds of Pentas are currently available. The smallest ones, called 'New Look' Pentas, are used as summer annuals throughout Florida. The larger Pentas are short-term perennials in south and central Florida, living about three years and blooming the entire time.

Far left: Starburst and Dwarf Lilac Pentas combine with Blue Daze and Yellow Lantana. The green groundcover is Juniper.

Near left: Starburst Pentas and Mend Bromeliads. The Starburst are particularly well-suited to shade.

Below: Starburst Pentas, Blue Daze, and Mend Bromeliads.

Year-Round Color: Winding-Path Gardens

are simple ways to display your botanical collection. Simply lay out a path in a shape you like, take out the grass, and start planting!

Left: This ecletic plant collection is unified by the winding path. Crotons and Tis are mixed with Pentas, Lantana, and Blue Daze.

Right: Tropical garden with Sanchezia, Flax, and Variegated Peperomia contrasting with the darker Ti Plants.

Before

Year-Round Color: Pentas and Shrimps

combine with Ruellia Purple Showers to provide constant color in this residence. The Ruellia blooms at least half the year, and the Cranberry Pentas and Golden Shrimp Plants bloom constantly. This garden is also shown on page five.

Ruellia

Shrimp

Pentas

After

Year-Round Color: Bromeliads

'Perfection'
Bromeliad

'Perfecta'
Bromeliad

This page: Bromeliads with leaf color offer year-round color. Two that worked well in our trials included the 'Perfection' and the 'Perfecta' Bromeliads. The 'Perfection' is larger, darker, and takes more sun.

Opposite: Peace Lilies, Tis, and Bromeliads provide year-round color in this entry garden.

Before

After

Year-Round Color: Perennials arranged by size; numbers indicate hardiness zones in Florida.

Under 1'

Dwarf Crown of Thorns 10-11

Gold Mound Duranta 10-11

Mend Bromeliad 9b-11

Perfecta Bromeliad 9b-11

Perfection Bromeliad 9b-11

Purple Queen 9-11

1' - 3'

Anthurium 'Lady Jane' 10-11

Arboricola 'Trinette' 10-11

Black Magic Ti 10-11

Cranberry Pentas 9-11

Dracaena Reflexa 10-11

Dwarf Crown of Thorns 10-11

Gold Mound Duranta 10-11

Imperial Bromeliad 9b-11

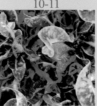
Mammey Croton 10-11

New Look Pentas 8-11

Orange Angelwing Begonia 9b-11

Starburst Pentas 9-11

Tricolor Ti 10-11

2.5' - 4'

Arboricola 'Trinette' 10-11

Black Magic Ti 10-11

Cranberry Pentas 9-11

Dracaena Reflexa 10-11

Icetone Croton 10-11

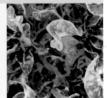
Mammey Croton 10-11

Mardi-Gras Copperleaf 10-11

Petra Croton 10-11

Piecrust Croton 10-11

Pink Angelwing Begonia 9b-11

Purple Prince Ti 10-11

Red Pentas 9-11

Red Spot Croton 10-11

Sanchezia 10-11

Sherbert Ti 10-11

Shrimp Plant 9-11

Silver Buttonwood 10-11

Snowbush 10-11

Ti Red Sister 10-11

White Pentas 9-11

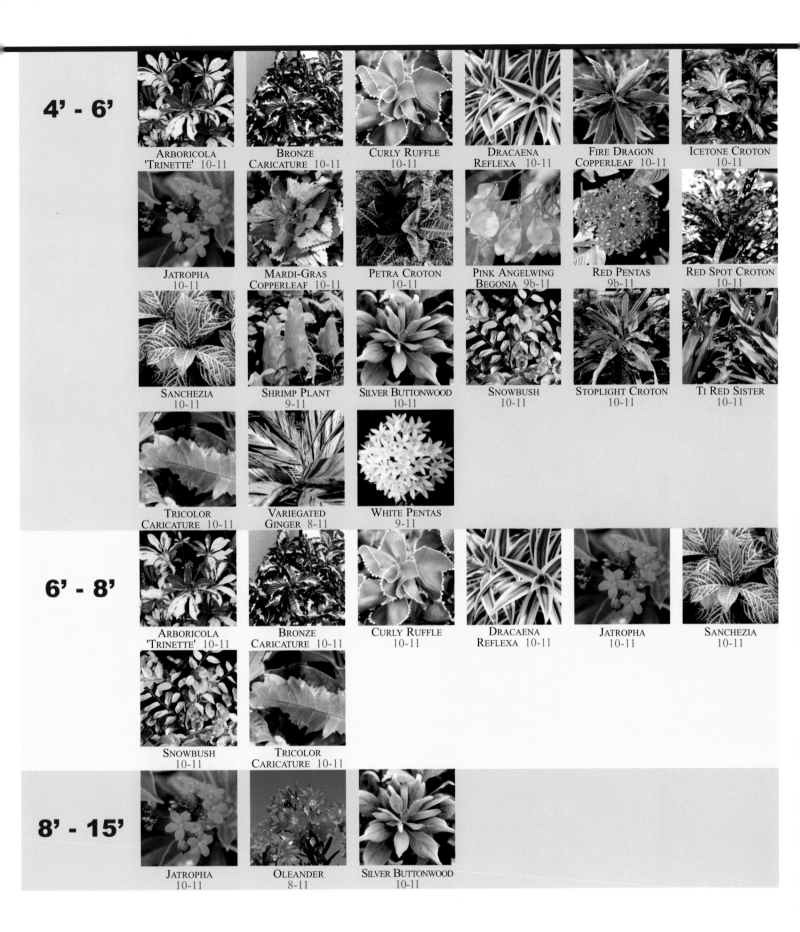

4' - 6'

ARBORICOLA
'TRINETTE' 10-11

BRONZE
CARICATURE 10-11

CURLY RUFFLE
10-11

DRACAENA
REFLEXA 10-11

FIRE DRAGON
COPPERLEAF 10-11

ICETONE CROTON
10-11

JATROPHA
10-11

MARDI-GRAS
COPPERLEAF 10-11

PETRA CROTON
10-11

PINK ANGELWING
BEGONIA 9b-11

RED PENTAS
9b-11

RED SPOT CROTON
10-11

SANCHEZIA
10-11

SHRIMP PLANT
9-11

SILVER BUTTONWOOD
10-11

SNOWBUSH
10-11

STOPLIGHT CROTON
10-11

TI RED SISTER
10-11

TRICOLOR
CARICATURE 10-11

VARIEGATED
GINGER 8-11

WHITE PENTAS
9-11

6' - 8'

ARBORICOLA
'TRINETTE' 10-11

BRONZE
CARICATURE 10-11

CURLY RUFFLE
10-11

DRACAENA
REFLEXA 10-11

JATROPHA
10-11

SANCHEZIA
10-11

SNOWBUSH
10-11

TRICOLOR
CARICATURE 10-11

8' - 15'

JATROPHA
10-11

OLEANDER
8-11

SILVER BUTTONWOOD
10-11

CHAPTER 15

COLOR FOR BUTTERFLIES

After

Before

Butterflies need nectar and larval food plants.

The nectar plants are the flowers, like Pentas and Firespikes, that the butterflies drink the nectar from. They drink from thousands of different flowers, as shown on the plant charts later in this chapter. If you want a lot of butterflies, plant many different kinds of flowers because they like variety, just like we do. You wouldn't want to eat the same meal all the time!

Larval food plants provide food for the caterpillars that will soon become butterflies. And, the caterpillars are quite picky about which plants to eat. For example, the Pipevine Swallowtail caterpillars eat mainly Pipevine leaves and flowers. The female butterflies lay their eggs underneath the leaves so that the baby caterpillars will have lots to eat the minute they hatch. Larval food plants are like pet food - expect to see lots of chewed up leaves and flowers. But, the benefit is a lot of butterflies! And these caterpillars are very considerate - they don't eat the rest of the plants in your garden.

Since this is a book about color, this chapter focuses on color for butterflies, particularly color that shows up well for people. For serious butterfly gardeners, look at green plants and plants with subtle color as well - particularly the Florida natives.

Above and left: A front yard butterfly garden featuring some of the best of the nectar plants for butterflies, Pentas, Porterflowers, and Lantana.

Butterfly Gardens

The 'Before' photo shows a fence in need of flowers.

The 'After' photo shows garden planted with butterflies in mind. Pink Porterflower is the large shrub in the center. It looks best surrounded by other plants that hide the leggy form of the shrub. This garden attracts a lot of butterflies because they like the variety of plants.

Before

After

Butterfly Gardens

Patience is important for butterfly gardeners! Look at the 'Before' photo below. Then look at the 'Just Planted' photo below it. Obviously, a lot of work went into planting this garden without immediate rewards for the homeowners because the newly-planted flowers are just too small to show up. To either people or butterflies. The flowers need to be profuse and large enough for the little butterflies to see them before they begin their feast.

If butterflies are already living on your property or nearby, they may show up on planting day to try the new flowers, even if they are small. But, more than likely, it will take a few weeks or months before you see many of them.

The 'After' photos show the rewards of patience!

Before

Just planted

Three months after planting

Eight months after planting

Color for Butterflies: Annuals and perennials arranged by size; numbers indicate hardiness zones in Florida.

Under 1'

Blanket Flower 8-11

Dwarf Hibiscus 9-11

Moss Rose 8-11

Pansies 8-11

Petunias 8-11

Purple Lantana 8-11

Purslane 8-11

Sweet Alysum 8-11

Torenia 8-11

1' - 3'

Annual Salvia 8-11

Azalea 8-9

Black-eyed Susan 8-9

Bolivian Sunset 8-11

Coneflower 8-9

Coreopsis 8-11

Cosmos 8-11

Cranberry Pentas 9-11

Daylily 8-9

Dwarf Hibiscus 9-11

Fruit Cocktail 10-11

Geranium 8-11

Ground Orchid 10-11

Impatiens 8-11

Ixora 'Petite' 10-11

Melampodium 8-11

Mexican Sage 8-11

Milkweed (L) 9-11

New Guinea Impatiens 8-11

New Look Pentas 8-11

Pink and White Salvia 8-11

Reed-stem Orchid 10-11

Starburst Pentas 9-11

Torenia 8-11

Victoria Blue Salvia 8-11

Yellow Lantana 8-11

2.5' - 4'

Azalea 8-9

Blue Porterweed 10-11

Canna Lily (L) 8-11

Cranberry Pentas 9-11

Dwarf Powderpuff 10-11

Firebush 8-11

340   BEST GARDEN COLOR FOR FLORIDA

(L) = LARVAL FOOD PLANT

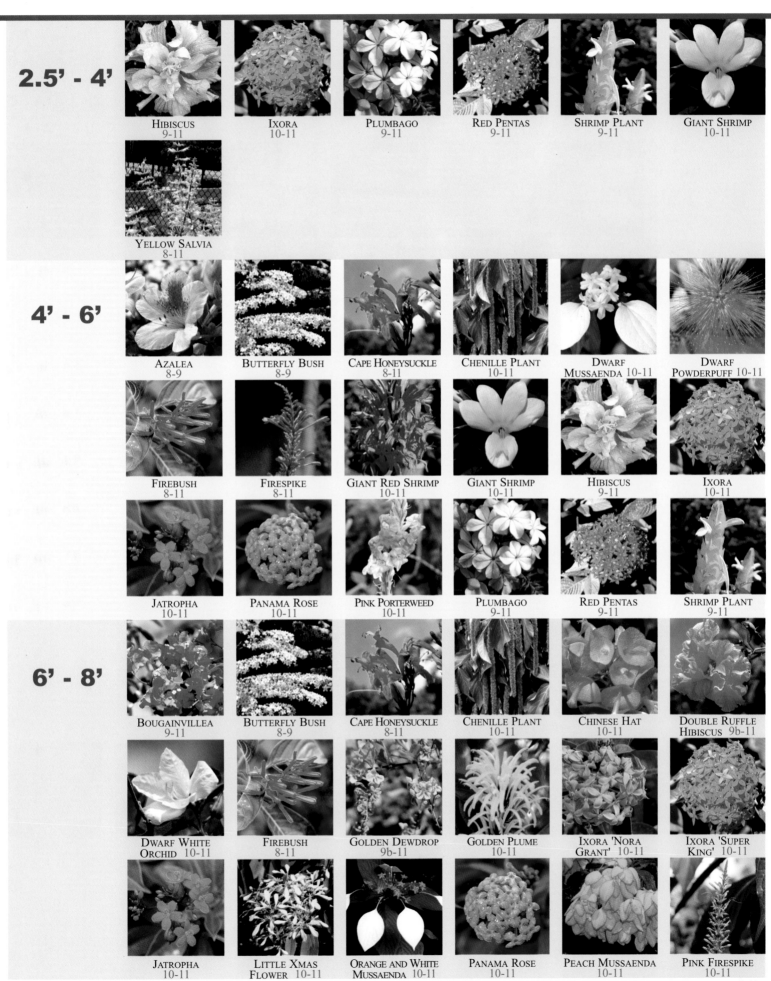

2.5' - 4'

HIBISCUS
9-11

IXORA
10-11

PLUMBAGO
9-11

RED PENTAS
9-11

SHRIMP PLANT
9-11

GIANT SHRIMP
10-11

YELLOW SALVIA
8-11

4' - 6'

AZALEA
8-9

BUTTERFLY BUSH
8-9

CAPE HONEYSUCKLE
8-11

CHENILLE PLANT
10-11

DWARF
MUSSAENDA 10-11

DWARF
POWDERPUFF 10-11

FIREBUSH
8-11

FIRESPIKE
8-11

GIANT RED SHRIMP
10-11

GIANT SHRIMP
10-11

HIBISCUS
9-11

IXORA
10-11

JATROPHA
10-11

PANAMA ROSE
10-11

PINK PORTERWEED
10-11

PLUMBAGO
9-11

RED PENTAS
9-11

SHRIMP PLANT
9-11

6' - 8'

BOUGAINVILLEA
9-11

BUTTERFLY BUSH
8-9

CAPE HONEYSUCKLE
8-11

CHENILLE PLANT
10-11

CHINESE HAT
10-11

DOUBLE RUFFLE
HIBISCUS 9b-11

DWARF WHITE
ORCHID 10-11

FIREBUSH
8-11

GOLDEN DEWDROP
9b-11

GOLDEN PLUME
10-11

IXORA 'NORA
GRANT' 10-11

IXORA 'SUPER
KING' 10-11

JATROPHA
10-11

LITTLE XMAS
FLOWER 10-11

ORANGE AND WHITE
MUSSAENDA 10-11

PANAMA ROSE
10-11

PEACH MUSSAENDA
10-11

PINK FIRESPIKE
10-11

Color for Butterflies: Annuals and perennials arranged by size; numbers indicate hardiness zones in Florida.

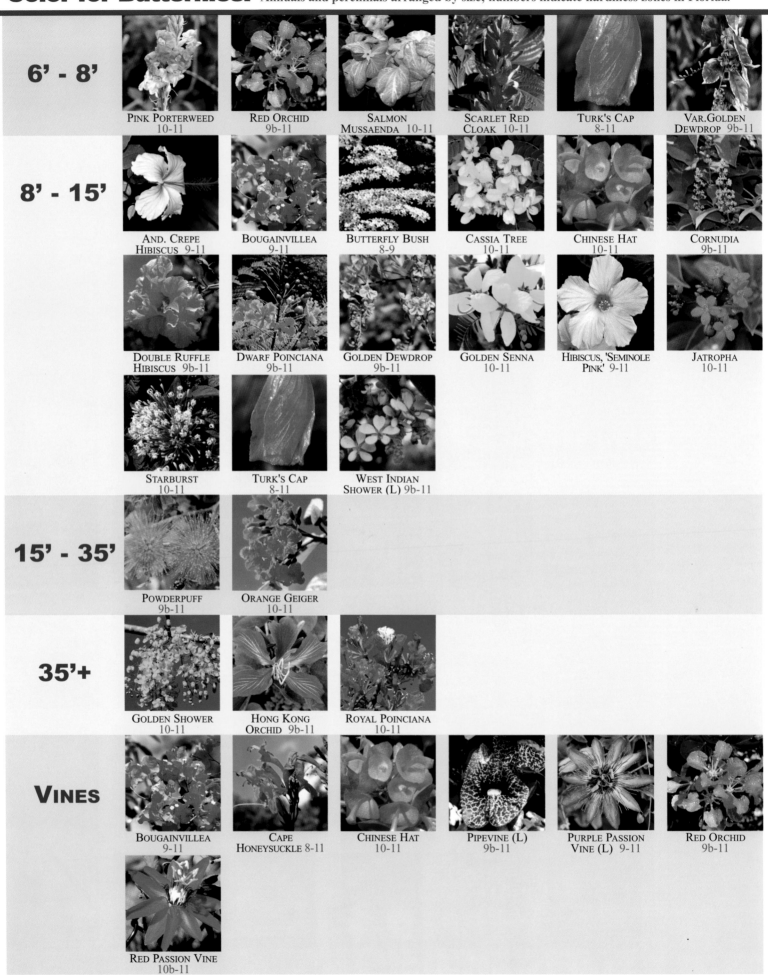

6' - 8'

PINK PORTERWEED
10-11

RED ORCHID
9b-11

SALMON
MUSSAENDA 10-11

SCARLET RED
CLOAK 10-11

TURK'S CAP
8-11

VAR. GOLDEN
DEWDROP 9b-11

8' - 15'

AND. CREPE
HIBISCUS 9-11

BOUGAINVILLEA
9-11

BUTTERFLY BUSH
8-9

CASSIA TREE
10-11

CHINESE HAT
10-11

CORNUDIA
9b-11

DOUBLE RUFFLE
HIBISCUS 9b-11

DWARF POINCIANA
9b-11

GOLDEN DEWDROP
9b-11

GOLDEN SENNA
10-11

HIBISCUS, 'SEMINOLE
PINK' 9-11

JATROPHA
10-11

STARBURST
10-11

TURK'S CAP
8-11

WEST INDIAN
SHOWER (L) 9b-11

15' - 35'

POWDERPUFF
9b-11

ORANGE GEIGER
10-11

35'+

GOLDEN SHOWER
10-11

HONG KONG
ORCHID 9b-11

ROYAL POINCIANA
10-11

VINES

BOUGAINVILLEA
9-11

CAPE
HONEYSUCKLE 8-11

CHINESE HAT
10-11

PIPEVINE (L)
9b-11

PURPLE PASSION
VINE (L) 9-11

RED ORCHID
9b-11

RED PASSION VINE
10b-11

     (L) = LARVAL FOOD PLANT

Bibliography

"Rose Culture" by S. E. McFadden. Circular 344, Florida Cooperative Extension Service, Institute of Food and Agricultural Sciences, University of Florida. First published: June 1990. Reviewed: March 1991.

Bar-Zvi, David. *Tropical Gardening.* New York: Pantheon Books, Knopf Publishing Group, 1996.

Black, Robert J. "Bedding Plants: Selection, Establishment and Maintenance". Circular 1134, Florida Cooperative Extension Service, Institute of Food and Agricultural Sciences, University of Florida, March, 1994.

Black, Robert J. "Daylilies for Florida" . Circular 620, Department of Environmental Horticulture, Florida Cooperative Extension Service, Institute of Food and Agricultural Sciences, University of Florida, Revised: June, 1997.

Black, Robert J. "Vines for Florida". Circular 860, Florida Cooperative Extension Service, Institute of Food and Agricultural Sciences, University of Florida. Publication date: April, 1990.

Broschat, Timothy K. and Meerow, Alan W. *Betrock's Reference Guide to Florida Landscape Plants.* Hollywood, Florida: Betrock Information Systems, 1999.

Brown, B. Frank ED.D. *Crotons of the World.* Valkaria, Florida: Valkaria Tropical Garden, 1992.

Brown, B. Frank ED.D. *The Cordyline, King of Tropical Foliage.* Valkaria, Florida: Valkaria Tropical Garden, 1994.

Clebsch, Betsy. *A Book Of Salvias.* Portland, Oregon: Timber Press, 1997.

Cooke, Ian. *Tender Perennials.* Portland, Oregon: Timber Press, 1998.

Culbert, Daniel. "Oleanders for Florida". Fact Sheet ENH-116, Environmental Horticulture Department, Florida Cooperative Extension Service, Institute of Food and Agricultural Sciences, University of Florida, Gainesville, Florida. October, 1995.

Haele, Robert G., and Brookwell, Joan. *Native Florida Plants.* Houston, Texas: Gulf Publishing Company, 1999.

Ingram, Dewayne L., and Midcap, James T. "Azaleas for Florida". Fact Sheet OH-37, Environmental Horticulture Department, Florida Cooperative Extension Service, Institute of Food and Agricultural Sciences, University of Florida. July, 1990.

Knox, Gary W. "Magnolias". Circular 1089, Environmental Horticulture Department, Florida Cooperative Extension service, Institute of Flood and Agricultural Sciences, University of Florida. June, 1993. Revised: April, 1994.

Mathias, Mildred et al. *Color for the Landscape.* Arcadia, California: California Arboretum Foundation, Inc. 1976.

MacCubbin, Tom, and Tasker, Georgia. *Florida Gardener's Guide.* Franklin, Tennessee: Cool Springs Press Inc., 2002.

McFadden, S. E. "Rose Culture" . Circular 344, Florida Cooperative Extension Service, Institute of Food and Agricultural Sciences, University of Florida. First published: June 1990. Reviewed: March 1991.

Meerow, Alan W. *Betrock's Guide to Landscape Palms.* Hollywood, Florida: Betrock Information Systems, 1999.

Menninger, Edwin A. *Flowering Trees of the World.* New York: Hearthside Press Inc. 1962.

Menninger, Edwin A. *Flowering Vines of the World.* New York: Hearthside Press Inc. 1970.

Morton, Julia. *Plants Poisonous to People.* Miami, Florida: Hallmark Press. 1995.

Nelson, Mark. *Nelson's Guide to Florida Roses.* Orlando, Florida: Waterview Press. 2003.

Ross, Susan, and Schrader, Dennis. *Hot Plants for Cool Climates.* New York: Houghton Mifflin Company. 2000.

Seidenberg, Charlotte. *The New Orleans Garden.* Jackson, Mississippi: University Press. 1993.

Sperry, Neil. *Neil Sperry's Complete Guide to Texas Gardening.* Dallas, Texas: Taylor Publishing Company. 1991.

Southern Living Annuals and Perennials. Birmingham, Alabama: Oxmoor House, Inc., 1998.

Southern Living Big Book of Flower Gardening. Birmingham, Alabama: Oxmoor House, Inc., 2003.

Stebbins, Mark K. *Flowering Trees of Florida.* Sarasota, Florida: Pineapple Press. 1999.

Watkins, John V. and Sheehan, Thomas J. *Florida Landscape Plants.* Gainesville, Florida: University Presses, 1975.

Welch, William C. *Perennial Garden Color.* Dallas, Texas: Taylor Publishing Company, 1989.

Index

Bold page numbers indicate main plant information pages.

Italicized page numbers indicate additional photos or information.

* This topic is covered in this books companion, "Easy Gardens for South Florida", which will be expanded to cover the whole state in 2004. The new title will be "Easy Gardens for Florida."

Index

Bold page numbers indicate main plant information pages.

Italicized page numbers indicate additional photos or information.

* This topic is covered in this books companion, "Easy Gardens for South Florida", which will be expanded to cover the whole state in 2004. The new title will be "Easy Gardens for Florida."

A Note from the Author

My book, "Easy Gardens for South Florida", is the first of a series of books designed to educate both gardeners - and the professionals who work with them - about the keys to achieving a beautiful landscape. It describes in detail the first (and easiest) 100 plants that survived my extensive trials and includes chapters on garden planting and maintenance that are critical for the success of the Florida garden. It tells you how to water, plant, fertilize, control pests, mulch, trim, and control weeds. I hope that these maintenance instructions will keep people from making all the mistakes I made when I began gardening here. I share years of research and experience that should save you years of mistakes and frustration.

Florida Gardening Series, Volume 1

Easy Gardens for Florida

• companion to *Best Garden Color for Florida*
• simple landscape plants and gardens
by Pamela Crawford

This book also includes a lot of design ideas from 65 local gardens. Readers are especially fond of the many before-and-after photos.

It is available from your bookseller now. Ask for ISBN number 0-9712220-0-2. If you have any problems locating it, contact me at my Web site www.easygardencolor.com.

My first book will be expanded to include the whole state in 2004. The new title will be "Easy Gardens for Florida". I use my own data from our Florida and Mississippi trial gardens as well as information from experts throughout the state. If you would like the release date, contact me at my Web site, www.easygardencolor.com.

My second book, "Best Garden Color for Florida", is for the gardener who loves color! It details the second 100 plants that survived our trials - plus some traditional choices for further north in the state. While most are easy, some are more maintenance-intensive than the ones described in the "Easy Gardens" book. Bougainvillea is a good example. It didn't fit in a low-maintenance plant book because of the work involved in trimming it each summer. However, it certainly fits well in a book about color, since it is one of our most spectacular winter bloomers. Annuals are also included. _**This book does not duplicate any of the plants or care information included in my "Easy Gardens" book. The two work together to give you the necessary information for beautiful garden color.**_